PRACTICAL THEOLOGY

STUDIES IN PRACTICAL THEOLOGY

Series Editors

Don S. Browning

James W. Fowler

Friedrich Schweitzer

Johannes A. van der Ven

PRACTICAL THEOLOGY

HISTORY · THEORY · ACTION DOMAINS

Manual for Practical Theology

Gerben Heitink

Translated by

Reinder Bruinsma

WILLIAM B. EERDMANS PUBLISHING COMPANY
GRAND RAPIDS, MICHIGAN / CAMBRIDGE, U.K.

Originally published as
Praktische Theologie
© Kok–Kampen, 1993
English translation © 1999 Wm. B. Eerdmans Publishing Co.
255 Jefferson Ave. S.E., Grand Rapids, Michigan 49503 /
P.O. Box 163, Cambridge CB3 9PU U.K.

Printed in the United States of America

05 04 03 02 01 00 99   7 6 5 4 3 2 1

Library of Congress Cataloging-in-Publication Data

Heitink, Gerben.
[Praktische Theologie. English]
Practical theology: history, theory, action domains: manual for practical theology /
Gerben Heitink; translated by Reinder Bruinsma.
p.   cm.   — (Studies in practical theology)
Includes bibliographical references (p.   ) and indexes.
ISBN 0-8028-4294-1 (pbk.: alk. paper)
1. Theology, Practical.   I. Title.   II. Series.
BV3.H4513   1999
253 — dc21   99-11227
                                             CIP

Contents

Series Foreword

In many countries around the world practical theology is gaining a new shape. It is stepping out of the shadow of being viewed only as the application of findings and guidelines developed by the so-called foundational theological disciplines of exegetical, historical, and systematic theology. Rather, the new practical theology is reminding all of theology of its practical nature, just as many of the great theologians of the past, from Augustine to Martin Luther and beyond, were in fact practical theologians.

In addition to the claim that all theology is practical, this movement is also asserting that practical theology is an academic discipline of its own and that its nature does not consist in merely being applied exegesis, dogmatics, or theological ethics, although it fully realizes the importance of its relation to these disciplines. This new identity of practical theology is not limited to a particular school of theology or to a particular country. Rather, practical theology has become the focus of an emerging international discussion that can be understood only by taking into account the various contributions from many countries and continents — North America, Europe, South America, Africa, and Asia.

Practical theology is a theoretical undertaking that builds on a practical basis. Although this discipline has much to learn from reflective practitioners — and in some of its forms actually begins with questions, problems, and descriptions from the field of religious practice — it is not an academic discipline to be identified solely with the processes going on in the field of religious practice nor with strategies and methods of stimulating these processes. The academic discipline of practical theology is a theory of the epistemological foundations, ethical norms, and general strategies of religious praxis in its various contexts. As a discipline, it should not be confused with the praxis itself, although it is highly relevant to all actual religious practice.

Practical theology should be understood as an empirically descriptive and critically constructive theory of religious practice. The empirical and descriptive dimension, which is pursued in close cooperation with other disciplines in the field of cultural studies, prevents practical theology from wishful speculative thinking and contributes to empirical theory building. The critical and constructive dimension, which is aimed at evaluating and improving the existing forms of religious practice, prevents practical theology from empiricism or positivism and contributes to a theology of transformation in the name of true religion.

Within the empirically descriptive and critically constructive framework of practical theology, religious practice may be studied on three different levels: with reference to society and culture, with reference to the church, and with reference to the individual. Christianity is not limited to the church, and practical theology should not be limited to a clerical paradigm. Its threefold focus is on ecclesial practices, on religious aspects of culture and society, and on the religious dimensions of individual life, including the interrelatedness of all three.

Consequently, this series includes major pieces of work in all fields of practical theology, with an emphasis on the emerging international discussion. The traditional subdisciplines of practical theology — from homiletics to catechetics and liturgical studies — are to play an important role in this series, but one should not consider them exhaustive of the entire discipline of practical theology. Rather, in addition to these subdisciplines we will sponsor more general practical theological studies on major topics within society and culture as well as investigations into the disciplinary nature and shape of practical theology itself. Furthermore, the series includes research that is based on various types of methodology — hermeneutical and historical, empirical and critical, quantitative and qualitative.

The books to be published within this series are addressed to a wide readership of all those with an interest in practical theology. Pastors will profit from them as well as students of theology and researchers or practitioners in the allied fields of sociology, psychology, cultural studies, social work, and medicine.

Don S. Browning, *Chicago*
James W. Fowler, *Atlanta*
Friedrich Schweitzer, *Tübingen*
Johannes A. van der Ven, *Nijmegen*

Note from the Translator

When translating a text into English at the request of an American publisher, a translator would normally be expected to adapt the translated text as much as possible to the American situation. When I began this project I soon realized that this practice would be impossible in this case. On almost every page this book reflects a European, and often more specifically a Dutch, context. With some notable exceptions the author refers to Dutch and German authors. But rather than being a problem, I believe this gives the book an added dimension not readily available in works by contemporary American practical theologians. Where possible, references to English translations are cited in brackets following the original references.

Translating Professor Heitink's text presented a number of interesting challenges. One of these is his frequent use of terms that have no adequate English equivalent. His use of the term *agogie* and related words is but one example. I have anglicized this word, encouraged by the fact that it appeared some years ago in the title of another book published by Eerdmans. The meaning will be apparent from the context in which this word and its related forms appear. Another word that needed to be anglicized in a similar way is *diakonologie*, which I have translated as "diaconology." No precise English equivalent exists for the concept of *kerkopbouw*. I have, following some others, translated this as "church development," but unfortunately this term fails to do justice to the combination of vertical and horizontal aspects the Dutch word implies. I trust the context will prevent confusion where I occasionally have taken some liberties in anglicizing these and other Dutch words.

Reinder Bruinsma

Preface

In recent times practical theology as a theological theory of action has experienced a rapid development. This Manual of Practical Theology offers a survey and draws the contours of the theory of this discipline.

This book is in some ways unique. For it has been a very long time since an introduction to practical theology was published in the Netherlands. Looking at older introductions, one usually finds a short historical introduction, followed by a survey of the various fields of study within practical theology. This book does not follow such a pattern. I emphatically intend to offer a theory for the entire discipline of practical theology that emphasizes its underlying unity.

This book belongs to the tradition of practical-theological theorizing that has developed at the Free University in Amsterdam and in Kampen. Since 1970 I have had the privilege of contributing in this area. The intense cooperation with colleagues finds its echo in the way in which the questions this book addresses are defined and answered. This practical-theological tradition is characterized by its concern for the praxis of church and faith, with the aim of arriving at a renewal of action in the service of the gospel.

This book has opted for an open dialogue with representatives of other traditions and disciplines, both within and outside the sphere of practical theology, and for integration of divergent views which may all be helpful for the formulation of our theory. In this way, I hope, some justice will be done to the *inter*confessional, *inter*disciplinary, and *inter*national character of this branch of theology.

In writing this book I have had various groups of readers in mind. My primary audience is advanced theology students, who may use this book as a textbook. I presuppose a certain level of basic theological knowledge. My own teaching experience has shown that students who have been exposed to theology for a few years should have no problem with the content of this book. I also hope that the book may be useful for postacademic training.

In addition, I want, in dialogue with colleagues, to make a contribution to the development of the theory of practical theology, for practical theologians and others. The study of practical theology is an integral part of theology in general and needs close cooperation with representatives of the social sciences.

Finally, a few words about how this book may be used. Considerable attention has been given to references to other authors, the index, and the bibliography, to ensure that the book would be a reference tool. Moreover, there are constant references in the text to other sections in the book. When referring to publications, I mention in every first instance the name of the author, with the year in which the work was published, followed by the page(s) to which the reader is referred.

Bennebroek, May 1993   Gerben Heitink

CHAPTER 1

The State of Practical Theology

Until relatively recently, the term *practical theology* served as a collective name for a number of dissimilar disciplines with one basic common denominator: their relation to ministerial practice. At the state universities in the Netherlands these areas of study form part of the curriculum that is sponsored by the church. In Reformed circles they are usually referred to as "pastoral subjects," and among Catholics as "pastoral theology." In both instances the relation to the ministry, and in particular to its pastoral aspects, is underlined.

In recent decades this situation has changed remarkably. Since the end of the 1960s pastoral theology has evolved quite rapidly, and it now presents itself at the academic level as a separate branch of theology. It is no longer satisfied with the subsidiary role of a *theologia applicata,* to which it was relegated in the past, but now identifies itself as a theological *theory of action,* with a methodology that is closely linked to the social sciences.

This development, which started roughly in the 1960s, is visible in publications that have since then appeared in the Netherlands, as well as in Germany and the United States.

Some Dutch studies may be cited as examples: J. Firet (1968 [1986]) about pastoral practice; P. J. Roscam Abbing (1980) about the work of the local pastor; H. Jonker (1983) about the praxis of theology; B. Höfte (1990) about the political-critical dimensions of pastoral theology; and J. A. van der Ven (1990 [1993]) about the methodology of empirical research in the area of practical theology. These books are written by Protestant as well as Catholic practical theologians. Although they all differ in their approach to this discipline, they all — from their

1

own particular point of departure — presuppose the unitary nature of practical-theological theorizing.

The German literature offers several *Grundrisse* (Introductions): A. D. Müller (1950) and O. Haendler (1957), and more recently G. Otto (1986) and D. Rössler (1986). The books from the 1980s differ significantly from those published in the 1950s. The older books offer mostly an inventory of the various practical-theological subdisciplines. The newer publications attempt to go beyond this division into separate fields of study and to develop a comprehensive theory.

One can detect a similar development in the United States. The introduction by Seward Hiltner (1958) already strongly emphasizes the unity of the entire discipline, but still assigns a central place to the work of the pastor. The more recent introduction by Don S. Browning (1991) is presented as a *fundamental* practical theology.

These developments are characteristic for the present state of affairs regarding practical theology. This introductory chapter offers a general survey of the situation. From a historical perspective, one can view practical theology as a crisis discipline (1.1). This point of departure determines to a large extent the overall character of this book (1.2). This, in turn, leads to a definition of practical theology (1.3) as the basis for the ensuing sections. A sketch of the present state of the discipline in the Dutch context (1.4) is followed by some observations regarding the organization of this book (1.5).

1.1 Practical Theology as a Theory of Crisis

Several publications argue that the emergence of the new paradigm of "practical theology as a theory of action" is related to the changing views in the 1960s regarding the problems theology must address.

In this period Western society went through a deep authority crisis. Society dealt a final blow to the last vestiges of authoritarian culture. The traditional authority of parents, teachers, politicians, and even spiritual and political leaders was no longer accepted at face value. Western Europe was on its way to a "fatherless society," as the title of A. Mitscherlich's book (1963) poignantly suggests. The "fathers" were no longer with us. The process of democratization, input in the decision-making process, and shared responsibility were unstoppable, and even the last hierarchical bastions in society were affected by it.

At the same time, in the churches the authority of the Scriptures, the authority of the clergy, and spiritual authority in general were topics of intense discussion. This new "emancipation" greatly influenced the participation of the people in the life of the church. Church attendance dropped. New groups and movements were born, as the churches were apparently unable to satisfy the religious needs and feelings of the people. But the most significant trend is that more and more people left the church. In 1947 17.1 percent of the Dutch population did not belong to any church. In 1979 this number had risen to 27 percent, while recent, less formal, research suggests that 52 percent of all Dutch men and women no longer consider themselves members of any church (Dekker 1992, 34). For the first time the church in the Netherlands found itself in a minority position. In 1964 the first chair for practical theology (officially still referred to as pastoral theology) was initiated at the Catholic University in Nijmegen. Even though this university, with its theological department, was founded in 1923, until then no need whatsoever had been felt to add such a chair to the existing program. The clergy were not aware of any problems: "The Catholics believed in their church, their priests, and their bishops." They believed in their cause (van der Ven 1985, 10). This changed in the 1950s. In his inaugural lecture in 1968, F. Haarsma, the first professor in this field in Nijmegen, referred to a growing divide between the teachings of the church and the convictions of the church members, and he went as far as to mention the expression "crisis of faith" (1968, 23).

In the same year Jacob Firet appeared on the scene as the first professor of practical theology at the Free University of Amsterdam. He also observed that the church could not simply continue in its former ways. The automatic continuity had been broken and modern society no longer had a clear model to follow (1968, 7-8). Taking his cue from H. Schelsky, he introduced the concept of a "theory of action," and under his leadership the Institute of Practical Theology (IPT) was founded.

Against this background one can more fully appreciate the fact that practical theology is often referred to as a *theory of crisis*. As G. Rau (1970, 27ff.) states: In times of crisis, when we see major upheavals in society and when the traditional approaches within the church lose their plausibility, we find a great need for advice as to how we should act. Since, indeed, we no longer know how to proceed, a "theological futurology" (Firet 1968) is needed to clear a way toward the future. The expectations were high.

Many insufficiently realized, however, that the discipline which was supposed to deliver the solutions was itself part of the problem. Practical theology shared this ambiguity with the social sciences. The social sciences owed their development to the modernization of society, but they, in turn, further stimulated this modernizing process. This was also true for an action-oriented discipline like practical theology. It "demythologized" the work of the church and its officials: God's work became the work of human beings. It also suggested how this work might be carried out in the best possible way, on the basis of sound theological and agogic principles. But because of its understanding of society, it could also manipulate the praxis and, once again, attempt to direct things in a way that simply pleased higher ecclesiastical authorities.

In the current crisis of the church and of faith itself, practical theology constantly hovers between adaptation and renewal. This is inherent in the phenomenon of crisis, which is viewed in different ways. Some regard it as a threat to the status quo, while others hail a crisis as a chance for renewal. Progressive and conservative forces in church and theology are at times negative, and at other times positive, toward this new discipline.

Practical theology has borne this character of a crisis discipline since it originated at the end of the eighteenth and beginning of the nineteenth century. The full-blown crisis of our times has had a long period of incubation. In his cultural-historical study about "the lost Father," F. O. van Gennep (1989) finds his point of departure in the period of the Enlightenment, which marks the ascent of modern autonomous humanity and the beginning of modern times.

Church and faith did not escape the influence of so-called modernity. It led in the Protestant churches to a bitter controversy between conservative and liberal Christians, resulting in a number of schisms. This also happened in the Netherlands, where the Reformed Churches in the Netherlands (RCN) vigorously rejected modernism, while the Netherlands Reformed Church (NRC) tried to deal with this development within its own ranks and sought to integrate it. Already in the nineteenth century the Roman Catholic Church forcefully condemned these ideas; in 1910 Pius X required all priests and theology professors to take the antimodernist oath. But from the 1960s onward, even the Catholic Church and the Reformed Churches fully shared in the crisis of modernity, and this, among other things, called for a practical theology.

Friedrich Schleiermacher, the first theologian who tried to formulate an answer to the Enlightenment, also became one of the founders of practical theology. In his well-known *Kurze Darstellung* (*Brief Outline;* 1811), he became one of the first theologians to create a space for this discipline. In 1821 the first Protestant chair for practical theology was established at the University of Berlin. But as early as 1774 F. S. Rautenstrauch reserved a slot for pastoral theology in his reorganization plan for the Catholic study of theology in Austria (Vienna) (Müller 1974, 42ff.).

This perspective of a theory of crisis, at the crossroads of restoration and renewal, is an important insight for a good understanding of the emergence of practical theology. It is here that this book also finds its point of departure.

1.2 The Character of This Book

This Manual for Practical Theology (Handboek praktische theologie) is designed to explain the underlying theory of a practical theology. I must give considerable attention to the unique position and function of practical theology within theology as a whole, and to the unique character of practical theological study. At the same time, I must clearly show the interdependence of the various elements of this discipline.

Several different approaches may be considered. Each path offers certain advantages, but also has its own limitations. The approach of this book fits with the theological tradition within which it originates. This might be summed up in three word pairs: historical-interpretive, hermeneutical-critical, and practical-constructive.

The method to be used may first of all be characterized as *historical-interpretive*. Practical theology is, as we saw, a historical phenomenon. The development of this theological theory of action dates from the beginning of the nineteenth century. We must describe, analyze, and interpret this development if we are properly to understand practical theology. As is apparent from the subtitle, this is in particular the subject of the first part of the book, but also has its impact on the other sections. I prefer the term *historical-interpretive* to *historical-analytical,* since analysis is based on a subjective interpretation of the literature that has been surveyed.

Second, I describe the approach as *hermeneutical-critical.* This characterization applies to the entire book, but even more so to part II. This term refers to the positioning of this book within a hermeneutical approach to theology. This particular method attempts to link tradition and experience, seeking to understand this tradition within the frame of reference of modern people. Actions are directed toward this goal. The word *critical* provides a link with the previous section. As soon as one accepts that the mediation of the tradition is influenced by historical processes, one wants to interpret this development through a critical theory. The hermeneutical tradition may use more than one of such critical theories. This also happens in this book. But priority is given to the conviction of the gospel itself that the appearance of the kingdom of God into this world may be seen as the basis of a critical-historical theory.

The third term, *practical-constructive,* serves as a presupposition for the entire book, but applies more specifically to the third part. The word *practical* in "practical theology" refers to action. In this book this term implies that any involvement with this discipline cannot be limited to an understanding and explanation of the praxis of believing and of "being church," but must also have as its purpose to influence and change this praxis. For that reason a theory of action is devised that includes various theories of communication that are related to this action. This also affects the role of the practical-theological theory in the professional training for the ministry, to which this discipline makes a significant contribution.

The word combinations are not at variance with the concept of the *empirical,* which so far has not yet been mentioned explicitly but does refer to an important intention of this book. Any study of practical theology that chooses its point of departure in human experience and in the current state of faith and of the church will have an empirical orientation. This empirical orientation allied to the development of social scientific theories will therefore have an important place in all three parts of this book.

1.3 A Definition

The choices made so far may now be translated into a definition, which serves as a guiding principle in the writing of this book and is defended and elaborated in the chapters that follow.

In this book practical theology as a theory of action is *the empirically oriented theological theory of the mediation of the Christian faith in the praxis of modern society.*

Since this definition is explained at length in the three main parts of this book, a few observations here may suffice.

Practical Theology

I prefer the term *practical theology* over other terms that limit the object of the discipline to ecclesiastical or ministerial practice. This is true for the terms used in the Reformed as well as in the Catholic tradition. The term *empirical theology,* coined by van der Ven to highlight the perspective from which he approaches practical theology (1990, IX), embodies just one of the approaches of the discipline. It is less suitable as a label for this entire branch of theology.

But even the term *practical theology* is open to misunderstandings. Through the years the word *practical* has given rise to incorrect expectations on the part of many. This happens when "practical" is seen as the opposite of "theoretical," since theory is the opposite of practice. But this branch of theology is not just practical, in the sense that it deals only with actual practice; rather, just like other subdisciplines, it also attempts to share in the development of theological theory in general. We have to live with this problem, since the term has been generally accepted, nationally and internationally. In Germany the usual term is "Praktische Theologie," while in the United States the name "Practical Theology" more and more replaces that of "Pastoral Theology."

Another objection against the term *practical theology* is that it says little about the unique object and the theological character of this discipline. In reality this is hardly the case. The object is — as one can already read in the lecture notes of Schleiermacher (1850, 12 [1988, 89]) — the "Theorie der Praxis" (the theory of praxis). I must note that "praxis" does not mean "practice" but "action, activity." This is the object. In addition, the word *practical* does in a real way express the theological nature of the discipline. One might think in this connection of the Greek name of one of the books of the Bible: Acts, *praxeis apostolōn*, the divine action through the ministry of the apostles, and of Romans 12:4, which refers to the different functions *(praxeis)* of the members of the church as the body of Christ. Thus practical theology deals with God's activity through the ministry of human beings.

An Empirically Oriented Theological Theory

The definition speaks of an "empirically oriented theological theory." This phrase does more justice to the content of this book than any description as an empirical-critical or critical-empirical theory.

A practical theology, which chooses its point of departure in the experience of human beings and in the current state of church and society, is indeed characterized by a methodology that takes empirical data with utter seriousness, takes these as its starting point and keeps them in mind as it develops its theory. This manner of "doing" theology differs from exegetical, historical, or philosophical approaches, which are distinctive for other subjects, even though practical theology does use exegetical, systematic, and historical methods.

Praxis — Two Concepts

One can properly understand the definition only by distinguishing between the two different concepts of praxis that it includes. The definition refers to *the mediation of the Christian faith* (praxis 1) in *the praxis of modern society* (praxis 2). Much of the confusion regarding the unique object of practical theology has to do with the failure to make a logical and methodological distinction between the two.

Praxis 1 indicates that the unique object of practical theology is related to intentional, more specifically, intermediary or mediative, actions, with a view to changing a given situation through agogics.

Praxis 2 emphasizes the context, where these actions take place, as a dynamic context in which men and women in society interact, whether or not their actions are religiously motivated while pursuing various goals.

To make this distinction does not in any way deny that praxis 1 and praxis 2 constantly interrelate. This interconnectedness must be adequately stressed when developing a theory.

The Mediation of the Christian Faith (Praxis 1)

Practical theology is focused on the mediation of the Christian faith. This mediation has to do with the core of the Christian conviction: "God's coming to humanity in the world." This is "a constant and ever-recurring event that takes place *through the intermediary of human ministry*" (Firet 1987, 31). God's action mediated through human action is the theological center of gravity of practical theology. In this connection Firet borrows the Greek word *paradosis* (handing over, tradition) from the parable of the talents (Matt. 25:14-30).

This point underlines that the continuity of the Christian faith in the lives of men and women and in the church depends on tradition, the mediation of the tradition through various channels. Such mediation takes place in an educational setting between parents and children, between teachers and students, and between pastors and church members in celebrations and various forms of church work. This mediation also occurs through radio and television, and in all sorts of organizations. It happens when people come together in all kinds of different ways: in personal encounters and conversations, in small groups, in worship, and through the media. It takes place within certain structures in the church, the family, and the school. This mediation takes shape in forms of communicative action, that is, in communication processes that occur within specific structures. Practical theology studies how these processes take place, and how these structures can be so adapted that there can be a real transmission of the Christian tradition.

The Praxis of Modern Society (Praxis 2)

When referring to "the praxis of modern society," one looks for description and explanation. The society may be described and explained as a praxis, as a domain of action, where individuals and groups, motivated by their personal ideals and driven by varying interests, make specific choices and pursue specific goals. This happens in people's daily experience — in their mutual relationships, in marriage, and in the family. It also happens in the work place, and in political, economic, and social contexts. In all these cases one finds intentional actions, with ethical implications, regardless of whether they are based on a specific religious conviction or worldview. The word *praxis* is therefore broader than *practice*. It also refers to theory because of the values, norms, and interests involved.

The Word *in*

The two-letter word *in* conveys that praxis 1 and praxis 2 are closely related. Praxis 2 may be favorable for praxis 1, but there may also be a tension between the two. For centuries, the praxis of society has been influenced by the Christian tradition. At the same time the Christian tradition has been subject to the influence of divergent developments within society. There were processes of adaptation that demanded an (ideological-) critical evaluation.

Although practical theology first of all focuses on praxis 1, it is always linked to praxis 2, as is clear from empirical practical-theological research. This link to a large extent determines the manner in which praxis 1 receives form and content. Praxis 1 can therefore never be detached from the context of praxis 2. Thus the exercise of practical theology does not have the church, but rather society, as its horizon.

The interdependence of praxis 1 and praxis 2 can best be illustrated by looking at the church itself. The church is the foremost channel of mediation through Word and Spirit. This is its most basic function. In its worship, its teaching, and its ministry it embodies praxis 1. But in the past the church was also a social institution — and that to some extent is true even today — that influenced the praxis of society and the behavior of the people. For that reason, the influence of the church may be viewed from the perspective of praxis 1 as well as from that of praxis 2. In interrelating Christian faith and society, as in my definition, one transcends the actions of the church. This seems adequately to reflect the current situation.

1.4 Practical Theology in the Netherlands

The pursuit of practical theology in the Netherlands has been characterized by an intense discussion about the basic assumptions and the methodology of the discipline, as is apparent from a series of publications that reflect the different schools of thought. The professional journals play a key role in the academic discussion. The journal *Praktische Theologie* (Practical theology) has been published since 1974 as the Dutch journal for the pastoral sciences. It resulted from a fusion between three precursors, the Roman Catholic journal *Theologie en Pastoraat* (Theology and the pastorate), the predominantly Protestant *Ministerium,* and the "mixed" *Tijdschrift voor Pastorale Psychologie* (Journal for pastoral psychology). Since 1988 an international periodical, the *Journal of Empirical Theology,* has been published in Nijmegen.

Protestant and Roman Catholic practical theologians cooperate in these and other ventures. They have so much in common that, by comparison, confessional differences play a minor role. This also has to do with the inductive approach of the praxis, which is typical for this discipline, in which normative-theological views do, of course, play a role, without ever dominating the discussion.

But the position of this field of study at the state universities differs from that at the private universities. The state universities are governed by the *duplex ordo,* which divides theology into subjects taught by the state and those taught by the church. So far there is little provision for research for the church-sponsored subjects, under which practical theology resides. Recent discussions between the universities and the participating churches about equal treatment for all subjects give hope that this situation will improve. At the other institutions, which do not have such a dichotomy, all subjects, including practical theology, receive equal treatment.

Since 1980 Dutch practical theologians have met in a working group for practical theology and scientific religious research, which is part of a foundation that seeks to foster this type of research. This group of more than one hundred members has close ties with a similar association for doctoral students who specialize in this area. The latter association is a step in the direction of a research institute for theology and religion, with participation of eight theological schools and universities.

International conferences and the recently founded International Academy of Practical Theology (Princeton) provide contacts with colleagues in other countries. It is typical for the Dutch development of this branch of theology that it continues to represent its own theological tradition and to create its own climate, albeit in a constant and open dialogue with its peer groups in

Germany and North America. By contrast, German and American literature has only in recent years paid attention to what happens outside their own borders.

1.5 Organization of This Book

In creating an outline for this book, I let myself be guided by a concrete image that more and more forced itself upon me: that of a building, a nineteenth-century edifice, well maintained, with a central section and two side wings. The three parts of this building represent the three parts of this book. I decided to draw a floor plan of this book, which I have included in this introductory section with some explanatory remarks. I hasten to stress that this drawing has no more than a heuristic meaning, with no other intention than to provide some insight into the structure and content of the book.

The building is part of a much larger complex of buildings, that of theology as a whole. For a few moments I will serve as a tour guide. Each room in the building represents a chapter of the book.

We now find ourselves in the hall, the introductory chapter (1), which provides an entrance to the three wings of the building. Behind the hall is the central section, to the left and to the right the two side wings. The reader may choose, after having studied the floor plan, to enter the main entrance to the scientific-theoretical part (II), but the preferred route would be to follow the signs to the left wing, the historical-interpretive part (I).

The door to part I leads to one large room, which has been subdivided into three parallel areas. The enlightenment of the subject (2), the modernizing of society (3), and the continuing relevance of the social question (4) constitute the three threads along which one may describe and interpret the development of practical theology since the nineteenth century. These are three interconnected perspectives, which have lost nothing of their actuality, for they continue to determine how (post-) modern humans see their situation. These three areas open up to a wide transverse hallway. This room provides a survey of the theological reaction to the development that has been outlined: the modern pluralism in church and theology (5). Here we discern how practical theology begins slowly to acquire a theological shape. For this reason, at the beginning of this century theology boarded up this part of this wing. The nineteenth century had been superseded! But today we realize the continuing importance of the nineteenth century for theology. A more detailed explanation is provided in room 6: the history of pastoral theology as the precursor

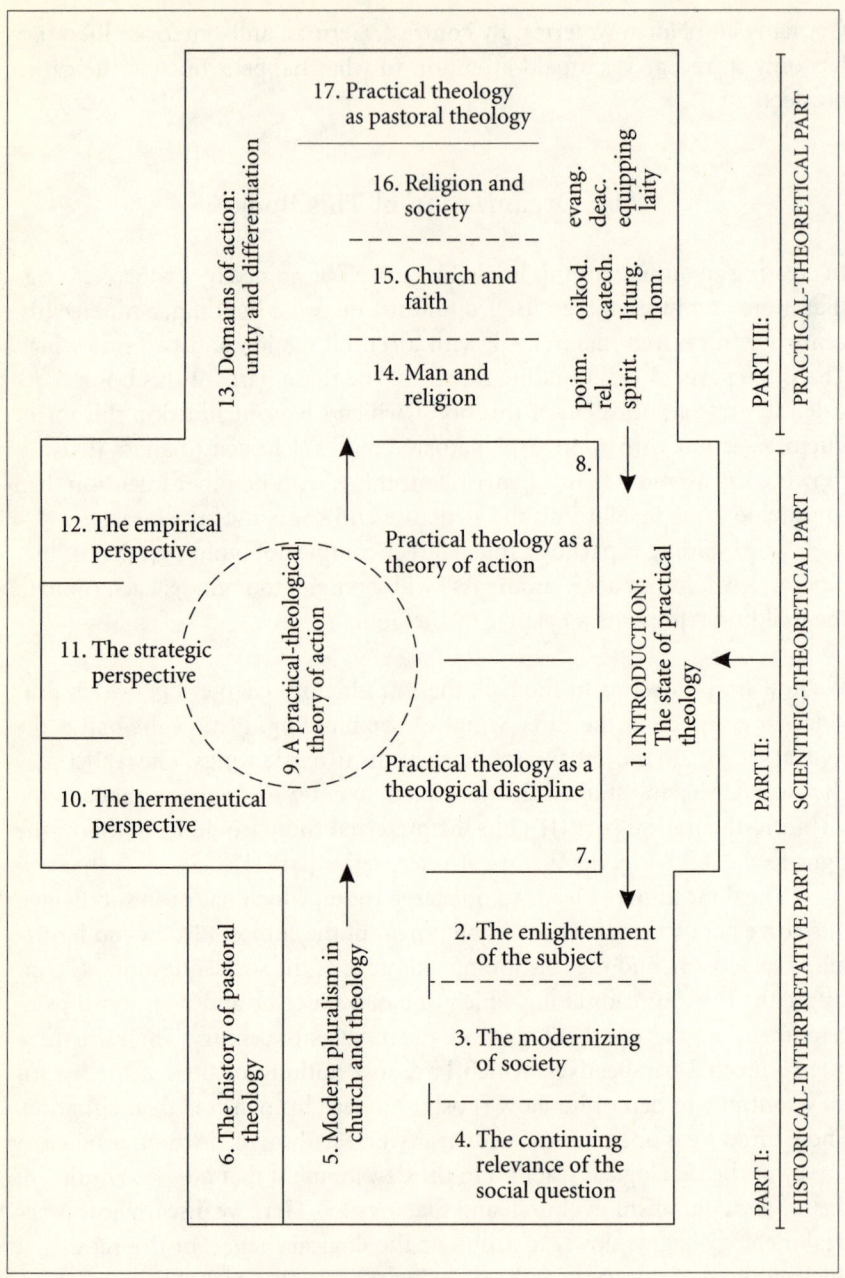

Figure 1: Floor plan of *Practical Theology*

of today's practical theology. For, as one might expect, even prior to the nineteenth century important decisions were made regarding the way in which the church and the clergy function.

Through the room that allows us a view into theological pluralism, we enter the central section, the scientific-theoretical part (II) of this book. The central space is occupied by the "theory-praxis room," in which the theory of action is discussed (9) — the heart of the matter. This room is in open connection with five other rooms. In order to get a good overall view, we first proceed toward the front. Here we find two interconnected rooms. In one of them (7) practical theology is developed as a theological discipline, while in the other (8) practical theology is developed as a theory that guides our actions. They are linked to each other, in particular in the area of the theory of action, through converging lines issuing from theology and the social sciences. To provide for a further elaboration of this theory of action, three other rooms have been reserved at the back, where one specific theological theory of action is developed along three different lines: from the hermeneutical perspective (10), from the strategic perspective (11), and from the empirical perspective (12). In this way this second part offers a comprehensive theory of practical theology as a whole. Having taken this in, the reader proceeds through the theory-praxis room to the right wing of the building.

In the practice-theoretical part (III), we get acquainted with practical theology's various domains of action. The central space emphasizes the unity in the theoretical foundation (13). This forms one part together with the four rooms that are in open connection with it. It becomes clear that one basic theory is fundamental to the various theories of practice. Then, once again, we find a differentiation along three distinct lines, reminiscent of part I. We can distinguish three separate foci of action, which overlap in part only in the current state of the differentiating process in society. These are the domains of humanity and religion (14), church and faith (15), and religion and society (16). They express private, ecclesiological, and public Christianity, and are approached through the development of anthropological, ecclesiological, and deaconological theories, respectively. Inside each of these rooms some theories for practice have been developed that also exert their influence into other rooms. It would therefore be incorrect to lock each branch of the discipline into one particular cell. The final area in this wing is the essential transverse connection: pastoral theology (17), the history of which we already explored in the first part.

This completes our tour of the building. At the beginning of each of the three parts of this book the structure and content will be clarified in further detail.

The Development of
Practical Theology

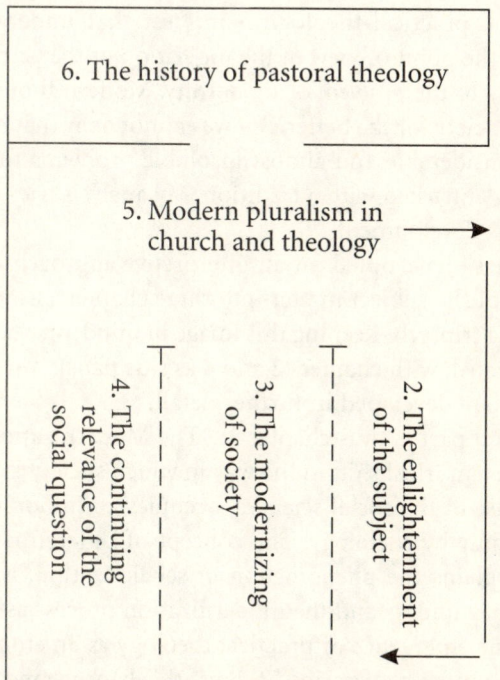

6. The history of pastoral theology

5. Modern pluralism in
church and theology

4. The continuing
relevance of the
social question

3. The modernizing
of society

2. The enlightenment
of the subject

Figure 2: Part I

The mediation of the Christian faith has become problematic in modern society (praxis 2). When understood as a theory of action, practical theology is in fact a theory of crisis (1.1). Viewed from the perspective of church and faith, it reflects the crisis of our modern times, usually referred to by the single term *modernity*.

One can understand what practical theology is only by subjecting it to historical analysis. The history of the origin of this discipline is a history of understanding. Therefore part I of this book is not just a historical part that deals with the history of practical theology, but a historical-interpretive part that attempts to clarify the thinking that led to the current practice of this branch of theology. The crisis of the 1960s, which gave birth to practical theology in its modern form, was rooted in the crisis that, ever since the Enlightenment, has permeated European culture like a leaven.

Resulting from the process of modernization that has occurred in Western society, modernity is an extremely broad and complex phenomenon. Scholars often distinguish among economic modernization, political modernization, social modernization, and cultural modernization (van der Ven 1993, 18-19 [1996, 30]). Here we can look at only a few aspects. The selection is based on the practical-theological interest that undergirds this book. Speaking from the point of view of the mediation of the Christian faith, I refer intentionally to the *problem* of modernity. Modern thought has in many ways changed society for the better. But we cannot deny that in our time it has also created considerable and almost insoluble problems for the church, as the community entrusted with a tradition. My analysis tries to provide more insight into this development.

In this part I have opted for an interpretive approach along three lines and a division of the subject matter into three chapters. Chapters 2, 3, and 4 may be seen as a triptych. Keeping this image in mind, one can view chapter 3 as the central panel, with chapters 2 and 4 as side panels, on which some important motifs are developed in further detail.

The central part is thus chapter 3: "The Modernization of Society." In this section the empirical shift in the way in which society is viewed, brought about by the rise of the social sciences, occupies an important place. Here I am guided mainly by sociology. The concept of differentiation, which to a large extent explains the phenomenon of secularization, is the core of the chapter. One may understand the modernization process as a process of differentiation. The emergence of practical theology as an empirically oriented theory of action must be described against this background. From the nineteenth century onward one detects that, under the influence of a more functional way of thinking, the discussion about the church as a social institution also takes on empirical traits. This is the main line, which is paralleled by two other lines.

Apart from its social interest, practical theology is also clearly interested in anthropology. The mediation of the Christian faith in the praxis of modern society is a human undertaking. One's understanding of the tradition is subject to a process of knowing and of raising awareness that has been profoundly influenced by the process of modernization. Modern autonomous humanity differs in many ways from humanity in the pre-Enlightenment era. Chapter 2, "The Enlightenment of the Subject," attempts to give more insight into the process of subjectivizing and individualizing that is basic to the way in which modern humans realize themselves — a process that is still ongoing. Considering the hermeneutical interests that underlie this book, I opt for the perspective of the human sciences. Philosophy and the science of psychology that evolved from it will guide us in this section. Following this line, we meet Schleiermacher, who took this new awareness of the problem of modernity with utter seriousness and thus made a contribution to the origins of practical theology as a theological discipline. The history of the beginnings of practical theology prompted me to begin with this chapter.

The counterpart of chapter 2 is chapter 4, the other side panel that throws additional light on the birth of practical theology. This is the socioeconomic perspective, which is related to the perspective of diaconal action of practical theology, and with the coming of God's kingdom, of peace and justice for all people. From this springs the critical interest that forms the foundation of this book and maintains a strong tension with the hermeneutical interest of chapter 2. The modern subject is unmasked as a bourgeois subject, a representative of the privileged class of society. This becomes visible in yet another development in the nineteenth century: the impact of the social question. Here I focus on the thoughts of Marx and the critical theory. In so doing I confront critical questions regarding the agogic approach, which is unavoidable as one thinks in terms of mediation. To what extent are we faced with an attitude of control that aims at self-protection and the status quo? To what extent did the church and the Christian faith stimulate or hinder the emancipation of various groups in society? Practical theology: *Cui bono* (for whose benefit)?

In this scenario the problem of modernity is studied from three different perspectives. Chapter 2 corresponds with the process of cultural modernization, while political and economic modernization are discussed in chapter 4.

This division is also supported in the publication *Sociologie*, by W. Ultee et al. (1992). Within the domain of sociology the author distinguishes three main lines of inquiry, corresponding to three central theories. The main problems are: (1) diversity (sometimes referred to as the problem of stratification); (2) cohesion (the degree of correlation in societies); and (3) rationalization (or the problem of modernization). These three lines of inquiry correspond with theories attached to the names of Marx, Durkheim, and Weber, respectively. I bring the lines of Durkheim and Weber together in chapter 3 and discuss the line of Marx in chapter 4. Ultee et al. (1992, 189) do not feel that, from a sociological perspective, a fourth line, that of the individual, should be distinguished. But from the point of view of the human sciences it would seem natural to pay attention to that aspect. This I do in chapter 2.

These three foundational chapters raise the question how the process of modernization is related to the developments in church and theology, as important spiritual and social forces in society. Where are the links? In what way did church and theology react, positively or negatively, to this development? Inspired by practical-theological interest, I try in chapter 5 to determine how sensitive theology is to the problems of today. Once again I opt for a hermeneutical-critical reading, but always also from an empirical angle. This approach further adds to our understanding of the origins of practical theology. At the end of the chapter, this leads to a position that serves as the basis for the other parts of the book.

I conclude this first part with chapter 6, which fathoms the historical depths. Practical theology was preceded by pastoral theology, which continues to play an important role. Through the centuries, the church has reflected on its pastoral and ecclesiastical activities, as these gave shape and content to the Christian tradition. Important decisions were made that continue to have their impact even today.

This concludes the section about the early history of practical theology, seen in the light of the record of the "history of understanding."

CHAPTER 2

The Enlightenment of the Subject

The Enlightenment (Dutch *Verlichting;* German *Aufklärung*) is a period in the history of European culture, more or less coinciding with the eighteenth century and ending at the time of the French Revolution in 1789. The term *Enlightenment* describes what this period did with regard to the process of raising certain issues to the consciousness of the people — a process that has its impact even today. An enlightened person has become a different kind of person. Each has become the subject of her or his own experience. This leads to a new understanding of religion and church that rebels against all forms of authoritarian faith and develops through subjective reflection and rational deliberation.

Taking this as a point of departure, I describe in this chapter a first perspective on practical theology. After the Enlightenment a new era commenced (2.1). The great philosopher Kant (2.2) marked the end of the Enlightenment and the beginning of a new time *(Neuzeit)*. Practical theology owes its origin to Schleiermacher (2.3), the first modern theologian, who, recognizing the value of the Enlightenment, wanted to build a bridge to modern humanity by reflecting on the Christian faith on the basis of the experience of the subject. In his *Kurze Darstellung* (2.4) he provided the basis for practical theology. The process of subjectivizing (2.5) became an important theme within the culture of this new era, and also a basic theme for the further development of practical theology.

2.1 The Consequences of the Enlightenment

The optimistic view that humankind experiences a process of progress was characteristic of the nineteenth century. Human possibilities were rated highly, in particular the use of reason as the test of truth. For Kant the Enlightenment signified human beings' release from the immaturity they had inflicted on themselves. He formulated the crux of his view in 1784 in these words: "Habe Muth, dich deines eigenen Verstandes zu bedienen" ("Have the courage to use your own brain"; van Laarhoven 1974, 69).

The Enlightenment has often been presented as an attack on the Christian faith. That idea is one-sided. It forgets that this movement could in fact originate within a culture that had for centuries been influenced by Christianity. The Christian faith helped to prepare the way for the self-reliance and new self-understanding of modern humanity. Rössler (1986, 78) points out that the Enlightenment continued not only the lines of the Renaissance and of Humanism but also those of the Reformation and Pietism — movements in which the modern subject also began to emerge. Christianity not only has to deal with the consequences of the Enlightenment — it also helped to create the environment in which the Enlightenment could originate.

The philosopher Th. de Boer states that the philosophers of the Enlightenment had a high regard for religion and for a Supreme Being (1989, 59). He argues that the antithesis between the God of the philosophers and the God of Pascal is rooted in Greek philosophy, which differentiated between truth in the sense of scientifically demonstrated knowledge *(epistēmē)* and opinion *(doxa)* based on sensory perceptions. The later controversy between faith and reason is similar. In the period of the Enlightenment the tension between the narrative tradition of Scripture as a source of information and that of the rational content of knowledge was brought to a head. Revealed information is based on opinion! Truth cannot be proved. Real knowledge is limited to what is absolutely certain. But all philosophers of the Enlightenment continued to believe in God (de Boer 1989, 16).

Nonetheless, the tension increased, in particular in the area of culture and pedagogy. The education of the bourgeoisie implied a liberation from the influence of the church. Until then education and teaching had been the exclusive domain of the church. In his *Emile* (1762) Rousseau employed words like *freedom, nature,* and *reason* as he was getting ready to attack the current educational practices of the church. Van Laarhoven (1974, 69) points out that the *Déclaration des droits de l'homme et du citoyen* (Declaration of the rights of humanity and of the citizen; 1789) — the beginning of the French Revolution — must be viewed as an educational decree rather than a manifesto of liberation. This declaration, in turn, was heavily influenced by the American Declaration of Independence (1776), which put its indelible mark on American culture and religion: "All men are created equal." Self-reliance is a core value in this philosophy of life. It is a concept that can be linked to the Bible as well as to the republican tradition and would characterize the culture of the United States (Bellah et al. 1985, 55).

2.2 Immanuel Kant

This development made theology as science a highly questionable venture, as is clear from the writings of Immanuel Kant (1724-1804). In his *Critique of Pure Reason* Kant designed a new epistemology. This "pure reason" asks: What can I know? Two roads lead to knowledge: (a) experience, through the use of the senses; and (b) reason, through the use of arguments. These avenues provide knowledge about the world of phenomena. One cannot, however, know the essence of the things one experiences ("Das Ding an sich," the thing in itself). The entire world of the phenomena is the object of science. The spiritual realm (God, soul, immortality) lies beyond this and can be met only with agnosticism.

This approach led to the modern positivistic view of science. Science focuses on the increase of knowledge, on the basis of what can be seen, experienced, or reasoned. This has major consequences for theology. God cannot be an object of science. This discussion about the object of theology dates back to the Middle Ages, but has lost nothing of its force (Berkhof 1981, 22ff., 208ff.).

But, as we saw, Kant was not prepared to do away with all religion. He did not approach religion with "pure reason" but rather with "practical reason," through "the window of morality" (Berkhof 1985, 20ff. [1989, 8ff.]). This, however, means that the question has shifted from, "What can I know?" to other questions, which his epistemology could not answer: "What must I do? What can I hope?" This is the domain of the moral will. The idea of duty is inherent in the human spirit. Kant spoke in this connection of a categorical imperative, an absolute command. This was based on three presuppositions: (a) human freedom ("Du kannst, denn du sollst!" — If you can do it, you should do it); (b) the immortality of the soul (because in this life virtue and happiness do not coincide); (c) the existence of God (to answer the question of ultimate meaning, through a faith that has not yet come to doubt a higher order). I find it difficult to empathize, in particular, with this last aspect, for "Why could the world not be absurd?" (de Boer). These presuppositions do not represent knowledge in the strict sense of the word, but they can serve as the basis of morality.

Thus although common sense "almost forces us to believe" (Störig 1985, 2:77), Kant maintained that religion cannot be based on science. That was the crucial issue. In this context I will ignore that in his third part about the *Critique of Judgment* Kant referred to feelings and fantasy, and, in particular, to the doctrine of aesthetics. In his observations on nature, he defended the teleological principle of an objective usefulness of all things. Berkhof (1985, 25 [1989, 10]) feels that, although Kant was a dualist in his thinking, he appeared to be a "monist in hope." In his "postcritical" period he wrote a book about *Religion Within the Limits of Reason Alone,* in which he even concluded that Christianity was the only morally perfect religion (Störig 1985, 2:78). But this book deviated so far from the teachings of the church that it was censored, because this enlightened philosophy was allegedly abused to create "disruption and humiliation of various doctrines about the Holy Scriptures and Christianity." Theology and faith were put on the defensive. Nonetheless, Berkhof (1985, 36 [1989, 18]) concludes: "Kant's aim was to save both God and the Enlightenment — both with equal passion."

After Kant, theology as a scientific discipline in the university was more and more up for discussion. Indeed, this eventually left room only for the study of the phenomenon of religion, that is, for theology as the science of religion (Adriaanse et al. 1987, 80). Practical theology, in those days still understood as *theologia applicata,* had no place in this. The Dutch *duplex ordo* at the state universities (1876) rested on the same conviction.

2.3 Friedrich Schleiermacher

Much has been written about the significance of Friedrich Schleiermacher for practical theology. Nonetheless, it is far from simple to evaluate his concrete contribution. The welcome given to Schleiermacher in this discipline may be viewed as a "history of misunderstanding" (Drehsen 1988, excursus 3).

One might ask with reason whether Schleiermacher should really be regarded as "the father of practical theology." One can certainly not refer to Schleiermacher if one regards the unique aspect of practical theology as a "shift to the empirical," as is now the common perception. For he still belonged too much to the era of Idealism. The empirical approach originated at a later date and was first encountered in another candidate for the "fatherhood" of practical theology: C. I. Nitzsch (3.4).

Also, there is a major imbalance in Schleiermacher's thoughts on practical theology. Several scholars have pointed out that he failed to fill, in any material way, the encyclopedic space he formally assigned to practical theology, based on his views of the theory of science. He did not feel that a separate chair for practical theology "is even desirable," as he wrote in a letter to Wilhelm von Humboldt at the time (1810) when the University of Berlin was established (Krause 1972, 7). Due to a well-known, but one-sided, interpretation, his views on how the church must act remain stuck in a "clerical paradigm."

Below I pay further attention to this when I deal with his well-known *Kurze Darstellung*. But there is another reason why many refer nevertheless to Schleiermacher's work as the beginning of practical theology. If it is correct to view this branch of theology as a reaction to and a fruit of the awareness of the problems of modernity that resulted from the Enlightenment, one may regard Schleiermacher as the first modern theologian who took the new era into account as he formulated his theology.

Friedrich Schleiermacher (1768-1834) was born in Breslau. He owed his first name to the enlightened King Frederick the Great, whom his father served as chaplain. His education was strongly influenced by the schools of the Hernhutters he attended. Here an authentic sense of religiosity was awakened in him. But, at an early age, he felt also impressed by the works of Kant, and he began to doubt the orthodox doctrines. These two lines remained visible: an openness toward the rationality of the Enlightenment, which he fully accepted, and at the same time a tendency toward self-reflection and an intense interest in experience as the essence of faith.

Having finished his theological and philosophical study, and after a few years as a ministerial intern, he became a chaplain in a Berlin hospital in 1796. Here he was heavily involved with the Romantic Circle, a somewhat less than down-to-earth group, which he himself helped to found — an intellectual elite in the city that rejected one-sided rationalism and focused on the unity of life in which nature, the human psyche, feeling, individuality, and love were most important (Berkhof 1985, 48 [1989, 32-33]). In Potsdam (1799) he served temporarily as court chaplain. Here, at the country house of "Sans Souci," he completed his first major work on religion.

According to Willems in the introduction to his recent translation, this book "about religion: addressed to the educated and those who despise them," is "the first passionate attempt to give faith and religion its own place within the modern view of life" (Schleiermacher 1990, 7). Some of these "despisers" to which the title refers were his own friends, who had turned their backs on Kant and opted for a romantic pantheism. Schleiermacher's second major theological work, *Der christliche Glaube (The Christian Faith)*, appeared in 1821. Berkhof (1985, 61 [1989, 39]) maintains that his thinking had hardly changed since his first book.

The fundamental concept "schlechthinnige Abhängigkeitsgefühl" (feeling of absolute dependence) has often been misinterpreted as referring to individual emotion. But Schleiermacher's own words clarify the real meaning: "it means that we are conscious 'of being absolutely dependent, or, which is the same thing, of being in relation with God'" (Berkhof 1985, 58 [1989, 44]). He tried to link the *fides qua* with the *fides quae*. We would speak of "experience," or "a sense of transcendence." He chose human experience as his point of departure, but linked it, from the very start, in a relational way to transcendent reality. When faced with the choice between the objectivity of thought and the subjectivity of feeling, he opted for a form of intersubjectivity, in which God and human interact.

His use of the word *feeling,* in particular, has often been misunderstood. For Schleiermacher "feeling" was not the opposite of "knowledge" or "will," but was closer to our concept of "sense of direction" or "inner conviction." It is the heart of the human person and goes beyond knowing and willing (Birnbaum 1963, 22).

Thus the knowledge of faith may be described as a "feeling of absolute dependence." This feeling is an essential part of human piety or religious experience. "Absolute dependence" is the kind of dependence, says Neven, that renders any resistance meaningless. It describes what might also be called a *sensus divinitatis.* With regard to God this knowledge — to which, as a foundational kind of knowledge, Schleiermacher assigned an epistemological meaning — links proximity and distance. On the basis of this comprehensive religious consciousness he also offered a critical correction on Enlightenment thought patterns: "In so doing he wanted to prevent that the feeling of dependence would be played off against the modern consciousness of freedom" (Neven 1993, 33).

Berkhof is of the opinion that Schleiermacher had such a profound understanding of the problem of faith in this "new era" that he remains as relevant for us as he was for his contemporaries. By comparison, van Laarhoven (1974, 75) says, Catholic theology remained far behind.

2.4 The *Kurze Darstellung*

It is also against this background that one must understand his encyclopedic study, which deals with practical theology in a more explicit way. This *Kurze Darstellung des Theologischen Studium (Brief Outline on the Study of Theology)* is a construction of a number of theses with a total of 338 short sections. The reader should keep in mind that it was written from the perspective of this new awareness of the problem of modernity, which made both the scientific nature of theology and its unity, even within its own university department, a matter of discussion (Jüngel, Rahner, and Seitz 1968, 23).

Courageously and defiantly, Schleiermacher chose his point of departure in the Christian faith, which he viewed as a praxis that develops in the course of history and demands a critical-scientific reflection. As time went by, this reflection has spread, as a result of unavoidable differentiation, to a number of disciplines. It is historical, systematic, and in part also empirical. With regard to this last aspect, one may refer not only to the emphasis on historical research but also to an interest of the social sciences in church and society: the domain of statistics (§§95, 195, 233).

That he viewed praxis as the basis and organizational principle for theology as a whole (Rössler 1986, 27) is clear from his understanding of theology as a positive science.

Pannenberg mentions Schleiermacher's "famous and epoch-making description of theology as a positive science" (1973, 247 [1976, 248]). The *Kurze Darstellung* begins with this premise: "Theology is a positive science, whose parts join into a cohesive whole only through their common relation to a particular mode of faith, i.e., a particular way of being conscious of God. Thus, the various parts of Christian theology belong together only by virtue of their relation to Christianity" (§1). The term *positive science* means that such a science does not evolve from the way in which science as such is organized, but that it attempts to solve a practical problem: the Christian community of faith needs leaders with an academic training. Doing theology, therefore, is rooted in the praxis of faith, church, and Christianity in the context of a changing society. He borrowed the concept of positive science from Schelling, who put theology on the same level with the study of law and medicine — corresponding to Kant's three "higher faculties." He did, however, give this concept a more historical and empirical character rather than just using it as an organizational principle (§21; cf. Drehsen 1988, 160).

This determines the character of theology: "Christian theology . . . is that assemblage of scientific knowledge and practical instruction without the possession and application of which a united leadership, i.e., a government of the church in the fullest sense, is not possible" (§5). In his *Kurze Darstellung* Schleiermacher employs three distinct concepts: *Kirchenregiment* (church government), *Kirchendienst* (church service), and *Kirchenleitung* (church leadership). The first term is rather general, without any focus on a particular organizational form (§3). The second term refers to leadership in the church, more specifically the local congregation (§274), while the last term refers to leadership in general in the church and in Christendom (§271). Thus there is no question of a reduction to a "clerical paradigm," as has often been suggested. All activities in the service of a "further development" of Christianity are included.

Schleiermacher wanted to give theology its place in the scientific arena. Theology offers a reasoned apology for the Christian faith, as a real contribution to the well-being of humans and their world. He followed Schelling in his incorporation of theology in the "organism" of science, on the condition that theology also uses proven scientific methods.

In his organization of theology, Schleiermacher opted for the trichotomy of philosophical theology, historical theology, and practical theology, with historical theology as the material core. While philosophical theology provides the link with science, historical and practical theology ensure the relation with the church and the *Kirchenleitung* (church leadership). In the first edition of the *Kurze Darstellung* (§31) he could therefore refer to practical theology (by enlisting the metaphor of a tree) as the "crown," "since practical theology must make the problems of modern time its specific theme" (Drehsen 1988, 158).

In this encyclopedic work practical theology occupies an integral place. Schleiermacher extended the distinction between *Kirchendienst* and *Kirchenregiment* into the organization of the discipline (§275), and he placed restrictions on practical theology (§260). Practical theology has nothing unique to add to philosophical and historical theology in determining the essential tasks of the church. But these tasks *(Aufgaben)* must be worked out in instructions *(Vorschriften),* which may be classified and grouped on the basis of the concept of *Kirchenleitung.* They are like "rules of 'art'" (§265), consisting of "methods" (§263), and based on an "art doctrine" or "technology," also referred to as "hermeneutics" (§132).

During his career Schleiermacher prepared six series of lectures in practical theology. The notes of these lectures were published posthumously by J. Frerichs, in consultation with C. I. Nitzsch, in 1850. They are in essence similar to the *Kurze Darstellung,* except that some concepts are defined more precisely. In these notes Schleiermacher argued that the name "practical theology" is not quite correct, since practical theology should not be equated with praxis, but is rather the theory of praxis (1850, 12 [1988, 99]). The "crown" metaphor reappears: "Practical theology is the crown of theological study because it presupposes everything else;

it is also the final part of the study because it prepares for direct action" (26 [99]). He did not want to limit practical theology to a clerical paradigm, but gave it a much wider domain of action: "We do not have to limit the scope of practical theology to what is actually involved in carrying out the office of ministry. It will include every action in the church and for the church for which rules can be given" (27 [99]). In this same context he clarified the relation between experience and practical theology: *"The task of practical theology is to bring the emotions arising in response to events in the church into the order called for by deliberative activity"* (27 [99-100]). To steer these "emotions" into the right channels is thus of central importance. He referred to this as *psychologia* or "guidance of souls," directed toward the building of faith (40 [109]). This is the basis for the motivation to act, and it requires certain techniques. An artist, for example, a painter, can express her emotions only if she has the skills to depict them with paint on a canvas. Technique never stands alone but serves a creative process. The "rules" give direction to one's actions. Even the church is no goal in itself. He defined it in these words: *"The Evangelical church is a community of Christian life devoted to the independent exercise of Christianity"* (62 [126]). (He stated that this is quite different in the Catholic Church.) One can already hear in this description the differentiation between the individual (independence), the church (community), and Christianity as a whole that is so characteristic of our modern times.

Studying these statements carefully, one realizes that Schleiermacher was not yet able to give practical theology the integral place he here assigned to it. For in practice his approach does not yet go beyond that of an applied science, with a central role for the "church leaders," more specifically the charismatic leaders, who through their religious influence inspire "the mass" (§268). The latter restriction stems from the liberal sense of class structure, to which Schleiermacher and those around him were not unaccustomed.

But his propositions have a much broader potential. *Kirchenleitung* (church leadership) is, as we saw, a broad concept that does not limit the leadership of the Christian community of faith to the church. As Schleiermacher stated (1811 [1966], §263), no other means are available for the *Seelenleitung* ("guidance of souls") — for the impact of theological thought on church and Christianity — than to work on the feelings. The "technique" he refers to in this section does, however, exist today, with the result that the *Seelenleitung* (or as we would say today, "the mediation of the Christian faith") has now itself become the object of academic study. Thus practical theology has in the meantime much further developed in the direction of a desirable hermeneutic, through its own methodology, in a relation with the social sciences.

This completes the short overview of Schleiermacher's proposal for a practical theology within theology as a whole. As in all of his theological works, the believing subject is at the center. His point of departure is the Christian faith, and the purpose is the *Seelenleitung*, within and by the church, with a view to an independent realization of Christianity by the individual.

Comparing his encyclopedic work with the most important Catholic proposal — by Anton Graf (1814-1867), a scholar from the same period — one is struck by the fact that he also, against the background of the Enlightenment, went beyond the level of pastoral theology (Steck 1974, 27-41). The Catholic view of faith and church, however, placed a much stronger emphasis on the institutional church. In his introduction, published in 1841, the church itself occupied the central place. This is a significantly broader base than found in the proposal offered by F. S. Rautenstrauch (1734-1785), whose entire theology was focused on the work of the priesthood. Graf allowed considerable room for the "self-building" of the church. This approach has been developed further by Arnold, Schuster, and Rahner in *Handbuch van de pastoraaltheologie* (Manual for pastoral theology; 1966ff.).

2.5 The Subject in Practical Theology

In harmony with the trend of the Enlightenment, Schleiermacher's theology gave ample room to the awakening of the consciousness of the individual. Yet it also criticized the Enlightenment by correcting the exclusively rational understanding of the process of becoming a subject. He was influenced not only by the Enlightenment but also by Romanticism (van Laarhoven 1974, 75). He also dealt with the deeper levels of human experience, with religious self-understanding as its core.

This focus on the subject remains one of the most important themes in the culture of the new era (the *Neuzeit*) and constitutes, therefore, an essential part of the praxis of practical theology. At this point we are confronted with an ambivalence, which, depending on one's perspective, may be praised or criticized. Chapter 4, in particular, provides a critical assessment.

2.5.1 Subjectivizing and Individualizing

Some distinction ought to be made between attention for the subject and attention for the individual. The individual predates the subject. One could argue that the individual already came to the forefront in the period after the

Middle Ages, in Renaissance and Humanism, but also in a movement like the Reformation. This is expressed in Luther's well-known question: "How do *I* get a merciful God?" Humankind broke away from the collective and became an individual. As time passed by, this individual became more and more dependent on him- or herself. Through self-reflection one must sort out who one is. One can detect this, for example, in the Pietist movement. Here the modern subject announced his/her arrival.

The subject was the human being, who, searching for truth, questioning, doubting, and hoping, conscious of the problems of a new era, tried to stand on his or her own spiritual feet. The term *subjectivizing* means that "the subjective experiences, the perceptions of the people, become more important than what is objectively given or prescribed. This implies a change in the human consciousness. People begin to see things differently, and, as a result, change their approach toward values and truths" (Dekker 1987, 117). Schelsky refers to this form of consciousness as *Dauerreflection* (continued reflection; 1957, 159ff.).

From then onward the process of subjectivizing became part of the consciousness of almost all. In this context individualism often carries a negative connotation. It supposedly depicts humans as occupied only with themselves and, indeed, satisfied with themselves. The *I* sense replaced the *we* sense. But one can also view the individualizing process in a positive light, as individuation always takes place through participation. The one who can truly be her- or himself lives in an open relationship with others. This allows de Lange (1989) to present a plea for individualism. The line of individualism is further extended in 13.3.

2.5.2 The Projection Theory

According to Han Fortmann, a Dutch cultural and religious psychologist, the emancipation of the individual consciousness, which expresses itself in a greater individual autonomy, must be seen as a cultural phenomenon. He argues that the root of the word *criticism* is the Greek *krinein* (to separate). In primitive cultures one hardly finds any distinction between individual and collectivity, between I and not-I, between subject and object, between the inner and the outer, between the conscious and the unconscious (Fortmann 1971, 29). Everything participates in everything. From a cultural perspective the boundary between the self and the outside world is flexible. One cannot always clearly distinguish objective reality and subjective perception. If we find a "shining apple attractive" (an example given by Fortmann) our perception and experience clearly add something to the object we perceive. In between the two is an element of *projection*.

Fortmann maintains that in the last few centuries Western culture has moved in the direction of separation and distinction. The "I" begins to live a life of its own. This leads on the one hand to autonomy and self-realization, but on the other hand to isolation and disintegration. There is enrichment but also impoverishment, since the reflecting consciousness gets separated from its unconscious roots, from the maternal womb of collectivity, and thus loses its potential to participate and symbolize. The separation between subject and object in the world of human experience is a characteristic of modern culture. This development has its consequences in the area of religious experience as well in that of spiritual health, as Fortmann demonstrates in his major work (1964-68), in which the theory of projection occupies a central place.

The theory of projection once again brings us back to a contemporary of Schleiermacher, Ludwig Feuerbach (1804-1872), a disciple of Hegel. He detached himself from his master by concentrating more exclusively on sense perceptions. He saw theology as anthropology: humans define their own essence as they define God. Religion serves to satisfy human needs and desires. With this theory Feuerbach influenced the thinking of both Karl Marx and Sigmund Freud. Thus the theory of projection became a strong criticism of the Christian faith, even until our times, as it raised important questions with regard to the praxis of practical theology.

2.5.3 The "Bourgeois" Subject

The modern subject is often referred to as the "bourgeois" subject. This has to do with the privileged position of the progressive-liberal bourgeoisie, to which the *Hervorragenden* (opinion leaders) of Schleiermacher, in contrast to the *Masse,* belonged. The "burgher" became the central figure in nineteenth-century society. The burgher's view of reality was characterized by the idea of the autonomy of the individual and her or his needs. This has also been called *utilitarian* individualism (Ultee et al. 1992, 189).

H. Luther states: "This ability of systematic self-reflection is a prominent feature of the bourgeoisie consciousness" (1992, 89). This ability resulted in a continuity in existing relationships, stability in society, and economic expansion. In this way society became manageable and self-realization and self-protection were achieved.

"The program of self-realization is supported by a rationalistic worldview, in which the 'burghers' themselves, as subjects endowed with reason, use their ability and will to determine how they want to direct their life toward virtues they prefer and in ways they regard as sensible, and to arrange their life, especially in the area of work and society, in a rational, that is, regulated and disciplined, manner." The quotation from Drehsen (1991, 105) provides a striking picture of the bourgeoisie culture, with its emphasis on self-realization, education, and *Bildung* (formation), and with the concept of individualized religion as one of its components. To this the developing practical theology was subjugated.

De Lange (1989, 86) points to individualism and subjectivity as a recent phenomenon in the history of just one culture (Western), a fact that is often forgotten. The problem is that as soon as one begins to see oneself as an individual, in the eyes of many one apparently ceases to be a social being. Höfte is of the opinion that the dominance of the subject dates only from the twentieth century: "I believe that the history of the Netherlands since the Second World War must be understood as the irreversible breakthrough of the subject and his or her perception of reality" (1990, 26). This is further reinforced by the economic perspective, the possessive individualism, which leads to an unrestricted satisfaction of needs, with one human being competing against another.

In spite of the liberating character of this new subject awareness, this perspective cannot suffice for the development of practical theology. In an analysis of the bourgeoisie subject, Willms (1969) justifiably criticizes this perspective.

2.5.4 The Awakening of Consciousness and Angst

But also from within, this modern subjectivity already faced criticism in the nineteenth century. Subjectivizing can lead to deep anxiety, as one can see in the works of another giant of the nineteenth century, the Danish theologian and philosopher Søren Kierkegaard (1813-1855). Like no one else he castigated the spirit of the modern "burghers" ("our kind of people"), who from the cradle had learned to ask questions that threatened their own safety. Humankind is the abysmal product of the "time of rationality," of inventive calculations. This type of culture, according to Kierkegaard's satire, produces children, "who, before they have taken the time to admire the beauty of a plant or an animal, want to know what these things can be used for" (Scholtens 1979, 91). Kierkegaard undermined the self-confidence of modern humanity, for he saw anxiety (angst) as the deepest stratum of human existence. Therefore, he could view faith only as a paradox, an act that touches one's total existence, not based on doctrinal certainties but on "fear and trembling." God and religion are not the same! He regarded Jesus as the one who thwarts human plans, and in his writings he therefore fulminated against the institutional church of his day (Scholten 1982). In the twentieth century this opposition against liberal Christianity received its massive theological expression in the dialectical theology of Karl Barth (5.2.1), who was very critical not only with regard to religion but also with regard to this young cuckoo in the nest of the nineteenth century: practical theology.

Toward the end of the nineteenth century, the insight that the self-realization of the modern subject is indeed threatened by deep unconscious anxieties led to the discovery of the unconscious — the multilayered inner being of humans — and to the birth of psychoanalysis: the work of Sigmund Freud (1856-1939). Humans are less rational than was commonly assumed. From the earliest phases of life, human behavior is largely determined by emotional factors. What is called rationality is in fact often a rationalization of emotional needs and desires. Humans are unfree rather than free. J. H. van den Berg describes the ascent of psychoanalysis as a cultural phenomenon that fits with the bourgeoisie culture of that time (1973, 12). Deep insight into the counteracting forces in the psyche is needed if one is to meet the high demands of the new time on the reflecting subject. Psychological processes render humans unfree. Deep in the subconsciousness neuroses and psychoses are born that hamper one in the way one functions and land one in a crisis. Psychoanalysis is the road toward freedom. Since Freud, psychotherapy in all its different forms and traditions has become firmly established in Western culture. For a survey of the relation between psychoanalysis and practical theology, I refer to Lindijer (1984).

In this context religion also comes under discussion. Freud saw religion as infantilism, a "father projection," a neurotic illusion. But C. G. Jung (1875-1961) considered religion as a careful handling of archetypes (such as the shadow, animus/anima, and the Self) to be the deepest layer of the human personality, which is essential for the health of every human being. Today Jung's work strongly influences such movements as the New Age.

In the twentieth century religion and meaning, religious experience, and spiritual health become important themes in the developing psychology of religion. The first, now classical, work in this area is *The Varieties of Religious Experience* by William James, an American (1902). Subsequently, pastoral psychology finds its origin in the search for links between theology and psychology, which has grown in our time into an important branch of practical theology.

Finally, I should note that so far I have spoken in a rather undifferentiated manner about the awakening process of the human consciousness. That men and women are at different stages within this cultural development is an important insight that we owe to feminism, as well as to the emancipation movement that originated in the nineteenth century as a fruit of the Enlightenment (van Gennep 1989, 140ff.). What this meant for church and faith was not really apparent until the 1960s when feminist theology emerged.

Although through the centuries some women have claimed their rights and exerted an influence in a wider circle, the emancipation of women did not receive systematic attention until the Enlightenment. At the end of the eighteenth century, at the time of the American Revolution and the French Revolution, women in England, America, and France rose up and insisted that women have rights. The right to education was the primary demand. After 1830 the first schools for girls were established in the United States. Aletta Jacobs was the first Dutch woman who, in 1871, succeeded in being admitted to the university. But it was not until 1919 that Dutch women received full active and passive suffrage. This first feminist wave was followed more recently by a second, which focused on autonomy and independence for women.

2.6 Conclusion

In this chapter I developed the first perspective on the birth of practical theology as a theory of crisis. In this light one must understand practical theology as a *theology of the subject.*

I followed the cultural and philosophical trail of the Enlightenment, through the nineteenth century to today's therapeutic society, by looking at philosophers and psychologists, from Kant to Freud. Along this route subjectivity, self-realization, the awakening of consciousness, and liberation were prominent themes. But the insight that we are dealing with the spiritual heritage of an elite group placed this development also in a critical perspective.

In theology we first find the shift toward the subject in the writings of Schleiermacher, who for that reason and because of his *Kurze Darstellung* has justifiably become known as the "father" of practical theology. Faith and religious experience are important themes in connection with this process of becoming a subject.

Schleiermacher's proposal for a practical theology leads toward "a view of the church that regards the individual as the only important component" (Luther 1992, 9). His conception of this discipline can be formulated as "practical theology as guidance for human souls" *(Seelenleitung)*. Important themes such as meaning in life, religious experience, and spiritual health have kept their relevance until today.

This sketch of the development of practical theology suggests that one can understand it as a process of adaptation to a cultural process of subjectivizing. But this does not take away from the responsibility of practical theology to relate to this process in a theological-*critical* way, as it formulates its theories.

CHAPTER 3

The Modernization of Society

In this chapter I intend to develop a second perspective on the origins of practical theology. The subjectivizing of modern humans must be studied within the broader context of the modernizing of society. *Modernizing* is a general term to describe the processes of change that have occurred in society in the last few centuries, with modernity as its end product.

This development runs parallel to the empirical shift in society and to the rise of the social sciences, sociology in particular. While in the previous chapter I focused primarily on philosophy, in this chapter sociology provides the most important concepts. It is a new science that has gained its independence from philosophy. The empirical categories developed by this new discipline help us to understand and explain society in terms of rationalization and differentiation (3.1). Rational techniques allow us more and more to control and guide societal developments. This means considerable progress in a number of areas.

But this development has another side to it (3.2). The modernizing process has a number of side effects, for example, the bureaucratization of society and the dehumanization of humanity. Religion and church are increasingly confronted with secularization. Remarkably, the social sciences have from their start shown a keen interest in the development of religion (3.3). The work of Max Weber is the most important example of this trend.

There exists a clear link between this modernization process and the development of practical theology, as becomes evident in an empirical interest in the way the church functions as an acting subject. This is clear in the proposals of Schleiermacher's disciple, C. I. Nitzsch (3.4), who played a major role in the further evolution of practical theology. After him, practical theology developed in a direction inspired by the social sciences.

3.1 Modernization as a Process of Differentiation

My description of the concept of modernization must be limited to some general observations. Modernization is "the development in society that is characterized by the attempt to solve problems from the perspective of rationality" (van der Ven 1993, 18 [1996, 5-6]).

Sociologists clearly agree as to what must be seen as the hard "core" of the modernization process. It is the concept of differentiation. I first discuss the differentiation process, and then look at a number of related phenomena: pluralism in society and the ongoing, ubiquitous specialization. We are here dealing with a historical process, which I approach retroactively in this section; that is, I view it from the perspective of "modern society" as the final product.

3.1.1 The Process of Differentiation

Sociologist of religion F. X. Kaufmann (1989, 217-18) argues that "a functional differentiation of society" is accompanied by a "structural individualization of interpersonal relationships." He points out that this insight can be traced to such classical sociologists as Emile Durkheim and Max Weber, and has been formulated in different ways in our time, among others by Jürgen Habermas.

Social differentiation may be described as "the process by which social entities are split into separate units, which, often with their own distinct functions, begin to lead a life of their own" (Dekker 1987, 113). The "unitary structure of life" has been broken, and relatively autonomous sectors, such as the economy, science, and politics, come into being through a "societal division of labor" (Laeyendecker 1992, 26). Each of these sectors has their own specific goals (profit, knowledge, power, respectively). These three sectors constitute the core of *the public domain.* Relationships within this domain are functional and businesslike. Large bureaucratic organizations are required for the proper functioning of these sectors. In contrast to the public domain there is *the private domain,* the world with personal relationships and smaller networks. This provides a sketchy but accurate picture of a differentiated society.

This distinction between two domains, the public and the private, has a major impact on the experience of people. While in the past most people were quite able to link these two related spheres, they now experience them as totally separate. This discrepancy in the two spheres of experience is referred to as *privatization*. The public domain is increasingly seen as autonomous and abstract, as a world of functionaries who speak their own jargon. It is a complex world that has become less and less accessible as a result of ever-increasing bureaucratization. The public domain is ruled by cold rationality, while only the personal domain allows for emotions. As soon as they have left their place of work, many people therefore withdraw into their private domain, where personal relationships are important and where they can be who they are. This stimulates a separate culture for free time and hobbies, where everything is as relaxed as possible. Media and commerce reinforce this picture.

Thus one can speak of a personal and an impersonal world (Dekker 1987, 127). Social differentiation runs parallel to a differentiation in values, as the gap between different sectors widens not only structurally but also culturally. This process of privatization has significant consequences for religion and church life. The latter becomes more and more confined to the sphere of free time and private life.

3.1.2 Pluralization and Specialization

This differentiation has its bearing on other phenomena. It is linked to a pluralization of culture, which manifests itself in a greater variety of values and norms, and of religious convictions. We are confronted with a complex phenomenon that plays at different levels. We see how different cultures and subcultures coexist in society. The more closed such a culture is, the more people experience it as a unity, as was the case in the past. Until the 1960s, Dutch society was segregated along religious and ideological lines: Catholics, Reformed, but also Socialists. Each group had its own culture with a strong credibility and an intense *plausibility structure* (Berger 1969, 43ff.), since their convictions could count on social affirmation and support. This was particularly true in groups that owed their origin to emancipation movements. In an open society people live simultaneously in different spheres. They participate in different cultures, and thus there is more interaction between the groups. People begin to put a greater value on other cultures and are less inclined to regard only their own ideas as true and good. A plurality of value orientations is the result. This also affects how people experience themselves; they become pluralistic. Their identity is usually nothing but a plural identity (Dekker 1987, 121).

Differentiation is also accompanied by specialization. There are more and more people who, within a very limited sphere, acquire almost unlimited skills and knowledge. The generalist disappears from the scene. One sees such specialists not only in medicine and politics but also, for instance, in the world of theology and church. This specialization leads to the acquisition of further skills through professionalization. Our modern world demands good testimonials, in the form of diplomas obtained through continuous education programs. The autodidact is ever rarer. This leads to new distinctions, also in the domain of church and religious organizations, for instance, between experts and laity, and between professionals and volunteers. In the latter case the distinction is further expressed in the contrast between paid and unpaid labor.

3.2 The Consequences of the Process of Modernization

We owe it to the empirical shift, in particular to the rise of sociology, that processes in society can be analyzed and explained. As a result, we are able to objectify social phenomena in society. Drehsen (1988, 166) states that the "self-thematization" of society is in itself already a form of modernization.

Modernization is accompanied by a rationalization of society. In this connection I am thinking first of all of a cognitive-instrumental rationality (van der Ven 1993, 24 [1996, 12-13]). By this I mean thinking in terms of means and goals, in order to control processes in an optimal way. What is the shortest route toward achieving a certain goal? What is most useful? Utilitarianism and acting in a rational way with a clear goal in mind are part of an attitude of the mind in which questions such as "What does it do for me?" and "What does it give me?" dominate. Every activity has a purpose.

This thinking in terms of usefulness also has an impact on the private sphere. One may think, for instance, of the rationalization of much domestic work that has given women, in particular, more freedom. But there are also sectors in society, such as recreation, art, and religion, where things are done without ulterior motive, without some clearly established goal. People may be harmed when, even in the private sphere, strict utilitarian thinking gains predominance. When the various bonds between individuals and groups, which are the very fabric of society, are seen only in terms of usefulness, interpersonal relations become more and more businesslike. With Habermas (8.4.1) one could then speak of a "colonization" of "lifeworlds."

Rationalization leads to a functional mode of thinking, which sees human beings first and foremost in the role they play and the position they occupy. Van Peursen (1976, 80) sees this switch from an ontological mode of thought to this functional mode of thinking as the characteristic par excellence of our time. He regards this development as positive, but does not ignore the negative side of this functional attitude: operationalism, which he defines as the sole focus on action, on operations (103). This leads to a reduction of reality.

Though modernization is usually understood as renewal — the fruits of which are harvested gratefully even by the harshest critics — its accompanying objectifying has proved not to be without side effects. The social sciences, in their turn, strongly influence the human consciousness. One can see how forms of categorizing develop within social groups. Individuals and groups are "labeled" on the basis of certain external characteristics or attributes. Statistics express these things in percentages; the majority is usually treated as "normal," while the minority is regarded as deviating from the norm. Society is demythologized and becomes surveyable and controllable through compartmentalization and definition.

A current, and in some respects justified, criticism is that this development not only solves problems but also creates some new ones. For as soon as a group in society is stigmatized as a problem, people begin to realize that they belong to that group and begin to see this as problematic, afraid that others will regard them as such. This phenomenon has been referred to as "victim blaming" (Claerbaut 1983, 163). These people are subsequently offered social assistance, which itself is a product of this social scientific mode of thinking, and can therefore only to a limited extent contribute to a solution of the problems that have arisen (Achterhuis 1980).

These developments led to major changes in society but also put their stamp on humanity. Here one can detect a connection with the previous chapter. I could point to various kinds of profiles of modern humanity that have been suggested. D. Riesman (1950) pictures the modern person as "other-directed." "The person's inner being is replaced by radar equipment that searches the environment and provides the norms for one's actions" (Weima 1981, 7). This is in contrast to the "inner-directed" person of the past, who was inspired by an internal ideal and let him- or herself be guided by an internal compass. T. W. Adorno (1950) characterizes "the authoritarian personality" as the person who, for lack of inner conviction, because of his or her fundamental anxiety and insecurity, relies on external authority. Herbert Marcuse (1964) speaks of "the one-dimensional man," whose existence is characterized by emptiness and alienation in a culture dominated by rationalistic-technocratic thinking. Van Peursen (1976) confronts us with the human as a functional being, while Christopher Lasch (1979) regards the alienation people experience in the sphere in which they live as unhealthy; he speaks of a "culture of narcissism."

3.3 The Consequences for Religion and Church

References in the previous paragraphs already indicate that the modernization of society has far-reaching consequences for religion and for the church. For a new worldview not only changes the way in which humans see themselves, but also influences the way in which they look at God. For that reason the classical sociologists were already extremely interested in religion.

3.3.1 A Changing Worldview

One can detect this attention for religion already in the works of Auguste Comte (1798-1857), who developed the science of sociology from philosophy and gave this new discipline its name. M. ter Borg (1991, 110ff.) shows how Comte connects society and worldview. Each society needs a worldview as an integral and inspiring idea in which life and action are rooted. For a long time religion filled that role. But as a society developed wherein knowledge was based on sense experience, traditional religion gradually disappeared. Each branch of knowledge inevitably goes through three stages. Our knowledge of nature provides a good example. The stage of theological explanation was followed by the metaphysical stage, which in turn gave way to the positivistic stage. Religion and metaphysics gave way to logic and empirical perception (Korthals 1989, 88). Science replaced traditional religion as a means of orientation and thus led to its eclipse. But the need for a worldview that will give meaning to life remains, since existential questions cannot remain unanswered (ter Borg 1991, 14).

This one also finds with another classical sociologist, Emile Durkheim (1858-1917), who broadly distinguished the same stages as Comte and also had a profound interest in religion. He took the process of differentiation — more specifically the process of the division of labor — as his point of departure. He argued that in Western society this resulted in a new kind of solidarity: organic solidarity. People were increasingly dependent on each other. For division of labor entails specialization and assigning specific tasks. For that reason, in spite of increasing pluralism and individualism, people continue to need each other (ter Borg 1991, 135-36). Durkheim explained religion from the perspective of its social function, as an integrating factor in society: "Religion is the symbolic expression of human dependence on society" (Dekker 1987, 27). He saw in religion "the ultimate means of orientation that provides identity and culture": "At regular intervals and in times of crisis, religion, and the unity of society, is reaffirmed" (ter Borg 1991, 136). If this does not happen, social chaos — Durkheim used the term *anomy* — ensues. This is a serious threat to the social order and to individual identity. Individualism, understood as the maturation of the individual, is the only element that continues to bind all members in a given society together. The existential question, like the remaining religious question, can be answered only in the private sphere. Even though Durkheim's argument may be open to different objections, his paradoxical premise "that individualism is the final collective form of religion" remains intact (ter Borg 1991, 140).

Whether religion will disappear or will continue to exist as an existential question (the two possibilities that seem to present themselves), it is clear that both sociologists saw little future for the Christian tradition.

Comte and Durkheim represent the school of structuralist functionalism, one of the three most important theoretical traditions in sociology (Ultee et al. 1992, 77). This approach focuses on the way social institutions function in actual practice. Hobbes's (1588-1679) question: "How can people live together in peace?" is central. This has also been referred to as the problem of order, described by Durkheim as "the problem of cohesion." A society must display a clear coherence (structure), including certain norms and values. Religion plays an important role in this. To the degree that a society is integrated, which is manifested in close intermediary groups, and thus shows a greater cohesion, there will be less cause for anomy (social chaos). This will also result in lower suicide statistics. (Cf. Ultee et al. 1992, 76-92.)

3.3.2 Max Weber

Max Weber (1864-1920), another of the classical sociologists, made the theme of the rationalization of Western culture the core of his work. He studied law, but his academic interest was much broader and included economics, history, and philosophy. He taught at several universities in Germany and Austria.

His method may be described as *verstehende sociologie* ("understanding" sociology), the interpretive understanding of social actions, in order to explain the causes and effects of these actions. Three questions demand an answer: What does the actor say (do)? What does the actor intend to say (do)?

Why does the actor say (do) what she or he says (does)? (Brand 1978, 806). Behind these questions is his premise that social actions have meaning. Meaningful action is based on values. This explains Weber's interest in religion.

His specific interest concerned the question, What has rationalization, especially the rational organization of labor, meant for Western culture? Thus he saw in "capitalistic action" the meaning of constant, methodical diligence, thriftiness, levelheadedness, and a sense of individual responsibility for professional tasks (Brand 1978, 810).

This leads us to his well-known work on the relation between Protestantism (Calvinism) and capitalism (Weber 1920 [1930]). His interpretation of this relation goes back to the Jewish religion, characterized — in its orientation toward ethical behavior — by a this-worldly tendency and a measure of reciprocity between God and humanity, based on the perspective of the covenant. The Jewish laws also emphasize asceticism. In times of crisis charismatic leaders (prophets) would arise to urge obedience to God and a new commitment *(Gesinnung)*.

Calvinism is also this-worldly, rational, and ascetic (ter Borg 1991, 122ff.). In this context "this-worldly" is to be understood as being focused on life here on this earth. This is accompanied by asceticism, since the ultimate goal is found in a higher life. This religious orientation has a bearing on the rationalization process, which is part of the basis of modern society. The world loses its magic and is opened up to scientific inquiry.

The main inner difference between Calvinism and Judaism is the former's emphasis on the individual and one's relationship with God, as expressed in the importance attributed to election and the requirement that one must live to the honor of God. This places one in the world with a sense *(Gesinnung)* of temperance, self-control, and thrift, which leads to a labor ethic that stimulates modern capitalism. Profession and calling coincide. "Promoted by Calvinists and Puritans, rationalization, asceticism, a this-worldly orientation, and control over nature create a world that differs from all that went before" (ter Borg 1991, 127). In this "this-worldly" rationalization everything turns on human effort, to the extent that God slowly but surely disappears.

In limiting the scope of his inquiry, Weber wanted to avoid misunderstandings. But in so doing he in fact asked for them. The "Weber doctrine" has led to a torrent of praise and criticism. Critics argue primarily that Weber looked at the Reformation era through Romantic nineteenth-century glasses and portrayed eighteenth-century Puritanism rather than Calvin's Calvinism (Rothuizen 1980, 26ff.). Also, the "this-worldly" asceticism within Western culture was certainly not limited to the Calvinistic segment of the population. Nonetheless, only few sociologists would deny some link between Protestantism and capitalism (Ultee et al. 1992, 150). Weber's views continue to fascinate, because he connected religion with rationalization. In any case, he was right when he maintained that the Christian faith, as it developed within Western culture, opened up created reality to scientific inquiry, and thus paved the road toward rationalization.

Attempting to understand the relation between religion and modern society from the perspective of the classic theories (of Weber, in connection with those of Comte and Durkheim), one discerns two lines. The first points to the disappearance of traditional religion and institutional Christianity as a result of the secularization process. The second points to the survival of religion in some form or another, since religion is part of the spiritual baggage of every human being. The following sections deal with the secularization process in more detail.

3.3.3 The Process of Secularization

In the previous section differentiation and rationalization were singled out as essential aspects of the modernization process. The concept of secularization is closely linked to this. But it proves to be capable of many interpretations (Nijk 1968), and is often used not in a descriptive but in an evaluative sense (Drehsen 1987, 222ff.).

G. Dekker (1988, 32), a prominent Dutch sociologist of religion, uses the term *secularization* in three different ways. (1) Secularization as a decrease in the religiosity of the people. Religious activities and convictions decrease in number and in intensity. (2) Secularization as a restriction of the scope of religion. Sectors of society gain their independence and religion is pushed back to the private sphere of life. (3) Secularization as adaptation of religion. Religion adapts its content to developments in society and to the ways in which modern people see themselves.

L. Laeyendecker (1990, 12) describes the various stages in which these three aspects occur. As religion is pushed back to the margins of society, its scope becomes narrower. First, religion is restricted to the private sphere of life (privatization). Then secularization even touches that private sphere of life. Individual religiosity, as expressed in church attendance and prayer life, diminishes. This implies a change in religion itself: concepts of God become vaguer and more diffuse and lose their personal character.

Dekker points out that these three processes do not necessarily coincide and are not always simultaneous. This explains the different developments in Europe and the United States. In the United States the process of adaptation (internal secularization) has been much stronger. As a result, individual religiosity has not decreased as in Europe, where the gap between religion and modern society has been much wider.

A further distinction can be made between a cultural and a structural dimension of secularization (Dekker 1975, 42; van der Ven 1993, 137 [1996, 154]). The cultural dimension is related to the process of rationalization, as described by Weber. Social reality is desacralized and this affects belief in God. Empirical research shows, at least in the Netherlands, that among members of all churches belief in an impersonal God becomes stronger to the detriment of belief in a personal God (van der Ven 1993, 138 [1996, 154-55]). The structural dimension is primarily related to the differentiation process. Autonomous institutions tend to give meaning within their own frames of reference. Thus ideologies give meaning to life with and without a specific worldview, which may or may not be religious. Nowadays the Dutch population derives its meaning for life more and more from a nonreligious worldview. This development leads to a further pluriformity in the search for meaning and in an increased marginalization of the Christian religion (van der Ven 1993, 139 [1996, 157]).

Any value judgment on secularization must remain ambivalent. On the one hand it brings autonomy and emancipation, which are experienced as liberation, while on the other hand it brings forms of loss. There is a "loss of reference," as believers receive less reaffirmation from those around them; there is also a "loss of relevance," as in many areas of life norms and values are no longer derived from religion, and a "loss of transcendence" because belief in God is replaced by a secular worldview (Heitink 1988, 164-65). Justifiably, many see this as a serious threat to the Christian faith, even though it does not imply that all religiosity disappears. Sociologists also feel that, considering the regularly occurring revivals and periods of revitalization of religion in the past, the possibility of a reversal of the secularization process may not be totally excluded (Peters 1993, 22).

I pointed to a second line that provides an enduring link between rational action and religiosity: the human need for a worldview that inspires. Along this line M. ter Borg develops his theory of "a dispersed eternity." The traditional religious worldview is replaced by a plurality of worldviews, a multitude of charismatic projections of individuals and groups, as expressions of a this-worldly secular religiosity, that help people to deal with the existential questions of life. Religiosity cannot disappear, since it relates to a fundamental aspect of human existence, the human predicament (ter Borg 1991, 105).

Nonetheless, there is no doubt that, as a result of the secularization process, the mediation of faith has become problematic. This helps to explain the emergence of something like practical theology. Here I retrieve the main thread of my argument and have to discuss the work of C. I. Nitzsch.

3.4 Carl Immanuel Nitzsch

Practical theology evolves against the tide of modern society. As long as religion and the church continue to exist as a matter of course, any reflection on the manner in which they function is superfluous. But as soon as the functioning of the church becomes problematic, study must be given to the empirical church. Here the social sciences prove their usefulness, for they make it possible to speak about the church in a new way, not in theological images of the ideal but in descriptive and explanatory languages, based on its actual situation.

F. X. Kaufmann (1989, 6) points out that it was not until the nineteenth century that the church was also perceived as a social organization of Christians. Due to that insight, ecclesiology could become a separate topic. Empirical thinking enables one to make the church itself an object of analysis. "This leads, as the discussion within practical theology shows, to the inevitable focus on the church as a social organization for communication and action" (Kaufmann 1989, 14).

The first practical theologian in an empirical sense, C. I. Nitzsch (1787-1868), was a disciple of Schleiermacher but transcended him in this aspect. More than his teacher, Nitzsch put his stamp on the further development of practical theology (Rössler 1982, 6). V. Drehsen warns against overvaluing the work of Nitzsch in relation to that of Schleiermacher. But they complement each other, with Schleiermacher drawing the basic contours, and Nitzsch filling in the details that had been left undefined in the work of his teacher (Drehsen 1988, 142-43). G. Otto is of the opinion that Nitzsch's concept, which assigns the church a central place, more easily leads to a reduction of practical theology to just the activities of the clergy than that of Schleiermacher, who chose the broader area of religion as his point of departure (Otto 1986, 45). History has proved him to be largely correct, for Otto shows how pastoral theology, which had been superseded with the help of Schleiermacher, made its return through the back door of the congregation. This, however, was certainly not Nitzsch's intention. But, in whatever way one evaluates this approach, all interpreters agree that since Nitzsch ecclesiology must be viewed as one of the most important themes in practical theology (Rössler 1982, 20).

In his three-volume study on this discipline, Nitzsch defined practical theology as the "theory of the church's practice of Christianity" (1847, 123ff.). Neither the historical nor the doctrinal church concept is the source of practical theology. Its essence is rather "the grounding, development, and mediation in the actual life of the church, its experience and action." Noteworthy is his view of the methodology, which should leave room for an empirical approach. In this context he remarks: "Our knowledge and our learning from praxis must always have a clear practical goal and must always give us direction, analyze experiences, explain what takes place, find its basis, and develop principles. Therefore we should, first of all, employ the empirical method. But we must also pay attention to conceptual aspects, and, third, use a more regulative approach; and in none of these approaches should we be accused of being nonmethodical." Thus he suggested a multimethodical approach. The church must explain events and trends empirically, but also pursue a theological study of the various concepts, while it formulates certain rules and regulations for its praxis. These three, Nitzsch argued emphatically, are part and parcel of a single approach. This division in three has not lost its actuality (cf. chapters 10-12 below).

Based on the elaboration of his definition of practical theology, one may conclude that Nitzsch brought the discussion about the foundations forward in a number of areas. First, he gave practical theology its own object and, in so doing, its own place within the discipline of theology as a whole. Nitzsch understood theology as a "scientia ad praxin," which finds its climax in a "scientia praxeos" (Rössler 1986, 34). Second, however, he also viewed the church as an acting subject, thereby surpassing Schleiermacher, who regarded the church as object — with a focus on the leadership role of the responsible ecclesiastical authorities. This functional understanding of the church makes it possible to see the church as an object of inquiry with regard to its self-understanding and its course of action. The subject of the ecclesiastical embodiment of Christianity is the congregation in all its members.

Third — and this is the most important aspect in this chapter — the new self-consciousness of a modernized society is clearly expressed in this thesis. Nitzsch's distinction between church and Christianity indicates that he understood the increasing differentiation of religion and church in modern society. In his analysis of Nitzsch, Drehsen argues that there is no question of a reduction in terms of just the institutional church, since Nitzsch clearly extended the church's embodiment of Christianity to all sectors of life. In this connection one phrase is central to Nitzsch's work: "The Christian faith acts in the world as a community and relates to it through the actions of the institutional church" (Nitzsch 1847, 1:13).

This single sentence, in which he showed himself a good disciple of Schleiermacher (cf. the latter's definition in 2.4 above), implies a differentiation of faith, church, and society. Christian faith, as the experience of the subject, and Christianity, as the unfolding of the Christian faith in the various sectors of society, extend far beyond the confines of the church. Thus Drehsen maintains (1988, 153) that Nitzsch's view of the church can be understood within the horizon of the kingdom of God, as the eschatological finalization of the Christian faith.

This must serve as a tentative practical-theological response to the process of differentiation and secularization in society, and the pluralization of religion that goes with it. Both the individual and society now have their own spheres of action. Thus the challenge of the Enlightenment — the subjectivization of religion — can be met by the Christian community that understands itself as an acting subject. A functional and rational approach, of structures and of processes of "being church," requires empirical instruments if the church is to face the developments in society in an adequate way. Part III shows how this tripartition by Nitzsch — individual, church, and society — provides important clues for our own time.

3.5 The Shift toward the Social Sciences

Within the confines of this chapter I cannot possibly provide a complete picture of the empirical shift within practical theology as the fruit of, and as a reaction to, the modernization of society. A few general observations must suffice. For a more detailed study I refer the reader, in particular, to the definitive study about the basic presuppositions of this discipline by Drehsen (1988).

One should ever keep in mind that church and theology tended to take the defense against any form of modernization and to combat it with ecclesiastical authority, rather than to face these developments in society in a positive way. J. van Laarhoven chronicles the history of the Roman Catholic Church in this period under the heading "The Church on the Defense," while in conservative Protestant circles the idea of modernization is usually interpreted in doctrinal, not in social scientific, terms, that is, as the result of a detestable modernism. This is not so strange. Secularization, as defined above by Dekker, implies a loss of influence by the church and a lesser say in major sectors of life. The very things that are viewed as a liberation from the perspective of the subject are regarded primarily as a threat by the ecclesiastical establishment. Only as one is prepared, as happens in the current practice of the sociology of religion, to view secularization as an inevitable differentiation from other relatively autonomous spheres of life does another approach become possible. Drehsen (1988, 118) refers, among others, to Peter L. Berger (see 11.3.2 below) and continues to view the work of Max Weber as seminal. Their empirical insights can bear fruit in the pursuit of practical theology. This occurred only in a fragmentary way as the new discipline developed in the nineteenth century. It is often only in retrospect, as we saw in the analysis of Nitzsch's work, that one can discern some traces of an empirical approach. Church and theology first and foremost tried to control the modern developments and to deflect them through their ecclesiastical authority.

This certainly does not mean that those who began to notice the relation between the developments in the church and those in society adapted uncritically to the new situation. From the beginning, practical-theological reflection was characterized by the critical interaction of theology and empiricism. Schleiermacher's view of theology as a positive science certainly does not imply a choice for uncritical positivism. Critical remarks to that effect were already voiced by Nitzsch (Drehsen 1988, 162), who noted that Schleiermacher's theological program does not entail the necessary critical analysis of the actions of the *Kirchenleitung* (ecclesiastical authorities). But this does not in any way diminish the critical intention of even Schleiermacher's theology (Pannenberg 1973, 255 [1976, 255]).

Subsequent to Schleiermacher and Nitzsch there have been many significant contributions to the development of practical-theological theory. From the perspective of this chapter, I mention only a few and further refer to the surveys of Birnbaum (1963), Krause (1972), and Drehsen (1988).

C. Palmer (1859) clearly distinguished practical theology from dogmatics, but then linked it to another normative discipline, ethics, since both deal with "life under the conditions of Christianity" (Otto 1986, 49). Based on a nomothetical theory of praxis, R. Rothe (1880; cf. Birnbaum 1963, 75) arrived at the same critical but concrete notion: he also placed practical theology as a critical-empirical science in an ethical context. The establishment of such a normative context preempts objections against a purely functional theory of action. Rothe distinguished two major aspects in practical theology: "the study of church order and the study of pastoral leadership" (1880, 102).

The first fully empirical approach to practical theology is found with

P. Drews (1910), whose proposals have been called "the most radical" until that time (Birnbaum 1963, 134). The size of Drews's book — only eighty pages — is inversely proportionate to its influence. Drews's ideal was to develop an "empirical ecclesiastic." He had discovered the empirical manifestation of the church as a social reality, and pled for a reorientation of practical theology, from a doctrinal view of the church to a historical and empirical view. The evangelical *Kirchenkunde* (church science) that he developed must be regarded as epoch making (Birnbaum 1963, 135). Drews himself, in the meantime, expected that some colleagues might find his approach too realistic and too empirical (Drews 1910; Krause 1972, 260). In addition, he made a definite distinction between the exercise of practical theology as an academic discipline and the study of specific subjects as homiletics, catechetics, liturgics, and poimenics, which he wanted to relegate to a *Predigerseminar* (a seminary for preachers; 1910, 251).

From the last quarter of the nineteenth century onward, the great manuals were written, such as the work of C. A. G. von Zezschwitz (1876), who defined practical theology as "the theory of the progressive self-realization of the church with the goal of establishing the divine kingdom in the world"; of E. Ch. Achelis (1880), who primarily focused on ecclesiastical and ministerial practice; of F. Niebergall (1918-19), who felt a kinship with Drews and built his practical theology along the lines of the science of religion; and of M. Schian (1922), who related practical theology to the activities of the institutionalized church.

Thus one can see how the empirical shift in practical theology, which began with Nitzsch, slowly but surely penetrated all practical theology.

3.6 Conclusion

In this chapter I developed a second perspective on the emergence of practical theology as a theory of crisis. In this light practical theology is viewed as a *theology of the way in which the church functions*, without the inevitable consequence of a reduction resulting from a clerical paradigm.

I followed the social-public track that is visible in the process of the modernization of society. The empirical development of practical theology parallels the development of the social sciences. Differentiation, rationalization, pluralization, specialization, professionalization, and — linked to all this — secularization belong to the important themes to consider, if one is to understand modern society and the role of religion and church therein.

The shift toward empiricism within practical theology is first seen in the proposals of C. I. Nitzsch, who thereby filled a void in Schleiermacher's work. He had an eye for a certain degree of differentiation between faith, church, and Christianity, in order to do justice to developments in society.

Nitzsch strongly influenced the further development of practical theology. From then onward the church occupied a central position as an acting subject. This may lead to a reduction as the result of a clerical paradigm, but also to a further unfolding of practical theology in an empirical direction. Thus practical theology more and more became an empirically inspired theory of action of the church, usually not just in a functional sense but also in a critical sense, by always viewing the empirical data in the light of a critical, that is, normative, theory about how the church ought to function.

CHAPTER 4

The Impact of the Social Question

The political-economical perspective offers, as a third approach, important clues for understanding the development of practical theology. The social question marks a breaking point in nineteenth-century society. It throws a monkey wrench in the belief in constant progress. Self-realization, firmly stimulated by the Enlightenment, remains the privilege of the bourgeoisie. In their responsibility for the majority of the people, they are ill prepared for the emergence of the proletarian masses. The threat of revolution endangers that privileged position and demands an adequate response to the problem of poverty.

With the Enlightenment and the modernization of society, the social question is part of the crisis of the new era, and therefore constitutes an important spiritual challenge for theology in general and for practical theology in particular. At first only a few see the urgency of the matter. For a long time the realm of theology was restricted to the spiritual world and had little to do with material reality. Someone like Marx must first arise, who established a link between consciousness and being, superstructure and foundation, knowledge and self-interest, before this insight penetrated into the thinking of theologians.

In this chapter I choose the revolutionary year 1848 as the point of departure. In Paris the new, fourth, estate — of the laborers — comes with social demands and causes riots that result in the removal of the king. In this same year other cities — Vienna, Berlin, and cities elsewhere in Europe — experience revolt. There is a cry everywhere for political reforms and more democratic freedom. In this atmosphere of international tension, the Dutch king William II changed, according to his own words, within twenty-four hours from a conservative into a liberal, and in the very same year the country received a new constitution, with a more extended suffrage, under the government of the liberal J. R. Thorbecke. Still in this same year, Karl Marx, together with Friedrich Engels, wrote the *Communist Manifesto,* while J. H. Wichern held his well-known oration about the social question at the *Kirchentage* (massive gathering of believers) of Wittenberg, and P. Hofstede de Groot, a professor at the University of Groningen, gave a lecture "about the peculiar character of the humanitarian associations of our time," in which he enunciated the basic principles of "andragology."

This chapter is based on the premise that these divergent events in this particular year are interrelated and have a major bearing on the emergence of practical theology. The social question, described in the first section (4.1), is only gradually recognized as a problem for the church. But reactions would come. The critical thoughts of Marx and emergent socialism meet with much opposition (4.2) from the side of the ruling liberal bourgeoisie. A small minority in the church and among the theologians was willing to listen to this criticism and understood the needs of the time as a form of repression and injustice (4.3). Those who belonged to this group saw the social question not merely as a political and economic issue, but as a personal problem of people who had become the victims. The agogic thinking that began to emerge at this time attempted to translate the problem in terms of education and humanitarian assistance for the people (4.4). Here and there the church began to realize its diaconal duties, but since politicians and churchmen by and large remained inactive, privately organized Christian associations tried to meet the needs of the people (4.5). There remained, however, a clear tension between a political-critical approach on the one hand, and an agogic approach, in terms of education and humanitarian assistance, on the other.

Yet this critical approach was not totally lacking in the developing practical theology of the nineteenth century, as one can see, for instance, in the work of Philipp Marheineke (4.6). He allowed for a critical theory of action. Against this background this chapter opens a third perspective on the origins of practical theology.

4.1 The Industrial Revolution and the Problem of Poverty

Between 1750 and 1850 Western society experienced immense changes. Rationalization induced technological progress, which, in its turn, became the engine behind a broad industrial revolution. The migration from the rural areas to the cities caused urbanization. In addition to the new third class of the bourgeoisie, a fourth class of laborers was born. When the class-structured society disappeared, the call for democratization and political change became ever louder.

The Industrial Revolution, which in the Netherlands began considerably later than in the rest of Europe (Ultee et al. 1992, 170), had dramatic social consequences. The living conditions of the factory workers, who lived in small quarters in anonymous apartment blocks, left much to be desired. Working days of fourteen hours for men as well as for women were no exception, and even children were forced to work at an ever younger age, to supplement the family income. Regular working hours were instituted since machines now determined when the work had to be done. Much work was monotonous and dull. The atmosphere in most factories was unhealthy and caused great distress, especially when epidemics occurred.

There were no social provisions. Those who could not work had to depend on their families or on church charity. Many sought escape in alcoholism. When the economy stagnated, large-scale unemployment created terrible poverty. In the mid-nineteenth century 60-70 percent of the Dutch population belonged to the poorest class: "charity-cases and destitutes, or: paupers, workmen, laborers, and servants, or: untrained and casual workers and people with their own small trade" (van Loo 1981, 23).

As soon as there was an economic dip or illness struck, people plummeted under the poverty line. Prior to the Industrial Revolution poverty was primarily a personal problem resulting from laziness or caused "by the hand of God" (Heidelberg Catechism, Lord's Day 10). Wealth was proof of good conduct or of sharing in the divine blessing. For a long time this thinking in personal categories prevented people from viewing poverty as a social problem.

The Law on Poverty of 1854 in the Netherlands, which replaces the first official regulations of 1818, built mostly on the principle of solidarity and gives priority to church charity. P. A. C. Douwes feels that the law of 1854 "bears the stamp of the convictions of the bourgeoisie, who could not reconcile their norms of decency with the sight of people dying of hunger, but, on the other hand, did not want to see their power challenged by riotous paupers and beggars" (1977, 64).

Douwes describes the diaconal work in Rotterdam. Personal charity to help the poor was replaced by organized assistance with a lot of bureaucracy. In order to get things under control, between 1804 and 1909 the poor of this city were required to worship in a separate church building, the "church of the poor." Those who came to church would receive a ticket with the word

"Sunday," which entitled them to assistance during the following week. This church was inaugurated on April 1, 1804, with a sermon on the text "the gospel is preached to the poor," Matthew 11:5b (Douwes 1977, 209).

4.2 The Response of Karl Marx

In 1848 Karl Marx (1818-1883), together with Friedrich Engels, wrote the *Communist Manifesto*. It begins with the words: "A phantom haunts Europe," and ends with: "Proletarians of all countries, unite!"

Marx, the son of a lawyer, studied in Bonn and Berlin, where he became infatuated with Hegel. The Hegelian system, his dialectical view of history, later often linked to the philosophy of Feuerbach, became the basis for his thought. Marx maintained the Hegelian dialectic as his method, but filled it with a new content, diametrically opposed to that of Hegel (Störig 1985, 2:157). That content was his materialistic worldview. Hegel regarded the idea as reality, while matter was only the external form; but Marx turned around this relation between thinking and being: the material determines the spiritual. This is referred to as historical or dialectical materialism.

The distinction between substructure and superstructure in Marx's theory is of hermeneutical importance. This terminology derives from a ship (ter Schegget 1977, 18). The substructure is the hull, the engine room, and the rudder. In the superstructure the maps are studied and the course is plotted. This is where the thinking is done. This image may be applied to society. The superstructure consists of the social interactions that receive shape in the totality of ideas and ideals, ideology, law, morality, art, science, and religion. The substructure consists of the means of production and their interactions. But the superstructure must rely on the substructure, the engine room. As a result of the division of labor the superstructure tends to go its own way, following its own interests. "The dominant ideas of an era were always just the ideas of the ruling class," the *Manifesto* of 1848 states. Consciousness becomes detached from being, and thus turns into a false consciousness.

Labor holds the central place in Marx's approach. Labor, performed in a conscious and systematic manner, is the essential condition for human existence (ter Schegget 1977, 11). Labor as social activity is the determining factor for other social phenomena and relationships. The way in which a society develops is largely determined by its mode of production of material goods. Marx gave special attention to the question of production versus ownership. The means of production are in the hands of a small group of people, and this inevitably leads to exploitation of the workers. Capital is an important factor.

Das Kapital is also the title of Marx's best-known book, the first volume of which appears in 1867. It pictures in clear language the struggle between the classes. In society two groups oppose each other: the capitalists, who own the means of production, and the members of the proletariat, who can only contribute their labor and are exploited by the capitalists.

In the context of this chapter I want to discuss, in particular, Marx's anthropological insights, which strongly echo humanistic Enlightenment ideals. The young Marx perceived that there was a social problem. He was among the first to recognize the proletarian situation and to understand this in terms of an alienation or a dehumanization of humanity (van Dongen 1964, 7). J. C. van Dongen points out that Marx borrowed the term *Selbstentfremdung* (self-alienation) from Hegel, but gave it another, social, content, because he perceived the very real threat to humankind of proletarianization (1964, 11). In analyzing the concept of alienation, Marx distinguished several aspects. First, the work environment of the laborer must be seen as an alienating factor. The product of labor is taken away from the laborer. The labor is determined by one's boss and loses the character of a free and creative activity. Next, one sees alienation emerging in one's social life. In the basement apartment one depends on the whims of the landlord. One's relationship with others becomes that of a servant versus a lord. All this leads to a state of self-alienation, which touches one's very existence. "One's various spheres of life become autonomous, and are threatened by materialism, instrumentalization, and a meaningless gratification of needs" (van Dongen 1964, 20).

Marx's criticism of religion, which met so much opposition in Christian circles, must also be understood against this background.

Marx's view of religion was expressed in his "opium text," in which he — taught by Feuerbach — unmasked religion. "*Man makes religion,* religion does not make man" (Marx and Engels 1964, 41). In these words he summarizes his projection theory.

Since this phrase has given rise to many misunderstandings, I cite the core of Marx's argument: "Indirectly the battle against religion is the battle against that *world* which has religion as its *spiritual aroma.* The religious misery is the *expression* of real misery, but also of a *protest* against this real misery. Religion is the sigh of the creature in distress, the soul of a heartless world, as it is the spirit of spiritless situations. It is the *opium* of the people. The abandonment of religion as *illusory* happiness requires the establishment of *true* happiness. If we require someone to give up his illusions about his situation, we *demand that he give up the situation that makes the illusions necessary.* The criticism of religion is thus, in its *essence,* the *criticism of the valley of lament,* which has religion as its *aureole.*"

(Italics are according to the Dutch version by ter Schegget 1977, 84, who also comments on the text [cf. Marx and Engels 1964, 42].)

Reading the text, one is immediately struck by its dialectical character. The text is dominated by the tension between protest and opiate, with religion in the role of intoxicant. But the question is whether this would exclude a different understanding of religion, as protest, had this been available. Theologians who in later times sought inspiration from Marx have not necessarily thought so.

Later, less dogmatic neo-Marxists adopted the outlines of Marx's thinking. The most important representatives of this movement belonged to the Frankfurt School. Its ideas were known as "the critical theory." In the pursuit of a more just society, social theories were analyzed on the basis of their societal background, and of the relation between "theory and praxis" (Habermas 1968). Max Horkheimer, Thomas W. Adorno, and Jürgen Habermas, but also Herbert Marcuse, Erich Fromm, and Walter Benjamin are regarded as belonging to this school of thought. Fromm's work has a broad significance, since he, like Marx and Freud, links Jewish thought with elements of humanistic psychology.

(Neo-) Marxist thinkers stimulated emancipation movements in their struggle for equal rights, and liberation movements in their struggle for freedom. They also provided clues for the theories of political theologians, liberation theologians, and feminist theologians. The "critical theory" regarding the relation between theory and praxis also led to a political-critical stream among practical theologians (see 9.4.4).

4.3 The Response of Church and Theology

How did the church and the theologians react to the social question? I want to look at three reactions: the *Innere Mission* (Home Mission) in Germany, Abraham Kuyper in the Netherlands, and the papal encyclical *Rerum Novarum*.

4.3.1 *The* Innere Mission: *J. H. Wichern*

J. H. Wichern (1808-1881), the father of the German *Innere Mission,* was deeply worried by the social question. The concept of alienation also played an important role in his thinking. Like Marx, he understood how the humanity of humankind was under threat. In his social thinking and actions, Wichern was not led by any compromise with the existing order, but by the clarity of the insight of evangelical faith (van Dongen 1964, 31). In 1848 Wichern gave his well-known speech during the *Kirchentag* in Wittenberg.

In this address, he pled with the church to regard the work of the *Innere Mission* as its own work. Let the church declare: "Love is as important for me as faith!" He appealed to the church, which alienated the people from itself, to confess its mistakes, since this was a matter of collective guilt: "We are faced with accumulated guilt, not of the individual but of all; a guilt not just of this generation but one that has been inherited over the centuries; a guilt that must be atoned for in this new era. The penance will be the marker between the past and the future in our church. The new era with its fruits will be more glorious than the old that has come to its end." The text of this address has been preserved only in telegraphese and is found in Bayreuther (1962, 107).

Wichern interpreted *Entfremdung* as alienation from God and neighbor. He did not proceed from a social analysis. Wichern's answer was a pedagogic one. He saw the solution for this alienation in a solid Christian (but not Pietistic) education. His educational theory (derived from Pestalozzi) was based on teaching people how to help themselves, within the context of a "comprehensive approach" (van Dongen 1964, 49). This required that the youth be given a new community. This ideal prompted him to establish a home for boys, the "Rauhe Haus" in Hamburg. "When he speaks about alienation, Wichern finds his theological point of departure in the practical pedagogic approach — in providing freedom within the context of a community" (van Dongen 1964, 38). *Rettung* (salvation) is individualizing and educating toward community in freedom. "Proletarianization can be prevented only if all aspects of need receive equal attention. For Wichern this community is the family" (van Dongen 1964, 49).

According to van Dongen, Wichern did not know what to do with the emergence of large industries. The reformer was hampered by the educator. His approach showed some structural suggestions, but they were not fully developed. The tragedy of much of the charitable social work in the nineteenth century was its failure to formulate a structural answer to the social question, the more so when one considers the compassion and the great sacrifices that were made.

This same zeal and inventiveness also characterize the representatives of the Dutch *Reveil* (Awakening), such as O. G. Heldring (1804-1876), who not only established homes and schools in Zetten and Hoenderloo, but also dug a well in the sand of the Veluwe, and wanted to kill two birds with one stone by sending Christian workmen to the Dutch East Indies. Laborers who fell victim to poverty in the Netherlands could there contribute to the spreading of the gospel as workers-missionaries. He showed himself in all of his writings to be "a simple, practical man" (Reenders 1991, 70). As a result, a broad network of organizations developed. "The Christian association takes the place of the church and of the state" (van der Werf 1960, 57), to alleviate the needs in society.

4.3.2 The Red Booklet of Kuyper

Abraham Kuyper's (see 5.1.3 below) address during the first congress of Christian social workers in 1891, later known as his *Red Booklet*, was the only structural Protestant response. In this speech he indeed made some significant statements. "When rich and poor stood opposed to one another, he [Jesus] never took his place with the wealthier but always with the poorer" (Kuyper 1891, 16). He added the following analysis: "Thus in all of Europe a well-to-do bourgeoisie rules over an impoverished working, which exists to increase the wealth of the ruling class and is doomed, when it can no longer serve that purpose, to sink away into the morass of the proletariat" (22 [47]). He employed the term *false desire* in this context. He probably read Marx's *Das Kapital* as early as in 1874, and, in any case, knew all about the German and English Christian Socialists (Jager 1976, 18). He referred to the need for an architectonic criticism of society, in order to change its organization. Poverty should never be linked to the will of God. "If there are still some who, God forgive them, try to defend such abuse by an appeal to the words of Jesus: 'For ye have the poor always with you' (Matt. 26:11), then out of respect for God's holy Word I must register my protest against such a misuse of the Scriptures" (32 [61]). He pointed out that "all of our property is on loan from [God]; our management is only stewardship" (36 [66-67]). In his comments on Lord's Day 42 of the Heidelberg Catechism concerning the commandment "Thou shalt not steal," he referred to Proudhon's view that all possessions are obtained by theft. Kuyper felt that this view went too far, but the idea that much of what people own has in fact been stolen was not invented by Proudhon, but since 1563 could be found in the Heidelberg Catechism (Kouwenhoven 1989, 45). With these thoughts Kuyper helped to push the cause of emancipation, in particular through education and Christian action.

But his address also contains conservative elements. As an anti-revolutionary, Kuyper had not forgotten the terror of the French Revolution, which caused havoc in the organism of society. Kuyper thought in terms of evolution. He regarded society as an organism that evolves. As a result, he also thought in terms of harmony rather than conflict. His theology of creation, with its belief that all potentialities of creation are brought to development by "general grace," shows the great extent to which he internalized the belief in progress — the organism thinking of Idealism, of which Schelling was an important champion. Jager summarizes it well: "He saw the social question as a disruption of the organic, rather than as an interference with his organic worldview" (1976, 41). This helps to explain why in later years, in Kuyper the politician, conservatism more and more prevailed over the progressive ideals of the young Kuyper. In his captivating analysis of Kuyper's theology, Jager points to the great fear of uncertainty, which is so characteristic of Kuyper's personality structure and of those around him, and which goes a long way to explain his emphasis on authority and obedience, which were part and parcel of the bourgeoisie milieu of his time.

4.3.3 *The Encyclical* Rerum Novarum

The encyclical *Rerum Novarum* of Pope Leo XIII was published in the very same year that Kuyper gave his well-known address. In this encyclical the pope voiced the extreme concern of the church about the socioeconomic and political development. The document emphasized the poor living and working conditions of the working class and gave papal approval for the establishment of Catholic labor unions.

But here also one can detect a downside. The corporate worldview that preferred harmonious negotiations was nothing but a form of thinking in terms of organisms. The theory of class struggle did not fit into the Catholic view of society as a harmonious *societas perfecta*, say Noordegraaf and Tieleman (1992, 315), and was therefore rejected. These two authors show the ambiguity of the document: "The ambivalence of the encyclical is found in that on the one hand Leo XIII rejects the economic doctrine of the unrestricted 'free market' as being contrary to Christian ethics, but on the other hand feels unable to support the opposition of the Socialist labor movement, since that movement is regarded as atheistic, and thus presents a threat to the church and to faith and morals." This then is a third road between liberalism and socialism.

Like the two previous examples, *Rerum Novarum* showed that, although the representatives of church and Christianity were convinced of the seriousness of the social question and of the need for action, they were held back by their conservative background. Their loyalty to the gospel failed to lift them above the bourgeoisie consciousness of their day.

4.4 The Rise of the Agogic Action Theories

The disruption of social relationships and the distress of large groups of people contributed to the development of agogic theories to undergird the emerging charitable organizations that attempted to change this undesirable situation.

In the turbulent year 1848, P. Hofstede de Groot, a theologian in Groningen, gave an address at the occasion of the tenth anniversary of the association for women that he himself founded. The speech was entitled: "About the curious character of the charitable associations of our time" (Michielse 1978, 11). This event was later regarded as the beginning of the discipline of andragology. The "curious" thing about these associations is that they "try in our time more and more, through the personal involvement of their members, to influence the person who is in need." This exertion of influence is the central theme of the agogic sciences that subsequently emerged. In Christian circles in particular — the initiative of Hofstede de Groot, who was a man of great compassion (Vree 1984, 218ff.), is a good example — many were eager to work for what would later be called "the education of the people."

Already in 1784 the Maatschappij tot Nut van 't Algemeen (Society for the promotion of the common good) was founded in the Netherlands. A group of thoughtful Dutchmen, says Banning (1966, 42), was worried about the situation in which the common people found themselves and took the initiative to "ennoble" the people. The initiators felt "a tender sympathy for the condition of the common person." The brochure published at the inauguration of the society offered the following diagnosis: "Many of our fellow workers are ignorant about several useful sciences. Many of them will most likely be unable to present the simplest proofs for the presence of God and for the truth of the Christian religion, or to explain their human duty as citizens and Christians. Neither do they have knowledge of other arts and sciences that make them useful members of society, and good educators and caretakers of their children and other members of their family" (42-43). Banning states that this "patriarchal model of education" — these are the words he uses for this type of educational endeavor — breathed the spirit of the Enlightenment and of the bourgeoisie culture. The many initiatives in this area led, among other things, to the founding of a large number of institutions for adult education.

Banning distinguishes the patriarchal from the emancipatory educational model, which used development to further social and spiritual emancipation. This was inspired by a critical emancipatory consciousness, which also emerged with force in the nineteenth century and resulted in the founding of labor unions, and of emancipation movements such as feminism, and in the emancipation of large sectors of society, in particular among the Catholics and the Reformed, through the many influential Christian associations.

Agogic thinking thus, from the beginning, had a dual character, described by A. J. Nijk (1972) as "control and emancipation." Any society that wants to continue to exist must maintain a system of social control, and as the economic system increases in complexity, more models of control are required (Stevense 1979, 19). Social control does not necessarily have to be repressive, but can in the long term even support emancipation. The slogan "evolution through emancipation" fits with the nineteenth century (Hendriks 1981, 15). In this way a social-pedagogic and social-cultural response to the social question was developed that strove for change without any overly critical intervention in the existing social relationships. It did give impetus to the democratization of knowledge. It is more or less a middle road between Marxism and liberalism.

Against this background the agogic sciences developed to offer expertise in intentional change. A distinction was made between agogics (agogic action and theory) and agology (the study of social technology). Communication processes and processes of exerting influence and providing guidance were now the object of scientific inquiry. In the twentieth century, in particular after World War II, social assistance and social-cultural work have mushroomed. The helping professions have been professionalized to a high degree. A "market of well-being and happiness" develops. But once it passes a critical limit, there can be a total reversal, and people can fall victim to a new kind of dependence (Achterhuis 1980). This danger has been more and more recognized. See also 11.2.

4.5 Reactions from Practical Theology

There is a close tie between practical theology as a theory of crisis and a theory of action on the one hand, and agology as a branch of the social sciences on the other. In attending to the processes of change in the domain of faith and church, practical theology faces similar dilemmas. It cannot be neutral, but supports either progressive or conservative options, works with a harmony model or a conflict model, aims at the adaptation of the people to existing conditions, or the emancipation of people to new situations. What happens in the church is related to political and social trends in the world at large, and practical theology will therefore have to face the moment when it will need a critical theory.

Whether or not practical theology in its origins shares in a critical consciousness, which not only aims at the alleviation of suffering but also seeks to analyze the causes of the social question, is difficult to say. The same Hofstede de Groot, whom we met as "the father of agology," played a key role in the "Groninger richting" (5.1.1), a movement in the northeastern part of the Netherlands that sought to link theology to experience and social action. Within his survey of the total "body of knowledge," he left room for practical theology, though he was dissatisfied with it because it remained too inactive (Vree 1984, 248). He emphasized catechetics, which betrayed his agogic interests and his preference for an educational model based on dialogue. He also added a new subdiscipline: "church life," a precursor of church development. The task of this new subdiscipline was: "to make us conscious of the fact that we are members of the one and only Christian church, and to support the efforts to act in accordance with this consciousness" (Vree 1984, 248-49). He had in mind an *ecclesia missionaria,* a mission-oriented church. His thoughts were certainly quite progressive for his time and reached far beyond the confines of the church.

New forms of charity *(caritas)* developed within the Catholic Church. In the areas of the apostolate and the diaconate, most inspiration was gained from the sort of traditional Catholic thinking that fitted the nineteenth century. Home visitation was the means to establish a long-term contact with those in need. This provided the opportunity to develop empathy with their situation. But these and other new elements bear much more the stamp of "moral improvement" than of a critical view of society (Poeisz 1968, 82-83).

The vision of Kuyper and his followers on diaconal work has some far-reaching critical traits. In his *Encyclopedie* Kuyper started from a broad social perspective on the diaconate: "The work of the diaconate extends to all who are in physical need" (1894, 540-41). But W. van den Bergh, known as "the conscience of the Doleantie" (the secession from the Netherlands Reformed Church in 1886), maintained that this view of the work of the deacon over-emphasized the "purchase and distribution of bread, peat, and underwear." This, he felt, indicated that almost all efforts were geared "toward combating the consequences, rather than the causes, of the misery" (1888, 93). He pointed out that this type of assistance to the needy pushed them in the position of pariahs. Poverty is not a disease; it is an evil. This critical analysis, based on a broader view of the diaconate, corresponded with this phase in the emancipation of the Reformed. But shortly afterward, the work of the diaconate was reduced once again to caring for the poor (Heitink 1982, 16).

4.6 Philipp Konrad Marheineke

Following this third line, one soon encounters, after the contributions of Schleiermacher and Nitzsch, an important practical theologian: Philipp Marheineke (1780-1846), whom I here present as my most notable witness. After Schleiermacher, Marheineke was the first to offer a proposal for a practical theology (1837). Due to his deviation from the position of Schleiermacher in the University of Berlin, his work was somewhat undervalued, with most favoring that of Nitzsch, who did follow in the steps of his "master" (Lämmermann 1981, 27-28). But many of his contemporaries saw not Schleiermacher or Nitzsch but Marheineke as the founder of practical theology (Lämmermann 1981, 32).

Marheineke (1837) started with faith as a unity of knowledge and action. He distinguished between theoretical theology, which thinks from the perspective of the *possibility* of a relation between life and action, and practical theology, which is based on the *reality* of that relation (1837). As a disciple of Hegel, he formulated the goal of practical theology in a dialectical manner, separating the things that are temporal from those that are eternal (Birnbaum 1963, 44-45). As a result, the theory-praxis relation became the object of reflection, and practical theology received its own independent status. In this respect he went beyond Schleiermacher, who, in completely separating knowledge from action, could not allow practical theology to have its own unique content.

Contrary to Schleiermacher's thinking, Marheineke argued that practical theology should not be unilaterally tied to the institutional church (Lämmermann 1981, 34). Reconstructing the ground plan for his theology, we learn "that he saw reflection on the reality of religion in society as the specific task of practical theology" (Lämmermann 1981, 46). This reality could be approached only through a critical theory. He wanted to emphasize the freedom of theology as a whole, also with regard to the church. For that reason, practical theology should find its point of departure in the existing praxis, in its efforts toward improving concrete conditions in the society and in the church (51). This meant "that practical theology must manifest itself as a critical study of reality" (54). The focus for innovation had to be in the local congregation (Marheineke 1837, 29). The process must not be initiated by the leaders of the church, as Schleiermacher thought. Marheineke did not want to distinguish between clergy and laity; he regarded all members as fundamentally equal (68).

For further clarification of this point, I quote a segment from §35 of his book, where in a very astute way he rejected the distinction between the leaders and the common people as contrary to the real meaning of the church.

It is clear that this division hangs on extremely thin threads that can easily break. Recognizing the contrast between those who are in places of authority and those who are not, one cannot — however easy it may be to move between the two — avoid the danger that things turn around, which may bring the whole edifice down. The leaders have not always been in their present position, and they may not be able to prevent others from taking their place, with the result that the leaders are henceforth those who are led and those who used to be led are now the leaders. In this fluid situation, one has to resort to force if one wants to safeguard the status quo. The *Kirchenregiment* [church order] is an arrangement merely to assist the church in its wider spheres, but the *Kirchendienst* [elders and pastors] are also involved in church governance. The entire organizational model has been taken and developed from something that was available elsewhere, namely, in the analogy of the state, which also consists of legislation and government, but to which the church, in this respect, has no inner connection.

Lämmermann follows Marheineke. He feels that, in a dialectic of knowing and acting, practical theology must develop into an empirical theological discipline — not as an empirical-functional but rather as a critical-empirical theory of action. His tendency to be critical of both ideology and church led Marheineke close to the Frankfurt School, even though he failed to give sufficient attention to experience in his speculative approach (Lämmermann 1981, 111). In addition, his fundamental distinction between theory and praxis prevented him from completing his program. He arrived at a "theory for praxis," but not at a "theory of praxis" (131). The founders of the critical theory maintained that theory and praxis always affect each other. Every kind of praxis has a built-in theory, and every theory is influenced by praxis. Marheineke still failed to see this, even though all ingredients of a critical theory were present in his Hegelian approach.

Lämmerman's study of Marheineke has not remained totally unopposed. W. Gräb (1984, 56-57) criticizes him for playing Schleiermacher off against Marheineke and for making too much of the contrast between a functional and a critical approach. G. Otto, who agrees with Lämmerman as far as content is concerned, is of the opinion that this historical study casts Schleiermacher and

Marheineke too much in the straightjacket of today's problems (1982, 148-49). According to Drehsen, Lämmerman is correct in pointing to Marheineke's critical consciousness, but fails to see how he never fully arrived at a critical understanding of praxis (Drehsen 1988, 246).

4.7 Conclusion

In this chapter I developed a third perspective on the emergence of practical theology as a theory of crisis. In this light practical theology must be understood as *a form of political theology.*

I followed the political-economic track from the Industrial Revolution to the social question, from Karl Marx to Abraham Kuyper. The most important subjects along this route are the social question, poverty, the relation between theory and praxis, the harmony model and the conflict model, and humanitarian assistance.

The shift in practical theology toward praxis occurred through Philipp Marheineke. For that reason some demand that he be regarded as the father of practical theology. In this context the prominent themes are alienation, education, community, emancipation, and change.

This leads toward the concept of "practical theology as critical theory." Important themes are the theory-praxis relation, norms, and values, with a focus in our time on justice and injustice and a praxis of liberation. Within this perspective the spotlight on changing the existing situation becomes the primary interest of practical theology. As a result, the emphasis shifts toward the formulation of agogic theories within the tension of control and emancipation.

CHAPTER 5

Modern Pluralism in Church and Theology

The three previous chapters offer a historical interpretation of the development of practical theology, beginning in the nineteenth century when people became aware of the new situation in church and society. The enlightenment of the subject, the modernization of society, and the impact of the social question constitute the praxis in which practical theology as a theological theory of action developed and to which it has to respond.

In this chapter my approach shifts to the opposite. Since the nineteenth century the pluralism in the world at large has been accompanied by a pluralism in church and theology. Here we investigate how theological theories, in their relationship with developments in the church, reflect on this praxis and contribute building blocks for the construction of a practical theology. I use a practical-theological search model that the three previous chapters have presented.

Practical theology has many things in common with systematic theology, in particular with dogmatics. This chapter scrutinizes that relationship. The mediation of the Christian faith, as the object of practical-theological reflection, demands a hermeneutical approach to the content of the faith tradition in the light of the crisis of our modern era.

As in the previous chapters, we once again start in the nineteenth century (5.1), in the period of the emergent modernism in theology. The twentieth century initially provides a reaction (5.2). But later we find that the heritage of the nineteenth century must still be digested, as is apparent in the works of such modern Dutch theologians as Kuitert, Berkhof, and Schillebeeckx (5.3). These three examples help us to extend the three basic practical-theological lines from the previous chapters (5.4). In this connection, by way of conclusion, we can formulate two principles that provide direction for the next two parts of this book. These are the principles of integration and differentiation (5.5), that is, integration with respect to methodology (the linking of a hermeneutical, an empirical, and a critical approach) and of differentiation with respect to various domains of action (the individual, the church, and the society).

5.1 Rooted in the Nineteenth Century

This section will explore how theologians who had their roots in the nineteenth century attempted to address the challenges of the new era. All realized the discontinuity between Christianity and culture. Using various models they sought to bridge the gap.

5.1.1 The Impact of the Enlightenment on the Netherlands: The duplex ordo

The Law on Tertiary Education of 1876 continued the "encyclopedic" discussion (about how the study of theology should be organized) in the Netherlands that Schleiermacher began. This law also sought to deal with the tension between faith and science, but preferred a different solution: the *duplex ordo*. Interpretations differ (Meuleman 1982), but it would seem correct to say that this law, in fact, made theology into a science of religion. Not the Christian faith, but religious phenomena were the object of inquiry.

This law limited the academic study of theology to the historical (including the biblical) and philosophical disciplines, which could stand the test of rationality. Areas with a clear faith character, in particular dogmatics and practical theology, were excluded. They became "ecclesiastical" courses, for which the churches could appoint their own professors, who may, however, use the university facilities. Thus theology was split into a *duplex ordo*, of courses taught by the state and courses taught by the churches. This, among other things, hindered the development of practical theology as being the responsibility of the church.

What was the theological situation at these universities in the nineteenth century? The spirit of the Enlightenment was clearly discernible in

Leiden, in the theology of J. H. Scholten, who taught there from 1843 onward, and of L. W. E. Rauwenhoff, who began his teaching in 1860. At that time Leiden exerted a major influence. Reformed theologians like Abraham Kuyper (4.3.2, 5.1.3) and Herman Bavinck (5.1.2) studied at the University of Leiden and encountered its modernism. Scholten gave the old words of the tradition a totally new content, making rational thought the basis for knowledge of God (de Jong 1978, 330).

The Groninger School — with P. Hofstede de Groot, whom we met before as one of its representatives — first rejected but then embraced the theology of Schleiermacher, in particular his *Reden (Speeches)*. It felt a kinship with him in his emphasis on experience and in his apologetics (Vree 1984, 156-57). The apologetic school dominated in Utrecht. J. I. Doedes and J. J. van Oosterzee, two professors at Utrecht, tended toward orthodoxy and labeled themselves as "ethical-irenic." Together with their colleague N. Beets, also known as a literary author, they founded the association Ernst en Vrede (Earnestness and peace) and attempted to reconcile theological orthodoxy with the results of modern science. Soon a split occurred among them, between the ethical party, and another group, closely allied to the theological faculty in Utrecht, that wanted to give faith a biblical foundation. Thus we see how the Enlightenment evoked diverse theological reactions: acceptance, adaptation, and rejection.

A number of studies in the area of practical theology were written at the state universities and its institutions. The German work by L. Hüffell, translated by I. Busch Keiser, was the first manual of practical theology to appear in the nineteenth century. The writer suggested that practical theology had not developed to the point where it had a unified approach. He stated that the principal aim of the work of the ministry consisted in the "maintenance, nurture, and growth of Christianity among the people." He also referred to "the theological crisis of this time," but argued that "the presence of religion in the human consciousness or the presence of a bond between the human spirit and the eternal and divine" remained the firm foundation (1833, 2).

The Groninger theologians wrote their own books. Between 1851 and 1857 W. Muurling, since 1840 a colleague of Hofstede de Groot, wrote his widely acclaimed study on the practical aspects of the ministry, in particular in the Dutch Reformed Church. He defined practical theology succinctly as "the science of ministerial practice" (1860, 2). He gave first place to the teaching of the catechism, and then listed homiletics, liturgics, pastoral work, canon law, and missions.

The Utrecht professor van Oosterzee, mentioned above, also wrote a book on practical theology (1877-78). He focused on the various functions of the ministry, in spite of the fact that he defined practical theology as "the science of the activities of the kingdom of God in all its fullness." He emphasized the role of homiletics. In subsequent years, van Oosterzee's book was considered too detailed, and as a compendium rather than as a book for use by students. It was replaced by L. W. Bakhuizen van den Brink's Dutch revision of the German *Grundriss* by E. Chr. Achelis. This book appeared in 1906 and was built on the following premise: "Practical theology is the scientific study of the activities of the Christian church for its continuance and consummation."

5.1.2 The Search for Integration: The Ethicists and Herman Bavinck

In the period 1870-1920 the ethical tradition found its expression, in particular, in the work of D. Chantepie de la Saussaye and his supporters J. J. P. Valeton and Is. van Dijk. The term *ethical* has to do with the way in which God, as a moral Being, takes human beings with absolute seriousness in their responsibility and limitations. These theologians sought to address the problem of the decreasing plausibility of the Christian religion and wanted to reformulate the faith of the congregation (M. Aalders 1990, 189). In so doing, they moved between the poles of modern science and fundamentalism. They searched for an appreciation of the new scientific findings that would leave the gospel of God's grace in Jesus Christ intact. They tried to rephrase the gospel in words that would be acceptable to modern humans.

The following passage from Aalders is striking: "Fundamental for their self-perception was the realization that God enters in Jesus Christ into a relationship, and this conviction bound them to the tradition of the church. The recognition that God does not overpower humanity with his revelation, but assigns humanity as his partner a concrete role in his covenant, offered them the possibility to do justice to humanity's independence, limitations, and responsibility. God does not reveal supernatural doctrinal truths, but enters into a relationship with humanity and takes the human limitations and situations into consideration. Human beings, on their part, are responsible for the intellectual formulation of what they experience in that relationship, and for putting this in writing" (1990, 189).

This quotation shows how the ethicists tried to integrate Christian faith and modern consciousness by doing justice to humanity's own responsibility, and thereby taking leave of supernaturalism. They defended humanity, which had rediscovered freedom in the face of a transcendent God, who in Christ enters into a relationship with humanity.

Today these thoughts sound quite familiar. With the sociologist Peter L.

Berger, one might call this the inductive method: a dialectical approach to the relationship between tradition and the current situation, which we encountered in Schleiermacher and which, in modern theology in particular, has become the hermeneutical response to modernity.

J. H. Gunning Jr. (1829-1905) is the best known among the older ethicists. Through a "confessional shift" he detached himself from his younger colleagues, with whom he previously felt much kinship but whom he now accused of individualism. In his years of teaching in Leiden, from 1889 onward, he clearly distinguished between the science of religion and dogmatics. He now saw no possibility of a compromise between Christianity and modern culture. In a radical choice he opted for what is unique in the Christian tradition: the cross and the resurrection (A. de Lange 1987). The road of experience was thus torn up. It gave way to the concept of the unity of church and kingdom as the link with society. "Gunning sees the church as the subject, the bearer of this unifying tradition; the church already represents the new, true reality in the midst of the old reality." The church is the real humanity, and, for Gunning, theology is the essential science (A. de Lange 1984, 25). For Gunning, working for a new humanity meant working through the church. For him this was a spiritual matter, and it is therefore no wonder that his relationship with the more strategically thinking Abraham Kuyper was one of major conflict.

As we read in a frank letter to Herman Bavinck (de Lange 1984, 153), Gunning felt a kinship with Bavinck, the Reformed theologian of the *Afscheiding* (Schism of 1834), in whom he failed to detect "the cynicism and arrogance" of Bavinck's supporter and opponent, Kuyper.

In 1874, after a year of study in Kampen, Herman Bavinck (1854-1921) moved to Leiden. Here his theological education began, during which he developed into the most important theologian in the Reformed Churches in the Netherlands. In 1882 he was appointed as professor in Kampen. In 1902 he transferred, together with P. Biesterveld, the professor of "ministerial" subjects, to the Free University in Amsterdam. Through his four-volume work on Reformed dogmatics, which appeared from 1895 onward, he exerted great theological influence. His theology manifested a clear openness to modern culture. Many of his later writings were in the area of pedagogics and psychology. He was the first president of the Dutch association for religion and psychology. His psychological interest led him also to give ample space in his dogmatics to human experience (Heitink 1977, 172). In 1911 he became a member of the First Chamber of the Dutch Parliament (Senate). He took a progressive stand with respect to topics like universal suffrage, the colonial question, and the war. After Bavinck's death the theological climate in the Reformed Churches in the Netherlands became more inflexible and less open, and a time of controversies and schisms began. Viewed from a sociological perspective, the goals of emancipation in the Reformed Churches in the Netherlands have been largely accomplished (Hendriks 1971, 218). On Bavinck see especially R. H. Bremmer (1961, 1966).

Bavinck also wanted integration. "General revelation" offered him the space where Christians and non-Christians could meet — a standpoint opposed by O. Noordmans (Hartvelt 1981, 201). Bavinck worried about the short circuit between faith and modernity. The "dowsing rod" used by Bavinck in his search for integration was the concept of the "organic," derived from nine-teenth-century thinking. This was transferred "from 'nature' to 'history'" (Hartvelt, 182). Bavinck spoke, for example, about the organic inspiration of the Scriptures, thus giving a rightful place to the human element and creating room for hermeneutical theological study. He tried, within a dynamic view of creation, to "relate God as closely as possible to this reality" (188).

All those mentioned in this section — and that certainly includes Bavinck — shared an irenic spirit that inspired them to open dialogue with others.

5.1.3 The Emancipation of the "Small Folk": Abraham Kuyper

Kuyper's response to the law of 1876 was the founding of the Free University (1880), "free" from both church and state. Kuyper saw Calvinism as a complete worldview. "It is a spiritual, all-encompassing vision, yes, a historically rooted renewal of Christianity" (Klapwijk 1987, 61). There are three central issues: the utter sovereignty of God, the absolute equality of all people (including clergy and laity!), and the universal calling of all Christians. With his "Neo-Calvinism" Kuyper "created" a new reality, encompassing humanity, culture, and society, and forming a structure that allowed a segment of the population — protected by the "antithesis," and thus operating from a minority position — to achieve emancipation (Hendriks 1971).

In his three-volume work on the "encyclopedia of sacred theology" (1894), he took the organic character of science as his basis. The corpus of science that has evolved over time is an organic whole. The existing disciplines focus on "human beings themselves," on "the nature that humanity controls," and on "one's God, by whom he is directed" (van der Laan 1979, 155). Humanity is the subject of science. A person also wants to know about "one's God." This is not possible through experience. Unlike Schleiermacher, Kuyper found his point of departure for theology in the supernatural character of divine revelation. The Holy Scripture is the *principium divisionis* for theology.

Kuyper referred to practical theology as "deaconology, divided according to the offices, which, instituted by Christ, function as the organs in the ecclesiastical organism" (van der Laan 1979, 156). His democratic principle led him to distinguish not only the area of the *didaskalia* (the minister), but also those of presbyterial studies (the elder), diaconal studies (the deacon), and courses dealing with the equipping of the laity. The last ones focus on the Christian responsibility for life as a whole, and for the interaction in church, state, and society. A broad view of the work of the deacon involves the church in social concerns and in Christian charity. P. Biesterveld, the professor who taught these courses (from 1894 in Kampen and from 1902 at the Free University), followed the encyclopedic views of Kuyper (Biesterveld 1894, 1902).

Kuyper (1837-1920) began his studies in Leiden in 1855, worked for some time as a pastor, and served from 1880 as the first professor at the Free University. He separated from the Dutch Reformed Church in the *Doleantie* of 1886. In 1874 he became a member of Parliament, and from 1901 to 1905 he served as the prime minister. He was the chief editor of the daily newspaper *de Standaard* and of the weekly publication *de Heraut*.

He wrote extensively in the area of theology. A. A. van Ruler argued that the concept of rebirth was Kuyper's only fully developed theological category (1940, 26). Grace is "particular grace." But what to think of the good things life has to offer for all, even for those who do not belong to the church? Kuyper introduced the concept of "common grace," which brings the whole of created reality under human responsibility. The distinction between the church as an institution and as an organism runs parallel to that between "particular and common grace" (van der Werf 1960, 41). The former also issues from the concept of being born again. Kuyper saw the church as an organism, that is, as the community of Christians who are present everywhere in society through the Christian organizations. This he viewed as essential: the church as an institution is of secondary importance and must serve the organism. In his pluriform view of the church, Kuyper could easily accommodate a pluralism in belief. What counts is that the second birth will penetrate the whole life and, from this renewal of humanity, will lead to the renewal of the world. Kuyper opposed antithesis as a matter of principle, for the elect of the Lord constitute the center of the nation. A concentration of elected believers is, however, important to serve the whole.

In all of his work, whether in the area of the church, science, politics, or social concerns, Kuyper created his own world as an alternative to the modern world. As he liked to phrase it, he wanted to bring theology "in harmony with the consciousness of the times."

This served as a proposal for a strategy to emancipate a segment of the population, which, through their own schools, their own associations, their own newspaper, their own political party, and their own university, soon experienced a tremendous upward mobility and was able to occupy an important place in society.

At the same time Kuyper, though probably without being aware of it, created space for modernity by stimulating independent thinking and individual responsibility. This led in the longer term to a form of internal secularization, through an ever stronger adaptation of the Christian faith to this modern outlook. As a result, the world of the Reformed Churches in the Netherlands was, after the completion of the emancipation process, broken open from the inside. But until circa 1960 Reformed life remained largely intact (Dekker 1992).

5.1.4 The Emancipation of the Roman Catholics

J. van Laarhoven (1974) characterizes the period 1848-1880 as "the church on the defensive." The encyclical of Pius IX *Quanta cura et Syllabus seu collectio errorum* (1864) serves as a prime example. This dealt in extenso with all objections against modernism and liberalism. It increased the tension between the church and the world and made it more difficult for them to relate to each other (van Laarhoven 1974, 182). In this entire period the university was the weak point. The church had no creative response to the advance of science. The empirical approach in the positivism of Comte and others was regarded as a denial of divine revelation. Most theologians were hesitant and vacillating, often seeking escape in a strong defense of Christian truth against the "spirit of the time" (185-86). Theology experienced an artificial revival of Scholasticism, in which the defense of church teachings developed into an immense fortress (188). In the first part of this century Neo-Thomism experienced its golden age. Vatican I brought an ecclesiastical centralism and a reinforcement of the hierarchical structure. Many felt called to the priesthood, which would indicate that the clergy were highly respected. The monastic orders also attracted many.

The establishment of the first chair for pastoral theology, in 1774 in Vienna, proved to be a difficult process. This new initiative, realized with the clear approval of Empress Maria Theresa, was intended to help "through its teaching to educate not only good Christians but also good citizens for the state and true friends for human society." For "the good Christian is also a good citizen." As "one of the more important members of society," the pastor must not forget that he himself "is fed by the state" (J. Müller 1974, 17). Could the alliance between theology, church, and bourgeoisie culture have been phrased more strikingly?

For centuries Catholicism in the Netherlands, though comprising almost 40 percent of the population, was mainly a matter of clandestine churches. The Constitution of 1848 changed this. The hierarchy was reestablished in 1853. New dioceses were created in Roermond, Den Bosch, Breda, Utrecht, and Haarlem. From then onward, many churches were constructed, schools were established, and Catholicism enjoyed a rapid development. Under the leadership of H. J. A. M. Schaepman (1844-1903) and W. H. Nolens (1860-1931) the emancipation of the Catholics got under way. W. Goddijn (1973) refers to the Dutch Catholic Church as a "controlled church." The Netherlands was in the forefront in the area of practical Christianity, and for a long time remained immune to modernism (Schoof 1968, 144).

But the emergence of the *théologie nouvelle,* which originated in the 1930s, led to theological renewal. At that time young theologians like Chenu, Congar, de Lubac, and Daniélou focused on the "rediscovery of the sources." This led to a biblical-kerygmatic theology (van Laarhoven 1974, 292). In more recent times high expectations were awakened by the *aggiornamento* of Pope John XXIII and Vatican II, but these were soon squashed.

In 1923 the Catholic University of Nijmegen was founded. Theology served first and foremost as the core of the education of seminarians. Not until 1964, as we saw (1.1), was a chair in pastoral theology established. Around 1966/1967 about thirty seminaries fused into four theological schools at the tertiary level. The traditional seminary belonged to the past, as the church opted for a university context, which helped to end the theological isolation. From the 1960s onward a process of modernization also affected the Catholic Church and its theology. Presently the Netherlands has three Catholic theological schools at the university level: Nijmegen (after a fusion with Heerlen), Utrecht (after a fusion with Amsterdam), and Tilburg. A new seminary was, however, founded in Rolduc.

5.2 The Reaction of the Twentieth Century

The shift from the general to the particular, which we saw in Gunning, characterized the development of theology in the first six decades of the twentieth century. The dialectical theology of Karl Barth, the most important exponent, offered a sharp reaction to the nineteenth century.

5.2.1 The Influence of Dialectical Theology: Karl Barth

Studies of the significance of Karl Barth for practical theology often ignore the critical content of his theology. This is understandable from a formal perspective. Barth viewed theology as the task of the church: Theology is a critical reflection on the pronouncements of the church. His dogmatics received the title *Church Dogmatics*. This led Barth to a tripartioning of theology (Birnbaum 1963, 196): Does the church receive its words "from Him"? (exegetical studies; studies of the sources); are the words of the church directed "to Him"? (practical theology); do the words of the church "correspond with Him"? (systematic theology). The underlying basis was proclamation. Within this one-directional system practical theology was simply left with the question, *How?* Preaching is the primary channel of proclamation, but religious education and pastoral care must also be included in proclamation. The latter aspect has been elaborated in Eduard Thurneysen's book on pastoral care (1957 [1962]).

There was little room for a methodical approach. The exclusive role of the Spirit implied that God could only come to humans through the Spirit. Any methodical directions might hinder this. Furthermore, there was no link with human experience, for "religion is unbelief." The content of the proclamation could never be partially determined by the human situation. As a result, dialectical theology put the breaks on the development of practical theology as an empirical theory of action.

This is in a few words the well-known view of Barth. But his *Church Dogmatics* already indicated that something more could be said. One may, for instance, refer to the way in which he dealt with phenomenology and relational thinking in his theological proposal for an anthropology (vol. III/2), and, not to forget, for his soteriology (vol. IV/3), which outlined his missionary ecclesiology in four key concepts: call, sending, task, and service. In serving the world the church must leave all tutelage behind. One section in IV/3 bears the motto of J. C. Blumhardt as its title: "Jesus is Victor." A focus on eschatological victory inspires people for action.

This readiness for battle is typical for all of Barth's oeuvre, which, in spite of its dialectical character, is extremely contextual. This "theology of crisis" reflects the sense of crisis that penetrated the lives of the people in the period around World War I (Zahrnt 1967, 9-10 [1969, 11-12]). Barth resolutely distanced himself from the liberal theology that felt at home with the civil authorities. If something in Europe could yet be saved, then something "totally different" had to happen, and that could occur only through "the One who is totally Other." In his well-known Tambacher address during the congress of German Christian Socialists in 1919, Barth made his political choice. His theological view demanded that he detach his choice for Socialism from any dream of creating God's kingdom, but he nonetheless urged all Christians to opt for Socialism as a consequence of their faith. This alliance between theology and politics enables us to understand Barth's theology as a "critical theory" (Grözinger 1986, 184). How critical his theology was became abundantly clear in the stand of the Confessing Church against National Socialism.

5.2.2 Reformed Diversity: O. Noordmans, A. A. van Ruler, K. H. Miskotte

Dutch twentieth-century theology cannot be detached from the work of Barth. Yet in this century the Dutch Reformed Church has had three very creative theologians, who, until today, have put their stamp on the praxis of theology and church, including practical theology: O. Noordmans, A. A. van Ruler, and K. H. Miskotte. Each of these in his own way has come to terms with the problems of the new era.

O. Noordmans (1871-1956) was a theologian from outside the world of academia (Neven 1980). He spent his whole life in the ministry. In 1931 he founded an association for the nurture of the church, which became the precursor of a similar organization initiated by H. Kraemer (Bruin 1992, 18). All his work focused on "the spot of light around the cross," which is present in all of us. He formulated his theology in the context of modern industrialized society, about which he was rather pessimistic (Neven n.d., 6). Noordmans gave special attention to the message of the Bible for those who were on the lowest ranks of the social ladder, at the bottom of society. He pleaded for a church "for the people," for the underprivileged. His theology, says Neven (n.d., 17), reveals his criticism of an aggressive male culture. Neven adds that Noordmans would have appreciated the criticism of the liberation theologians. He moved beyond a theology that gave a central place to modern subjectivity in order to give a voice to marginal human beings as subjects. Thus the presence of Christ as "the neighbor par excellence" became visible. His critical-theological position was, for instance, apparent in his well-known meditation entitled "Sinner and beggar" (Noordmans 1946).

A. A. van Ruler (1908-1970) is best known in the area of practical theology for the so-called theonome reciprocity — derived from him by R. Bohren — which refers to the God-human relationship under the aspect of the work of the Spirit. "For the Spirit never acts alone, but always through, and as, humanity" (van Ruler 1965, 100). Van Ruler, who stated that he owed much to Noordmans and that he began as a pure Barthian, felt that the latter left too little room for pneumatology. Giving a relatively independent role to the work of the Spirit, van Ruler's theology is broad, this-worldly, focused on human culture and all created reality, and, in an eschatological sense, on the establishment of the kingdom. Based on this pneumatological perspective, J. J. Rebel (1981) develops a theology of the pastorate. Similarly, van Ruler attempted to offer a theological response to the reduction of the Christian faith resulting from the differentiation process in society. This became apparent in his theocratic thinking, in which he extended the line of P. J. Hoedemaker — the great counterpart of Kuyper. He understood theocracy in different ways. It is a "political profiling of life from within the church," but even more "an all-encompassing view of life, characterized by a unique understanding of reality" (van Hoof 1974, 39). Finally, I draw attention to van Ruler's interest in mysticism, as encountered in the Nadere Reformation (the Dutch version of eighteenth-century Pietism; van Ruler 1971, 43-44).

K. H. Miskotte (1884-1976), as a theologian of the Word, was even more than the others a disciple of Barth. But he had his own emphases, such as his attention to the Old Testament heritage, and his openness toward Jewish culture, for learning together, and for his interest in culture and literature. His disciple ter Schegget summarizes Miskotte's main concern: "His first concern was not the christening of the life of the people, but rather that, through the powerful testimony of the Christian communities, the world would remember what no human heart had thought, but what had been prepared by God" (1976, 305). Though rejecting any religious point of reference in humanity, Miskotte, probably more than any other theologian, understood the inner feelings of the modern person. He saw nihilism as the most dangerous threat (1956). Nihilism in the shape of national socialism could be combated, but it is much more difficult to deal with as a basic philosophy of "the fourth man" of our time. He began his theology from God's a priori, not as a statement but as "as an experience of faith, in the strict sense of what has happened to us and therefore has become communicable" (J. T. Bakker 1984, 210).

5.2.3 The Nonreligious Interpretation of the Gospel: Dietrich Bonhoeffer

Dietrich Bonhoeffer (1906-1944) was a theologian who felt totally involved with the mood of the new era. His work is a source of inspiration for many practical theologians. His family background made him a representative of the "educated elite." From his prison cell he wrote with a measure of pride in a letter at the occasion of the baptism of his nephew about "being called to bear a great responsibility for the common good and to spiritual achievements and leadership" (1972, 246). In this letter he made much of these bourgeoisie ideals.

F. de Lange (1986, 14) points out how the middle-class citizen has two different faces: that of a calculating capitalist and that of a refined humanist. Bonhoeffer represented the latter: bourgeoisie with a human face. That enabled him to survive. In his entire life and in all his works this admittedly somewhat conservative man radiated the power of a self-perception rooted in the Enlightenment. To become a real subject, a true individual, is something positive. De Lange calls Bonhoeffer "a bourgeois in *optima forma*."

In his studies Bonhoeffer focused much of his attention on the theme of community, and he based all his research on the empirical data of the sociology of his day. This is apparent in his *Sanctorum Communio* (1986 [*The Communion of Saints,* 1963]), which he completed at age twenty-one! His theological reflections became far more radical when he was imprisoned because of his involvement in preparations to assassinate Hitler. His premature death left his work unfinished, but his diary from his prison cell sketched in a preliminary way the new trends in his thinking (Bethge 1968, 894ff. [1970, 700ff.).

In this book he dared to draw the ultimate conclusion from the ongoing modernization process: the world will be emancipated, and its inhabitants will be without religion. The church should never attempt to belittle that emancipation, but will have to work toward a nonreligious interpretation of the gospel. In this new situation of being a minority church, it must safeguard the tradition, living from the *disciplina arcani* (the secret discipline in the catechumenate of the early church). These three themes were linked in Bonhoeffer's work (Heitink 1988b, 31ff.), thus assuring that the church would remain true to its calling: "to exist for others" (1972, 317 [1972, 382]).

We find reflections of Bonhoeffer's work in the theology of the World Council of Churches, in the work of J. C. Hoekendijk (a Dutch theologian), and in the German practical theologian E. Lange.

5.2.4 The Hermeneutics of Correlation: Paul Tillich

Paul Tillich's (1886-1965) theology ties in with the general climate of existentialism and to some extent parallels Heidegger's philosophy. Tillich presupposed a correlation between existential questions and theological answers.

"God answers man's questions, and under the impact of God's answers man asks them. Theology formulates the questions implied in human existence, and theology formulates the answers in divine self-manifestation under the guidance of the questions implied in human existence" (Tillich 1968, 1:61). The despair of being alienated from the self drives one to ask questions. The subject is torn by feelings of anxiety and despair (Heidegger) and searches for integration and harmony.

Within major sectors of the discipline of practical theology the correlation principle has become somewhat like a hermeneutical principle, both with regard to preaching and with regard to religious education and pastoral work (Berkhof 1985, 287 [1989, 294]). S. Hiltner (1972) uses this principle in his theological work, as he searches for "theological dynamics," in which psychological and theological notions are hermeneutically linked together. W. Zijlstra (1989) uses Tillich's polar anthropological approach in his pastoral theology. In so doing, he creates a bridge between the Christian tradition and the experience of modern people, who share in the alienation they are subjected to in their individualized situation. Achieving total independence may bring the middle-class person from anomy to the deepest despair.

Speaking of borderline experiences, M. van Knippenberg refers to Tillich as "a guest of honor at the court of pastoral theology" (1989, 5). This is probably most applicable in Catholic circles, since Tillich seemed to agree with their basic theological view that humanity's being is inclined toward divine grace. The Dutch New Catechism (1966) begins with a chapter about humans as questioning beings: whenever things lose their obviousness humans begin to ask questions. As a result a reinterpretation occurs of the doctrines that had been cordoned off by the Scholastic tradition.

5.2.5 The Rediscovery of Christianity's Jewish Roots

The Holocaust may well have been the greatest shock for the self-confidence of the middle-class citizen. Since then we speak of a "theology after Auschwitz." This theology wrestles intensely with the theodicy problem, and is, more than any theology in the past, conscious of the Jewish roots of the Christian tradition.

However much they suffer, Jews have no time for apathy. The Viennese psychiatrist Viktor Frankl, an Auschwitz survivor, regards it as his calling to defend the value of life. On that basis he developed his "logotherapy" in which the question of meaning is central (Frankl 1979). Humans are free to choose in what way they want to relate to suffering. That freedom enables them to survive (Jongkind 1991, 107).

Not surprisingly, Jewish novelists, together with Jewish philosophers, have exerted a major influence on postwar thought. Martin Buber, Abraham Joshua Heschel, and Emmanuel Levinas are prime examples. Their work provides important anthropological insights for practical theology. In this connection reference also ought to be made to the work of E. H. Friedman (1985), a family therapist, and R. L. Katz (1985), a specialist in the area of pastoral counseling. The question remains whether these persons fully represent the Jewish tradition, or must be viewed as modern thinkers of Jewish descent who have been heavily influenced by Western culture. Both aspects are probably true, and it may well be the linkage between the two that appeals to so many.

5.3 The Return to the Nineteenth Century

There appeared to be a dividing line between 5.1 and 5.2. It is as if theologians of the twentieth century forcefully shake off the dust of the nineteenth century. This is clearest in the case of J. H. Gunning, who made a "confessional shift," leaving him with feelings of not being understood by his former ethical supporters and of being isolated. Likewise, Neo-Scholastic Catholic theology, Reformed orthodoxy, and dialectical theology were ventures that either denied the nineteenth century or attempted to transcend it. These ventures succeeded until shortly after World War II, but then, in the 1960s, the nineteenth century hit back. Once again we faced a deep crisis. Secularization intensified, and more and more people left the church, while all around the world suffering and poverty grew to new extremes.

Modernity has not been defeated. In this new situation several theological initiatives attempt to deal decisively with the nineteenth-century heritage. Three Dutch theologians from different ecclesiastical traditions will serve as examples. I consider their approaches as examples of a theological reaction to each of the three lines of thought developed in the previous three chapters, and I think they provide direction in developing a contemporary practical theology.

5.3.1 The Emancipation of Modern Humanity: H. M. Kuitert

The desire to do justice to the emancipation and the autonomy of modern humanity is a central theme in the theology of H. M. Kuitert. In *De spelers en het spel* (1964 [*Signals from the Bible,* 1972]) we already see how he reads the Bible with new eyes. The concepts of covenant, partnership, reciprocity, and voluntariness are foci of attention (Kuitert 1964, 31-35 [1972, 19-22]) and create space for the subject. These become basic themes in his later theological endeavors.

He follows his own unique road in his "encyclopedic" study of the philosophy of theology (Kuitert 1988) in order to assure that theology remains what it traditionally was but at the same time also becomes a true science. He maintains that, if theology wants to keep its place at the university, it must stick to the rules of the sciences. He therefore provides theology with an "anthropological basis." Viewed from the anthropological perspective, religion is an ingredient of human nature. Through their faith images human beings picture their perception of reality in a religious way. They extend these perceptions with the notion of God (43). People give a significance to their lives, which they come to see as their "ultimate meaning." This Kuitert describes as "basic" faith. Religious ideas fill our experience and make it into something that provides ultimate meaning (61). A multitude of ideas of what God is like abound. It is the task of theology to test the viability of these ideas. Thus in the context of our culture, we should allow Christian theologians to operate from the basis of a Christian theology (72). This can be done without fear, for "a God who is not really God does not survive eternally; his profile will not remain valid as society changes" (94). Theology is both a science and a preparation for a profession (95), and this provides the link with the church. Practical theology also has its place: "It studies, first of all, the problem the Christian faith tradition faces as it seeks to transmit its beliefs" (24). This fully agrees with our remarks about the "mediation" in the relationship between praxis 1 and praxis 2. The place given to ethics, quite separate from theology, is remarkable. Ethics can function without theology (106). Morality is something independent of religion. One might call this an ongoing differentiation.

Kuitert officially concluded his academic career with an oration about "Autonomy: an awkward late arrival in the world of ethics" (1989). His book *Het algemeen betwijfeld christelijk geloof* (1992 [*I Have My Doubts: How to Become a Christian without Being a Fundamentalist,* 1993]) became a bestseller. The secret of this book is, I believe, that Kuitert succeeds in a truly authentic way in joining tradition with how modern people feel and think. This creates the liberating perception that one can be a modern person and a believer at the same time. The book creates, in one word, plausibility. Not surprisingly, parallels have been drawn between Kuitert and Schleiermacher (Neven 1993). Thus Häring refers to "the last certainty of an enlightened theology" (1992).

This provides an important launching pad for such concepts as subject, experience, and search for meaning.

5.3.2 The Bond of Love and Freedom: Hendrikus Berkhof

In his systematic theology Hendrikus Berkhof starts from the basic conviction that "divine salvation and earthly reality are complementary concepts; it is only in relation to each other that they can become visible" (Berkhof 1973, 4 [1979, 4]). This idea runs like a red thread through his entire theology. On the one hand he tries to safeguard the unique character of faith by asking his readers to make a "leap," while on the other hand insisting on the unity of the experience of faith and the experience of reality. J. T. Bakker wonders whether "we should emphasize this 'leap' as something that defies explanation and is contingent, or whether the author in fact places a higher value on his notion of 'a series of leaps,' which, in spite of fractions and tensions, seems to suggest a continuity of process" (Bakker 1976, 151).

Berkhof allows for both notions. He thinks in terms of processes, when dealing with experience as well as when dealing with history. Revelation is an encounter, focused on life within the covenant relationship (59 [56]). Humanity is invited to "join all nature in the salvific history of God for man," for "We are nurtured from below while being called from above." To a degree salvation remains "provisional" and "unfinished" (178 [169]). The eschatological perspective unveils a way of change, as God's future pulls our world toward him. This processlike thinking gives Berkhof's theology a strong empirical content and betrays a kinship with the social sciences. Nonetheless, Berkhof leaves no doubt that God has the first and the last word in the covenant relationship between God and humanity. Salvation has an abiding priority vis-à-vis our reality and remains normative. With regard to practical theology, the connection between the two provides a hermeneutical key, which I have elsewhere referred to by enlisting the concept of "bipolarity" (Heitink 1977, 170).

Much from the previous sections receives, as a cumulative experience, an echo with Berkhof. He has traversed the Barth era, but has not relinquished his kinship with the ethical school. Aalders's description of this school of thought (see 5.1.2) could have been a quotation from Berkhof. The idea of the covenant between God and humanity has a central place in his relational approach. This forms the basis for his anthropology. As a "responsive being," humans are — in Berkhof's terminology — "designed" or "constructed" to encounter God "in love and freedom." Humans must have freedom, and love provides the highest mode where this freedom can be realized (194 [184]). Later, love and freedom reappear in the chapter about the renewal of humanity (476ff. [455ff.]).

Thus Berkhof lays an anthropological groundwork for social involvement and, at the same time, for his ecclesiology, which, in the light of tradition, could be called a slimmed-down ecclesiology. The covenant is first of all to be understood as community (356 [339]). The individual and the community are interdependent. The institutional church acquires a human face. The institution must "participate in the covenant relationship," and the secret of that participation is in pneumatology. Within the context of the covenant the Spirit uses elements that serve as "mediating activities" or conductors. Berkhof mentions nine of these elements, among them not only the Lord's Supper but also discussion or dialogue. When we mention the word *Spirit,* we also say *human,* and thus the entire covenant event opens itself to "transmission," to a mediating process. This offers a clear invitation to construct a practical theology. The church as the "mediating agency between Christ and the world" has three dimensions: that of institute or institution, of community, and of orientation to the world. "The institutional church mediates Christ toward the community; likewise, the community in turn mediates him toward the world" (429-30 [410-11]).

In summary one may say that, building on the faith of the community of believers, Berkhof in all openness seeks the encounter with the spirit of contemporary life.

5.3.3 Resistance against Suffering and Oppression: Edward Schillebeeckx

Edward Schillebeeckx is my third example. Reading his books on Jesus (1975, 1977 [1979, 1980]) one cannot fail to be impressed by the immense exegetical work this systematic theologian had to do in his attempt at "re-sourcing." He apparently must first grind his way through the thick layers of the Scholastic tradition. In explaining why he wrote his books, Schillebeeckx remarks that the post–Vatican II renewal followed just one single track: that of "re-sourcing" or going "back to the sources" (1978, 13 [1981, 3]). But after this "return to the sources," theology had to pass the "new and even critical threshold" of contemporary experience. Theology finds its inspiration not only in the tradition of the great Jewish-Christian movement, but also in the new, contemporary, human experiences of Christians and non-Christians. The human sciences have a major bearing on this latter aspect (13 [3]). In his books on Jesus, Schillebeeckx describes the relations between the two sources in these terms: "to see the second source, the actual situation in which we live today, as an intrinsic and determinative element for understanding God's revelation in the history of Israel and of Jesus, which Christians have experienced as salvation from God for men and women, i.e. the first source" (13 [3]). One can discern the hermeneutical circle. We are not told that we must first know the tradition before we can apply our knowledge. We can use the word *God* in a meaningful way only as we experience it as a liberating response to real life problems. That was true in the past, but it was restricted to the experiences of a small elite, while today it applies to everyone's experience. The experience of alienation becomes apparent in a poignant way in a secularized world. Revelation transcends experience, but it can only be perceived *through and in* human experiences (19 [11]). In this connection the close relationship between experience and interpretation in certain models of thought should not be overlooked.

The historical-critical consciousness in Schillebeeckx's theology, which brings him in close proximity to the critical theory, is remarkable. This is manifest, in particular, in his approach to the baffling problem of suffering, which calls us to a praxis of resistance (1977, 667 [1980, 726]). "God wants *men's salvation,* and in it victory over their suffering" (671 [730]). When discussing the problem of suffering Schillebeeckx introduces the concept of an "experience of *contrast*" as essential for a contemplative and emancipatory praxis (755-56 [817-18]). Such "experiences of contrast" arise from the experience of injustice and relate in a critical manner to other forms of knowledge. Thus "under the aspect of the experience of *contrast* or critical negativity, the experience of suffering forms a bridge towards possible action which might remove both suffering and its causes" (755 [818]). In his last book he explains this further, typifying negative "experiences of contrast" as "a basic human experience which as such I regard as a pre-religious experience and thus a basic experience accessible to all human beings" (1989, 24 [1990, 5]). In our contemporary world "believers and non-believers have the basic experience of an absolute limit, of radical finitude and contingency" (96 [77]), in the face of suffering, illness, and death. He regards this religious concept as far more dynamic than Schleiermacher's feeling of total dependence, which continues to reflect too much of the nineteenth-century outlook.

Schillebeeckx's theology has a distinct affinity with certain forms of liberation theology, which confront us in a critical way with accounts of suffering. This also opens the way toward the praxis of historical theology as "a praxis of conversion and liberation" (Höfte 1990).

5.4 Practical-Theological Basics

In the final section of this chapter I intend once again to summarize the basic principles that I have presented and elaborated in the first part of this practical theology.

The first three chapters manifest a degree of ambivalence. There may be a considerable degree of appreciation for the enlightenment of the subject, recognizing the liberating influence it has exerted on many. To illustrate this line of thought we have, by way of example, referred to the theology of Kuitert, who showed how one can deal in a positive way with the consequences of the Enlightenment for the faith of individuals. Many will here find a point of recognition. But our trust in human reason and human autonomy has its limits. The twentieth century has presented us with a world that was characterized by a lack of freedom, in particular as we realized to what extent our lives, and society as a whole, are often predetermined — which was confirmed by most thinkers in the social sciences. Anxiety and aggression are key factors in our human experience, and social factors to a large degree determine human behavior. The Christian faith knows about this and calls it "sin." Although the individual may, in a process of trial and error, come to considerable achievements (in this salvific consecutive order), we will have to remain hesitant and suspicious with regard to one's free potential. Modern humans are much less free than many tend to think. Therefore, a social and societal correction on the tendency to think from the perspective of the individual is suggested.

We encountered a similar ambivalence in our discussion of the second line of thought concerning the modernization of society. The rationalization process has led to great technological progress in many areas and to a mode of social scientific thinking that has been of immense significance for our understanding of human relationships and social interactions. In this line of thought a leading role was attributed to Berkhof. His entire theology, in particular in the area of dogmatics, is characterized by a great affinity for empirical questions. But in the analysis presented in chapter 3 we also encountered some side effects of the rationalization process, for instance, the objectification of social phenomena and the depersonalization of humanity. Awareness of this brings us back to the subject, which, through a deeper personal experience and acceptance of personal responsibility, must refuse to become a mere object. Practical theology is able to make a contribution in this area when it operates from an agogic-emancipatory perspective.

This almost automatically brings us to the third line, that of the critical theory, which became visible in the fourth chapter, as we analyzed the social question. This expresses what many of us discovered in our society in the 1960s, as we saw the process of political awakening and realized that many things were now assuming global dimensions. In our world large groups of people fall victim to the exploitation of those who are powerless by those who are in power. Here, by way of example, we can point to Schillebeeckx, who discerns an excess of suffering and evil in history. "There is a barbarous excess, for all the explanations and interpretations. There is too much *unmerited* and *senseless* suffering for us to be able to give an ethical, hermeneutical and ontological analysis of our disaster" (1977, 666 [1980, 725]). His concept of the "experience of contrast" has helped many to keep their faith under difficult circumstances. Schillebeeckx has exerted a strong influence among the so-called base communities. As a result, justice and solidarity have become central themes in contemporary practical theology. But along this line some ambivalence is once again inescapable. We must agree with Kuitert, who argues that everything is political, but politics is not everything. A political theology often tends to emphasize the collectivity to the extent that the individual is lost sight of. We also face problems when we try to apply the model of liberation theology to our own society, where — as K. A. Schippers once wrote — "most believers are not poor, and most poor do not believe." Nonetheless, many feel inspired by this approach to theology and become motivated to ensure that theology retains this critical perspective.

I believe that the three lines referred to above, which seem to govern the worldview of modern humanity and also of contemporary (practical) theology, can be integrated in a fruitful way. Every theologian, in her or his own unique way, must face the problems modern theology has to address — which I have described in this chapter. Several theologians have shown how certain emphases may help our understanding. Our experience is cumulative, and we continue to owe much to those who worked in the past. This concludes the contours of our theological basis, which remains of fundamental importance for a hermeneutical approach to practical theology.

The choice of the theologians highlighted in this chapter remains, of course, subjective and selective. We could have developed certain perspectives by referring to other theologians, for example, Dorothee Sölle, Jürgen Moltmann, David Tracy, or Clodovis and Leonardo Boff. Their work also shows a kinship with practical-theological themes. Students should choose their own heroes from whom they seek inspiration. It is usually prudent not to focus too exclusively on one particular theologian or current of thought. By becoming "the voice of one's master," one loses any originality one might have. Integrated thinking safeguards against undesirable one-sidedness and polarization.

5.5 Integration and Differentiation

This brings us to a preliminary conclusion of the first major section of this book. The road I have suggested has consequences for practical theology, first of all for any inquiry into its basic premises and in determining its methodology. Following my definition of practical theology (1.2), I used the word pairs historical-interpretive, hermeneutical-critical, and practical-constructive, in the context of an empirically oriented methodology. This approach now takes on a more definite shape. Following the historical-interpretive track, I developed three perspectives, taking their points of departure in the individual, the social life, and the politico-economic situation. Wherever humanity arrives at understanding, a further clarification is needed through an interpretive (hermeneutical) approach. Daily life in society demands an empirical orientation. The relevance of a critical theory becomes evident in the context of a politico-economic approach. All three interact, and — though not without tensions — cross-fertilize each other. This may be referred to as integration.

We operate on the implicit assumption that contemporary philosophies of science do allow for a complementary approach through a hermeneutical method, an empirical method, and a critical method. The second part of this book must deal more explicitly with this tension-laden complementarity. The expectation that this may lead to an integrative practical theology seems justified.

From what has been said above, one may deduce a second premise regarding the object of practical theology. Differentiation is an important hallmark of modern life, in connection with on the one hand individualization and privatization, and on the other hand a greater separation between the various sectors of public life (3.1; 3.2). This has consequences for the situation of religion and of the church, and demands in my view a differentiated practical theology. In the mediation of the Christian faith, the spheres of the individual, the church, and society must be treated as distinct domains of action.

Research indicates that a narrow focus on the role of the church will limit our influence to a minority of the Dutch population — only those who are actively participating in the life of the church (Dekker 1992, 34-35). But not all who are inactive in the life of the church are nonreligious. Around those who are active in the church, there is a significant current of individual Christianity and a broader religiosity. An anthropological approach, which fits with the way in which these people — whether or not they are on the membership list of the church — see the world, will be needed if faith is to be mediated in this situation.

One finds a similar situation when one looks at society. The time has passed when all links between church and society were institutionalized in Christian organizations. Today the churches seek direct access, individually or through the Council of Churches, to the government and public institutions (Dekker 1992, 171). But their influence has greatly declined. This makes it even more urgent that individual church members, driven by their Christian conviction, play an active role in society. Remarkably enough, in spite of deconfessionalization and secularization, Christian organizations in the areas of politics, education, media, and social care continue to play an important role in Dutch society. Some refer to this as a form of "cultural Christianity" that no longer meets specific doctrinal criteria but nonetheless is saturated with Christian traditions, norms, and values. This type of "civil Christianity" also demands our attention.

This differentiated approach to a large extent agrees with Rössler's tripartition in the German situation (1986, 79). For the American situation, we may refer to such concepts as "public philosophy" and the "public church" (Marty 1981). For a further discussion, see part III of this book, which deals with the various separate domains of action of practical theology.

In pursuing the three different lines drawn in the previous section, justice must be done — simultaneously, but at different levels — to these aspects of integration and differentiation. Through a hermeneutical, empirical, and critical approach, and from this perspective of a differentiation in church and society, an integrative practical theology will study the mediation of the Christian faith in:

Individual	Church	Society
on the microlevel	on the mesolevel	on the macrolevel
directed toward the individual	directed toward the group	directed toward society
through an anthropological approach	through an ecclesiastical approach	through a diaconological approach
focusing on greater awareness	focusing on communicative activities	focusing on social action
aiming at individual Christianity	aiming at institutional Christianity	aiming at "public" Christianity

5.6 Conclusion

The two previous sections conclude this chapter and the interpretive model developed in part I. The next chapter stands to a large extent by itself. The three perspectives summarized in the last section can be separated only on paper. In reality there are no precise demarcation lines, and there will always be a degree of overlapping. Part II deals in more detail with this integrative principle. In part III we return to the differentiation principle.

CHAPTER 6

The History of Pastoral Theology

Situating the origins of practical theology in the nineteenth century may give the impression that praxis was never before in history the object of reflection. This chapter wants to remove that impression. From the earliest days of the Christian church, elementary and more elaborate forms of pastoral theology did exist. Note that I use the term *pastoral* theology rather than *practical* theology. The reason is that this aspect of theology occurred in an ecclesiological context and was limited to the development of "a systematic doctrine of the pastoral ministry." The term *theologia pastoralis* is first mentioned in the sixteenth century within the Catholic tradition.

Today's practical theology has much to learn from this tradition of pastoral theology. It contains a centuries-old treasure of experiences, with the Scriptures as the guiding principle for faith and practice. Even today, this manner in which people, led by Word and Spirit, with all their limitations and shortcomings, attempted to give form and content to their faith can help one in finding answers to many questions.

I start with the praxis of the New Testament (6.1), and continue with the earliest development of a pastoral theology, in the early church and in the Middle Ages (6.2). The Reformation occurs in the sixteenth century. From that time onward one must distinguish between a Reformed (6.3) and a Catholic tradition (6.4), which were often sharply opposed to each other.

6.1 The Praxis of the New Testament

One already finds an elementary form of pastoral theology in the New Testament. The Acts of the Apostles *(Praxeis Apostolōn)* emphasizes the role of the Spirit in extending God's acts in human activity. God's revelation creates room for "mediation." Men and women receive spiritual gifts *(charismata)*, enabling them to proclaim the gospel *(kerygma)*, to support each other in the establishment of a community *(koinōnia)*, and to be servants in the kingdom of God that is being established in this world *(diakonia)*.

The Pauline Letters reflect the earliest forms of these patterns. Writing about the church as "the body of Christ" (1 Cor. 12–14), Paul paints the picture of a charismatic community, with a multicolored spectrum of spiritual gifts. In addition to the gift of tongues, of healing, service, compassion, knowledge, the discernment of spirits and leadership, other charismata are more structural in nature. They are referred to by names like prophet, evangelist, pastor (or shepherd), and teacher (Ridderbos 1966, 499-50 [1975, 446-47]). One gets the picture of a democratic community, a church "from the bottom up."

The Pastoral Letters (1 and 2 Timothy, Titus) paint another picture. There a group of elders and "overseers" exercise authority *over* the church. Unlike the previous one, this model most likely has a Judeo-Christian background. The elder is the *presbyteros,* who, in the Reformed tradition, becomes the "presbyter" (elder), and in the Catholic tradition develops into the priest. The word for overseer is *episkopos,* from which the word *bishop* derives. By the second century the *episkopos* (bishop) had become the head of the *presbyteroi* (elders). The deacons, who are also mentioned, at first performed a variety of services, but, as the hierarchical structure grew, gradually became the assistants of the bishop. Thus some structure developed within an originally rather pluriform praxis.

Structure was needed to assure the continuity of a community. The church began to reflect on this more intensely when the young community faced its first major crisis: the belief in the impending return of Christ. The early Christians were firmly convinced — as is clear from, for example, 1 and 2 Thessalonians — that Christ would soon return and that the end of time was nigh. In this limited time frame there was little need to pay much attention to church organization. But when the second coming did not materialize, they had to look for a way in which the tradition of Christ's death and resurrection — that "dangerous memory" (J. B. Metz) — could be transmitted to the following generations, while maintaining a balance between "remembering" and "expecting."

A further echo of this crisis occurs in the parables, in particular in Matthew, where this time perspective has been stretched out. Firet states that the parable of the talents (Matt. 25:14-30) might well be regarded as the "magna charta" of what we now refer to as the object of practical theology. The master in the parable travels abroad and entrusts his possessions to his slaves, who are expected to work with these talents (charismata) in God's kingdom, and must give account upon the master's return. "The *paradosis* of the Lord (the key concept of the parable, v. 14) makes the coming of God, constantly and ever anew, an actual event *through the service of human beings*" (Firet 1987, 30). Humanity becomes the subject in progress of the history of salvation. Pneumatology offers the framework. Speaking about the Holy Spirit, one should emphasize that God prefers to work through people. Humanity is enlisted *as humanity* in God's service (van Ruler; see 5.2.2).

The place of action is in essence "the church as it meets together." Firet (1968, 60ff. [1986, 43ff.]) distinguishes three slowly emerging separate modes: *kerygma, didachē,* and *paraklesis,* as the basic core of what would develop into proclamation, catechesis, and pastoral care. The New Testament also has a number of key terms for the nurturing of the church. Bolkestein (1964, 87) refers to such verbs as *espiskopein* (to oversee), *stērizein* (to strengthen), *katartizein* (to equip), *nouthetein* (to discipline), *elenchein* (to defend), and *oikodomein* (to build). These basic terms presuppose a broad spectrum of activities for the nurturing of the church. Some very precise instructions are found in the parenetic parts of the letters. A clear example is found in the Letter to the Hebrews, directed to Christians of the second generation living in oppression: "Do not forget to entertain strangers [*philoxenia,* love for strangers]"; "remember those in prison [those who are persecuted because of their faith], as if you were their fellow prisoners" (13:1-3). What other example of empathy does one want?

6.2 The Origins of Pastoral Theology

The lines of the New Testament are extended into the early pastoral-theological writings that reflect on the practice of the Christian ministry. These writings were of great benefit in the missionary context of the church in the early centuries and the beginning of the Middle Ages, to the increasing number of clergy who often had little formal education. The reflection on the role of the ministry received a central place within the hierarchical concept of the church. This was especially true for the office of the bishop. Cyprian (third century) stated: "Ecclesia est in episcopo" (The church is in the bishop;

A. D. Müller 1950, 82). The people are dependent on the church, and thus on the bishop, for the same church father maintained: "Extra ecclesiam nulla salus" (There is no salvation outside of the church).

Holding a church office entails a heavy responsibility. Who is suitable for such a task? According to A. D. Müller (1950, 20), this is the central theme of the earliest pastoral theology. He attaches great value to three writings: "Peri phygēs" of Gregory of Nazianzus (ca. 265), "Peri hierōsynēs" by John Chrysostom, (ca. 385), and "Liber regulae pastoralis," written by the well-known Pope Gregory the Great (540-604), at the threshold of the Middle Ages (H. Jonker 1983, 58-59).

The first two writings emphasize the flight motif. When called to an office in the church, the natural reaction is to flee. This motif led the authors to identify with biblical prophets like Moses, Jeremiah, and Jonah, who also ran away before they eventually obeyed. Already at an early stage, being a minister was associated with asceticism, a turning away from the world, and celibacy. These things set the clergy apart from the laity. Gregory's rule already offered a more detailed theology of the ministry. A central aspect was that of being a shepherd, but also the work of the Holy Spirit was strongly emphasized. The Christian minister was not primarily a theologian, or a professional, but one who was filled with the Spirit.

Augustine's (354-430) Confessions are a moving piece of pastoral-theological autobiographical writing. Recent translations (e.g., by G. Wijdeveld in Dutch; 1985 [by H. Chadwick in English; 1991]) make this document easily accessible. Augustine is the best-known individual from antiquity. We are also well informed about his work as a minister, as is apparent in the excellent study by F. van der Meer (1957) about the work of this church father. His De catechezandis rudibus, written for the benefit of the catechumens, belongs, together with the "mystagogical catecheses" of Cyril of Jerusalem, to the most important catechetical manuals in the early church.

From the very beginning women, who were after all the first witnesses of Christ's resurrection, played a major role in the ministry of the church — a fact that has often been underreported by later (male) historians. Although the New Testament stressed the equality of men and women (Gal. 3:28; 1 Cor. 11:11-12), the relationship soon became one of subservience and exclusion from church office. Reading the New Testament one notices the list of greetings in Romans 16, headed by the deaconess Phoebe and including women like Prisca, Tryphena, Tryphosa, and Persis, who are listed because of their ministry. Men and women shared in the gift of prophecy, as well as in public prayer (1 Cor. 11:5). The Pastoral Letters imply that there was a distinct role for widows, in an office with specific entrance requirements (1 Tim. 5:9), and that there may have been female deacons (1 Tim. 3:11). In the early church women filled important missionary assignments. In the ancient world they had sole access to the living quarters of women, where they baptized, taught, and were responsible for pastoral and diaconal care. This situation changed when the church became the state church and the priests received a much wider range of responsibilities (Jelsma 1975, 31). From that time onward, all women who did not enter a religious order were marginalized.

The church entered a new era when Emperor Constantine (284-337) converted to Christianity; in 380 it received the status of state church. This led to a significant increase in the tasks and responsibilities of the clergy. But even before Heering's book about "the fall of Christianity" appeared, A. Kuyper pointed to the rather dubious character of this development: "The conversion of Constantine was for the Church the signal to wed itself with the power of the world, thereby cutting the nerve of her strength" (1891, 19 [1950, 31]).

The need was felt for an efficient organization to cover the whole empire. Following the pattern of the state, the church was divided into dioceses (districts; the word derives from Greek *dioikein*, "to rule one's household"). This term replaced *paroikia*, "community of outsiders, parish," which reminded the church of its eschatological position (Arnold 1966, 15). Its future lay elsewhere. But the established church was of this world!

This gave rise to the basic pastoral model that, in particular under the influence of Charlemagne, spread over all of Europe as a network of ecclesiastical communities (Schippers 1989, 89). This decentralization was needed if all people were to have access to a priest. The model can be referred to as "one man, one building, and one territory" (90). It has proved to be an unbeatable formula, with the result that until today the cleric officiates in the worship services. The distance between laity and clergy continued to increase. This model retained its significance during the Reformation.

In the course of the Middle Ages pastoral theology became more and more a subdiscipline of a structured theological education. The Fourth Lateran Council of 1215 (A. D. Müller 1950, 23) determined that churches in provincial centers must have a magister, who must lead the presbyters and the laity in the "cura animarum," the care for the souls. This was linked to the obligatory auricular confession, instituted by this same council. For this reason canon law and moral theology became subdivisions of pastoral theology. Later, the separate subdiscipline of "ascetics" focused on the spiritual formation of the priest and dealt with *meditatio, oratio,* and *tentatio* (how to face temptations).

The confessional practice has its roots in the Celtic tradition, where a discipline for the correction of errors had developed. In the seventh century

Irish missionaries carried this custom to the European continent, where it soon replaced the penitential practice of the early church. "Instead of being public and rare, confession and penance become private, frequent and common to all" (McNeill 1965, 112). The rules are spelled out in penitential manuals, Columbanus's Rule being the oldest in that genre. This change in practice led to an extensive casuistry. The Reformation objected primarily not to the confession but rather to its obligatory nature, the "obligatory remorse" and the absolution. The examination in the confessional was therefore replaced by the confessional examination! This continued to be reflected in the "question-and-answer" model of the catechism, which was borrowed from the penitential books (Neidhart 1967, 237-38).

6.3 Pastoral Theology in the Reformation

Reformation pastoral theology heavily emphasized the office of the minister. But some of the accents were shifting. The new stress on justification by faith switched the emphasis from administering the seven sacraments to the proclamation of the Word.

Likewise, the role of the clergy was toned down because of the new accent this renewal movement placed on the general priesthood of the believers. This was particularly true of the Lutheran tradition (Thurneysen 1957, 261 [1962, 294-95]). Calvin and Bucer allowed for democratization through a differentiation of the various church offices: lay leaders could be appointed as elders or deacons. The basic pastoral model was utilized in the division of Geneva into quarters, with elders in charge of home visitation and church discipline, and with deacons dealing with the social needs. Church discipline was especially important, as the jurisdiction was shared by the church and the government (Plomp 1969). The church, through its diaconate, carried a heavy responsibility for the care of the poor, as well as of the sick and the needy. Calvin linked his tripartioning with the threefold work of Christ: prophet (minister of the Word), priest (deacon), and king (elder). In addition, he mentioned in fourth place the office of the doctor (teacher of the church or professor of theology). This view on the offices within the church was adopted by the Dutch churches, where women were initially allowed to serve as deacons.

The Reformation required a broad reorientation with regard to canon law, liturgy, proclamation, catechesis, pastorate, and church development. Martin Bucer was the first to propose the outlines of a pastoral theology in his book about "the true care for the soul and the appropriate service of the pastor" (1538). This work emphasized the church as the body of Christ, where the community of the Word, the sacraments, and discipline must receive their rightful places. To achieve this, the Lord works through his faithful servants, in order that his kingdom may be extended. The church must elect these individuals in an orderly manner. Based on the five groups mentioned in Ezekiel 34, Bucer distinguished five distinct tasks in the area of pastoral care. The aim was "to search for, and find all the lost sheep, to bring back those that were chased away, to heal the wounded, to strengthen the weak, protect and tend those that are healthy." Bucer said that he was "being charged by those who collaborate with me in Strasbourg in the Word of the Lord" (1991, 143). G. Rau (1970) believes that the Reformed concept of the plural office has done more for the development of pastoral theology than the Lutheran view of the one, single office.

One finds a first all-encompassing approach with Andreas Hyperius (i.e., from Yperen), 1511-1564, a professor in Marburg. His book *De Theologo sive de ratione studii theologici* (1556) identified a number of disciplines, which together constitute the *praxeis* of the church: church history, canon law, church leadership, poimenics, and liturgy (A. D. Müller 1950, 24). He assigned a particular importance to the "cura animarum," as new pastoral procedures had to be developed to replace the confessional practice. His student Wilhelm Zepper (1550-1607), in Herborn, urged — inspired by Hyperius — the appointment of a "professor practicus."

In the Netherlands, the General Synod of Dordrecht (1618-19) decided not only to prepare a new translation of the Bible but also to regulate in detail — by means of the Church Order of Dordrecht — the way in which the church operated and the offices functioned, with special attention for the work of the pastor. The pastor was, of course, a man. After he had completed his university education, the church decided whether he would be admitted to the ministry through a "preparatory" and a "peremptory" (final) exam. This was already prescribed by the Convent of Wezel (1568). Also referring to Hyperius, the Synod of Dordrecht pointed to the importance of an education in the sphere of the *theologia practica* and of the practical exam (A. D. Müller 1950, 24). The faculty in Leiden, however, showed little enthusiasm for the introduction of such a course, in spite of considerable pressure from the Synod of the Province of South Holland (den Dulk 1992, 4-5).

Gijsbertus Voetius (1589-1676), professor at Utrecht, was the first to use the term *theologia practica* for the courses in pastoral theology in his encyclopedic introduction to theology — in the third volume of his *Selectae disputationes theologiae* (1659). This *theologia practica* was divided into three major parts: "theologia moralis aut casuistica" (ethics), "theologia ascetica" (ascetics or spirituality), and "politica ecclesiastica" (comprising liturgy, canon law, and homiletics). His treatment was a kind of appendix, a training to prepare the students for the practice of the ministry.

In this time and for several centuries to come, when few people had an academic background, the pastor remained primarily a scholar, a teacher who lived among his books, rather than a shepherd who lived among his flock. In the nineteenth century the status of the minister increased: "more and more pastors have double names" (de Jong 1969, 55). Double names remind one of men of noble birth. In the major Protestant churches women were not admitted to the ministry until the 1960s. Some smaller churches, the Doopsgezinden (Dutch Mennonites) and the Remonstranten (a small liberal denomination), had preceded the larger churches. Today women are usually in the majority among theological students, even though most of the professors are still male.

In our time the profession of the ministry has become problematic and is "like a reed in the wind" (W. J. Jonker 1970). Once again there is a need for a contemporary form of pastoral theology, as a specific focus within the discipline of practical theology. The two-volume work on pastoral theology by M. Josuttis (1982, 1988) is an example.

6.4 Pastoral Theology in the Roman Catholic Church

According to F. X. Arnold, the criticism of the Reformation was to a large extent based on "the flaws and the abuses of the religious-liturgical practice." "As a result, pastoral care and piety often became a matter of an exaggerated objectivism that expected too much from objective sacramental acts, while undervaluing the subjective personal involvement and the ensuing ethical impulse" (Arnold et al. 1966, 25).

Trent gave birth to the Counter-Reformation, and therewith to a new era for pastoral work (i.e., the role of the clergy) in the church. The Council named after that city (1545-1563) would put its mark on pastoral theology and the work of the priest until the Second Vatican Council (Arnold et al. 1966, 26). The council wanted to safeguard the pastoral care in the church and the development of its core activities. In an attempt to solve the conflict between the mendicant orders and the secular clergy, who were often at loggerheads with each other, the parochial principle was clearly enunciated. In addition, the liturgy received much attention. In reaction to the theology of the Word of the Reformation, considerable stress was laid on the catechesis and the sermon.

The Reformation had some tragic consequences: "With almost dialectical necessity the Catholics pushed those points to the background that were strongly emphasized by the Protestants, while giving too much prominence to certain aspects rejected by the Protestants" (Arnold et al. 1966, 35-36). The change in the organization of the content in the catechisms of Peter Canisius and Robert Bellarmine may serve as an example. Besides the classical catechetical sections — Credo, Decalogue, the Lord's Prayer — a separate expansion was seen of two controversial subjects: the doctrines of the sacraments and of Christian justice. The separation of faith from the *iustitia christiana* intensified the controversial reproach of legalism (37). The Catholic sermon likewise shared in the shift of the Counter-Reformation (38). Thus the entire pastoral area (the life and work of the church) became enthralled in polemics, resulting on both sides in a doctrinal imbalance. Faith was more and more superseded by correct doctrine.

When the academic studies were reorganized in Austria, pastoral theology became — for the first time — an independent discipline (1774); cf. 5.1.4. In spite of the way in which the reorganization has been effected, there was a general consensus that Rautenstrauch's new curriculum took the changing circumstances and the requirements of theology as a whole into account (Arnold et al. 1966, 44). The curriculum indicated clearly how the new subject must be taught. An introduction was followed by three parts. First, the duty of the pastor to teach (catechesis, preaching, pastoral care). Then followed a section on the safekeeping and administering of the sacraments. The third part, finally, dealt with the duty of nurturing, focused on the Christian life, in private, in the parish, and in society at large. All traditional courses found their place in this curriculum, and all aspects of the work of the future priest were included (Arnold et al. 1966, 47).

The term *pastoral theology* was probably first employed by Peter Canisius. As early as in 1591, a book entitled *Enchiridion theologiae pastoralis* (Handbook on pastoral theology) appeared, written by Peter Binsfeld, the suffragan bishop of Trier. As time went by, the tendency to give central place to the role of the clergy shifted to the view of A. Graf, which, as we saw earlier (2.4), emphasized the inner growth of the church.

The Protestant Republic of the United Provinces did not leave much room for a seminary for Catholic clergy. The only seminary to survive this period was in Roermond. Most priests received their education in other countries. But in the nineteenth century the Catholics became citizens with equal rights. This led to the founding of seminaries, where students could live in dormitories in relative isolation. Separate, preparatory seminaries with boarding facilities were established to provide for secondary education. Several orders and congregations established similar institutions for the training of future monastics. In the era of emancipation the priests became the spiritual leaders of their communities.

The seminary tradition in the Netherlands ended around 1966-67. With the creation of new schools for higher education, later renamed universities, the number of female theology students increased sharply. Many of them found a position in the church as pastoral workers, but they remained barred from the priesthood.

6.5 Conclusion

This chapter provided a bridge, via the tradition of pastoral theology, to the modern situation, when practical theology arose as a theory of action. The development of practical theology since the nineteenth century was surveyed in the previous chapter. We are now ready to proceed to part II, which deals with epistemological aspects.

I return to the pastoral theology tradition in 9.4.5 and, finally, in chapter 17, where I discuss contemporary questions about the present position of pastoral and ministerial work.

Practical Theology as a Theological Theory of Action

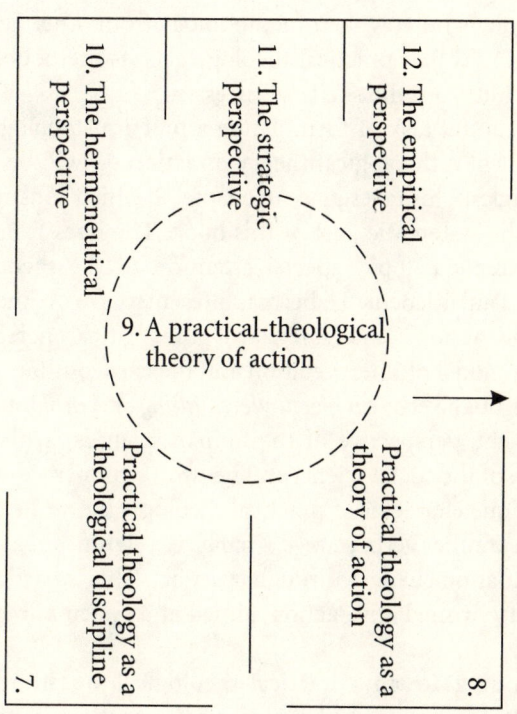

Figure 3: Part II

In this book I define practical theology as *the empirically oriented theological theory of the mediation of the Christian faith in the praxis of modern society* (1.3). I systematically explain this definition in part II.

A consensus has emerged among the specialists in this discipline that practical theology must be viewed as a theological theory of action. Reference is usually made to the programmatic definition of N. Mette: *"Practical theology must be conceived of as a theological theory of action within a theology that is understood as a practice-oriented science"* (1978, 9).

Chapters 7 and 8 take this definition as their point of departure and as the foundation for practical theology, by describing this theory from two emerging perspectives. Speaking about practical theology as a theological theory of action, I intend to state that (1) we are dealing with a *theological* branch of learning, and (2) more precisely, with a *theory of action*. Chapter 7 focuses on the theological aspects, while chapter 8 takes a closer look at the concept of a theory of action.

As a branch of theology, practical theology is tied to theology as a whole. But as a theory of action it derives its paradigm and methodology from another area of science: the social sciences. This is not unique. All branches of theology borrow their methodology from other fields of inquiry. The peculiar thing is that practical theology gets its methodology not from the humanities but from the social sciences.

Thus the central task of formulating a practical-theological theory — the development of a theological theory of action — will be clarified from two different angles. This takes place in chapter 9, which constitutes the theoretical core of the systematic part of this book. The lines from the previous chapters are extended. I pay special attention to the theories of Jürgen Habermas and Paul Ricoeur. Habermas presents us with the paradigm of "communicative action" and safeguards the critical perspective, while Ricoeur offers a model of interpretation and the basic outlines for a methodology that — through verbs such as *understanding* and *explaining* — links the hermeneutical (the perspective of the human sciences) with the empirical (the perspective of the social sciences). The two verbs form an important element in the unique character of practical theology: the strategic perspective, encapsulated in another verb: *change*. Change is a significant aspect of any action. A given situation changes through every act. This is particularly true for any intermediary or mediative action, aimed at a systematic intervention in reality.

In responding to any practical-theological question, one faces a hermeneutical, an empirical, and a strategic perspective, all of which closely interconnect. This insight is in essence already found in the first methodological description of practical theology, by Nitzsch (3.4), who linked a conceptual theological appraisal with an empirical explanation and a regulative approach to praxis.

This determines our course in the next three chapters (7–9). A practical-theological approach, which at a certain point expresses the tension between tradition and experience, is (a) interpreted by means of a hermeneutical theory, (b) analyzed by means of an *empirical* theory, and (c) translated in terms of action through a *strategic* theory. This presents us with three theoretical tracks, which I deal with in the following three chapters (10–12). The order of treatment is: hermeneutical, strategic, empirical. This book gives priority to the hermeneutical approach, but the two other lines of inquiry are no less important. The order strategic-empirical has been adopted for the sake of the flow of the argument. Practical theology as a theory of action must be developed from a hermeneutical perspective (chapter 10), from a strategic perspective (chapter 11), and from an empirical perspective (chapter 12). The three lines converge into one single theory in the *integrative* approach adopted in this book.

There are different schools in the study of practical theology, each with its own accents and emphasis on one or some of the various aspects. Chapter 9 provides a survey of these various currents of thought.

CHAPTER 7

Practical Theology as a Theological Discipline

Modern practical theology had its beginnings in the 1960s. Since then a considerable consensus has emerged regarding the view that practical theology is a theological *theory of action.* In this chapter I discuss the first half of Mette's definition (1978, 9): *"Practical theology must be conceived of as a theological theory of action within a theology that is understood as a practice-oriented science."* These words assign practical theology its own place within theology as a whole: practical theology is a *theological* discipline.

First, in three separate steps, I explain and develop Mette's statement, taking into account the original character of the discipline of theology. Theology began as a practical science (7.1). Second, I then pay attention to the medieval notion of theology as a *theologia practica,* where the term *practical* refers at least to a dimension of theology in general (7.2). Third, following this route I look at the encyclopedic approach as the final stage in a differentiation process within the discipline of theology, which assigns the subdiscipline of practical theology its own place within theology as a whole (7.3).

This provides an adequate response to the preliminary questions raised by Mette's definition and opens the way for an elaboration of the theological character of practical theology along hermeneutical lines (7.4). Following this, I survey the development of practical theology in a number of language areas (7.5).

7.1 The Practical Nature of Theology in General

There is no simple answer to the question, What is theology? It makes all the difference whether one poses that question from "the heart of the matter" that is at issue in theology, or within a university context during a discussion among professionals. At the very least there is a tension between these two that also touches practical theology.

Considering the original aim of theology, one might defend the thesis that all theology is practical. Firet thus described theology as "a systematic reflection on our faith to help others believe" (1987, 21). One finds such a form of theology already in the Bible itself. According to its subtitle, Herman Ridderbos calls his study of the letters of Paul "an outline of his theology, a description," which is fitting for "so profound and complicated a phenomenon as the manner in which the Apostle Paul has given form and expression to the gospel of Jesus Christ" (1966, 5 [1975, 13]). In any case, the result is not immediately accessible to the average Bible reader. Faith demands thought and explanation: "Fides quaerit intellectum" (Anselm). From its inception there was also an apologetic motive: the desire to make the faith intelligible for others by removing possible intellectual stumbling blocks. Even today, most theological students who intend to enter the ministry usually derive their personal motivation from this practical purpose of their reflection on their faith.

This latter aspect is not remarkable and hardly differs from what one sees in other disciplines. All learning is based on prior, nonscientific experience, and usually has a practical purpose. "The prescientific experiences must therefore not be seen as simply the kind of knowledge that existed before there was any science, but rather as human knowledge in general that continues to constitute the basis of all contemporary scientific, that is, methodically arranged, knowledge" (Beerling et al. 1980, 23). Science develops from a closer look at the various streams of experiential knowledge, in a process of selection, ordering, measuring, that is, through objectifying the data derived from this experiential knowledge. Thus it is true of all pretheoretical experience that "it is not in the first instance aimed at the establishment of a scientific theory or a deeper insight, but has a practical orientation" (23). Scientific language describes and categorizes; it aims at explanation and verification. "The language of the prescientific experience is usually a language of action — asking someone to do something, to avoid a danger, to make a decision" (24). In the same sense theology is based on experiential knowledge and is aimed at faith and action. From its very beginning theology had a practical purpose.

In the past the relation between faith and knowledge was not very problematic. For the knowledge about God was very similar to other kinds of knowledge. Theology means literally "speaking about God," and the realm of the divine was simply part of a general, broad reservoir of experiential knowledge. Theology describes our love for God with our whole mind, and this God can be the object of our reflection.

Augustine began to differentiate between theology and philosophy (Pannenberg 1973, 12 [1976, 8-9]). He understood the Christian teachings as *sapientia* (wisdom), which he distinguished from *scientia* (knowledge, science). The sciences deal with the temporal world, while wisdom has to do with the eternal, with God as the highest good. They do not totally exclude each other, for even the sciences can be directed toward that highest good and can lead to wisdom. Philosophy is *ancilla theologiae* — it serves theology that encompasses true wisdom. Other ancient thinkers agreed with Augustine on this point. Augustine claimed Pauline support for linking knowledge and wisdom with Christ's incarnation: God in Christ, "in whom are hidden all the treasures of wisdom and knowledge" (Col. 2:3). This view remained dominant until well into the Middle Ages.

As we shall see, this notion of theology as a practical discipline remains an important undercurrent within theology as a whole.

7.2 *Theologia practica* as a Way of "Doing" Theology

As the medieval world changed, this view of practical theology as a practical branch of learning came under pressure. Edward Farley (1983, 31ff.) points to the increasing ambiguity of the concept of theology: between theology as a personal knowledge of God and all that is related to him, and theology as an academic discipline, as a conscious, scholarly attempt at increased understanding. The idea of *habitus* is introduced, the personal attitude of the theologian. This duality is also apparent in the Aristotelian concept of *epistemē* (Latin *scientia*), which can refer to "pure" knowledge but also to an organized body of knowledge or to the inquiry that seeks to arrive at such a body of knowledge. These aspects were separated from each other at the time of the Enlightenment. Theology as habitus gradually disappeared from the theological curriculum, to the detriment of the whole enterprise of theology. As a result, in the ensuing period theology became fragmented into a series of independent subdisciplines.

This dual nature is related to the rise of the universities. The modern concept of theology (as *logos,* "doctrine" or "speaking," about God) originated with the establishment of these institutions, which assigned the *facultas theologica* its own place (Pannenberg 1973, 12 [1976, 8]). The first universities were established around 1200, when professors in Paris and Bologna joined students in a "universitas magistrorum et scolarium" or "studentinum" (Schelsky 1971, 14). In this connection Schelsky remarks that the basic reason for the rise of the universities in the Middle Ages was the desire to know the truth rather than to provide training for a profession, even though an academic degree was usually seen as positive for someone in search of a position. The university had a significant degree of autonomy; it was a place of freedom, but also of loneliness. This concept of a university, which later was also supported by Wilhelm von Humboldt, played a dominant role in the establishment of the University of Berlin (1810), for which Schleiermacher acted as adviser with regard to the theology department (Krause 1972, 3). According to this view, university education was participation in the process of scientific inquiry. This tradition would not have known how to relate to an educational process based on a modular system!

This idealistic tradition, typical of European culture, was unlike the Anglo-Saxon concept of a university, as expressed, for instance, by J. H. Newman (1852). He saw a university as "a place of *teaching* universal *knowledge*" (Meuleman 1991, 6). With his focus on a "habit of mind," he fit in with the habitus tradition referred to above, also supported by Farley. In this view, as in the previous one, the university did not offer professional training in any strict sense, even though it prepared one for various positions in society.

Many medieval universities had a theology department. This did not create any controversy, but there was, as one would expect from what has just been said, a difference of opinion about the nature of theology. On the one side was Thomas Aquinas (1225-1274), who regarded theology as a science *(scientia)* in the Aristotelian sense of the word. Theology thus fit perfectly within the academic definition of science. On the other side, Duns Scotus (d. 1308) disagreed. He also saw theology as a science, though a peculiar one, and not as a *scientia* in the Aristotelian sense (Meuleman 1991, 21). He remained skeptical toward Thomas's view of theology as a speculative theory and defended, fully in harmony with the *sapientia* tradition, theology as *scientia practica* (Pannenberg 1973, 230 [1976, 232]), directed toward the highest good — a view for which he also claimed support from Aristotle. Typical for this concept of theology was that it included not only *knowledge* about God as its object, but also *knowing* God (Firet 1968, 14 [1986, 5]).

Protestant theology of the sixteenth and seventeenth centuries largely followed the line of Duns Scotus and William of Occam (1290-1349). Luther had no doubt whatsoever that theology was not a speculative but a practical discipline: "*Vera theologia est practica — speculativa igitur theologia* belongs with the devil in hell" (Pannenberg 1973, 233 [1976, 235]). Luther saw the object of theology in the relationship between humanity and God — between sinful humanity and a righteous God. "Thus with its acceptance by Luther as a practical science, theology became more existential and pastoral" (234 [235]). John Calvin largely agreed. At the very beginning of the first book of his *Institutes* (1559), he argued that our knowledge of God and our knowledge of ourselves are intimately connected. This unity between revelation and experience — to use modern terminology — also led toward the view of theology as a practical discipline.

Considering the firm link between theology and praxis, Karl Rahner also thinks that the label "practical science" would be more fitting than "theory" for theology as a whole (Mette 1978, 342). For theology is fundamentally a reflection on our faith. Therefore, even today many Protestant and Catholic scholars agree that theology is a *study of God*. In spite of differences in approach, most agree that theology as *theologia practica* is to be understood as at least a dimension of theology in general.

7.3 Practical Theology as a Separate Discipline

A totally different process of differentiation ran parallel to the development outlined above. In the early history of the university (the thirteenth century), one can see a measure of distinction between exegesis and dogmatics, between biblical and systematic theology, or — in the words of Schleiermacher — between historical and philosophical theology (Adriaanse et al. 1987, 85). Exegesis, the study of the original sources, received its own place beside systematic theology, which focused on the quest for truth. This explains why "theology" is often seen as synonymous with "systematic theology" (Pannenberg 1973, 350 [1976, 347]).

Church history did not acquire its own separate status until the time of the Reformation. In the controversy between Rome and the Reformation each side sought to defend its position against that of the opponent by appealing to the historical sources. Church history first appeared as a separate subdiscipline in 1583 (Adriaanse at al. 1987, 88), but only the historical consciousness of the nineteenth century made it fully independent.

In the eighteenth century, when the transmission of the Christian faith began to present problems, practical theology was more clearly distinguished from dogmatics. For instance, J. F. Buddaeus (1711) suggested that one part of theology should deal with the *agenda* (things that must be done), while another should deal with the *credenda* (things that must be believed) (Adriaanse et al. 1987, 89). According to this view practical theology provided the link with contemporary faith. As we saw earlier (2.4), Schleiermacher was the first to plead for a separate status of practical theology within theology as a whole. Toward the end of the nineteenth century missiology emerged from practical theology.

From the Enlightenment onward, the study of the various religions and of the phenomenon of religion found their place in the theological curriculum. The universities now opted for an objectifying approach to religion, thus missing the faith a priori of theology. As a result, they were able to pass the test of scientific criticism, as long as they kept enough distance from classical theology as a study of God. This is the view of Adriaanse et al., who use this line of reasoning to defend the *duplex ordo,* which had been introduced in the Netherlands in 1876. Empirical religious studies, such as the sociology of religion and the psychology of religion, which have arisen in recent times, also belong to the domain of religious studies.

With the birth of the nineteenth century the "encyclopedic" era began, typified by Edward Farley, an American scholar, as "the triumph of the fourfold pattern" (1983, 99). This pattern distinguishes four areas: exegetical, historical, systematic, and practical theology. Further subdivisions tended to lead to an ever increasing fragmentation of knowledge. Farley is unhappy with this development and considers this encyclopedic approach an unfortunate way of expressing the structure of theology. Few Americans have decided to take this road. In Germany, however, this general introduction *(encyclopädie)* becomes a separate subdiscipline with two main lines of inquiry: What is the relation between theology and other disciplines, and how do the different theological subdisciplines relate to each other? The Netherlands presents a similar picture.

One of Farley's objections against Schleiermacher's proposal is the "clerical paradigm" that results from regarding theology as a positive science and from the fact that historical consciousness and the historical method have their impact on all disciplines (102). He sees the separation between "theological education and church education," between formal learning and catechesis, as a major problem of any "encyclopedic" approach. This leads to a difference in position, and thus in power, between professional theologians and laypeople (131). Another problem centers on the concept of praxis. Academic praxis differs greatly from the praxis of liberation, which inspires feminist theology and liberation theology. These are based on a close connection between reflection and action. Farley therefore asks for renewed attention for theology as habitus (132). "Encyclopedia" is a principle of organization rather than a model for training. He pleads for the restoration of an ancient theological tradition, the *theologia practica,* which has shifted to the background in the university environment.

I deal with this point at considerable length, since this clearly shows the difference in the way practical theologians in Europe and America view their discipline. European theologians think primarily in encyclopedic terms, while American theologians think primarily in hermeneutical terms (R. E. Palmer 1969). The Europeans first of all search for the proper distinctions by clarifying differences, while the Americans focus on good correlations and possible connections. This also clarifies the tension between academic theology and forms of liberation theology. These theologies with a special focus assign a central place to the experience of the subject as an avenue toward knowledge, and in that respect they are a peculiar type of *theologia practica,* which more easily fit into the American than the European academic tradition. Below I look at possible bridges between these various traditions.

7.4 A Hermeneutical Approach

The previous sections have clarified in three steps the consensus formulated by Mette, that practical theology must be conceived of as a theological theory of action "within a theology that is *understood as a practice-oriented science.*" This implies that this practical theology, which has developed into a separate practice-oriented discipline — based on the view that theology is *theologia practica* — must not be allowed to be functionally independent. One must ever keep in mind what theology is all about: the unity of knowledge, faith, and action. This inevitably leads to the following question: How can practical theology as *a theological discipline* contribute to that aim?

In answering this question I have opted for a hermeneutical approach. This, first of all, must elucidate the object of theology, in its literal meaning of "the science of speaking about God." As knowledge of God becomes less and less self-evident, it is increasingly difficult to see God as the object of academic inquiry. At the very least we are dealing "with a very peculiar object of a very peculiar academic discipline" (Berkhof 1981, 31). I intend to go a step further and find the point of departure in the anthropological shift that is apparent in theology since the days of Schleiermacher. Not God himself, but the human experience of God, the Christian faith, now takes central stage as the object of inquiry. Pannenberg suggests that this view may be regarded as a counterpart of the concept of the *theologia practica* found with Scotus and among the early Reformers. Theology thus comprises not only knowledge of God but also knowing God. "The subject of theology is now man, and its theme is man's constitution, his goal as a member of the human species" (Pannenberg 1973, 309 [1976, 307]). We know God's revelation only indirectly, in the form of human experience. Thus we may distinguish between the direct and the indirect object of theology (van der Ven 1990, 120 [1993, 103]). Faith is the direct object of theology. God, the indirect object, cannot be the topic of inquiry. God is only the direct object of our faith.

This opens the road to a hermeneutical approach to theology in its entirety. The object of Christian theology, of theology as the science of divinity, is therefore the Christian faith, as we know it through its (1) sources, (2) through its tradition, and (3) in its past and (4) present manifestations of belief. This sentence is intended to underline that the distinction between theology as profession and theology as habitus is not as sharp as many might think. Even if we start our theological enterprise with faith, in the combination of *fidea quae* and *fides qua*, of faith content and faith experience, it does not rule out a degree of differentiation in (1) biblical, (2) systematic, (3) historical, and (4) practical theology. They no longer stand next to each other as separate disciplines but are hermeneutically tied together. After all, hermeneutics is a matter of "saying," "explaining," translating" (R. E. Palmer 1969, 12ff.), of "knowing," "interpreting," and "acting."

This can be illustrated with the image of a hermeneutical circle. Theology aims at understanding (discernment), explaining (definition), and grasping (internalization). Comprehending the Word demands thought and interpretation of that Word in contemporary language, through exegesis, so that people will grasp what it says, in the context of their own world. This is not one-way traffic, for this understanding presupposes in its turn the experience and presuppositions of the subject, who tries to understand, interpret, and communicate the Word on the basis of her or his own experience.

The hermeneutical point of departure is of great importance for any attempt at practical theology. With Firet I must emphasize the unity of the hermeneutic and the agogic moment in practical theology: "the word has the power to clarify, by which understanding arises; and the power to influence, by which change occurs" (1968, 124 [1986, 93]). With van der Ven I view the praxis of practical theology as a hermeneutical-communicative praxis. This brings us to the matter of defining the object, but not before we have looked in the next chapter at the concept of a theory of action.

This hermeneutical interpretation corrects the objectifying, encyclopedic approach. It creates the necessary unity in the theological enterprise as a whole and assigns practical theology, in its attempt to bring people to fuller understanding, its own place. This fits with the description of the object of practical theology in the definition (1.3): the mediation of the Christian faith in the praxis of modern society.

7.5 New Developments

I conclude this chapter with a short survey of the developments in the domain of practical theology that have occurred along these lines from the 1960s onward. In this section I mention many practical theologians and place them in their historical context. Elsewhere in this book I return to the contributions some continue to make to the further development of the theories undergirding practical theology.

7.5.1 Practical Theology in Germany

Barth's theology (5.2.1), which dominated Protestant theology until the 1960s, left little room for an inductive development of practical theology. The most conspicuous proponent of this approach to "theologizing" is R. Bohren, who defines practical theology as "the science of the present gathering and sending of the church" (1964, 9; 1975, 189). "God's becoming practical," understood in the aesthetic sense of "God's becoming beautiful" (1975, 14), is central. This "making God practical" by human beings is, however, a form of religion in the Barthian sense of the word. Daiber (1977, 12) maintains that Bohren reduces practical theology to practical dogmatics or practical pneumatology. Bohren uses as his hermeneutical principle that of "theonomic reciprocity" — a concept borrowed from van Ruler (5.2.2).

One sees an empirical shift in H. D. Bastian, who feels that Barth has contributed to the decline of practical theology. His "theology of questions" (1969) signals his resistance against a theology that immediately knows all the answers and loses sight of the questions faith evokes, and that fails to do justice to humans as questioning beings. He tries to find bridges to various nontheological disciplines. Just as the historical-critical method led to a demythologizing of the biblical text, an empirical approach will lead to a demythologizing of praxis (Bastian 1968, 32). One could, for example, defend the thesis that preaching is the proclamation of God's Word and therefore must be beneficial, but how can this be harmonized with the reality of a poor communicative praxis, which, according to empirical research, makes many sermons utterly ineffective? He sees a threefold task for practical theology: a critical task with regard to tradition, an empirical task with regard to the way the church acts in the present, and a prospective task with regard to planning for the future.

· The pastoral manual prepared under the leadership of F. X. Arnold, H. Schuster, and K. Rahner is a breakthrough in the Catholic camp: from pastoral theology to practical theology. It has an ecclesiological design, opting in the wake of the Second Vatican Council for a dynamic view of the church: the church as the people of God (priests and laity) en route. Practical theology is defined as "the scientific-theological discipline that deals with the self-realization of the church" (1:111). In contrast to other disciplines, the focus is here on the church of today. This manual has been very influential, also through a translation into Dutch (1966ff.).

To celebrate the two hundredth anniversary of the establishment of the first chair for pastoral theology, a collection of essays appeared entitled *Praktische Theologie heute* (Practical theology today), edited by F. Klostermann and R. Zerfass (1974). This joint project of Catholic and Protestant practical theologians shows the growing consensus regarding the view of practical theology as a theory of action. R. Zerfass proposed a hermeneutical model (1974, 167), which has exerted a major influence on subsequent theories. (See fig. 4.) He showed in this study how practical theology starts from the description of a concrete, and usually unsatisfactory, praxis. Something must be done! Reflecting on this situation solely on the basis of church tradition does not lead to any real improvement. Praxis must first be examined with the use of a series of instruments from the social sciences. As a result, tensions become visible, leading to the emergence of impulses to act, with a view to renewal and improvement of the existing praxis. Practical theology has the task to lead in this process of change in a way that is responsible from the perspective of both theology and the social sciences.

In 1967 G. Krause became the first to apply the concept of a theory of action to practical theology (Rössler 1986, 7). A further analysis from various angles of the nature of a theological theory of action is found with K.-W. Dahm (1971), K.-F. Daiber (1977), N. Mette (1978), and G. Lämmermann (1981).

A few practical theologians develop a vision on the entire scope of practical theology. M. Josuttis (1974) places practical theology in a middle position, between politics and religion. The gospel interacts with the private worlds of individuals, but is more than just religion; it is also directed toward the praxis of liberation, but goes beyond mere politics. He defines practical theology as "a critical theory of the praxis of the church, inspired by the biblical gospel" (1974, 258). Thus he opts for a hermeneutical position. Josuttis's definition resembles the approach of G. Otto, who earlier described practical

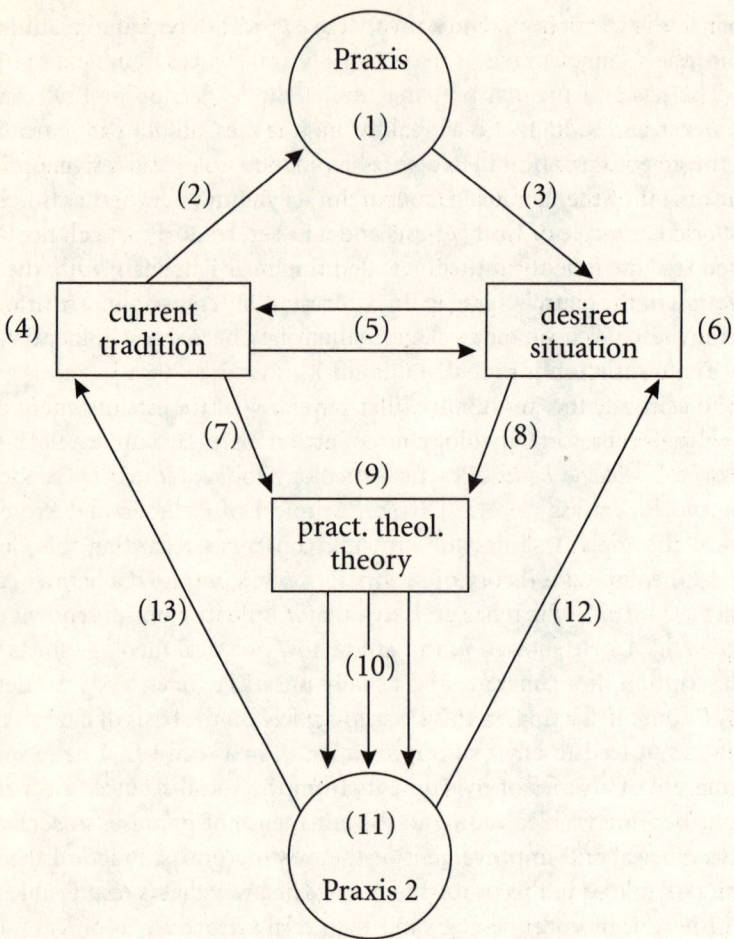

Figure 4: R. Zerfass (1974, 167)

theology as "a critical theory of a praxis that is religiously mediated within a given society" (1974, 195-96). In so doing, Otto agrees with the way in which the followers of the Frankfurt School connect "knowledge" with "interest." Society, religion, and church are so much interwoven that the church in its historical manifestation mirrors the existing social situation. He elaborates his point of view in two volumes (1986, 1988). Here, in a transparent way, he links as a matter of course "perspectives of reflection" with "domains of action" (1986, 71). (See fig. 5.) A. Grözinger proposes a "practical theology as aesthetics." He sees the tension between the freedom of the Word and our human methodical involvement with the Word as the basic problem and opts for the aesthetic praxis as the hermeneutical road to transcend this problem (1987, 215).

Ernst Lange (1927-1974) made a unique contribution to the development of practical theology. His impressive oeuvre was written in the concrete environment of the famous "Ladenkirche" in Berlin (E. Lange 1981), and of the World Council of Churches in Geneva, where he worked with the liberation pedagogue Paolo Freire. He applied the latter's emancipatory vision on education to the local congregation (E. Lange 1980). Lange is also known for his innovative work in the area of homiletics (van der Laan 1989b).

The most recent proposal is that of D. Rössler (1986). His understanding of the problems of modernity determines his differentiation within praxis among the spheres of religion, church, and society. H. Luther (1947-1991) developed his practical theology as a theology of the subject, in relation to the process of individualization. He distinguished between "individualizing *of* religion" and "individualizing *through* religion" (1992, 12). A veritable gold mine for the study of the development of practical theology is the comprehensive treatment of its foundations by V. Drehsen (1988).

7.5.2 Practical Theology in North America

American practical theology represents another tradition. We already saw how the American approach to practical theology closely follows the *theologia practica* tradition. That is the reason why until recently there was no place for practical theology as a separate discipline. The pragmatism that is characteristic of American society led already at an early date to an empirical form of pastoral theology.

The most complete example of this is found in the proposal of S. Hiltner, who, with "the organization of theological knowledge and study" as his organizational principle, makes a distinction in "the body of divinity" between "logic-centered fields" (the domains of biblical, historical, systematic theology) and "operation-centered areas" (shepherding, communicating, organizing), with a constant interaction between the two (Hiltner 1958, 28). (See fig. 6.) Hiltner is best known as the theologian of the "Pastoral Counseling Movement." The founder of this movement, A. T. Boisen (1960), looks at the human being, in his or her concrete existence, as a "living human document." Besides the psychology of Carl R. Rogers, the correlation theology of Paul Tillich heavily influences this movement.

The shift from "pastoral theology" to "practical theology" takes place

115

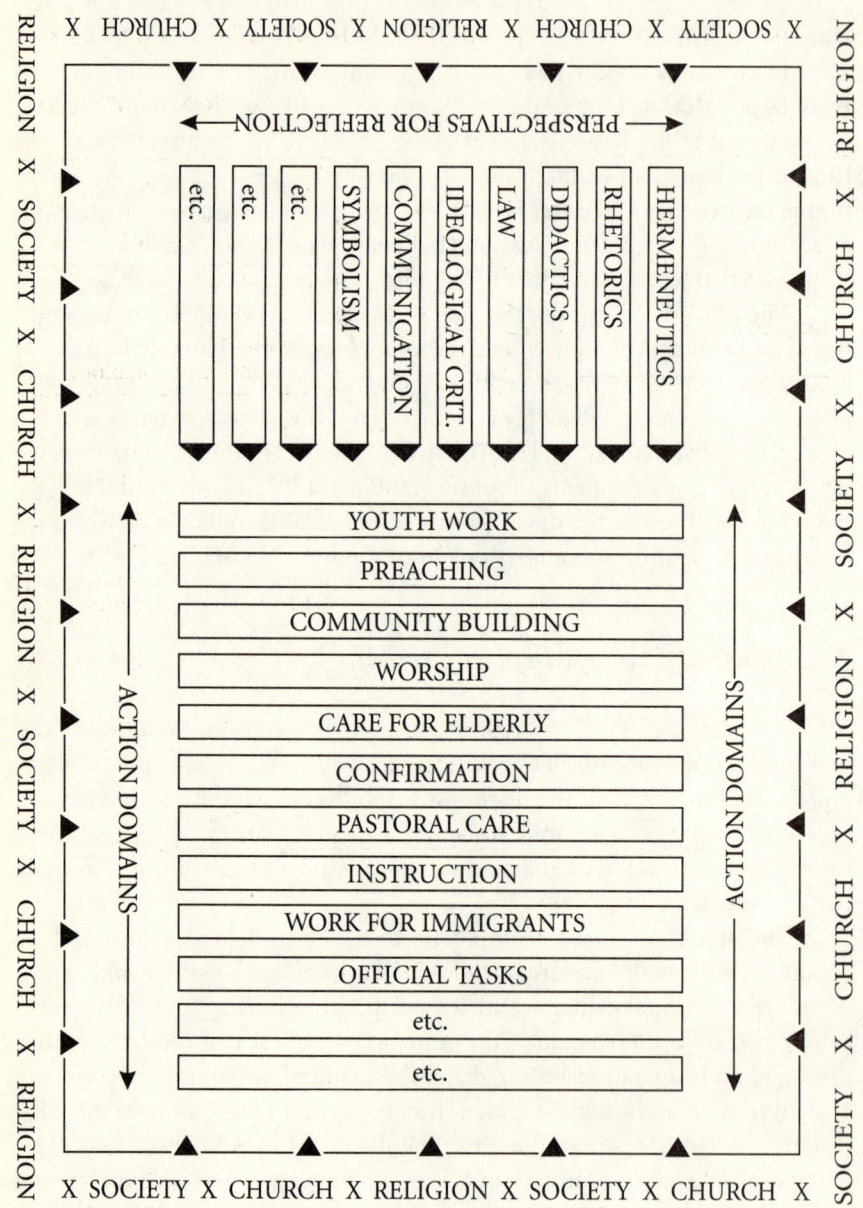

Figure 5: G. Otto (1986, 71)

THE BODY OF KNOWLEDGE

THE ORGANIZATION OF THEOLOGICAL KNOWLEDGE AND STUDY

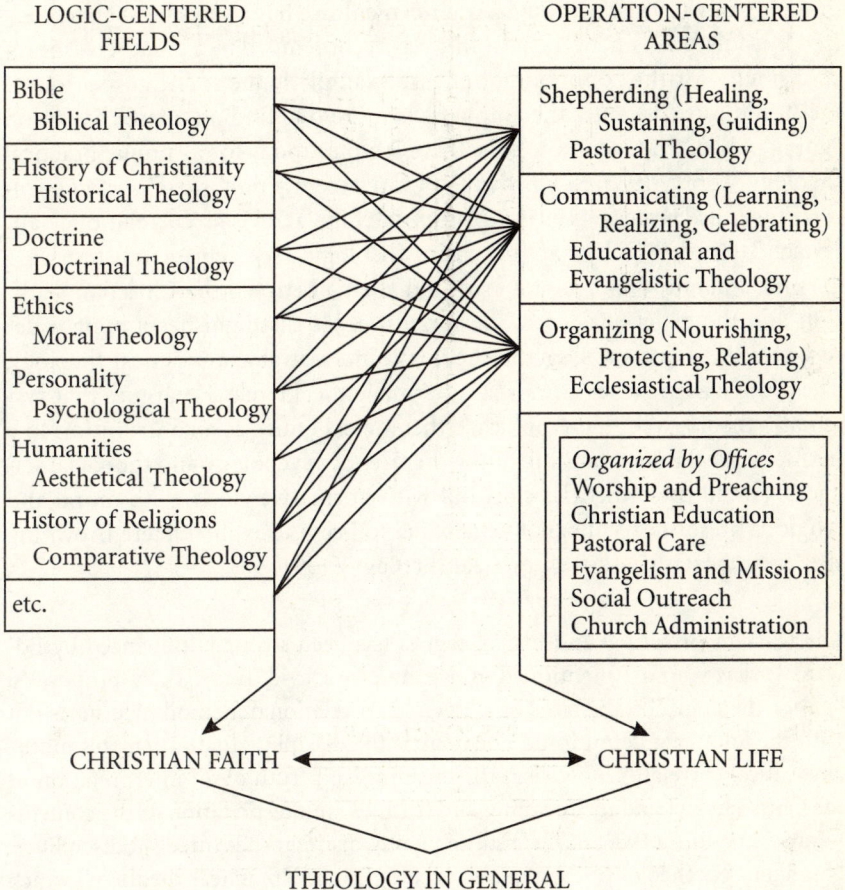

Figure 6: S. Hiltner (1958, 28)

under the leadership of Don S. Browning, who published a first series of essays under this title in 1983. He observes that the concept of "practical theology" is suddenly recognized from all sides as a fundamental theme, but without any precise idea of what it encompasses. Is it a new approach to theology or a new discipline? One thing is clear: "There seems to be a growing desire to make theology in general more relevant to the guidance of action and to

117

bridge the gap between theory and practice, thought and life, the classical theological disciplines and practical theology" (1983, 3).

An important aspect in this is no doubt the growing separation between private life and the public sector, as Robert N. Bellah et al. have shown in their study (1985). Although American culture has always been characterized by individualism, in the past this was accompanied by a great sense of responsibility for the common good. One example is the social gospel movement. But more recently the emphasis is more on "finding oneself" than on "going public." In reaction to this, there is a plea today for a "public practical theology" (Tracy 1983, 61). Browning more recently published *A Fundamental Practical Theology* (1991), a proposal for "a revised correlational approach." He also feels that the entire theological enterprise must serve a "practical habitus," aimed at a critical dialogue between the Christian tradition and the experience of modern culture. He distinguishes among a descriptive theology, a systematic theology, and a strategic practical theology. These three approaches comprise a hermeneutical circle. He argues that systematic theology should emphasize theological ethics as a contribution to a hermeneutical understanding of the theories of psychology and the social sciences. For all these theories start out with normative views, with moral and religious presuppositions that usually fail to become explicit. Here Browning sees an important task for practical theology (1991, 98).

The work of Browning and his colleagues has been strongly influenced by Edward Farley, whom I mentioned above, and by David Tracy. Tracy proposes a "public theology," on the basis of a "revised correlational method." He starts out with the following definition: "Theology is the discipline that articulates mutually critical correlations between the meaning and truth of an interpretation of the Christian fact and the meaning and truth of an interpretation of the contemporary situation" (1983, 62). He subsequently distinguishes three subdisciplines: "fundamental theology," "systematic theology," and "practical theology," which he defines as follows: "*Practical theology* is the mutually critical correlation of the interpreted theory and praxis of the Christian fact and the interpreted theory and praxis of the contemporary situation" (1983, 76). The concrete actions are to be seen not as "practice" but as "praxis," since the actions are theory-laden. He seeks support for this hermeneutical approach of the theory-praxis relation from such political theologians as J. B. Metz and from representatives of the critical theory.

Key concepts in this new approach to practical theology are "hermeneutics," "transformation," and "beyond clericalism." James W. Fowler (1983) sketches a model for practical theology comparable to that of Zerfass. (See fig. 7.) He

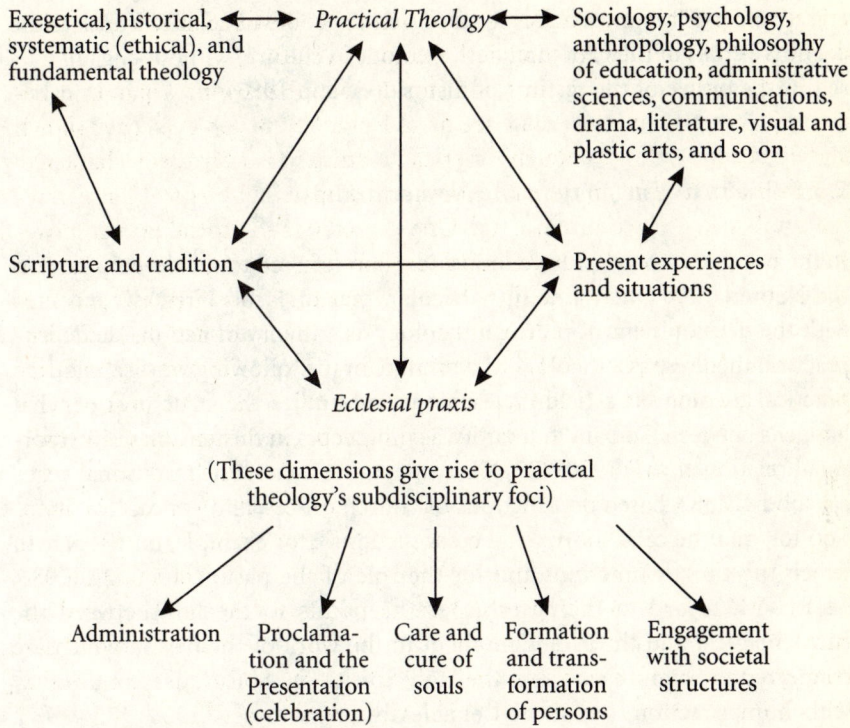

Figure 7: James W. Fowler (1983, 153)

also bases his proposal on the hermeneutical circle. He establishes a relation with the other branches of theology on the one hand, and with the social sciences on the other. The praxis of the church remains central for him: "I believe that the enterprise of practical theology draws its energy and experiences its primary vocation in relation to the concrete *ecclesia*" (154). This choice is typical for much research under the heading of "congregational studies" (Wheeler 1990).

The focus on "transformation," not only of people but also of society as a whole, gives a political dimension to practical theology. D. P. McCann and C. R. Strain (1985) make a clear connection between practical theology and social action, and regard this as a program for an American approach to this branch of theology. Rebecca S. Chopp offers a critical approach from the perspective of liberation theology and feminist theology. She criticizes the "revised correlation method" of Tracy and Browning, identifying it with a purely academic way of "doing" theology, more specifically of "doing" modern liberal theology. This approach is focused on the problems of modernity, as the cognitive crisis of the Christian faith in modern culture, without engaging itself in the praxis of the victims of history (Chopp 1987).

7.5.3 Practical Theology in the Netherlands

In the previous sections I have time and again referred to the development in the Netherlands. One name in particular, that of Jacob Firet, is connected with the development of practical theology as a theory of action. He defines practical theology as a theological discipline in the following words: "Modern practical theology is a field of learning that studies the structures of what happens between God and humanity, as this occurs in the tension of interpersonal relationships" (1970, 329). He wants to transcend the traditional vertical subdivisions, based on functions of church offices, and appeals for attention for what he calls "horizontal cross sections": for example, for the way in which the church functions and for the role of the pastor (1968, 22 [1986, 12]). With regard to the latter aspect he points to the link between the hermeneutical and the agogic moment in the work of the pastor, which are connected through the work of the Holy Spirit. The Spirit does not do away with human action, but indeed enables humans to act (1968, 175 [1986, 134]). As far as the empirical aspect is concerned, he has developed his practical theology particularly in an agogic direction, aiming at an improvement of the actions of the congregation and the pastor. Subsequently he pleads for a broader conception of praxis: "I now tend to view the praxis that forms the object of pastoral theology less exclusively as the way in which the church and the pastor function. This does not imply a lesser degree of appreciation for the church, but it is based on a clearer perception of the possibility and the reality of God coming through other ways than only ecclesiastical institutions" (1974, 7). As a result, he is later able to summarize the paradigm of practical theology as "communicative action in the service of the gospel" (1987, 260).

Frans Haarsma plays a similar role in the Catholic camp. His personal involvement with Vatican II allowed him to experience the *aggiornamento* of church and theology from nearby. He became an important spokesman of this trend within practical theology. Since his dissertation on the theology of O. Noordmans (1967), his approach to theology has been characterized by his attempts to link pneumatology and ecclesiology. This leads to a dynamic view of the church that transcends the traditional hierarchical and institutional emphasis and is open for ecclesiastical renewal. This thinking is reflected in two books (1981, 1991). "His entire oeuvre may be summed up as a constant attempt to transcend clerocentrism" (van der Ven 1985, 19). In later works he begins to refer to pastoral theology as a theological theory of action. It deals with "God's activities, through human beings, in the advance of God's kingdom" (van der Ven 1985, 26). This directs attention not only to individual salvation but also to the historical conditions of evil and liberation.

Haarsma's successor, J. A. van der Ven, takes a fresh approach. He assigns such a central place to empirical-theological inquiry that the name of his department changes from "pastoral theology" to "empirical theology." He has given a solid defense of his proposal for an empirical theology, based on a tradition of fifteen years of research (9.4.3), conducted from a theological and from a social science perspective (1990 [1993]). In 1993 [1996] his empirical-theological study of the development of ecclesiology in the context of modern society appeared in the series in which the present book is also published.

Other Catholic practical theologians show a politico-critical approach, for example, R. van Kessel (1989) and his student B. Höfte, who understands theology as liberation theology. His dissertation offers a thorough theological and philosophical defense of this position (1990).

In spite of the restriction that the *duplex ordo* imposed on the development of practical theology, even at the state universities, in Groningen in particular, a broader vision on the discipline developed. G. D. J. Dingemans, who wrote the volumes on catechetics (1986) and homiletics (1991) in the series on practical theology referred to above, opts for a hermeneutical approach. He describes practical theology as "an independent branch of theology that studies the praxis of faith and faith communities" (1986, 16). The discipline has both a descriptive and a normative character, with the improvement of action as its main goal. He sees its uniqueness in "the analysis, the standardizing, and the regulating of the ecclesiastical or Christian religious praxis" (1989, 211). He has worked this out in further detail (1990, 142) inspired by the model of Zerfass, which he wants to extend into three hermeneutical circles, targeting the past (Christian tradition as norm), the present (analysis with support from the social sciences), and the future (improvement of praxis through agogics). (See fig. 8.)

The Dutch language is also used in Belgium (Flanders) and South Africa. In Belgium practical theology is taught at the University of Louvain (Catholic) and Brussels (Protestant). E. Henau, who teaches in Heerlen (Nijmegen) and Louvain, concentrates on homiletics and ecclesiology (1989). The journal *Praktiese Teologie in Suid-Africa* (Practical theology in South Africa; since 1986), and the work of C. Burger (1991) provide a picture of what is happening in the

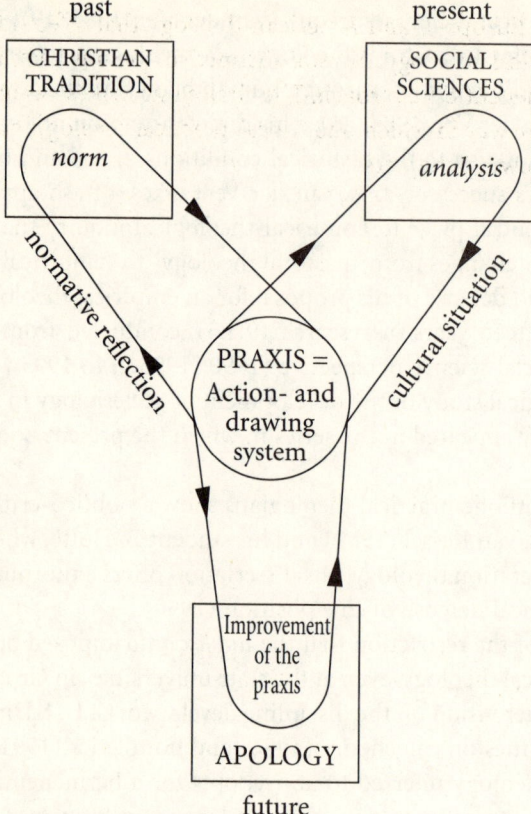

Figure 8: G. D. J. Dingemans (1990, 142)

area of practical theology in South Africa. This is heavily influenced by the work done in the Netherlands; see, for example, H. J. C. Pieterse, who combines a hermeneutical approach with empirical research (1991).

7.6. Conclusion

It would be correct to say that practical theology developed as a theological theory of action in many different countries from the 1960s onward. The two diverging views of theology, the encyclopedic approach and the *theologica practica* view, meet in the hermeneutical approach, within which practical theology has its own distinct place. I have noted important differences in emphasis between European and American theology that affect the discussion regarding practical theology. Several distinctive streams may be discerned within the hermeneutical approach. The choice one makes has important implications for the way in which one "does" practical theology, as will become clear in the following chapters.

CHAPTER 8

Practical Theology as a Theory of Action

In this chapter I concentrate on the other part of Mette's programmatic definition: "Practical theology must be conceived of as *a theological theory of action* within a theology that is understood as a practice-oriented science" (1978, 9). This definition poses a number of questions: What precisely is a theory of action? What is a theological theory of action? How does such a practical discipline, with its focus on faith and daily life, relate to theology in general? In view of the importance of these questions, one can hardly be surprised by the flood of literature that has appeared since this concept of a "theological theory of action" was introduced in the 1960s. This chapter cannot go into any great detail. But one cannot avoid facing the question whether the social sciences are like a Trojan horse, smuggled into the fortress of theological inquiry that is inspired by the human sciences, or whether this development of practical theology signals a more general theological renewal.

Inspired by its usage in Germany, the Dutch term *handelingswetenschap* (theory of action) was first introduced in the Netherlands in 1970 by Jacob Firet (1970, 328). Ten years later, however, the same author writes: "Characterizing practical theology as 'a theory of action' does not say anything about its theological content or about its academic status" (1980, 12). Today, doing away with the term would be unthinkable. But this does not imply that the formulation of this theory has so far progressed that we have a convincing concept of such a theory of action at our disposal.

In this chapter I take some important steps. I first look at the introduction of the expression "theory of action" by H. Schelsky (8.1). Then I survey the theological reception of this concept (8.2) and more precisely delineate this "action" as the object of practical theology (8.3).

The second part of this chapter deals with the philosophical and social scientific implications of the concept of a theory of action as the basis for a practical-theological action-oriented theory. Here I build on the classical theories of action, which I reviewed in part I (chapters 2–4). I prefer theories that combine the hermeneutical, empirical, and critical perspectives (5.5).

This leads me to choose the theory of communicative action, proposed by the German social philosopher Jürgen Habermas (8.4), an integrative thinker who succeeds in blending divergent points of view from a number of different sciences. His work has greatly influenced the current state of practical theology and therefore deserves due attention. My second choice is the French philosopher Paul Ricoeur (8.5), who establishes a bridge with the social sciences on the basis of hermeneutical philosophy, and thus contributes to the development of a paradigm and a methodology for the human sciences. This, I believe, constitutes an acceptable basis for a theological theory of action.

8.1 The Expresssion "Theory of Action"

When describing the origin of the expression "theory of action," most scholars point to H. Schelsky's well-known book about the organization of German universities (1963). Schelsky argued that the social sciences had been emancipated, as "a third type of science," from the humanities.

Disciplines like economics, sociology, political science, and psychology came from the womb of philosophy, in particular practical philosophy, better known as ethics. Other areas of study, like pedagogics (later also agology) and cultural anthropology, have — though not without causing tension — left the cluster of the humanities and joined the domain of the social sciences. From a functional perspective, this new group of studies has moved closer to the natural sciences. Schelsky characterized this "tertium genus" in these words: "Its characteristic is that, because of the nature of its knowledge — that is, also as 'theory' — it may lead to immediate consequences for social action, since the 'politics' that emerge from it affect directly social action; this aspect distinguishes it from historical disciplines that emphatically distance themselves from any such fundamental, immediate influence on present action" (Schelsky 1963, 213).

Firet, however, is of the opinion that Schelsky's list combines apples and oranges: sociology and psychology cannot be lumped together with pedagogics. Daiber (1977, 61) also feels that theories of action, often referred to as human sciences or behavioral sciences, cannot be restricted to their descriptive-analytical task. The practical-theological interest goes much further. It seems therefore reasonable to differentiate between theories of action that want to *describe* and *explain* social and human reality and theories of action that want to *influence* and *change* that reality. The latter aspect is related to the anthropological fact that humans can make choices; they can intervene in the course of events and can be held responsible for them (Firet 1987, 261).

My definition of practical theology (1.3) combines both perspectives. This leads to a description of action such as Geulen's (1982): "To act is to pursue a goal, to work toward an intentional and active realization of certain plans, by utilizing specific means in a given situation." Action always takes place within a social context, and must be defined within the framework of a theory of social action, viewed as an intersubjective event. According to A. van der Beld, an action is "an intervention in the course of events, controlled by an actor" (1982, 46).

Not all theologians have welcomed the introduction of the concept of a theory of action as a fitting description for practical theology. Some fear that this threatens the unity of the theological enterprise, which at least in part is based on its ties to the human sciences.

Pannenberg sees a close link between dogmatics and practical theology, which studies the praxis of the church. The Christian faith brings its own relation of theory and praxis along, since it has the work of Jesus Christ in this world as its content. Action is based on the experience of meaning. For that reason, ethics and practical theology cannot be detached from dogmatics, the branch of theology that gives access to the reflection on this experience of meaning. Practical theology also must take this praxis of faith as its theme and as a basis for models for a contemporary praxis of the church (1973, 439 [1976, 437-38]). He apparently fears that praxis might become empirically self-contained. Appealing to Luther, G. Sauter states: "Theology is practical in nature, because it offers *salvific knowledge*" (1974, 127). The essential aspect of this praxis is that one can fulfill one's calling before God and discover those life situations in which one can experience the newness of one's being. This approach can hardly be reconciled with a praxis that chooses the empirical manifestation of faith and church as its point of departure. R. Bohren (1975, 124ff.) likewise fears that the concept of a theory of action detracts from the "praxis of the *pneuma*."

126

One should note, however, that those who want to develop practical theology as an empirical theory of action certainly do not want to cut all ties with dogmatics. (I refer in this connection to chapter 5.) But they do want to free the discipline from its image of an applied science, and do intend, from an empirical perspective, to build a separate, independent approach to the object of theology. This means that the empirical character of practical theology must always be understood in relation to its fundamental hermeneutical character (7.4).

8.2 Reception of the Concept of a Theory of Action by Practical Theologians

Following Schelsky, G. Krause in 1967 introduced the concept of a theory of action within the sphere of practical theology in Germany (Mette 1978, 314). He wanted to take the relation with the social sciences with full seriousness. He understood the concept of a theory of action not only in its analytical sense but also in its aims to develop adequate strategies for action.

In this context an increasing openness developed for an empirical orientation within practical theology, as is evident in the work of H.-D. Bastian (7.5.1), H. Schröer (1969), A. Hollweg (1971), and K.-W. Dahm (1971). Schröer wanted to develop his practical theology in an empirical-critical direction. He regarded its function as a critical support of church actions and as the creation of goals and strategies to improve these actions. While Bastian tended toward the critical rationalism of Karl Popper (9.1.1), which is primarily interested in the quest for truth and focuses on the falsification of statements, G. Otto (1970) joined another current within the social sciences: that of the critical theory. In this critical approach to religion, action is placed in a political framework. B. Päschke (1971) also followed Otto's line.

The studies of Y. Spiegel (1974), K.-F. Daiber (1977), and N. Mette (1978) have particularly contributed to a further clarification of the concept of a theory of action.

Spiegel, who already uses the term *empirical theology,* makes a helpful distinction between two forms of practical theology: a theology that is totally focused on action, and a theology that focuses on praxis. The first form sees its task in the critical interpretation of theological statements that penetrate the words and actions of the church. The second has the task to develop theological theories of action. He joins the American sociologist Robert K. Merton in referring to "theories of the middle range," that is, theories with a limited range, in particular targeting the activities of the church and the ministry. These theories must clearly indicate which kind of actions they address, before they begin (reference is made to G. Otto) their critical interpretation and then emphasize new actions and the education and training of personnel (Spiegel 1974, 179-80). This distinction throws some light on the discussion in the Netherlands.

Daiber pleads for establishing clear boundaries for the concept of a theory of action. He argues that practical theology should not deal with human actions in general, not even if these are interpreted in a religious sense: "It should deal only with forms of action and their conditions within a particular social range" (1977, 73). This leads him to the following concretization: "The task of practical theology is to develop action-oriented theories for congregations and churches in the context of the praxis of society" (74).

He thus distances himself from proposals that want to significantly broaden the field of inquiry by including any Christian or even religious activity. His choice is based on pragmatic grounds. He wants to keep practical theology in close proximity to the church and the theological profession. For instance, choosing "the praxis of oppression and liberation" in general as object leads one into the domain of social ethics. A clear demarcation will guard practical theology against crossing borders within theology into such fields as dogmatics and ethics, and outside theology into the social sciences.

Mette maintains that, in spite of differences in opinion, all approaches to the concept of a theory of action have some elements in common. They opt for the inductive method, use empirical methods, select an interdisciplinary strategy, and are geared toward "employing anything that may help to give direction to present and future actions of Christians and churches" (1978, 318-19). This statement intends to say that a practical-theological theory cannot stop at an analysis and interpretation of praxis, but must also deal with the consequences of actions. In this context he refers to Zerfass's model (7.5.1), which shows how a new praxis may be developed from an existing praxis.

This section then indicates a preference for a concept of a theory of action that does not, in a broad manner, aim at a description and interpretation of all religious phenomena, but concentrates on mediative action: the praxis of the "mediation of salvation." This explains the initial emphasis on the activities of the church and the ministry.

8.3 Action as the Object of Practical Theology

In the Netherlands the discussion also concentrates on a more precise definition of the kind of "action" that becomes the object of practical theology as a theological theory of action. Over the years, a consensus has developed that the object of practical theology is broader than that of earlier pastoral theology. It is generally felt that this action should not be restricted to the activities of churches and ministers.

J. H. van der Laan provides a survey of the discussion of this broader definition of action (1979, 164-65). He shows how there has been a gradual process. The first extension was that practical theology no longer dealt exclusively with the work of the professional pastor but also with that of other church workers. Kuyper's concept was still broader, because of the introduction of courses of study that dealt with the activities of the laity. This extended the praxis to such domains as religious education in the family and the school, political issues, the relationship between employers and employees, and the mission to society. All of this found its place in the *diakonia*, the service to society inspired by faith. A further broadening occurred when praxis was defined as the praxis of the church, with the church viewed not only as the object of practical theology but also as the subject of action. Definitions that originated in the 1960s and 1970s illustrate this point. This leads to the establishment of a subdiscipline of church development. Subsequently, attempts are made to do away with ecclesiocentrism. Praxis is described as "the realization of God's kingdom" (A. D. Müller 1950), "the cause of Jesus" (Biemer and Siller 1971), the "praxis of the gospel" (Josuttis 1974), "God's becoming practical" (Bohren 1975), "the event between God and humanity" (Firet 1970).

Vossen (1987, 240ff.) and Höfte (1990, 85ff.) describe the similar discussion among Catholic theologians.

How can this action be defined more precisely? Firet and van der Ven are the champions of two different camps in the Netherlands.

In discussing the concept of a theory of action, Firet states: "Practical theology does not deal with human action in general, neither with the action of the believer nor the person who acts in the service of God, but specifically with action that has to do with the actualization and the maintenance of the relationship between God and humanity, and humanity and God" (1980, 13). In the range of action theories, practical theology is closer to pedagogics than to sociology. Firet distinguishes between action and behavior. He argues that sociologists like Weber and Parsons lead us astray by describing action as a central sociological category. They view action as human behavior, to which the actor assigns subjective meaning. Later he describes "the disciplinary matrix" of practical theology as "communicative action in the service of the gospel" (1987, 260). The words "in the service of the gospel" not only limit the area of attention but also refer to a normative and critical element in the theory. He further describes these words as "all efforts to ensure that the gospel of the kingdom of God reveals its power in the human situation in general, or in the concrete situation of a specific individual or some individuals" (1987, 261). Action viewed from the actor perspective is not simply behavior. Communicative action occurs in the interaction between subjects. Along similar lines van der Laan also describes practical theology as a theory of action, as "the theology of acting in the service of the gospel, with emphasis on the *mediative* aspect" (1990, 270).

Firet concludes (1980, 13) that the concept of "a theory of action" can be useful only if it contains the following elements:

- It must deal with concrete domains of action.
- It must analyze the context of the actions and the actions themselves in the present situation and with regard to their potentiality.
- It does this — also on the basis of an empiricism-transcending critical theory — with the purpose of developing action models and strategies for the various domains of action.

J. A. van der Ven also assigns a central place to mediative action. He describes practical theology as "the theological discipline of religious-communicative action, which is the focus of pastoral activity" (1985, 193). Subsequently, he distinguishes between the formal object in a broad and in a narrow sense. In its broad sense, we are dealing with "the factors, processes, and structures that determine and foster today's personal and social life from the perspective of the kingdom of God." In the narrow sense, we are dealing with the pastoral practice: "to foster religious communicative action in the personal and social life of today through pastors, other professionals, and volunteers" (193-94). He sees the uniqueness of practical theology in the empirical-theological approach both in a broad and in a narrow sense. Considering the latter aspect, he opts for the term *empirical theology*. Later he refers simply to a "hermeneutic-communicative praxis" (1990, 47 [1993, 41]), based on the normative principles of Habermas. In this connection I remind the reader of a statement by Vossen (1987, 246), that, also within this empirical-theological concept, action is to be differentiated from behavior by "the intentional quality, or the teleological structure of the action." "Human action cannot simply be reduced to behavior that is determined by external factors, since it intends to realize certain goals that are related in an intersubjective way" (Vossen 1987, 246).

Both approaches have much in common, as mediative action is central to both. But while Firet focuses in particular on the hermeneutical and agogic reflection of this mediative action, van der Ven develops, within the confines of practical theology, an empirical-theological approach, which studies conditions that in a modern society govern religious-communicative action in a broader sense. This demands extensive empirical research, aimed at describing and interpreting the actual situation of faith and religion in today's world. It gives rise to an empirical-analytical current of thought, often referred to as empirical theology, which differs from the hermeneutical-mediative stream represented by Firet, and the political-critical stream to which B. Höfte belongs.

Höfte sees "human action, inasmuch as it is determined by the interchange of religious meanings" (1990, 326), as too narrow a basis for defining the object. He proposes to understand the specific object of practical theology "in terms of human action, on the economic, political, and ideological level" (372). He relates the discussion about the object to that about the subject of action. He believes that practical theology develops its theory in dialogue with, and in the service of, modern humans (93). He finds his own point of departure in a liberation theology that points to the poor as the real subjects of Christian and ecclesiastical action.

I have thus far referred a few times to the formal object of practical theology. Some authors, for example, van der Ven and Höfte, distinguish this from the material object. The formal object is "the formal perspective through which theology in general and practical theology in particular differ from nontheological views of reality" (Höfte 1990, 90-91). One might say that theology sees reality in its relationship to God or to the kingdom of God. The material object has to do with the specific task of practical theology in distinction from other theological disciplines. One may describe this as, for instance, "religious-communicative action" (van der Ven) or "communicative action in the service of the gospel" (Firet).

I return to these various currents of thought in the next chapter (9.4). At this point it suffices to say that the disparities are mainly differences in emphasis, as is evident from the approach proposed in this book. This approach fits with the hermeneutical-mediative tradition of Firet, who, however, fully agrees with the immense importance of empirically oriented practical-theological research. I started in my definition of praxis (1.3) from the basis of a duality in praxis. I proposed a certain distinction between praxis 1 (the mediation of the Christian faith) and praxis 2 (the praxis of modern society, within which religious and church-related actions can find a place as forms of meaningful social and human action). This distinction, to which I return later (9.3), agrees to a large extent with what van der Ven refers to as the formal object in a broader or a narrower sense, although I view the latter aspect as the direct object of practical theology. Chapter 1 concluded with the choice for an integrative approach, "a hermeneutical-critical approach within an empirically oriented practical theology." This ties hermeneutical, empirical, and critical aspects together and leads toward a practical-theological theory of action, which I spell out in more detail in chapter 9, on the basis of what has been said in this and previous chapters.

But first I want to take a closer look at what recent philosophers and social scientists have said about the concept of a "theory of action." I do so by concentrating on the work of Jürgen Habermas and Paul Ricoeur.

8.4 The Theory of Action of Jürgen Habermas

From the 1970s onward, one finds references to the work of the German social philosopher Jürgen Habermas in the practical-theological literature. His magnum opus about the theory of communicative action appeared in 1981 (Habermas 1981 [1984-87]). In subsequent years theologians, particularly Catholic (practical) theologians, have usually understand the concept of a theory of action in Habermas's terms. This section deals first with the cultural-historical and philosophical background of Habermas's work. This is followed by a synopsis of his theory of communicative action. Finally, I look at how practical theologians received his theory.

8.4.1 The Cultural-Philosophical Background

Interpreters of Habermas's oeuvre, which he has built since 1954, point to its continuous line and to his ability constantly to integrate into this basic framework the insights of the philosophers, sociologists, psychoanalysts, and linguists he has studied. As a result there are different stages in the development of his thinking, leading to differences in interpretation.

J. Keulartz (1992) analyzes these various interpretations, arguing that many interpretations of Habermas's work suffer from imbalances. In this connection he refers to two interviews with Habermas, in 1981 and 1985. The first of these interviews is highly relevant for our present purpose, as it puts us on the track of Habermas's "theology."

A quotation from 1985: "My theoretical interests have from the very beginning constantly been determined by the philosophical problems and questions regarding the nature of society that have emerged from the development of thought from Kant to Marx. Around the mid-1950s, my intentions and basic convictions were shaped by Western Marxism, through a confrontation with Lukacs, Korsch, and Bloch, with Sartre and Merleau-Ponty, and, of course, with Horkheimer, Adorno, and Marcuse. The sole significance of everything I have further absorbed relates to the project of a new social theory, which follows naturally from this tradition" (Keulartz 1992, 11-12).

This image of Habermas as a Neo-Marxist, Keulartz says, dominates the secondary literature, but it is incomplete. In this connection he points to an interview in 1981, where Habermas comments on the real source of inspiration for his "theory of communicative action." Habermas refers explicitly to a "dogmatic core" in his work.

"My thought follows a distinct motif and a basic intuition, which finds its roots in religious traditions; among these are Protestant (e.g., Jakob Böhme) and Jewish mystics (e.g., Isaak Luria), but also Schelling. The underlying motif is the reconciliation of a modernity that has become divided in itself; the idea that a society can be created in which true autonomy and dependence are in peaceful balance, without relinquishing the differentiations which make modernity possible in the cultural, social, and economic spheres; that it is possible to be genuinely oneself in a community that is untainted by the dubious character of substantial commonalities. This intuition comes from the sphere of interaction with others; it has to do with experiencing an unscathed intersubjectivity, less secure than anything history has so far produced, as far as communicative structures is concerned — a closer and closer, continuously more delicately woven fabric of intersubjective relationships that nonetheless leaves room for a relation between freedom and dependence that one can only imagine through interactive models" (Keulartz 1992, 12). This is the "faith" that the young Habermas, growing up in postwar Germany, reclaimed from his historical reality.

Keulartz argues that this tradition believes that we live in a world where "hate dominates over love, evil over good, harshness over mercy, darkness over light, the external over the internal" (13). We live in "the wrong world." Conversion or a turning around is required to restore the original order. "Depending on the phase or context in which they occur, Habermas refers to two types of basic attitudes, actions, cultural lifestyles, social spheres of reproduction, intentions of learning, and methodologies of inquiry."

Habermas's philosophy establishes a link between the metaphor of conversion and the perspective of time. His way of dealing with time betrays the influence of Ernst Bloch, Walter Benjamin, and, in particular, Martin

Heidegger. Heidegger's view of temporality may be formulated as follows: "Only when we decisively anticipate the future can we return to the past and are we free to shape the present as we want" (Keulartz 1992, 20). This expresses the modern consciousness of time, which relates in a different manner to both the future and the past than was formerly the case. It is not a matter of building on the past but of anticipating the future, and from there critically remembering the past. Keulartz calls this the dialectical bond between anticipation and anamnesis, which is also characteristic of Habermas's work (22). The motif of anticipation stems from Bloch and his "principle of hope." It is the utopian dream of a society where all controversy has been eliminated. Language becomes the vehicle that opens up a new world. Habermas cites Bloch's "advent" philosophy: "Reason cannot blossom without hope, and hope cannot blossom without reason" (21). Benjamin gives first place to remembering, the anamnesis. Habermas views this as a radicalization of the modern consciousness of time. Benjamin's philosophy is one of mourning, a thinking that starts from ruins, from brokenness and fragmentation. One's thinking about the future must take the frustrated desires of past generations into account. The liberating power of remembrance must repay the guilt of the present to the past (21).

This clarifies the connection between the metaphor of turning around and the preoccupation with history: "Our world will show itself as the wrong world only when viewed in the light of the anticipation of the future; and the only reason to allow for the possibility that this situation of 'corruption' will ever cease to exist is to view this situation as the result of a radical change that has taken place under historical, and therefore contingent, circumstances" (22). The critical theory, with its emancipatory core, puts the origin of this corruption in past history. Habermas's thinking of this anticipation leads to "the ideal context for dialogue" as the essence of his theory of communicative action.

Thus the metaphor of a turning around, together with the dialectic of anticipation and anamnesis, leads to two aspects that constitute the core of the theory of communicative action that I am about to discuss: the colonizing thesis and the idea of an ideal context for dialogue. This, of course, is also only one interpretation, but it is an important one in the context of this study. It could be referred to as "the gospel according to Habermas."

One of the older works of Habermas that should be mentioned is his well-known *Erkenntnis und Interesse* (1968 [*Knowledge and Human Interests,* 1971]). Practical theologians often cite this work as an example of critical theory. It distinguishes between instrumentary action based on technical knowledge, communicative action based on practical knowledge, and emancipatory action based on a critical knowledge. Emancipatory knowledge allows for a critical approach of reality, aimed at the liberation of humans from structures that overpower them and keep them dependent. Power structures are often ideologically defended and can be made transparent only through a process of critical self-reflection. In this respect Habermas agrees with psychoanalytic theory (Keulartz 1992, 230).

8.4.2 The Theory of Communicative Action

Friend and foe agree, says Keulartz, that Habermas's critical theory of action is one of the most interesting developments in the social sciences. Habermas is able to bring divergent philosophical and sociological strands together in his broad conception of rationality, and can thereby build a bridge between different theories of science. His focus on rationality and "pure" knowledge and his practical and political intentions offer a connection between rationalism and critical theory. He also joins historical and systematic insights and argues on the metatheoretical as well as methodological and empirical levels (Keulartz 1992, 9).

The central question in Habermas's theory of action is: "How do societies continue to exist? First of all, they must be able to link action and the consequences of action in such a way that a somewhat stable network emerges. This linking of actions results from the use of language. Habermas therefore speaks of a symbolic reproduction through communicative action. But societies must also have material reproduction for their survival: they must offer their members material goods, such as clothing. Material reproduction results from the use of systems." This is according to Korthals (1989, 141), in his interpretation of Habermas's theory, which I follow in outline in this section.

A central concept is *communicative action*. This is the tool the actors use as they negotiate their aims and the circumstances in which they find themselves. Through negotiation they coordinate their actions into networks. As they negotiate, the situation is categorized into existing facts, norms to be followed, and feelings of the actors. Through language, Habermas thus partitions communication into three worlds: facts, norms, and feelings. In this context one must accept three validity claims: that the alleged facts are true, that the norms are correct and fair, and that the feelings are genuine. The actors want truth, fairness, and genuineness. They must reach a preliminary consensus on this. Then a discourse begins, in which the validity claims with regard to truth (theoretical discourse), fairness (practical discourse), and genuineness (esthetic-expressive discourse) are successively tested on the basis of arguments. When this does not occur, the actors embark on strategic action, using mere power to exert influence. This can happen in all kinds of situations.

Since this explanation remains rather abstract, it would seem useful to borrow the following seemingly petty, but rather striking, illustration of what communicative action is: "Suppose a family is watching something on a recently acquired video recorder, and the mother says to her youngest son: 'I am thirsty, please get some milk from the fridge.' Or translated into Habermas's terminology: the mother is convinced that there is milk in the fridge; she assumes that the norm that parents can ask their children to perform certain tasks is fair, and she feels genuine thirst. If the son addressed accepts the validity of those three elements and thereby the categorization of the situation, he will get the milk and the coordination of action has met with success. If he does not accept these claims and refuses, he may start negotiations. He may want to argue that there is no milk in the fridge, or to deny the validity of the norm. Or he may doubt whether his mother is really thirsty and has expressed a true feeling, and may argue that she simply wanted to get him out of the room because of some scenes in the film she regarded as unfit for children" (Korthals 1989, 142). When the mother decides not to negotiate any further, but exercises her authority (e.g., by issuing a command or by bribery), she embarks on strategic action, which may well result in a strategic reaction.

I here mention Habermas's definition of the concept of strategic action, since this plays a role in this book, albeit with a somewhat different meaning: "We call an action oriented to success *strategic* when we consider it under the aspect of following rules of rational choice and assess the efficacy of influencing the decisions of a rational opponent" (Habermas 1981, 1:385 [1984, 1:285]).

Even experts agree that this study about "the theory of communicative action is an extremely complicated and at times almost incomprehensible book" (Keulartz 1992, 9). In the Netherlands H. Kunneman (1983) has provided a much-used introduction to the book.

The social order should as much as possible be established through democratic negotiations. An order based on strategic action lacks stability. In these negotiations individuals share many aspects of their sociocultural situation. They act from the same presuppositions. Habermas refers to this common background as the *lifeworld*. This provides common frames of interpretation and creates mutual solidarity, while the partners in the discourse assume each other's rationality. Habermas distinguishes three components in this lifeworld: "*culture*, which provides individuals with the frames of reference to define and interpret new situations; culture establishes in essence how the facts, norms, and feelings are to be understood; *society:* the entire complex of legitimate forms of solidarity; and the *personality,* the personal identity" (Korthals 1989, 143). A society reproduces itself in these three areas. Habermas speaks of cultural reproduction, social integration, and socialization.

Besides the symbolic reproduction through communicative action, a society is also involved in material reproduction. Habermas refers to this as a *system.* In modern society the state and the economy have created their own worlds on which our negotiations have but little impact. In these worlds power and money are all-important. In the marketplace, where goods are bought, one does not inquire about the genuineness of the buyer's feelings or the fairness of the buyer's norms. Only thin threads (e.g., parliamentary control) remain between the systems of economy and state and the lifeworld.

The relation between lifeworld and system has changed in Western society. The lifeworld is subject to a process of rationalization, as Habermas concludes in agreement with Weber (3.3.2). Thus a rationalized lifeworld takes over. Differentiation in culture gives rise to three kinds of validity claims. The areas of science, law, and the arts receive their independent positions. Social integration creates institutions that regulate solidarity. Individuals have "fluid identities," which lead to role conflicts. This rationalization process brings "gradually, but never completely," the ideal communicative society (Korthals 1989, 144).

"Exchange relations" between lifeworld and systems are of great importance. Our lifeworld consists of two areas: the private sphere and public life. These contribute to the maintenance of systems and are influenced by the systems. The systems of economy and state exact their toll on our lifeworld (Korthals 1989, 145). As a result we play four different roles: employee, consumer, client (of public services), and citizen (voter). This is necessary to comply with the demands of the systems. Habermas calls this increasing influence of systems on our lives, which is in fact a process of erosion of the private and public spheres, *colonization* (Habermas 1981, 2:275ff., 489ff. [1987, 172ff., 356ff.]).

In this context of rationalization and colonization, methodological discussions often refer to what, on the basis of Habermas's thought, might be called a reduced rationality. This occurs where objective truth claims begin to dominate the normative sphere and personal experience. The emphasis shifts to effective action (rationality in purpose), which is not wrong in itself but, if detached from communicative action, leads to dehumanization.

8.4.3 The Reception by (Practical) Theologians

The two previous sections have shown the considerable impact of modern philosophy on recent theology. The modern consciousness of time, the dialectic between anticipation and anamnesis, can be translated theologically with the term *eschatology*. The kingdom of God, as the polar tension between the "already" and "not yet," invites one to anticipate the future in hope, remembering (anamnesis) the death and resurrection of Jesus Christ. One finds a theological expression of the anticipation motif in Jürgen Moltmann's "theology of hope" (1964 [1967]), while one meets the anamnesis motif in the political theology of J. B. Metz, who calls theology — as the guardian of the public ideals of freedom and emancipation — back to its essential task: "the public witness and bearer of the tradition of the dangerous memory of freedom in the 'systems' of our emancipative society" (1977, 78 [1980, 89-90]). One can already detect these lines in H. Peukert's seminal study of theology as a theory of action (1976, 303). Following the "memory" thesis of Metz, Peukert points to an anamnetic solidarity with the victims of history as the ethical radicalization of the discourse. Thus Habermas's theory of communicative action receives a normative content from a universal, solidary, communicative society (Peukert 1976, 273ff.). However, this ideal often falls victim to an aporetic reality.

Restricting ourselves to practical theology in the Netherlands, we discover the influence of Habermas's work in the empirical theology of J. A. van der Ven (1990, 86-87 [1993, 73-74]) and H. J. M. Vossen (1985, 8ff.), as well as in the political-critical approach of R. van Kessel (1989, 65-66) and B. Höfte (1990, 37-38). It is remarkable how these Catholic theologians, who belong to a tradition that seeks a philosophical foundation for theology, absorb Habermas without much difficulty into their theological thinking, while a Reformed theologian like A. K. Ploeger (1989), with all the respect he has for Habermas's work, maintains a critical distance. I detect the same theological reservation with van Gennep, who nonetheless speaks of an amazing analysis (1989, 263). He sees points of contact for new forms of mesostructure as necessary social arrangements in society. Habermas's book *Erkenntnis und Interesse* (1968 [1971]) and his two-volume work on the theory of communicative action (1981 [1984-87]) play an important role in this reception.

I now attempt a preliminary analysis. What significance do Habermas's ideas have for the development of practical theology as a theory of action? (a) They possess an analytical significance by offering insight into the developments in society. (b) They also have a normative meaning, as they offer a critical appraisal of the way in which people interact and point to an ideal, intersubjective situation for dialogue. (c) This results in their methodological significance for various types of action in the church, which may reflect the rules of an ideal situation for dialogue. (d) Finally, some are willing to attribute a theological meaning to the theory of communicative action. This one discerns in van Kessel's study of faith in the track of truth, ethics, and justice (1989, 72-73). Höfte connects the anamnestic solidarity, through Peukert, with a praxis of change and liberation, in line with liberation theology. Vossen extends these lines into the pastoral situation: "Religious communicative action is therefore communicative action with regard to providing religious meaning in aporetic situations, aimed at explanation, that is, at a corporate testing of claims regarding truth, accuracy, and authenticity" (1985, 8). Van der Ven interprets the normative principles of Habermas — equality, freedom, universality, and solidarity — using the symbol of the kingdom of God as his point of departure (1990, 86ff. [1993, 73ff.]), and thereby giving it a theological connotation.

Ploeger remains critical toward a theology that emerges from this communicative action, as proposed by Peukert and van der Ven, with whom "the religious aspect nestles in a theory of action" (1989, 136). He shares with Eberhard Jüngel the idea of "faith as something that is given" (43). Israel's faith is a prophetic religion. God himself awakens faith through the Holy Spirit (152-53). He refers to a statement by Luther, that God is to be known only in his Word, for in the world he is the *Deus absconditus*. Ploeger believes that those theologians who speak of religious communicative action have sold out to philosophy (172), even though he does recognize that faith enables one to correlate various aspects of human life (217).

Generally speaking, Protestant theologians tend to maintain a greater distance between divine salvation and earthly reality. This makes them more hesitant to affix terms like "religious" and "faith" to human actions. But, on the basis of the *analogia fidei*, it is certainly defensible to see "parables" of God's kingdom in human acts, considering also that God's Spirit does not make human action superfluous, but rather makes human action genuinely possible (Firet; see 7.5.3 above).

In practical-theological debates the question is raised whether the hermeneutical-critical approach of Habermas is compatible with the empirical-analytical approach as proposed by van der Ven. Ploeger (1989, 225) thinks it is not. Philosophers, however, have pointed out that even for Habermas the two approaches are not totally incompatible. For instance, Widdershoven refers to the discussion between Habermas and Gadamer: "According to Habermas it is of the essence to develop systematic and methodological forms of interpretation, and to connect these in the social sciences with current empirical-analytical practice" (de Boer et al. 1988, 153-54). Also: "The fundamental problem of every theory of society is, according to Habermas, to establish a link between the inner-directed and outer-directed perspectives of hermeneutics and systematics, respectively. Habermas attempts to bring these two aspects together in his book about the theory of communicative action" (172). One must admit, however, that a systems-theoretical approach does presuppose a hermeneutical approach (173). This means that practical theologians may also adopt the more objectifying approaches of the social sciences.

Similarly, one should not see the distinction between communicative action and strategic action as an absolute contrast. Even Ploeger makes room for forms of action other than only communicative action and discourse (1989, 248). Practical theology attempts among other things to develop strategies for action for various forms of communication, in the service of the nurture of the church, liturgy, preaching, catechesis, pastorate, and diaconate; it cannot operate without forms of strategic action. For one is dealing not only with personal relationships but also with functional relations and with the structure of an organization. Thus the praxis of the Christian congregation may be positioned on the boundary between system and lifeworld (Bäumler and Mette 1987, 13).

One should never forget, however, that strategic action must be permeated by communicative action, by taking human beings seriously as subjects. If that does not happen, strategy will be lost in a type of action that is merely technical or utilitarian. The following chapters deal in more detail with the relation among the various perspectives.

8.5 Paul Ricoeur's Theory of Action

A second philosopher whose theory of action I consider of great significance for practical theology is Paul Ricoeur. One may distinguish several phases in the work of this French philosopher (b. 1913) that allow one to discern a clear development. Initially, his anthropological work emphasized the hermeneutics of the symbol. But as time passed, in particular since the 1970s, his hermeneutics has become much broader (de Boer et al. 1988, 90), developing into a hermeneutics of the text.

In his most recent publications he extends this theory of interpretation into the vast domain of the social sciences by building a bridge between the interpretation of texts and the interpretation of social reality. Hermeneutics focuses on exegesis: the interpretation of written documents. The concept of "understanding" that does justice to the interpreting subject, however, provides a legitimate extension to hermeneutics. Text and social reality are thus linked together.

Ricoeur develops the following hypothesis: "If there are specific problems that are raised by the interpretation of texts because they are texts and not spoken language, and if these problems are the ones that constitute hermeneutics as such, then the human sciences may be said to be hermeneutical (1) inasmuch as their *object* displays some features constitutive of a text as text, and (2) inasmuch as their *methodology* develops the same kind of procedures as those of *Auslegung* or text interpretation" (1991, 144-45). Two questions emerge from this: Is the concept of "text" a suitable paradigm for the object of the social sciences? Does the methodology of text interpretation offer a valid paradigm for the broader domain of the human sciences?

The confirmation of this hypothesis is of great importance for practical theology as a theological theory of action, since it attempts to bridge the gulf between text (Scripture and tradition) and action (the praxis of mediation). I therefore follow Ricoeur in his answer to both questions. I concentrate on the later phase of his work (Ricoeur 1976, 1981, 1990 [1992]).

8.5.1 The Paradigm of the Text

Ricoeur finds his point of departure in the *usage of language,* which he distinguishes from a language system or language code. Usage of language is an event. Both the spoken and the written word are included. The spoken or written sentence is the basic unit in our use of language.

The usage of language differs from a language system in four ways: (1) It is realized in time, in the present. (2) It demands a subject: who is speaking? (3) It deals with something, since it refers to a world. This shows the symbolic function of language. (4) Usage of language is directed toward the other, the partner who is addressed. These four characteristics apply to the oral and the written usage of language, but are realized in different ways.

1. Usage of language occurs in time, in the present. The spoken word is a fleeting event that demands to be recorded. What is recorded is not, however, the language event as an event, but the content of what has been said, the meaning of that event (the *noema*). Ricoeur points in this connection to the philosophy of language of J. L. Austin (1962) and J. R. Searle (1969).

The language theory of Austin and Searle is based on the view that a language event consists of two parts: the performative part, which records the illocutionary power, for example, "I promise you to . . . ," and the propositional part, which expresses some aspect of reality, for example, "to go to bed on time." Austin distinguishes three levels of action: the level of the locutionary or propositional action, the action of saying something; the level of the illocutionary action (or power): what one does while one says something; the level of the perlocutionary action: what one does by saying something, the intended effect on the audience. Illocutions can be categorized as constatives (to establish, pose), expressives (clear expressions of intention, conviction), pledges (agreeing to do something, such as "I promise"), and prescriptives (demanding something, such as "I want . . ."). Cf. Baart (1986, 86). Searle used the ideas of Austin in his more extensive theory of language.

Ricoeur gives the following example: "When I tell you to close the door, I do three things. First, I relate the action predicate (close) to two variables (you and the door): this is the act of saying. Second, I tell you this with the force of an order rather than a statement, wish, or promise: this is the illocutionary act. Finally, I can provoke certain consequences, such as fear, by the fact that I give you an order; hence discourse is a sort of stimulus that produces certain results: this is the perlocutionary act" (1991, 79).

These three levels in the use of language are also recognizable in the written word, although in a different manner. According to Ricoeur, propositional action, illucotionary power, and perlocutionary effect are in decreasing order suitable for the externalization of the intention in writing. The transition from saying to what has been said is defined in the following three points:

2. In the usage of language, the meaning rests with the person of the speaker. This referral is immediate. "Intention" and "meaning" almost coincide and are in many languages expressed by the same verb (*vouloir dire,* "to mean," *meinen*). In written language the intention of the author no longer coincides with that of the text. Putting words on paper separates intention from meaning. The meaning of the text takes precedence over what the author intends to say. Intention is replaced by interpretation.

3. Usage of language refers to a "world." A dialogue refers to the situation of the partners in the discourse. Written language implies a similar reference. The text not only opens a situation but also refers to a "world," for example, to the "world" of the Greeks. This world clarifies, as it were, our own situation. Written language opens a "world" to us, and provides a new dimension to our being-in-the-world (Heidegger).

4. When we use language we speak to someone, who becomes our partner in dialogue. The written word is directed to whoever wants to read it. Dialogue is replaced by understanding. The relation of writing and reading differs significantly from that of speaking and hearing.

To what extent is it possible to determine the object of the human sciences — Weber: "meaning-oriented behavior" — through the readability criteria mentioned above? Ricoeur sets out four criteria for "meaningful action":

First, Ricoeur deals with the recording of an action. One learns from comparison that meaningful action can become the object of scientific inquiry only if it can be objectified. "Understanding" differs from "interpretation." This is comparable to the recording of language in written form. As a result, the action is no longer just a transaction in the given situation. The *meaning* of the action can be detached from the *event* of the action. An action possesses the structure of a locutionary action. Action verbs are specific forms of predicates. Ricoeur clarifies this with the following statement: "Brutus killed Caesar in the Curia, on the Ides of March, with a . . . , with the help of . . ." (1991, 151). This sentence clarifies the *who, what, where, when,* and *how,* that is, the *structure* of a given event.

One must be able to define the ontological status of an action, if one is to transmit something that has been recorded. This may occur through "mental actions" (believing, thinking, willing, imagining, etc.). But the propositional structure of an action has some additional characteristics. In essence, this concerns the dialectic of event and meaning. Ricoeur refers to this as the noematic structure of the action. Thus the interpretable object is detached from the interaction.

The noema also has illocutionary characteristics. One may, for instance, offer a typology of action according to Austin's categories of illocutions, and link this to a criteriology for defining the rules governing a certain type of action. For instance, if one wants to know what a promise is, one must understand what conditions must be met before a certain action qualifies as a promise. If an action cannot be recorded in written form, how can it be recorded at all? As in the case of what is said, that which is *done* can also be compared with an inscription, as one indicates when one says that an event has left its traces.

Second, Ricoeur shows subsequently how the action gains an independent status. As a text detaches itself from the author, so an action detaches itself from the actor. In a simple action, meaning (noema) and intention (noesis) coincide. This is not the case with more complex actions. An action thus becomes a social event. Some actions are events that leave their stamp on history. There are abiding consequences and remaining structures. These structures could be seen as documents of human action, which are comparable to texts. The social record of action may be regarded as a document file. One might even refer to history as the file of human action. Chronicles provide such a register of human action. Some institutions emerge from these actions. The meaning then no longer lies in the intention of those who executed the work but in the work itself.

Third, this independence offers a link with the concept of meaningful action, the kind of action with a significance that transcends the original situation. Important actions result in meanings that can be actualized in new situations.

Finally, human action is accessible to others, similar to a text that is accessible to all who want to read it. Human action is open to a practical interpretation within the current praxis.

This dialectic of work and interpretation has its impact on the methodology to be used.

8.5.2 Methodological Implications

Having made clear that the paradigm of the interpretation of texts provides a paradigm for the interpretation of action, Ricoeur elaborates his thesis further in harmony with the methodology of the human sciences. In these sciences a certain tension has arisen between a hermeneutical approach that is characteristic of the human sciences, often referred to with the German word *verstehen* (to understand), and an empirical approach that is characteristic of the natural sciences, often referred to with the word *erklären* (to explain). But can the human sciences claim to be scientific if understanding is detached from explanation?

Ricoeur dares to suggest that there is a dialectic relation between explanation and understanding, comparable to that between writing and reading. This is not simply an extension of speaking-listening, the situation of dialogue. Ricoeur is critical toward applying the dialogue model to the hermeneutical approach to the text. He starts, as we saw, from the objective nature of the text. The paradigm of reading may, on the basis of the four characteristics referred to above, be viewed as an original paradigm. The objectivity of the text (distanciation) offers the possibility of explanation. The dialectic of understanding and explanation can be see as a dual movement: a movement from understanding toward explanation, and from explanation toward understanding.

The path from understanding to explanation may be portrayed as from guessing to validation. Guessing is a process without rules. When trying to interpret a text, guesswork is "divination," to use Schleiermacher's word: there is a sudden flash of insight. Validation rather represents the grammatical moment: examining the context to see whether the statement makes sense.

Ricoeur searches for a theory of guessing, with the intention of arriving at a construction of meaning. Interpretation as reconstruction of texts has a circular character. On the one hand, something complete is presupposed as one recognizes certain components. On the other hand, one proceeds from the details to the whole. But the final judgment remains a matter of guesswork. In addition, each text is unique. Through localizing and individualizing, a text slowly but surely acquires character.

Reading implies one-sidedness and gives a hypothetical character to an interpretation. A text is spoken with varying intonations and allows for several readings and interpretations. Validation will provide arguments that make one interpretation more plausible than others. The logic of subjective probability already provides a firm basis for a hermeneutical theory of the unique. This is further strengthened by extending the hermeneutical circle to include the circular relation of guessing and validation (1991, 159).

This dialectic of guesswork and validation has a paradigmatic value for the entire domain of the human sciences. The significance of human actions, historical events, and social phenomena is expressed through different voices and must therefore be constructed. Before one can interpret any action, one must understand the intention and motivation underlying the action. One is here dealing with the relation between the *what* and the *why* of an action. "I *understand* what you intended to do if you are able to *explain* to me why you did such and such an action" (1991, 160). Meaningful actions require a motive as *reason for,* not only as *cause of.* The aspect of reason points to intentionality in the action. This is particularly apparent when this occurs on the basis of the "desirability character" of the "wanting" or of the conviction, in which the forces of an action become visible. On this basis the meaning of an action can be discussed. This argumentation, which is acompanied by a certain distanciation, is comparable to the interpretation of a text. Actions can be tested. Ricoeur draws a further comparison with the judicial system as a form of validation, which is recorded in a verdict.

The opposite path leads from explanation to understanding. Here Ricoeur focuses on the act of reading. He opts for the structural model. A text is detached from its environment and viewed as an independent unit. The surrounding world is left out of the equation. This may be done on the basis of systems theory, which abstracts systems from processes. Structural analysis leads from the external structure of the story to the internal structure, to the depth of the text. Thus one learns what the text is about. To understand a text is to follow a movement, from that *which* is said in the text to that *about which* something is being said. Thus one detects the *meaning* of the text as an admonition to look at certain things in a new light.

This dialectic of explaining and understanding has a paradigmatic significance for the entire domain of the human sciences. Ricoeur argues that the structural model may also be applied to social phenomena (1991, 165). A language system may serve as a model for other systems. One may, for instance, speak of systems of action, working on the presupposition that social reality is fundamentally symbolic. Action is linked to providing meaning. Likewise, in the social sciences one may, through the use of structural analysis, move from an analysis of external aspect to interpretations of the deeper aspects. But these connections, which one attempts to detect through this deeper interpretation, can be understood only if one is personally engaged in a way comparable to assimilating a text. Does this not, however, open the way for all kinds of subjective interpretations? Ricoeur responds that this assimilation has to do with the dynamic significance that becomes apparent through the explanation (167). This in turn falls within the hermeneutical circle and thus becomes part of the correlation of explaining and understanding.

For an extensive survey of language theory in its relation to practical theology, I refer the reader to J. Thomassen (1986), and, in particular, to the *handboek* (manual) of A. Grözinger (1991). The latter pays attention to, among other things, linguistics (F. de Saussure), analytical philosophy (Bertrand Russell, G. E. Moore, Ludwig Wittgenstein), the sociology of language, literary criticism, and the theory of theological language. This summary provides an idea of what is being done in a broad range of disciplines. In addition, there is the significance of language in psychoanalysis in the tradition of Freud: "If sickness manifests itself in language phenomena, then language must also have the potential to bring healing" (Grözinger 1991, 54).

Among the important themes for practical theology are: the distinction between external, superficial structures and underlying, deeper structures (Firet 1980, 14ff.); the uniqueness of metaphorical language (van Es 1979; Veltkamp 1988, 176; Grözinger 1991, 94ff.); attention to literary genres like poetry and story (Baart 1986); and, most importantly, the area of rhetoric (Grözinger 1991, 70ff.; Dingemans 1991).

One would expect that, because of its hermeneutical basis, Ricoeur's theory of action is of great significance for the development of a practical-theological theory of action. It is my point of departure in the next chapter.

8.6 Conclusion

This chapter has provided greater clarity with regard to the options embodied in the concept of a theory of action, or the choices that must be made. Practical theology is theology in the full sense of the word (chapter 7), and as a theological theory of action it offers, in principle, a unique approach, with its own object and its own methodology. As a relatively young discipline, practical theology has seen a rapid development since the 1960s.

There exists a broad consensus to view actions as the object of practical theology, in terms of the mediative action of the Christian tradition within the context of modern society.

If practical theology is to realize its intention and pretension of a theological theory of action, it will have to provide a further elaboration on the basis of the action theories of the social sciences. Habermas's theory of communicative action and Ricoeur's interpretation theory offer some important suggestions in this respect.

From both a theological and an action-theoretical perspective, these last two chapters have provided the basis for a practical-theological theory of action, which I intend to develop in the next chapter.

CHAPTER 9

A Practical-Theological
Theory of Action

The two previous chapters attempted to chart the concept of a "theological theory of action" from two different angles: as a theological discipline (chapter 7) and as a theory of action (chapter 8). This chapter must connect those two aspects as I try to develop a theological theory of action as the core of a practical-theological theory. I must explain what I mean by an *integrative* practical theology, by clarifying how the hermeneutical, the empirical, and the critical perspectives interact.

The critical perspective manifests itself in the historical character of human knowledge and action. These occur in space and time: who does what to whom in what situation? Asking this question presupposes that all one's knowledge and all one's actions are, in principle, open to critical examination. I have developed this perspective with regard to practical theology in part I. There we discovered how theory and praxis interact continuously. Praxis is directed from, or interpreted on the basis of, a specific theory. This relation of theory and praxis demands a more systematic treatment, if it is to be applied in the context of a theory of action. This chapter begins with this aspect (9.1).

The hermeneutical and the empirical perspectives belong to the core of a theory of action, and we must keep in mind this close relation as we develop our theory. When considering their application in the context of practical theology — which chooses mediative action as the direct object of its inquiry — we must include another element, the strategic perspective. Working along these lines, we can bring into focus the outlines of a practical-theological theory of action in the second section (9.2). This theory of action is worked out in more detail in the next three chapters.

This leads to a more precise definition of the relation between "praxis 1" and "praxis 2," a relation that has a central place in determining our object: "the mediation of the Christian faith in the praxis of modern society" (9.3).

From there I return to the concrete situation where practical theology is "done" (9.4). The action theory to be developed offers the possibility to distinguish several currents of thought and to evaluate their respective merits.

9.1 The Relation between Theory and Praxis

The critical character of a theory of action may be discerned in the dialectic relation between theory and praxis, which is defined historically and on the basis of the given situation. The concepts of theory and praxis must be understood within a philosophical frame of reference (9.1.1) before they can be applied in practical theology (9.1.2).

9.1.1 The Philosophical Frame of Reference

Since the classical era, theory and praxis have been among the key concepts of philosophy. They provide humanity's answer to the world in which humans live. But while in our time theory and praxis, thought and action, order the world, the opposite was true in ancient times. Thought and action were the human answers to a predetermined world order, the order of the cosmos.

Theory was a concept on its own. The Greek word *theoria* means "being a spectator at solemn occasions," "observing." Greek philosophers regarded the attitude of critical contemplation, rather than practical life with all its restrictions, as the highest achievement in human existence: a form of knowledge for the sake of knowledge, and insight into true reality. This contemplation enabled humans to see the essence of things.

Aristotle distinguished this contemplative knowledge from practical action, which he subsequently divided between *poiesis* and *praxis* (Pannenberg 1973, 438 [1976, 436]). *Poiesis* is action that brings results, that produces something. It is based on *technē*, on skills. Both the construction of a house and the work of a medical doctor would fall in that category. By contrast, *praxis* is a form of life in which a human being acts on the basis of life experience. The action is a goal in itself. This would include seeing, thinking, reading, living. *Poiesis* becomes technology when it detaches itself from *praxis*. This distinction returns in modern philosophy.

Likewise, when we speak of the practice of faith, in the sense of "praxis pietas" or "orthopraxis," we think of a faith that lives through experience and manifests itself spontaneously. This belongs to the essence of faith. For that reason *poiesis* may not detach itself from *praxis* as we develop our practical-theological theory — something that may easily happen as the result of a one-sided view of professionalization.

As time has gone by, the classical view of the relation between theory and praxis has been replaced by a modern view. The philosopher René Descartes gave expression to the rift between the classical worldview and the new human self-consciousness (Grözinger 1987, 157). He verbalized the emerging subjectivity and the new self-consciousness in his famous words: "Cogito, ergo sum." Descartes mistrusted human observation. His fundamental attitude was one of systematic doubt. As a result, thought distanced itself from the rest of the world. The new self-consciousness was characterized by distance. The thinker was thrown back upon him- or herself. Since Descartes, the theory-praxis problem has regained its central place in philosophy, as it seeks to indicate how the distance between thinking and acting can be bridged.

In the nineteenth century, G. W. F. Hegel's philosophy offered a link between theory and praxis by suggesting that idea and reality were mediated along the path of history (Lehmann 1974, 85). Marx built on this in his famous eleventh thesis on Feuerbach: "The philosophers have given *different interpretations* of the world, but what counts is, to change the world" (Lehmann 1974, 86). He chose his point of departure in action. The Frankfurt School established the relation through a "critical theory," which, in view of its emancipatory character, is a form of praxis. Habermas (8.4) agrees with this Aristotelian distinction between *poiesis* (construction) and *praxis* (action). This enables him, according to Keulartz (1992, 25-26), to link the concepts of feasibility and personal involvement, and thus to develop a two-dimensional praxis concept (286), through the dialectic of labor and interaction, goal-oriented and communicative action, which must ever be held in tension, like strategic and communicative action.

Karl R. Popper's philosophy of science differs fundamentally in that it chooses the theory as its starting point. His philosophy is a reaction to all systems of thought and strategies for action of the twentieth century that betray totalitarian traits (Grözinger 1987, 163). He wants to develop a new nonideological, purely scientific way of thinking. The Socratic idea of "not-knowing" is his leitmotiv. What is presented as knowledge is no more than theory that has so far not been refuted. Thus falsifiability becomes a fundamental aspect of his philosophy of science (Korthals 1989, 49). Theories must be judged on the basis of the probability of their hypotheses. Thus he becomes the trendsetter for a critical rationalism. The empirical-analytical model of inquiry fits with this tradition.

9.1.2 Practical Theology: Theory and Praxis

Practical theology also recognizes this interaction between theory and praxis. These concepts are defined from a theological perspective and directed toward the praxis of mediation, as the specific practical-theological focus, but without isolating this action from society as a whole. In order to make them useful for practical theology, these concepts have been defined as follows:

Praxis is understood as the actions of individuals and groups in society, within and outside the church, who are willing to be inspired in their private and public lives by the Christian tradition, and who want to focus on the salvation of humankind and the world.

Theory is understood as a comprehensive hermeneutical-theological statement that relates the Christian tradition to experience, to the life and actions of modern humans.

Both definitions refer to the Christian tradition. The unity of the Scriptures presupposes a close bond with Israel. In my elaboration of the relation between theory and praxis, I use a few theses of the German practical theologian N. Greimacher (1974, 103ff.).

1. There is no pure theory of praxis. "Theory always receives the impact of history and is conditioned by society."

This thesis is the presupposition of part I (above), which examines the "theory of praxis" along historical-interpretive lines. In chapter 8 Habermas helped us to see how even the thought models of modern theology are to a significant degree determined by the consciousness of the new era. This puts question marks behind the possibility and the desirability of a deductive Word theology. Even the best listener is always a child of the times in which one lives: indeed, the understanding of the Word is *one's* limited understanding.

2. Though at times one is unaware of it, praxis always has an underlying theory. Praxis is always, at least in part, determined by theory. Failing to recognize this leads to an ideological praxis.

This thesis implies that we must always be careful in our actions — and this includes our theological actions. To mention one example: even the "simple faith" that prefers to accept things without explanation is a form of theory. In this theory a high priority is given to a state of dependence in human beings' relationship to God. There always are educators and authorities who have an interest in keeping people insignificant and dependent. Praxis is therefore often ideologically determined, as we know from some popular images of God, which seem to fit wonderfully well with particular views of society. Ecclesiastical action in our society often reflects a middle-class mentality.

3. The primacy of theory over praxis, long defended by practical theology, must be rejected.

Theology can detach theory from actual life, in terms of ontology and metaphysics. As a result people will say, "It may well be true, but why should I care?" Thus dogma becomes mere doctrine and loses its doxological, experiential character. It begins to function as an imposed truth, which always implies some degree of oppression. If that happens, the time has come — to refer once more to Habermas — to refresh our thinking again by looking at praxis.

4. Likewise, one must reject a primacy of praxis over theory — a view with Marxist elements, supported by some social scientists, and at times either consciously or unconsciously accepted by church leaders. Such a view would eventually result in the confirmation of the status quo in the church.

To argue that theory is totally defined by praxis is a form of determinism. Some interpretations of Freud's thoughts about humanity and Marx's philosophy of society might lead in that direction: "People are as they are and things happen according to fixed laws." But this deprives people of their responsibility to think critically about their situation and to resist any unacceptable praxis. In this view real change is impossible. One fatalistically accepts traditional forms, since it would be useless to "refresh" one's praxis by a new theory.

5. The relation between theological theory and ecclesiastical praxis is determined neither by a complete separation nor by an identification of the two, but by a bipolar tension-filled combination. The shift from theory to praxis, and vice versa, is a qualitative shift. Theory is in constant need of verification or falsification through praxis, while praxis must constantly be transcended by theory. Theory in the context of practical theology must always be critical theory.

This thesis shows practical theology fully operational. Theory must constantly be tested in praxis. This requires empirically oriented practical-theological research. At the same time, praxis must receive a constant critical review from theory. This demands an ongoing development of the hermeneutical theory. The question then emerges how this theory receives a critical content.

Bipolarity is not a correlation of question and answer, but creates a tension-filled, critical relation. The concept "critical" can be further defined from the perspective of the political theology that works on the basis of "critical theory," along the lines of the Frankfurt School, or from the perspective of liberation theology, based on the option for the poor. The concept can also be critically defined by means of verification through falsification of factual data, along the lines of critical rationalism. The path of hermeneutics offers yet another way of defining the polar relation of tradition and experience. We will find that practical theologians have varying preferences in this regard.

These are some of Greimacher's theses, with some of my comments. Such comments are inevitably colored by an additional factor: the context within which one thinks and acts. Every theory has its own conscious and subconscious presuppositions and can be falsified on that basis.

Dorothee Sölle is a theologian who shows herself to be extremely conscious of this contextuality. In her lectures in Buenos Aires, she leaves no doubt about her conviction that the theory-praxis relation in Germany differs sharply from that in Latin America: "I cannot bring you the theology you need. That would be arrogance and cultural imperialism. What I can do is to try to explain as honestly as I can why I, a white woman belonging to the middle classes of the First World, need faith. . . . I am attempting to be a Christian in the context of the rich and despairing world" (1981, 2-3).

Our theological language does not allow us, as human beings, to speak the last word or to formulate eternal truth. Truth is always subject to situations and relationships, and will be credible only if it is not frozen in verbal expression. This means that in our various actions we will more than ever have to depend on an intersubjectivity, in which people, on the basis of a shared commitment, become the veritable subjects of their own experience. This requires a constant interaction between text and context, theory and praxis.

Taking into account the hermeneutical-communicative praxis, on which the development of a practical-theological theory is focused, one may illustrate the interaction between theory and praxis as in Figure 9. Practical theology starts from the situation, the praxis. An experience people have (praxis) becomes the object of reflection on the basic theological statements (theory). This theory, which itself is the result of the thinking and actions of the past, and reflects the distribution of power of the past, apparently fails to

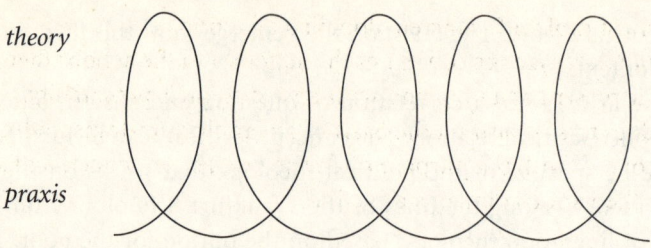

theory

praxis

Figure 9: Relation between theory and praxis

convince people in their contemporary praxis. Many ask critical questions: Did the people of the past arrive at an adequate understanding of certain biblical texts, in the light of their times? This leads to a rereading of Scripture, and subsequently to a revision of the theory. A new theoretical insight then asks critical questions with regard to the existing praxis. Why do things happen as they do? These and other questions lead to a reexamination of praxis. Which factors are determinative for the current situation? Why do people think and act as they do? Is there any alternative? This leads to further questions about the theory and any subsequent answers also have their impact on praxis. People recognize their situation and learn to view this with new eyes, in the light of a "fresh" theory. It prompts them to initiate and change things, which leads to a renewal of praxis. This, in turn, prompts further questions to the theory, leading to a circular process. This is often set in motion through mediative action, through education, group discussions, dialogue, or through participation in an action group that stimulates this process.

Habermas's theory offers many points for reflection in this critical analysis of action (8.4). Remember the relation between "knowledge" and "interests," which offers insight in the way in which authority functions; the importance of knowledge for emancipation; and the "colonization" of the "lifeworld" by systems, accompanied by a reduced view of rationality. A critical analysis of the relation between theory and praxis may bring these aspects to the surface.

9.2 Profiles of a Practical-Theological Theory of Action

The dialectical relation between theory and praxis provides insight into the situation of ecclesiastical and social action, but is in itself not adequate to understand, explain, guide, and direct that action. A theory of action is needed that must meet the following conditions formulated by Firet (8.3):

- It must deal with concrete domains of action.
- It must analyze the context of the actions and the actions themselves in their present situation and with regard to their potentiality.
- It does this — also on the basis of an empiricism-transcending critical theory — with the purpose of developing action models and strategies for the various domains of action.

This description presupposes a more precise definition of the concept of action. According to A. van der Beld, an action is "consciously and knowingly realizing something in the world" (1982, 1). The actor, who intervenes in the world and changes something, is a key element. Human interventions are not simply caused but are based on reasons (12). This intentional character differentiates action from behavior, which is often unconscious and unintentional. Actors usually know what they do. They can give reasons when asked why they do something.

As a theory of action, practical theology must define how it functions as an academic discipline (9.2.1), described below, in conjunction with the definition of its object (praxis 1 in relation to praxis 2), as "communicative action in the service of the gospel" (9.2.2); and it must have an adequate model of interpretation (9.2.3). This brings us to the core of a theological theory of action, the methodology, for which hermeneutics and the social sciences provide the building blocks (9.2.4). To this I add some conclusions with regard to the application of practical theology.

9.2.1 The Development of a Paradigm

Those who work in the field of practical theology cannot do without a paradigm or a "disciplinary matrix" (Firet 1987, 260). By this I mean a clear description of the elements that form the generally accepted basis on which this discipline is pursued. Firet refers to "communicative action in the service of the gospel" as a generally accepted paradigm. Here, once again, one can turn to elements in Habermas's theory.

First, we must establish a theological framework for our actions. "Communicative action" occurs in space and time. It is directed toward the "already" and the "not yet" of God's kingdom, in the dialectic of anamnesis and anticipation, of remembering and expecting. This provides a unique inspiration and motivation for action, understood as intentional and mediative.

This type of action is always communicative action, directed toward truth, authenticity, and justice, taking into account facts, norms, and feelings. In the Christian tradition these dimensions of our actions are critically examined on the basis of the norms and the experiential world that are embedded in the eschatological perspective of the kingdom of God (van der Ven 1990, 80ff. [1993, 69ff.]). In dealing with these issues, practical theology enlists the services of biblical theology, dogmatics, and ethics.

This communicative action forms the basis for forms of mediation, that is, of strategic action, that want to change reality in such a way that it answers to a greater degree to the perspective given to us through faith and in the hope of the coming of God's kingdom. This colors our actions in terms of love, freedom, solidarity, and justice.

For further details I return to Ricoeur's model (8.5). Actions that convey meaning, which become the object of the human sciences, may be studied through the paradigm of text interpretation, and, as far as methodology is concerned, through the reciprocal movement from understanding to explanation. I now apply this model to practical theology. Ricoeur's theory of the use of language and the dialectic between event and meaning may be pictured as follows:

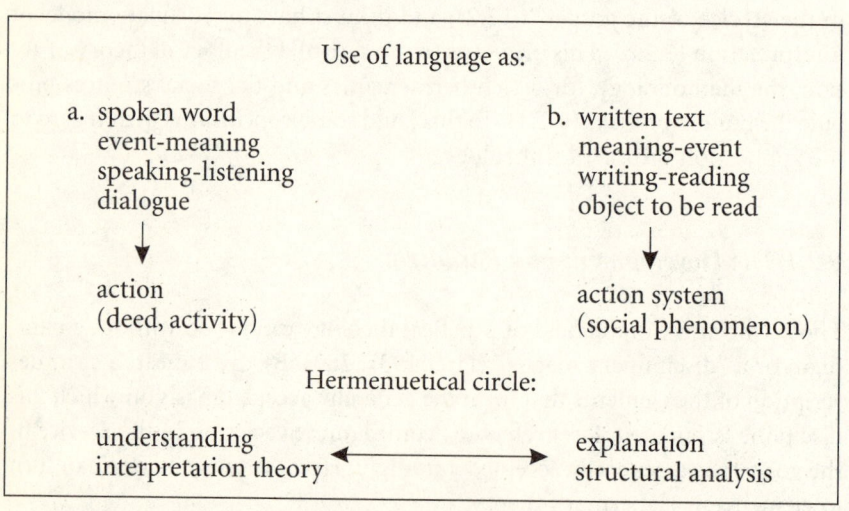

In this context some terms must be further defined.

A *model* is the first stage in the development of an empirical theory, by reducing reality to a scheme with an operational character.

A *paradigm* is the general framework for the development of the theory of a given discipline in a given era. The expression "disciplinary matrix" was coined by Thomas S. Kuhn (1977, 297). The paradigm is not to be confused with the *methodology,* the principles of the method to be followed.

An *action structure* refers to the way in which a complex phenomenon, such as an action or social system, is structured.

An *action system* is an interpretation of social phenomena as a collection of elements that manifest a specific pattern of relations.

The two concepts of "understanding" and "explanation" refer in the philosophy of science, respectively, to the hermeneutical method of the human sciences, and to the empirical method derived from the natural sciences. In the social sciences they are applied to what humans themselves produce: words and actions, texts and products (Riedel 1978, 15). As befits a practical discipline, the hermeneutical approach is directed toward the incidental and the individual. The empirical approach is directed toward the general and the universal. Individualization stands over and against generalization (22). In the first case one speaks of understanding, in the latter case of explanation.

9.2.2 Communicative Action in the Service of the Gospel

The shortest description of an action could be something like: "He walks." In that case one is dealing with a singular action or basic action. But most statements about actions are more complex. To understand fully the structure of an action, one must ask: *Who* does *what* (in relation to *whom*), *where, when, why,* and *how?*

This sentence poses questions about (1) the actor — who did this? (2) the kind of action — what did the actor do? (3) the modality — how did the actor do it? (4) the context — where, when, under what circumstances did the actor do it? and (5) the reason for the action — why did the actor do it? (van den Beld 1982, 7).

This description in the form of interrogative pronouns, also used in the interpretation of texts, reveals not only the structure of an action but also its implications as a social phenomenon. Such a phenomenon can be studied independently. An action system may be analyzed in the same way as a document, a language system, is interpreted through structural analysis. Considering the symbolic character of human action, one is in both instances confronted with the dialectic of event and meaning.

The following example illustrates this. On Easter Sunday in 1993, the minister of the Methodist congregation in one of the black townships near Johannesburg preaches about the hope of peaceful coexistence of people of different races that is embedded in the gospel of the resurrection of Christ and about the coming of the kingdom of God, while appealing to his audience to refrain from violence.

This is an extremely complex action statement. One recognizes the three levels Ricoeur distinguishes:

- The *circumstances:* reference is made to the context (place and time) and to the situation (the tension between black and white). A worship service takes place. This action has a structure (who, what, where, why, and how) that can be described. This may be called the locutionary level of the action. Something of the noematic structure of the action already becomes visible in the linkage between event and meaning.
- An *activity:* a worship service, or, to be more precise, a sermon about a text in Scripture. This shows the uniqueness of a theological action: reference is made to the written record of a tradition that needs to be interpreted. The present historical situation is interpreted from the perspective of the kingdom of God, and the resurrection is in a narrative way connected with the situation of resistance, here and now. This bond between event and meaning gives substantial power to the action. It implies a promise. This is the illocutionary level of the action.
- A *realization:* what the minister achieves with his action in this liturgical setting. He appeals for nonviolence, motivating the audience to a certain kind of conduct that will result in peaceful coexistence. This may evoke anxiety, but may also help the audience to sense hope rather than fear. This is the perlocutionary level.

In this tension between event and meaning, mental actions as believing and hoping furnish the action with a unique dimension. The action has to do with a concrete reality, while the inspiration derives from a faith reality, which is mediated by a text. Reality is seen in that particular light, giving it a symbolic character: the crucified and risen Lord in a world of cross bearers. In this interpretation the dialectic of event and meaning receives a unique dimension: the clear distinction between interpretation and text is no longer there. This gives the practical-theological interpretation its own character, but it must continue to operate within the established hermeneutical rules.

This interpretation must, of course, also allow for a critical perspective: In whose interest is this appeal? Does this minister in his appeal for reconciliation represent the interests of the established order, which currently seems to be a dis-order, or does he really put himself in the service of a new order of things? Any interpretation must take "prejudice" into account.

9.2.3 The Interpretation Model

Using this example, I now look in greater detail at the interpretation model. This provides insight into the structure of the action.

The central question is:

- Who does what (in relation to whom)?

This question leads to three, to some extent separate, perspectives:

- Who does what: why/about what?
- Who does what: where/when?
- Who does what: how/with what intent?

These perspectives may be referred to as the hermeneutical perspective, the empirical perspective, and the strategic perspective of an action.

Who Does What?

The "what" may refer to acting as an action (a deed, comparable to the spoken word, the dialogue) and to action as a social phenomenon that can be objectified (comparable to a written text). In the first instance, the interpretation of the action focuses mainly on the understanding, beginning with the question of the purpose of this particular action. Does this action make sense? Is it wise to do this in this manner to achieve the desired goal? The perspective of the participant is of primary importance. The "what" in our example is "the sermon of the minister."

In the second instance, one tends to regard a certain kind of human action more as an independent entity, as an action system, and attempts to explain this through methods comparable with structural analysis, in order to trace the meaning and to detect its deeper sense, which, in turn, can lead to new forms of action. In our example, the "what" is defined as "resurrection sermons in situations of oppression."

Both dimensions stand in a dialectic relation and may be understood in terms of a hermeneutical circle. They call for each other and complement each other.

The question of the "who" is extremely complex (Ricoeur 1990 [1992]). This is readily apparent when one tries to understand what motivated the minister, considering the tumultuous context of time and place. In such a situation how can the "I" be loyal to him-"self," in solidarity with his audience and convinced of the cause it defends? This is the matter of identity, the dimension of genuineness in relation to that of truth and justice. The time will come when history will have to pronounce judgment as it seeks to explain the role of the black ministers in the last phase of apartheid, based on the record of their sermons.

The ethical dimension of our action also becomes visible as we link the "who" and the "what." What kind of circumstances would make this type of action morally defensible? No action is neutral; it always has to be subject to moral evaluation. This points to the relation between theology and ethics.

A number of different perspectives emerge from the "who does what." Why does someone do this? What circumstances surround the action? How does the person in question act and with what intent? I now take a closer look at these perspectives.

Who Does What: Why/About What?

This immediately leads to the question "why," the intentional aspect of our actions. With Ricoeur one may distinguish between intention and motivation, with "intention" referring to the matter under discussion (the hope that is grounded in the gospel of the resurrection), and "motivation" referring to the personal involvement (conviction, faith). Considered from a theological perspective, this concerns the relation between *fides quae* and *fides qua*. This immediately poses another question. In the light of the meaning of the content of the text or the action, the connection between the "what" and the "why" also impacts on the "about what." This is the referential aspect of an action. Ricoeur calls this the movement from "sense" to referral, from what a text or action is saying to that about which a text or action is saying something. In this case: What is the content of the gospel of Easter? Does one understand it rightly if one draws such far-reaching conclusions from it?

This once again opens the way for a critical approach, based on the question, Cui bono? Who would benefit from the action? In whose interest are certain action structures and action processes? This touches on the moral aspect of the question "why."

This linkage between the "what" and the "why" affects primarily the hermeneutical meaning of a text or action. It is a matter of interpretation with a view toward arriving at understanding. What is the sense or meaning of a text or an action? This question has to do with both the symbolic character of an action and the underlying structure of an action system. Here also understanding and explanation need each other.

Who Does What: Where/When?

The "what" must also be connected with the "where and when," with the place and the time as the context of the action. This is the situational aspect. In that way the circumstances in which the action occurred become transparent. Every action is historically and contextually conditioned. In our example, place, time, and circumstances are carefully noted.

The situational aspect does not usually become apparent until the action has resulted in action structures, which can be interpreted as independent units. Every action confronts one with a number of variables, in this case: minister, audience, worship service, context. Placing these variables in a broader, theoretical framework enables one to compare this specific incident with other events. On that basis one may develop hypotheses that may lead toward knowledge with a more general validity with regard to such a phenomenon as "preaching in a situation of oppression." The distanciation that occurs (from the perspective of a participant to that of a spectator) allows for a better insight in the degree to which the action structures, which manifest themselves at a specific time and under specific circumstances, are conditioned by personal and societal factors. It also throws new light on the "who" and "why" of the action.

This opens the possibility of critical interpretations, of interpretations of the external and underlying factors. This method of explanation demands a kind of "structural analysis," rooted in an empirical methodology that assigns a central place to explanation.

Who Does What: How/For What Purpose?

The third connection is between the "what" and the "how." This brings the instrumental aspect of the action into the open, the kind of action chosen for this situation. In our example it is the medium of a sermon. The "how" must adequately serve the "what"; any form of mediative action must always serve the intended communicative goal. The latter element, the teleological aspect of the action, once again has a moral side to it: What goal sanctions what means? The "how" thus receives a depth of content by linking it to the "for what purpose."

This connection again occurs at two levels, that of action as a deed, and that of action as a phenomenon. In the first case, the medium utilized to achieve a certain goal is of primary importance. Mediative action intentionally uses different kinds of action strategies. These do not stand by themselves, but depend on the "what" of the mediative action, and may be empirically examined to ascertain their effectiveness. This connection also plays at the level of interpretation of actions, in the dialectic of understanding and explanation.

Therefore, an intentional action has — in similar ways to the use of language — a strategic meaning, as an illocutionary (in our example: the appeal) and perlocutionary (with a view to the intended effect) action. Any action is an intervention in the surrounding world and is directed toward change. The actor wants to achieve something. Along these lines one may develop a typology of action, which distinguishes between different kinds of change. In relation to the hermeneutical perspective, the action originates through a process of "understanding," but demands an explanation based on an empirically founded methodology.

All three perspectives are closely related, since they all focus in their own way on the core question of "who does what?" and since each question relates structurally to the others. This results in the following scheme:

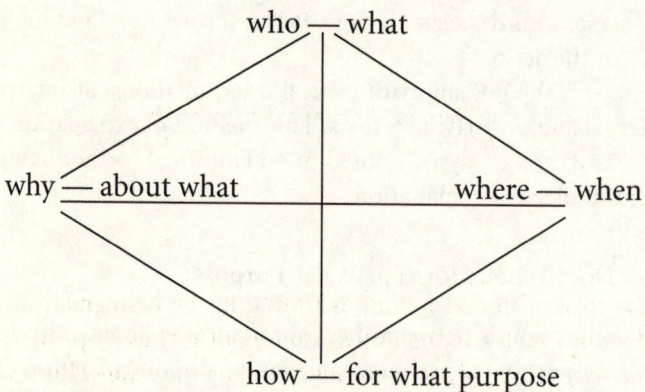

Figure 10: Action structure

For that reason one can only say about a particular perspective that it is *primarily* hermeneutical, *primarily* strategic, or *primarily* empirical. Having already established a link between the analysis of the structure of the action and considerations of methodology, I now take a closer look at these.

9.2.4 The Methodology of a Theory of Action

In the methodology of practical theology one meets three concepts: understanding, explanation, and change. Ricoeur regards understanding and explanation as the two foci of the hermeneutical circle. Both are of great importance for the methodology of practical theology. The third concept — change — is, as we saw, inherent to any form of action. An action is always an intervention in reality that leaves its traces. Change is also the direct object of practical theology, mediative action, and strategy for transformation. In this section we study the methodological relation of these three. One may picture the mutual relations as points of departures from within a triangle:

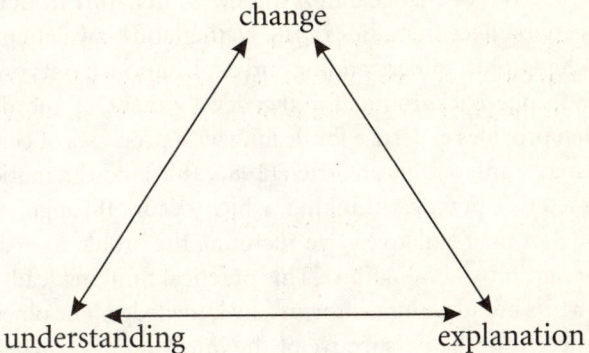

Figure 11: Methodology

The perspective of understanding is central in the hermeneutical theory of interpretation, which has the understanding of text as its primary task, but which one may also apply to the understanding of actions. Ricoeur refers to the reconstruction of an action structure as a movement from guessing to testing. This structure has a circular character, usually referred to as the "hermeneutical circle." The guessing has to do with the fact that one is dealing with the localization and individualization of a unique action. Such an interpretation will of necessity offer several possibilities. Nonetheless, one can argue that, from the point of view of truth, genuineness, and justice, one interpretation has more validity than the other. Ricoeur speaks in this connection of the logic of subjective probability, which provides a solid basis for the science of the individual, thus making it worthy of the name *science* (1991, 159).

The perspective of explanation is central in the empirical approach in the human sciences. It calls for a testing process, comparable to the judicial system, which is confronted with various interpretations of wrongful actions. Testing is required to arrive at a verdict that is valid, reasonable, and just. Similarly, it is possible, in a way comparable to structural analysis, to separate action systems from processes. Testing through falsification by means of the empirical cycle provides an adequate, scientific basis for the academic inquiry into the meaning and effectiveness of human action.

The essence of Ricoeur's methodological concerns is that the movements from understanding to explanation and from explanation to understanding interact, and together offer a meaningful methodology for the human sciences, with purposeful action as its object.

The perspective of change differs somewhat in nature from the two previous perspectives. Recent studies in the Netherlands have attempted to establish that change, like understanding and explanation, has its own scientific basis. This was the background for the development of the discipline of agogics, which provides expertise for dealing with processes of change. In this context one may want to join van Strien (1986, 18ff.) in his remarks about the unique character of practical thinking, which occurs through the methodological model of the regulative cycle (defining the problem — diagnosis — plan — intervention — evaluation). This practical thinking leads not to academic statements but to actions informed by knowledge. The object of the inquiry is studied from the perspective of the intention of change. It does not want to predict what will happen, but it wants to propose a possible action. But even though agogics has made a significant contribution to the development of a theory of strategic action, it has not succeeded in creating its own fundamental-theoretical basis.

For this I need to return to the dynamic of understanding and explanation, both of which possess an inner potential for change. When taken together, the perlocutionary character of an action, comparable to the power of language, and the insights in human behavior and social phenomena acquired through explanation offer pointers on how methods for dialogue, learning processes, and forms of community work might be developed.

It is important to state from the start that each perspective offers a circular process. (The next three chapters describe these processes.) This is true for the interpretation theory, the explanation theory, and the theory of change. The first two constitute the fundamental theory that emerges from the dialectic of understanding and explanation. The last, aimed at the development of methods, must constantly interact with the first two. This allows one to understand the unique character of the practical-theological method-ology, which may be illustrated as follows:

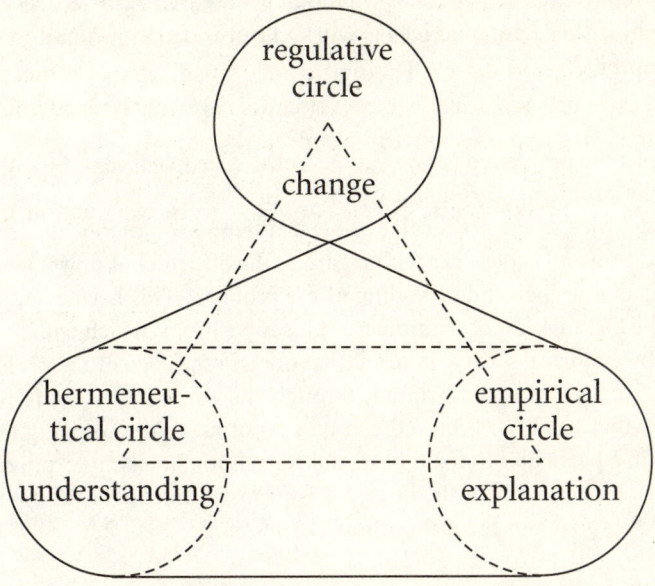

Figure 12: The methodology of practical theology

This figure shows three circles: the hermeneutical circle, as the interpreta-tion theory that is typical for the human sciences; the empirical circle, as the testing circle that is typical for the natural sciences; and the regulative circle, which is typical for the methodology in practical thinking. In the hu-man sciences, according to Ricoeur, the first two become part of an ellipse with understanding and explanation as its foci. The unique aspect in practi-cal theology as a discipline of mediative action is the interconnectedness of these three circles in a distinct circulation system or "circuit" of theory for-mation. The three circles correspond to the distinctive goals of the disci-pline: the interpretation of human action in the light of the Christian tradi-tion (the hermeneutical perspective), the analysis of human action with regard to its factuality and potentiality (the empirical perspective), and the development of action models and action strategies for the various do-mains of action (the strategic perspective). One can distinguish a number of action domains where one can apply this model. I return to this in part III.

The strategic perspective takes first place in the education and training of pastors and in pastoral praxis. The hermeneutical perspective relates to practical theology in general. The empirical perspective is the point of departure for practical-theological research. The distinct character of each of these perspectives is worked out in further detail in the next three chapters.

An example: the problem of prayer in our culture. People find it difficult to pray. What is the problem? Through a hermeneutical approach and on the basis of available knowledge, the practical theologian attempts to describe the tension between tradition and experience with regard to the difficulty of prayer, with a view to arriving at a deeper understanding of the problem. This hermeneutical circle leads to the formulation of a number of presuppositions, which will be explored or tested by empirical means, in order that one's knowledge of the problem may be enhanced. Then a second round, through the empirical circle, follows. The knowledge that has been acquired can now be utilized in improving the action strategies in a particular domain of mediative action, for example, prayer as part of religious education or of the liturgy. This translation consists of the formulation of a clear goal and the elaboration of a method.

9.2.5 Some Implications of This Model

In anticipation of a more detailed treatment of these three perspectives in chapters 10, 11, and 12, I may already draw some conclusions that are important for the development of a practical-theological theory.

- The new element in Ricoeur's model is, in particular, that it puts an end to the old controversy about method in the social sciences, which was based on the presupposition that a hermeneutical approach and an empirical approach cannot be combined. Through the dialectic of guessing and testing, understanding and explanation, each has its own place. Or to put it even stronger: they cannot function without each other.
- This model enables one to transcend the difference between intermediary or mediative action in the narrower sense of the word, as the direct object of practical theology, and social-communicative action in the broader sense. Both cases have to do with intentional actions, for which, from a perspective of meaning, reasons and not only causes can be adduced. Furthermore, all action aims at change. The only difference is

that the first case refers to the kind of action that is initiated by enlisting intentional strategies.

- The close interconnectedness of the hermeneutical, the strategic, and the empirical perspectives can be clarified through a study of forms of pastoral action. I mention, for instance, the research method of quasi-experimental design, which develops action strategies through empirical research within a hermeneutical field. This approach forms the basis of a number of research projects at the University of Nijmegen. There is also the method of "survey-guided development," utilized in research about the vitalization of church congregations at the Free University of Amsterdam. Processes of change have hermeneutical implications and must be guided by means of empirical research.

- The model also throws light on hermeneutical models such as those developed by Zerfass (7.5.1) and others. Linked with the hermeneutical and the strategic perspectives, these offer in particular an educational or training model, but fail to produce the movement of understanding and explanation in both directions. They must be complemented with a model of empirical research, so that the theory that is being developed may be tested. This aspect has been taken into consideration in figure 12.

- Finally, this model clarifies the critical aspect of our actions, in relation to the hermeneutical and the empirical aspect. The critical perspective appears to be a dimension of both rather than a distinct approach to science. It requires a critical use of the theory-praxis relation, as found in the theses of Greimacher (9.1.2), by paying attention to historical and contextual factors on the basis of a critical theory. This concerns the "cui bono" question, which gives the "who does what in relation to whom and why" an interpretive accent: "in whose interest?" This perspective is related to the moral perspective, as I have indicated in connection with the different combinations of interrogative pronouns.

9.3 The Relation between Praxis 1 and Praxis 2

The previous section also further clarifies the relation of praxis 1 (the mediation of the Christian faith) and praxis 2 (the praxis of modern society) in my definition of practical theology. Both are intimately connected in all aspects of human existence.

167

9.3.1 The Influence of the Context (Praxis 2)

Praxis 2 is not only the backdrop against which praxis 1 is played out, but constitutes the context of real life, where people, whether they are believers or unbelievers, are the actors who bear responsibility for their own life, for that of others, and for society as a whole. They all do this on the basis of their own norms and values, and must do so in a pluralistic society through communicative action that wants to be understood (Habermas), as is fitting within a democratic community.

Praxis 1 cannot be detached from this. Even where the mediation of the Christian faith has been institutionalized in various forms of church life, there can be no question of a totally separate domain, where only Christian norms and values call the tune. For believers also fully participate in modern culture, which they ingest through the media and everyday life. They are people who have been influenced by the Enlightenment and have adopted the camouflage of a bourgeois culture, so that the external life of Christians differs but little from that of others.

That is not to say that praxis 1 cannot have a positive, that is, partly corrective, influence on praxis 2, when the church and its members participate through different forums in communicative action, and on the basis of their faith accept responsibility for developments in society. The church continues to insist that prophetic speaking and priestly service have value for life in general.

9.3.2 The Mediation of the Christian Faith (Praxis 1)

I now need to define more precisely what I mean by praxis 1. What is this "mediation of the Christian faith"? The relation between theory and praxis requires "mediation." This word expresses reciprocity on the one hand, and on the other hand points to people and institutions who, as intermediaries, take on this mediative role. This is also true for the mediation of the Christian faith, although in this case the Holy Spirit becomes an all-important factor. For precisely the work of the Spirit, which is associated with freedom (2 Cor. 3:17), relates critically to every patronizing or belittling form of mediation that robs people of their independent judgment.

This praxis of mediation takes many forms in our modern society. For that reason, in contrast to many practical theologians quoted earlier, I understand this mediation not exclusively in a purely ecclesiastical sense. This mediation also occurs in the family, between parents and children; in the school, between teachers and pupils; in community work and adult education, between church workers and lay members, and between individual church members; in society through individuals and institutions, in groups that operate in society, through organizations or forms of community service, in public debates in the media, and in political and other public forums.

One may distinguish three main domains: the private life, social establishments (e.g., the church), and the public sector. In all three domains one finds a mediation of faith, but in many situations this occurs outside the immediate sphere of the church's influence. This tripartition is a given in modern life, as I concluded in part I. It has consequences for the division of practical theology in distinct domains of action, as becomes apparent in part III, where I work out in more detail the choice for a differentiated practical theology (5.5).

Nonetheless, it is clear that this mediation, this "communicative action in the service of the gospel," demands a form of church life as an organizing umbrella and an integrating force. This leads to a dynamic ecclesiology.

A good example of this is the ecclesiology of Hendrikus Berkhof (5.3.2): "The church . . . is the mediating movement between Christ and the people. As the institute mediates Christ to the congregation, so the congregation in turn mediates him to the world." Everything is focused on this latter aspect. "The fact of being church is thus not something static; it is a perpetual movement, a bridge-event" (1973, 429-30 [1979, 410-11]). One sees how praxis 1 immediately leads to praxis 2, as Berkhof states: "Since the Enlightenment, the 'evil world' becomes itself an articulate subject from which the church can evidently learn a great deal" (430 [411]). In this context he refers to theologians like H. Kraemer, A. A. van Ruler, and J. C. Hoekendijk.

All this requires the utmost from the methods utilized in this mediation. The aim of communicative action does not sanction all means, especially when one's intention is to serve the gospel. There must be reciprocity, openness, and truth, if the *poiesis* is not to be detached from the *praxis*. In the realm of church and faith communicative action must penetrate all strategic action. That is possible when dialogue is seen as the basic element of all action. This is expressed in the interrogative pronouns of the interpretation model described above.

9.3.3 The Object of Practical Theology

Regarding praxis 1 as the direct or material object of practical theology does not mean that one can detach this object from praxis 2. There are simply too many connections to allow this. But a logical distinction is desirable.

Theology as a whole is involved with a theory-praxis relation. On the basis of my hermeneutical view of "doing" theology (7.4), one can regard praxis 2 — the actual faith and life in society — as the praxis of all theology. From their own vantage point, systematic theologians, ethicists, and others are all partners in dialogue with people in all kinds of contexts. But practical theology comes with its distinct interests: "the actualization and maintenance of the relationship between God and humanity, and between humanity and God" (Firet). Here again, resulting from this interest, one finds in praxis 2 a broad field for practical-theological inquiry. Moreover, within this broad field practical theology meets other disciplines: philosophy, social sciences, economics, but also natural sciences and technology. Considering the normative points of departure, which play a role in every discipline, one finds various grounds for dialogue. In view of the common empirical methodology, particular attention is due to the relation with the social sciences.

Attention to the indirect object, the praxis of our modern society that is saturated by theory and ideology, is essential for the study of the direct object of practical theology, the mediation of the Christian faith. Modern society is not just the "address" where the Christian faith can deliver its message; it is — to remain with this metaphor — also the "sender" of its own messages, and thus, above everything else, a partner in the dialogue.

This interconnectedness of praxis 1 and 2 lends its synergistic character to the study of the direct object, "the communicative action in the service of the gospel." The relation between means and purpose, form and content, structure and culture, is never atemporal. The crux of the matter is what possibilities exist to ask questions about God in a situation that is in many ways aporetical (Heitink 1988b, 6ff.), or to remain silent by opting for another type of presence. The "bridge-event" does away with the perspective that leaves room only for what traditionally happened in the church: preaching, catechesis, and pastoral care. It points to a high priority for practice-oriented research and broadens the scope of the mediative action, which may be extended to "action in the service of the gospel, to foster the well-being of individuals, groups, and society as a whole as the (preliminary) realization of God's salvation for humanity and the world" (van der Laan 1990, 271).

9.4 Currents within Practical Theology

The theory described in the previous sections offers the possibility to identify a number of different currents within practical theology. I build on the developments described in 7.5, with some additions where needed. Surveying the field of these theories, one may identify five currents: a normative-deductive, a hermeneutical-mediative, an empirical-analytical, a political-critical, and a pastoral-theological current.

This division coincides largely with that proposed by others. Apart from some "mixed types," Mette (1978, 169ff.) distinguishes between an action-theoretical, an empirical-analytical, a dialectic-ideological-critical, a pastoral-theological, and a pragmatic approach. Höfte (1990, 103ff.) prefers three categories: hermeneutical, empirical-analytical, and political-critical.

9.4.1 The Normative-Deductive Current

This school of thought bases action on a normative theological theory and ascribes, where necessary and desirable, an ancillary function (Mette and Steinkamp 1983, 166) to social scientific methods.

One finds this approach in dialectical theology, which exposes human abilities and actions as religion (in the sense of unbelief) on the basis of the event of God's Word. The only possible form of mediation is the proclamation. The best-known example of this is *Die Lehre von der Seelsorge (A Theology of Pastoral Care)* by Eduard Thurneysen (2d ed. 1957 [1962]). R. Bohren (7.5.1), who defends Thurneysen against his critics, may be regarded as a modern and modest representative of this current. He believes that the social scientific perspective may easily become too narrow and may take away from other aspects of "God's becoming practical" (1975, 14) — a thought developed by him on the basis of his pneumatology. A modern Dutch version is found in the hermeneutical orientation of the "Amsterdam School" (van Uchelen 1979), which has become very influential in the preaching and catechesis in the Protestant churches through the Dutch Sunday School Association.

The danger this current of thought faces is that it remains stuck in exegesis and dogmatics and never arrives at a hermeneutical and empirical analysis of the theory-praxis relation. The critical character of Barth's theology is, however, undeniable and is, for instance, fully recognized by Catholic theologians like van Kessel (1989, 74).

One must make a distinction between this approach and another type of deductive method found in confessional-orthodox circles. Even though H. Jonker realizes that culture develops, he fears that moving toward a theory of action leads to a theological reduction. He pleads for a kind of practical theology that "in a deductive way, starting from the theological mystery, integrates the contributions of the auxiliary disciplines in a meaningful, comprehensive unity" (1983, 14). C. Trimp (1976) is even more critical regarding a hermeneutical dissolution of proclamation into dialogue. W. H. Velema in Apeldoorn is another representative of this Word theology (van Genderen et al. 1991).

Contributions from this group often excel in their historical analysis of practical theology and in their attention to doctrinal matters. But their tendency to stay as far away as possible from hermeneutical questions and to deal rather selectively with views from the social sciences results in a failure to address the real problems of praxis 2.

This traditional approach, based on a belief in objective truth, to some extent finds a parallel in a Catholic pastoral theology, which, focused on the clergy, gives great weight to the efficacy of the sacraments.

9.4.2 The Hermeneutical-Mediative Current

The term *hermeneutical-mediative* expresses that in this current a hermeneutical orientation is combined with a central place for mediative action (praxis 1) — the kind of action that fosters acting on the basis of faith and encourages improvements in action strategies that are directed toward that aim. The word *hermeneutical* does not apply exclusively to this current, as neither the term *empirical* nor the term *critical* does for the currents to be mentioned below.

This current places major emphasis on the aspect of professional preparation, and thinks from the position of the pastoral profession within the framework of the parish. By incorporating a strong agogic element into the pastoral profession and by working toward the improvement of methods used in pastoral and other church-related activities, progress is made toward a qualitative amelioration of forms of communicative action. Practice-oriented thinking according to the regulative cycle (11.4) provides direction. Practical-theological research is primarily understood as praxisbased research, with the intent of arriving at suggestions for further action. As in Zerfass's model, tradition and situation are brought together in a relation of reciprocity. As a result, theology and social science each makes its own contribution, but their independence assures that they can also function in their own right. This current shows some preference for qualitative research.

In the Dutch context I am thinking first of all of Firet, who chooses "God's coming to humanity in the world" as the central theme of his theology and pays close attention to the agogic moment (7.5.3). One finds this research tradition in the work of the institute for practical theology at the Free University. The same approach is followed in the study of K. A. Schippers et al. (1990) of pastoral care in old neighborhoods. The Catholic study of "community building" (Utrecht) also fits in this tradition. G. D. J. Dingemans (1991) and R. Bons-Storm (1984, 1989) can also be listed among the representatives of this hermeneutical current.

W. Greive (1975), R. Zerfass, and M. Josuttis (7.5.1) are among the German theologians who support this view. Josuttis states clearly: "Theology is now faced with the challenge to become practical, while remaining theological" (1967, 59). In the United States this hermeneutical orientation is found in the works of C. F. Caldwell (1978) and Don S. Browning (7.5.2).

The strength of this current is in its theological content and its practice-oriented thinking. Action research (not to be confused with research about what goes on in "action groups"!), which is partly in the domain of ecclesiastical policy making, therefore often faces difficulties in fully complying with the criteria of pure academic research. Solid empirical research is required. Examples of this can, however, be found within this current (e.g., Hendriks and Rijken-Hoevens 1976).

9.4.3 The Empirical-Analytical Current

The empirical-analytical current is primarily focused on research and usually prefers the perspective of the spectator over that of the participant. The German theologian H.-D. Bastian (7.5.1) has been foremost in pleading for objective empirical studies, "etsi deus non daretur" (1968, 31). As far as this aspect is concerned, representatives of this current feel a kinship with the school of critical rationalism (9.1). Methodologically they follow the empirical cycle, as developed by A. D. de Groot (12.3.3).

The most important Dutch proponent of this current is J. A. van der Ven (7.5.3), who has extensively documented his studies, usually described as "empirical theology," which are based on his research of many years (1990 [1993]). He wants to give maximum credit to the potential of social scientific research. This is expressed by the term *intradisciplinary*. It means that theologians must be fully conversant with the social scientific methodology and must utilize this in dealing with theological problems. This places the study in a hermeneutical-critical framework, while safeguarding possible connections with other practical-theological approaches. The intention is to avoid the criticism of a "narrow rationality."

The research aims to categorize, analyze, interpret, and evaluate the religious convictions, ideas, images, and feelings of the people. The inductive approach, starting from experience, is therefore followed by the deductive approach: developing theological concepts and making these operational, and testing them empirically. This research can thus contribute to the development of explanatory concepts and theories within theology as a whole.

So far a considerable number of studies has appeared, for instance: the study of H. J. M. Vossen (1985) about mourning; that of J. A. M. Siemerink (1987) about prayer in religious education; and that of M. van Knippenberg (1987) about death and religion. Several types of research are used: surveys, quasi-experimental designs, content analysis, and field research (van der Ven 1990, 148 [1993, 127-28]).

The strength of this model is in its attempt to make theological concepts operational, and in the empirical methodology, which confers a high academic status. Moreover, it seeks to link in an open manner quantitative and qualitative research, and the perspective of a spectator with that of a participant. Some studies raise the question whether they should not be viewed as empirical systematic-theological, and whether, in addition to providing academic information, they also result in a contribution toward the renewal of actions in terms of praxis 1 (Heitink 1991, 525ff.).

9.4.4 The Political-Critical Current

One of the currents may be defined by the term *political-critical*. As far as their theology is concerned, the representatives of this current move in the tracks of political theology, while they feel a kinship with the Frankfurt School in the area of the social sciences. G. Otto (7.5.1) was the first German theologian to emerge as a representative of this current when he described practical theology as "a critical theory of a religiously mediated praxis in society" (1970). B. Päschke (1971) is close to Otto in his thinking, and the study of G. Lämmermann (1981) follows the same pattern. The Catholic theologian N. Greimacher, from whom I earlier borrowed some theses, refers to practical theology as the "critical theory of the praxis of the church in society" (1974,

117). H. Steinkamp understands his "social pastorate" as "opting for the theology and praxis of liberation," inspired by Latin American liberation theology (1991, 9).

In the Netherlands I must mention not only the Protestant theologian K. Strijd (1978), but also the Catholic theologians R. van Kessel, H. Meeuws (1975), and B. Höfte (7.5.3). Van Kessel defines the task of practical theology as "designing a liberating praxis through a process of seeing (observation, experience, analysis), judging (evaluation according to established criteria), and acting (development and execution of projects), in a constant reciprocity according to a new relation of theory and praxis" (Höfte 1990, 116-17). Two themes are central: the knowing subject and the ideological and historical-practical impact of theories and practices.

Höfte deals in his study with the criticism of Latin American liberation theologians. This criticism against academic theologians is in essence "that in their 'ideals' and theories they do not adequately take into account the balance of power and the way in which people are dependent in modern society" (1990, 115). This demands a critical approach to ideology and a praxis of raising the awareness for the need of solidarity. The emancipatory interest allots a central place to the poor as the subject of theology, thus doing away with a pure, academic practice of the discipline. In the United States one finds this orientation toward liberation theology with, for instance, Rebecca Chopp (1986) and Daniel S. Schipani (1988).

This current also works with terms like *hermeneutical* and *empirical,* but they are defined from a political-critical perspective, with primary attention to the "cui bono" question. The knowing subject must not remain detached from the object of the inquiry. This, of course, has consequences for research and research methods. Here one finds a preference for qualitative action research from the perspective of the participant (Höfte 1990, 349ff.). The aim is not just the increase of knowledge, but also a change in the oppressive situation of those with whom the researchers have established a close bond. The usual academic rules, which demand an objectivizing distance, are given up. There is a kinship with the hermeneutical current (Höfte 1990, 341), but the representatives of this current remain critical with regard to the empirical-analytical methodology (350), since human action cannot be reduced to statistics. The relationship between the researcher and those who are being researched should be a subject-subject relationship.

The strength of this current is its engagement and involvement with those whom the gospel addresses emphatically: the poor and the persecuted. This bias may, however, lead to one-sidedness, since the preference for one perspective excludes other points of view. Moreover, representatives of the empirical-analytical stream question whether this type of inquiry produces reliable information (Vossen 1988, 94ff.).

9.4.5 The Pastoral-Theological Current

The pastoral-theological current is in part a continuation of the old pastoral theology (chapter 6). It shares the orientation toward the praxis of the church, in particular from the vantage point of the professional activities of the pastor.

This current is strongly represented in the North American tradition. It is closely related to the concept of theology as "habitus" (7.2). Seward Hiltner (7.5.2) pioneered this approach to theology at the academic level. His point of departure — the role of the pastor — leads him to give psychology a central place in his thinking, as far as the social sciences are concerned. He relies, in particular, on the psychology of Carl R. Rogers, which, in correlation with the theology of Paul Tillich, results in a number of "theological dynamics." Theological concepts thus acquire an experiential character.

In the Netherlands the professionalization of the pastoral ministry has also been regarded as a central theme. Since the 1960s it has found expression in the movement for clinical pastoral education, which has its roots in the United States. The place this current has been able to occupy at the universities is due largely to the current emphasis on the professional training aspect of practical theology. This is closely related, as we saw, to the emergence of practical theology as a theory of action. The idea of "learning by doing," combined with the model of training and supervision, provides a unique approach to the theory-praxis relation, in the form of a learning model.

In the Netherlands this current is represented by, among others, H. Faber and E. van der Schoot (1962 [1965]), W. Zijlstra (1969), H. Andriessen (1975), and P. W. M. Claessens (1988). The movement also had an impact on Germany and Switzerland, where D. Stollberg (1969), R. Riess (1973), and supervisors H. C. Piper (1973) and H. van der Geest (1978) contributed to the development of the theoretical basis. While in the United States the movement is strongly pragmatic, the emphasis in Europe is mainly on theological reflection. Zijlstra's work is an impressive example of the latter.

Methodological contributions by this movement are found in the case studies, initiated by A. T. Boisen (7.5.2) with his "living human documents": the verbatim analysis, the sermon analysis, and the supervision model (Haarsma 1974). These are also used as research instruments, but the subjective character of the available material makes this less suitable for empirical research. More recently, efforts have been made to fit the undeniable learning effect of training courses into the framework of a theory of learning (Vossen 1991) and to study this empirically (van der Ven and Rooijakkers 1989).

The significance of this stream lies most of all in its contribution to competent and communicative action and in "doing" theology in an experience-oriented manner. Its limitation is in the clinical setting of a psychological model and in the lack of involvement with the needs of society (Höfte 1990, 78ff.). Moreover, professionalization is a product with side effects.

9.5 Conclusion

The theory-praxis relation may be viewed from a critical perspective as an important problem practical theology must address. There has been a development in the theological and action-theoretical reflection on this relation. A bipolar approach safeguards against biases and provides the opportunity for a critical contribution from a theological angle.

The development of a theological theory of action may be seen as a central task in the shaping of a practical-theological theory. The paradigm of "communicative action in the service of the gospel" and the model of text interpretation provide it with an academic basis. The insights of Habermas and, in particular, Ricoeur prove to be of great value. A further elaboration must follow in the next few chapters, from, respectively, a hermeneutical, a strategic, and an empirical perspective.

Several distinct currents of thought have emerged with respect to the formulation of an adequate theory. But this does not necessarily prevent an integrative approach. One finds rather, at least in the Dutch context, that the three most prominent streams challenge each other, criticize each other, and strengthen each other, resulting in a fruitful interaction.

CHAPTER 10

The Hermeneutical Perspective

I concluded in the previous chapter that a practical-theological theory of action must be approached from three different angles: as a hermeneutical theory of action, as a strategic theory of action, and as an empirical theory of action. These perspectives are closely related and must therefore always be considered in their correlation to each other. I deal first with the hermeneutical perspective, and take up the thread from 7.4, where I pointed to the importance of the hermeneutical path for practical theology.

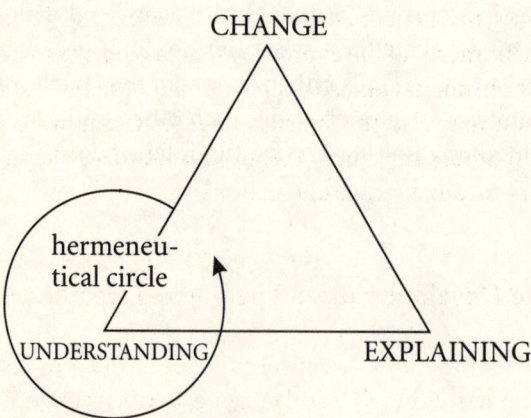

Figure 13: The hermeneutical perspective

The hermeneutical perspective links the "who does what" primarily with the "why" and the "about what." As a result, intention and motivation, which are the basis of an action, become apparent. Before one understands an action, one must grasp what motivates people and why they do what they do in this particular way. This allows one to move from *understanding* to *explanation,* and then to *change* — the two other perspectives we must deal with.

My first concern in this chapter is to get a better idea of the development and the significance of hermeneutics in the human sciences and the social sciences. For that reason I sketch this development from the point of view of theology (10.1), philosophy (10.2), and the social sciences (10.3). Building on the unity of understanding and explanation, I continue in a fourth section (10.4) with some additional comments on the basis of structuralism. This provides the groundwork for a hermeneutical approach to the main problems of practical theology (10.5), with emphasis on the *hermeneutical circle of understanding.*

What is hermeneutics? The Greek word *hermeneuein* has several meanings. It means "to say," in the sense of "to express" or "to announce"; but also: "to translate" in the sense of "to interpret" (R. E. Palmer 1969, 12ff.). The concept of hermeneutics has by now a history of several centuries behind it. Today hermeneutics means simply *the theory of interpretation.* Hermeneutics has a twofold task. It studies the basic principles of understanding and formulates the rules for actual interpretation. Ricoeur gives the following working definition: "Hermeneutics is the theory of what must be done in relationship to the interpretation of texts" (1991, 21).

More recently, hermeneutics has expanded to include the interpretation of nontextual phenomena, of life expressions, such as spoken words, gestures, and action, and of historical and social phenomena (de Boer et al. 1988, 11). This interpretation may also involve meanings that cannot be traced to the consciousness of authors or actors. This is referred to as "depth" hermeneutics, which occurs through structural analysis.

10.1 The Development of Theological Hermeneutics

One could argue that the hermeneutical problem is the most burning theological issue of modern times. A number of post-Reformation developments have had a major impact on the way in which we now read the Scriptures. We are all "post-Enlightenment people" (Runia 1992, 35).

The term *hermeneutics* had originally to do with the interpretation of texts. Its first appearance in a theological context dates from 1654, in the title of a book written by J. C. Dannhauer about the "hermeneutica sacra" (R. E. Palmer 1969, 34). Hermeneutics has traditionally been understood as "the science of the exegesis of Scripture" (Kuyper 1909, 3:90). It became necessary to establish such principles for exegesis when the Bible was no longer viewed as a timeless product of "mechanical inspiration," but as a collection of historical documents that demanded explanation. The language that had been transmitted no longer spoke for itself. Since explanation could not be a matter of arbitrariness, rules had to be established that would help us to understand the text. The insight gradually emerged that God's Word had come to us in human language. This resulted, as a fruit of the Enlightenment, in the development of the historical-critical method.

This philological tradition received — once again — a first extension through the work of Friedrich Schleiermacher, who distinguished between hermeneutics as a "theory of interpretation" and as a "theory for understanding." In a series of lectures in 1819 he stated programmatically that this latter aspect required a "general hermeneutics" (R. E. Palmer 1969, 84). This focused attention not solely on the text but also on the author. To arrive at a good interpretation it is necessary to reexperience the process that took place in the author, by totally immersing oneself in the text. Through this process of empathy the listener becomes a contemporary of the author, and thereby a "good listener" — a constitutive element in the interpretation of the text. In addition to the grammatical moment, the psychological moment receives its own meaning. This gives a new dimension to the hermeneutical circle of understanding. Through the medium of language, both the writer and the listener are able to participate in the subject that is discussed, along the path of "discourse." This does indeed presuppose that one can, through this empathy with the author, bridge the distance between author and reader. As we shall see, this line plays a major role in the development of philosophical hermeneutics.

One sees later currents of thoughts develop in biblical hermeneutics (our point of departure in this section) in which the attention shifts from the text to the author, then to the editor, and finally, through the *Wirkungsgeschichte* (the history of its impact) to the reader of a text. This is followed by the existential interpretation (Bultmann) and, in France and Italy, by structural analysis.

The latter approach stands more or less on its own. Structural analysis presupposes that each linguistic expression manifests a certain structure. The term *structure* refers to the interdependent laws of a language system. The word *text* is akin to the word *textile*, a fabric with a large number of threads in different colors. Readers will not understand the document if they look only at the threads. One cannot understand a part when it is detached from the whole (den Heyer 1979, 95). The structure, a re-creation of the interpreter, now receives all attention. Understanding the external structure leads to perceiving the deeper structure of a text. The result is an objectified analysis of texts, which, according to some, does not harmonize with the hermeneutical principle of empathy.

The concept of hermeneutics has recently been further broadened from exegesis to theology as a whole. For instance, Schillebeeckx maintains that faith in divine revelation always starts from our world, since "there are historical mediations" (1989, 57 [1990, 39]). "The mediation of revelation varies, depending on place, society and period, but it nevertheless comes within the interpretation of faith which is presented." In the transmission of faith we must build a bridge between the faith tradition of the past and our Christian experience in a new situation. This requires a reciprocal critical relation between tradition and experience, thus allowing that "present-day society and culture comes within the understanding of revelation" (59 [40]). Schillebeeckx further defines this by relating the understanding of faith in the context of the past to the understanding of faith in the context of the present. "The identity of meaning can only be found in the fluctuating 'middle field,' in a swinging to and fro between tradition and situation, and thus at the level of the corresponding relation between the original *message* (tradition, which also includes the situation of the time) and the situation, then and now, which is different each time" (60 [41]). This places hermeneutics also on the agenda of systematic theology and throws light on the unique questions practical theology must address.

In this approach one also hears the echo from philosophy and the social sciences. Considering the important role these play in the theory of interpretation, I must first elaborate this point.

10.2 The Development of Philosophical Hermeneutics

In Schleiermacher one discerns how the hermeneutical spark flies from theology to philosophy. One can extend this line, via Dilthey, Husserl, Heidegger, and Jaspers, to the hermeneutical theory of Gadamer. Their thinking is critical, since they proceed on the basis of a "subject-subject" relationship, in contrast to the "subject-object" scheme in the epistemological process. One can see a further broadening of scope in more recent hermeneutics. It develops into a theory of "understanding the manner in which people, within a given tradition, give meaning to their own private existence." Pannenberg speaks in this connection of hermeneutics as "a methodology for understanding meaning" (1973, 157ff. [1976, 156ff.]).

10.2.1 The Philosophical-Hermeneutical Tradition

Wilhelm Dilthey (1833-1911), a student and also the biographer of Schleiermacher and one of the great philosophers of the nineteenth century, regarded hermeneutics as a core discipline that could serve as a general foundation for the entire domain of the humanities and the social sciences. All these disciplines confront linguistic, historical, and anthropological problems, which may be objectified through established principles. This would do justice to humanity as a "historical" being and make hermeneutics the theory of the historical consciousness.

His hermeneutical formula rests on the concepts of "experience," "expression," and "understanding" (*Verstehen*; R. E. Palmer 1969, 107ff.). This distills from these various elements, within a specific context, a coherent meaning. Dilthey described "understanding" as something that happens from the inside out. The concept of "understanding" broadens the subjective empathy into an intersubjective accessibility of culture (Korthals 1989, 92).

As with literary texts, in interpreting cultural expressions understanding the components is essential for an understanding of the whole, and vice versa. The hermeneutical circle, which is related to this, assures interaction between the parts and the whole. In the same way one may approach a work of art, for example, a painting. The work is part of a wider oeuvre, belonging to a particular style or school. One cannot understand the isolated work of art if one has no knowledge of the wider context.

These insights, which stem mostly from Dilthey's later works, constitute an addition to a psychological empathy. This addition has exerted a major influence on the further development of hermeneutical philosophy, its related psychological orientation, and — more in general — on the quest for "understanding" *(Verstehen)* in the social sciences. Van Nierop maintains that Dilthey's views still have validity and continue to be of importance for the current discussion (de Boer et al. 1988, 50).

The philosopher Edmund Husserl, a somewhat later (1859-1938) contemporary of Dilthey, expanded these ideas in a phenomenological direction. Husserl referred to everything we observe through our consciousness — whether through seeing, imagining, thinking, evaluating — as a "phenomenon." The study of this consciousness thus acquired the name "phenomenology" (Störig 1959, 2:273). It wanted to observe the essence of things and to see their true meaning. That people understand each other is due to the fact that they all want to assign meanings that transcend the phenomena and are mutually exchangeable. Husserl explained this in the classical tradition: human thinking has access to "ideas" or eternal truths.

An example may clarify this phenomenological approach. Duijker (Duijker and Dudink 1970, 49) uses the example of the wheel. "We know what a wheel is. It has various characteristics. Every wheel has a color, but that is not essential. Wheels may have all sorts of colors, but they remain wheels. One could even think of wheels of glass and debate whether such wheels would have a color. Another characteristic of a wheel is that it is round. But, on second thought, is that always true? . . . We cannot exclude the possibility that there might exist, somewhere, octagonal, hexagonal, or even square wheels. This would result in a very bumpy ride, but we cannot say that it is absolutely impossible. The form appears to be more important than the color, but it does not seem to be truly essential. One other aspect, however, does seem to be imperative: a wheel must have the ability to turn around an axle. The axle does not necessarily have to be in the center, but it must be there. A checker piece is not a wheel, for it does not turn around an axle. Reasoning along these lines we find something that is essential, something that belongs to the essence of a wheel." On this basis one may say: "If somewhere in the universe, in the past, present, or future, there were, are, or will be living beings who use wheels, we can be sure that these wheels have at the very least the characteristic that they turn around an axle."

The line of hermeneutical philosophy is extended to Martin Heidegger (1889-1976), who in his work *Sein und Zeit* (1927 [*Being and Time,* 1962], dedicated to Husserl) linked elements from Dilthey and Husserl, as he developed a hermeneutical phenomenology (R. E. Palmer 1969, 125). Heidegger's ontological interest led him to begin with human *Dasein* (existence), in order to find access to "being," for what is can ask itself questions about its own being. This requires an existential-ontological analysis of Dasein. Dasein is "being in the world." It is having been "thrown" into the world, without having asked for it. It implies a state of anxiety, of "concern." Fear is a fundamental experience, for the human Dasein is, in its deepest essence, a "sein zum Tode" (being toward death). This confrontation with one's own mortality creates the urgency of the Dasein. This view of death reveals the aspect of temporality as the basis and limitation of human existence (Störig 1985, 2:297ff.). This leads to a hermeneutical *Vorverständnis* (preliminary understanding) that makes life accessible to an existential interpretation. Thus a new phase in philosophical hermeneutics has arrived.

Finally, I should also mention Karl Jaspers (1883-1969), a philosopher who began his career as a psychologist. He gave his own emphasis to the perspective of meaning by linking existence with transcendence. Although he believed that transcendence implies total hiddenness *(theologia negativa)*, it nonetheless makes reality transparent. Things become *chiffres* (secret codes), symbols of transcendence. Enlightenment is born in the depth of communication, as our existence is clarified. The categories of freedom, community, and history are central (Störig 1985, 2:289). This leads to an open, accessible, and somewhat mystical approach to life that is essential for the mode of understanding intended by the hermeneutical tradition.

Heidegger's view of human existence, in particular his concepts of *Sorge* (care) and *Fürsorge* (assistance), has its impact, for instance, on the theology of the *Seelsorge* (care of souls; humans as shepherds of being); cf. W. Jentsch (1965, 12ff.).

Jaspers has been praised by those who want a more spiritual, more experiential approach to practical theology. I refer to H. Jonker (1983, 91ff.), who pleads for an existential orthognosis (250ff.).

10.2.2 The Hermeneutics of Hans-Georg Gadamer

I had to take a few intermediary steps before arriving at Hans-Georg Gadamer and his influential book *Wahrheit und Methode: Grundzüge einer philosophischen Hermeneutik* (1960 [*Truth and Method*, 1975]). In this book one can detect the influence of Dilthey, Husserl, and Heidegger. Gadamer has elevated hermeneutics to a universal principle. He uses two concepts that modern science often looks down on, but that he regards positively: the hermeneutical circle and prejudice (Gadamer 1960, 250ff. [1975, 235ff.]; de Wit 1991, 77ff.).

In our attempts to understand texts or reality we all operate with our own biases. Understanding is always conditioned by the context of the one who explains. This elevates historicity to a hermeneutical principle. Objective historical knowledge does not exist. A recognition of this preliminary judgment does justice to the hermeneutical problem. But our prejudging of the situation raises questions that help us to better understand a text from the past. This anticipation of its meaning, which guides us in our acquisition of knowledge, opens up the meaning of a text to us. It is the task of hermeneutics to clarify the conditions that facilitate such understanding.

Gadamer is primarily interested in the understanding of texts. The reader stands at a great distance from, for example, the text of the Bible. How can this text be brought nearer? Influenced as he was by Romanticism, Schleiermacher wanted to become a contemporary of the author through a process of empathy. Gadamer, however, views the distance as positive. It helps us to discover the historical nature of our biases. Past and present are linked by the *Wirkungsgeschichte* (history of impact, or effective-history) of the past (Gadamer 1960, 284ff. [1975, 267ff.]). The historical consciousness itself is also under the influence of this *Wirkungsgeschichte*.

Our situation regarding tradition is hermeneutically determined by our own horizon of understanding, as the perspective from which we see things. This horizon, says Gadamer, is something into which we move and that moves with us (288 [271]). We must move from our own position if we want to place ourselves in someone else's situation. Making the tension between past and present explicit may lead to a "fusion of these horizons" (289 [273]). The particular and the unique message of the text may now be heard (de Wit 1991, 80). Genuine understanding takes place when the historical horizon is fused with our own horizon of understanding. Present and past are in a relationship of dialogue as a real "I-Thou" relationship. In the discovery of the original questions to which the text intended to respond all depends on whether the right questions are asked. The hermeneutical experience makes us see the world in a different light. This experience is embedded in language. Hermeneutics involves creating conditions that make understanding possible.

Gadamer's theory gives an added dimension to the hermeneutical discussion and adduces a new element to the hermeneutical circle through his emphasis on bias and our personal horizon of understanding. But some critics, though appreciative of Gadamer's theory of interpretation, would like to balance this with some historical-critical research to avoid interpretations that are too subjective and arbitrary (Dingemans 1991, 76).

Gadamer's hermeneutical theory has had a strong impact, in particular on Protestant practical theology with its tradition of Scripture and dogmatics. Though working on the basis of a broader praxis concept, David Tracy's (7.5.2) correlative model has been significantly influenced by Gadamer. I detect the same influence with Don S. Browning (1983, 38ff.). The theory has shown its importance for an understanding of the didactic process in catechesis (cf. Kuiper 1977, 264ff.), and no less for homiletics (Dingemans 1991, 74ff.).

10.2.3 Recent Developments

As already indicated, the work of Jürgen Habermas (8.4) and Paul Ricoeur (8.5) offer new developments. Habermas criticizes Gadamer because of the latter's lack of attention for ideological moments and related power structures (Keulartz 1992, 233). Nonetheless, together with that of Heidegger, Dilthey, and Husserl, Gadamer's work has exerted an undeniable influence on the theory of communicative action (Habermas 1981, 1:158 [1984, 1:107]). Habermas also sees interpretation as a process of dialogue; the point of view of the other is related to one's own point of view, and together they are related to the matter under discussion. Habermas's work may therefore be characterized as a critical hermeneutic, says Widdershoven, who provides an extensive survey of the debate between Gadamer and Habermas, also known as the debate between hermeneutical and ideological criticism (de Boer et al. 1988, 155). Habermas pleads for a relevant and well-founded methodology, which is able to criticize what happens in society. This is found in the theory of communicative action, as described earlier (8.4.2), which critically examines the validity of claims. Habermas recognizes the limitations of an interpretive approach and wants to supplement this with a critical perspective and research of the social sciences. For that reason he speaks of a hermeneutical circle between philosophical and empirical theory (Widdershoven in de Boer et al. 1988, 165).

This, finally, leads us to the work of Paul Ricoeur, who defines his philosophy as a hermeneutical phenomenology. Ricoeur begins by stating that texts are forms of language usage. Each expression through language aims at providing meaning. But a text always presents a discontinuity between author and reader. The gap between the two, for which he uses the term *distanciation,* is a precondition for understanding. The important thing is that readers immerse themselves in the world that is expressed in the text, and apply this to their own lives. The reading process includes internalization and analysis, and this creates a bridge between practitioners of hermeneutics and structuralists. The aim of this dialectic process is to help readers to understand themselves better, as they move from an understanding of the text to self-understanding. His philosophy also contains a critical perspective, for suspicion is an important element in arriving at a proper understanding. Since humans tend to have a misguided image of themselves, they must — if they want to attain to true knowledge of themselves — distance themselves from this image by opening themselves up to texts (M. van Buuren, in Ricoeur 1991, 14).

This brings us to the point where I introduced the work of Ricoeur as the basis for a practical-theological theory of action (9.2), since it bridges the gap between interpretive and empirical research in the synthesis of understanding and explanation. The structure of the text becomes the model for the structure of action, thus allowing for the hermeneutical perspective to be linked with the strategic and the empirical perspectives. In this way, hermeneutics creates a link between philosophy and the social sciences, which from their inception have known a hermeneutical tradition, as we shall see in the next section.

10.3 The Hermeneutical Tradition in the Social Sciences

The hermeneutical tradition in the social sciences also goes back to Dilthey and Husserl. Among the classical sociologists Max Weber (3.3) belongs to this *verstehende* (understanding) tradition.

The debate between the scientific method of the humanities and that of the natural sciences forms the backdrop for this section. They both have exerted their influence over the *tertium* of the social sciences. The two methods seem to exclude each other, but that was certainly not the case for the universal scholar — philosopher, theologian, physicist, and mathematician — Blaise Pascal (1623-1662), who had no difficulty in distinguishing between the god of the philosophers and the God of Israel (de Boer 1989, 12ff.). He also made the methical distinction between the rational mind-set of the natural scientist and the emotional approach of the heart. One meets these in the discussions of the philosophy of science as two roads toward knowledge. The path of the natural sciences is characterized by reason and explanation, that of the humanities by imagination and *verstehen* (understanding).

J. H. van den Berg illustrates the difference with an example: "Those who explain the rainbow on the basis of wave lengths and density do not want to hear a word about the landscape in which the rainbow glows. For those who are willing to listen to this will sooner or later be led into a world that once upon a time resisted the development of the natural sciences and that, in a struggle of centuries, has gained the upper hand" (1973, 47). Van den Berg believes that the struggle is over. The natural sciences also have their shadow sides. While the representatives of the humanities within the social sciences recognize the rightful place of the natural sciences, the reverse is usually not true.

There are many links between the two approaches of reality and there are mixed forms; the current consensus is that we are certainly not dealing with an absolute separation (Swanborn 1987, 341ff.). The most important hermeneutical or interpretive currents of thought, which are also of importance for practical-theological research, are symbolic interactionism, with ethnomethodology as a variant, and phenomenology.

10.3.1 Symbolic Interactionism

The term *symbolic interactionism* was introduced in 1939 by Herbert Blumer. The theory has two accents, that of social interaction and that of providing meaning. The word *symbolic* refers to the latter aspect (Wester 1987, 25). From the perspective of action, social reality is viewed as a body of social interactions. From the perspective of meaning, it is regarded as the product of the way in which people assign sense and meaning to that reality.

An example of interpretive research illustrates this: "In *Awareness of Dying* Glaser and Strauss study the interactions in hospitals between terminally ill patients and their relatives and the medical staff. The crucial element for the manner in which the interaction proceeds is what the interacting parties know, or pretend to know, about the seriousness of the state of the patient. Glaser and Strauss distinguish several contexts of awareness within which these interactions take place. Each of the contexts of awareness is further defined (closed awareness, awareness based on a premonition, open awareness, and awareness based on mutual pretense), and the question is posed what consequences these have for the actions of the interacting persons and what possibilities exist for changing the context of awareness" (Wester 1987, 31).

The insights that form the basis of symbolic interactionism stem from philosophers and sociologists who worked in Chicago before World War II. George Herbert Mead (1863-1931), often seen as the father of interactionism, occupies a central place (Zijderveld 1973, 73). Mead rejected the deterministic view of human behavior, as defended by the psychological school of behaviorism. But he was at the same time convinced that human behavior provides access to social and psychological reality. In line with Romanticism (Fichte), he attached great importance to the human self-consciousness, the I that can only realize itself through identification with the non-I. Mead found his point of departure in the communal life of individuals. Their interaction is determined by interpretation. For every action of the other is translated, and one "takes the role and attitude of the other." All communication is symbolic (77). Internalization of the attitude of the other brings "meaning," but also refection of "mind." Mead referred to these internalized attitudes, which are collectively absorbed, as "the generalized other," in contrast to some "particular attitudes," based on those with whom we identify in a special way (parents, friends, pastor, teacher, etc.). He called these people "significant others" (82). This makes life into a "role play." Mead differentiated between "the play" (the internalization of roles that are hardly coordinated) and "the game" (the interaction with specific others, the interaction being defined by the rules of a team). Within the human "self" a distinction can be made between the "I" (my own answer to the attitudes of others) and the "me" (what I have internalized, "society" in me). Even though Mead made little use of the concept of a system, he was certainly aware of the structure in which the parts are interdependent (Zijderveld 1973, 85). Habermas adopts the ideas of symbolically structured and normatively determined interaction in his theory of communicative action (1981, 2:11ff. [1987, 2:4ff.]).

The name of H. Garfinkel is associated with ethnomethodology, a particular form of this current of thought (Zijderveld 1973, 161). It places a strong emphasis on the situational context, the social order, within which we live. This characteristic is referred to by the term *indexicality*. Study is made of "the methods, used by the interacting people (*ethnos* = people) to clarify their (collectively) perceived reality, for themselves and for others" (Swanborn 1987, 347).

10.3.2 Phenomenology

As we saw, the aim of phenomenology is to clarify the essence of the phenomena. I commented on this in the discussion of Husserl (10.2.1). One finds this phenomenological approach in particular in psychology and psychiatry.

Under the influence of Heidegger and Buber, phenomenology links forces with an existential and relational view of humanity. In this connection, one may point to the anthropological school in psychiatry, with the Swiss psychiatrist and philosopher Ludwig Binswanger (1881-1966) as an important proponent. Over and against the deterministic view of humanity in Freudian psychoanalysis, Binswanger proposes his "Daseinsanalytische" (existence-analytical) method, which searches for reasons for any irregular development as the possible result of tensions in human existence, which should therefore be understood in terms of problems in finding meaning rather than in terms of illness. This allotment of the central place to the perspective of meaning also characterizes the work of the Viennese psychiatrist Viktor E. Frankl (1979).

Binswanger's idea of the "loving encounter" constitutes an inspiring motif in the prominent Utrecht existential-phenomenological school of J. H. Buytendijk. In retrospect, the fascinating possibilities as well as the historical limitations of his approach are seen clearest — after the second wave of feminism — in his well-known study of "the woman" (1958). What had been seen as the essential female element, in contrast to the essence of masculinity, was now explained on the basis of culture and roles.

Buytendijk had many disciples. I mention in this connection H. C. Rümke and his study of religious development — one of the few Protestant contributions to the psychology of religion (1939). Like Jaspers, Rümke based his theory on the distinction between understanding and explanation, not because he wanted to limit the sphere of explanation, but rather in an attempt to open up those aspects that are not accessible to explanation (the subjective elements of life) for methodical research (van Belzen 1991, 104).

Buytendijk has influenced Catholic psychologists of religion like H. Fortmann and H. C. I. Andriessen, who, in turn, have exerted a strong influence on the development of the psychology of religion and pastoral psychology in the Netherlands.

One finds a clear kinship with Buytendijk's thinking at the Free University in the anthropological school of L. van der Horst and A. L. Janse de Jonge, and with H. R. Wijngaarden (van den Berg 1973, 51ff.). Wijngaarden (1950) interprets adulthood as self-acceptance, acceptance of others (community, acceptance of the other [love]), and acceptance of the meaning of life.

The popular author J. H. van den Berg is, no doubt, with his original metabletic studies, the best-known Dutch representative of the phenomenological stream. His book about the psychology of sickness (1952 [12th ed. 1967]) remains required reading for the medical and pastoral profession and provides an interesting example of his approach. In the encounter with a patient, each separate moment is thematized and interpreted.

It remains a difficult question where to place psychoanalysis in the field of tension between the natural sciences and the humanities. Freud wanted to reduce psychological functions to physical phenomena, but van Strien is correct in his observation that he attempted in his analysis to reconstruct the life story of people (1986, 75). It is therefore hardly surprising that some regard his psychoanalysis as a hermeneutical method, more specifically as "depth-hermeneutics."

10.4 Structuralist Approaches

In more recent hermeneutics, the contrast between understanding *(verstehen)* and explanation has been greatly relativized. Ricoeur speaks of a dialectic relation between structural analysis and internalization (10.2.3). For that reason in this chapter I also pay attention to structuralist approaches, which may be regarded as complementary in the movement from understanding to explanation.

Structuralism plays a role in many disciplines: in linguistics (de Saussure), in philosophy (Foucault), in psychoanalysis (Lacan), in sociology and cultural anthropology (Lévi-Strauss), and also in the exegesis and hermeneutics of the Bible (den Heyer 1978). There is a cross-fertilization between the various disciplines. These theories do not assign any scientific value to life experience, which would lead astray. Structuralist hermeneutics seeks its point of departure in the natural sciences when dealing with the relation between these and the human sciences.

Michel Foucault regards the "humanism," which appears in many hermeneutical theories, as a totally opaque ideology. The subject has been decentralized! Humanity and human consciousness can no longer be taken as the point of departure. The self, Foucault believes, is nothing more than an element of a text within a language system. Foucault's theory is very critical of developments in society and leaves no doubt that structuralism operates with a hermeneutics that differs fundamentally from the kind of hermeneutics I discussed above.

The philosopher H. Achterhuis (1980, 190ff.) pursues the consequences of Foucault's work with regard to the interpretation of developments in society. He observes how Foucault detected a significant epistemological change, which occurred around 1900. A new type of knowledge emerged in the areas of, for instance, psychiatry, medicine, linguistics, and labor (196). People began to see the world with different eyes than before. In this new dimension our knowledge and actions are more or less prestructured. This new dimension of our knowledge helps to explain the origin of the police, the hospital, educational institutions, psychiatric institutions, community care, prisons, and the human sciences (197). Much of what today is presented as new and humane is not so new. In his book about prisons, Foucault describes society as a "system of dungeons," which serves as a model for other regulative institutions, for example, psychiatric hospitals. Due in part to the humanities, life and society have become highly predictable. An objectivizing structural analysis is the only means to trace the various determinants.

One finds a totally different approach with René Girard, a literary scholar and philosopher, who makes fascinating discoveries in the texts of novelists. Girard points to the decisive meaning of the phenomenon of imitation or "mimesis." The new element is, in particular — and this offers a transition to the language of (cultural) anthropology — that imitation also extends to our desires. We follow the desire of others in our own desire of things. Thus we make others our model, and this model becomes both obstacle and rival (Kaptein and Tijmes 1986). Since we desire through others, there is always the danger that violence will erupt. The other becomes, in the metaphor of Leviticus 16:20ff., the scapegoat (Girard 1986). Girard shows how widespread and entrenched the scapegoat motif is in our culture. This then becomes a hermeneutical key for the analysis of social relationships.

A telling illustration is "the black sheep of the family" that draws all aggression to itself, thereby creating a deep bond among the other family members. "Often the black sheep accepts the role it has been assigned. When that happens, the scapegoat motif is most effective: there is full unanimity, even the victim agrees with his or her guilt, and can feel a sense of belonging (albeit as the victim) with the community" (Lascaris 1987, 24). This mechanism explains many conflicts.

The structuralist approach also plays an important role in cultural anthropology and provides it with a distinct explanatory approach (Tennekes 1982, 33). This is in tension with a hermeneutical approach from the perspective of the participant, as we find, for instance, in the work of the American anthropologist Clifford Geertz (1973). But even here an attempt is made, for instance by the American practical theologian R. J. Schreiter (1985), to find a link between the inward-looking and outward-looking perspectives. He combines the perspective of the participant with a more structuralist approach (1985, 48).

10.5 A Practical-Theological Theory of Interpretation

A survey of the hermeneutical domain from the point of view of theology, philosophy, and the social sciences prepared the groundwork for a practical-theological theory of interpretation that does justice to the interpretation of texts and to a genuine understanding of social reality. The many viewpoints mentioned above enable one to develop variants within a theory of interpretation, depending on which philosopher or social scientist one wants to line up with. In this section I limit myself to the essentials.

The question of mediation between tradition and experience occupies the central place in a practical-theological theory of interpretation. How can the words of Scripture, which were beneficial for the people in the context of the past, be experienced in today's context as comforting and liberating and serve as a source of inspiration for action? How can they help the people to acquire knowledge of God and knowledge about themselves? How can this process of understanding through mediation bring meaning and change, and renewal of life?

I find a point of departure in pneumatology (10.5.1), before I briefly survey some models of interpretation (10.5.2). This route leads to the circular process that constitutes the core of a practical-theological theory of interpretation (10.5.3). It provides a hermeneutical circle, the movement from understanding to explanation. I conclude with some examples, using several patterns of interpretation (10.5.4).

10.5.1 The Pneumatological Basis

The central problem practical theology must face is the hermeneutical question about the way in which the divine reality and the human reality can be connected at the experiential level. This question focuses attention on the pneumatological basis of a theological theory of action. The fundamental choice to be made in this respect has its impact on the daily praxis in the church.

I am thinking, by way of example, of the candid confession of Eduard Thurneysen that his dialectic-theological vision made him shy and quiet in his pastoral contacts (1928, 199). This was related to his view of the work of the Holy Spirit, in which the mediation by human beings depends directly on God's gracious intervention, which comes to us only through the proclamation of the Word.

The reflection on the work of the Spirit, which is, in particular, inspired by the Johannine and Pauline writings, occupies a central place in recent theology, in which the problem of the mediation of tradition is among the key questions. The Spirit, as the firstfruit, is God's eschatological gift (Rom. 8:23) for the renewal of creation. The Spirit opens a new kind of existence in the here and now (2 Cor. 5:16), characterized by freedom (2 Cor. 3:17). As I said earlier, this is in total contrast with every form of patronizing or condescension. The church with all its members participates in the gifts of the Spirit, to be equipped for its mission in this world (1 Cor. 12:4ff.). The Spirit leads the church toward the truth (John 16:13) and convinces the world of sin, righteousness, and judgment (John 16:8, 11). These presuppositions are basic for the faith of the Christian church.

A correct view of the work of the Spirit has consequences for our actions. A core question in pneumatology concerns the relation between God's actions and human actions. Here the "theonome reciprocity" of A. A. van Ruler (5.2.2) offers possibilities for relating God's actions to our actions, as in the balanced approach of Jacob Firet (7.5.3), which I intend to follow: Divine action does not do away with human action but makes it possible. This may be seen as a pneumatological synergism (Veenhof 1987, 41ff.), in the positive sense of the word, for: "The Spirit himself testifies with our spirit that we are God's children" (Rom. 8:16). One could also refer to the charismata as "the talents the Spirit plays with" (Schoonenberg 1985, 47ff.). God's Spirit uses the gifts that are inherent in our humanness. This requires a willingness to open ourselves to the workings of the Spirit in an authentic spirituality, which enables us to proceed along the path of dis-possession, of being open toward the Other, who helps us truly to possess.

The work of the Spirit cannot be put in a framework of method, but it is possible to give room to the kind of communicative action that allows for a listening attitude, in mutual openness and receptivity. This then poses the question: What are the conditions that allow for this freedom of action, so that what cannot be done will nonetheless happen, when God's Spirit is willing to attach himself to it?

One finds other approaches to the work of the Spirit in the literature that point to differences in spirituality. Connecting the Spirit more closely with certain elements of the *ordo salutis* (rebirth, conversion) leads to a more dualistic concept with a greater emphasis on dependency. A sacramental view of the work of the Spirit results in an approach to the pastoral praxis that is primarily based on the ordination to the priesthood and a sacramental mediation of salvation. A charismatic approach usually leads to an enthusiastic, active praxis, with more emphasis on witness than on reflection.

It is therefore of great importance in any analysis to determine on which pneumatological concept one will base the hermeneutical work.

10.5.2 Theological Models

In reflecting on the work of the Spirit and on the relation between divine salvation and earthly reality, one must distinguish among a number of different hermeneutical-theological models. These models can, I believe, be put along a continuum, from an infinite distinction between the reality of God and humanity on the one hand, to total identification of the two on the other hand.

- The first model is that of diastasis, the presupposition of dialectic theology (5.2.1). This excludes natural knowledge of God and natural knowledge of ourselves. The distance between God and humanity can be bridged only by God's sovereign Word, which creates a horizon of understanding for itself. The social sciences are restricted to an ancillary role, while there is no room for religious experience.
- I have myself referred to the second model as that of bipolarity. It builds on the point of departure that I described, and suggests, with Hendrikus Berkhof (5.3.2), that divine salvation and human reality, though in tension, can be so related that the one moment cannot fully come into its own without the other (Heitink 1977, 170ff.). This creates room for elements like encounter and experience. Greimacher (1974) applies this model to the theory-praxis relation in practical theology.
- The third model is that of correlation, with a close link between question and answer. Tillich (5.2.4) suggests that theology formulates the questions that are embedded in human existence, and provides the answer of God's self-revelation that is somehow present in all those questions. Along the lines of Heidegger, Rudolf Bultmann provides a variant in his existential interpretation of the gospel (10.1). Tracy (1983) has further broadened this in his "revised correlational method."
- The fourth model is to a large degree built on the identification of human experience and religious experience, either from an anthropological or from a historical perspective. In the first case I think of the interpretation of human experiences of, for instance, happiness and desire in terms of an experience of the divine, or of the interpretation of psychotherapy in terms of salvation and liberation. This has been referred to as the paradigm of *Fremdprophetie* (prophecy from a "strange" source; Mette and Steinkamp 1983, 168). One might see this as a clarification of our human existence through depth-hermeneutics. The Catholic tradition, which finds hints of the supernatural in human nature (the *analogia entis*), often moves along this hermeneutical track. Another path, from the historical perspective, is that of an identification of experiences of suffering and liberation with the experience of the divine. One finds this in a particular current within Latin American liberation theology, "the theology of the oppressed people of believers" (Höfte 1990, 244ff.).

Each of these models requires serious theological decisions and has consequences for praxis. Once again it is true that "les extrèmes se touchent" (the opposites meet), for both the dialectical model and that of liberation theology lead to a critical-hermeneutical theory.

10.5.3 Interpretation as a Circular Process

As I have surveyed the hermeneutical process, from the angle of philosophy as well as from that of the social sciences, I have observed that it is circular in nature. This section looks at the way in which this process occurs from a practical-theological point of view. Even though understanding is largely a matter of guesswork, one may find rules of interpretation that could be helpful in this respect.

The hermeneutical circle of understanding, making understandable, and arriving at understanding (7.4) involves a complicated process in which one must distinguish several interacting factors. One must first of all acknowledge the bias, or the prejudging, determined by historical, sociological, and historical factors. How people understand the words of Scripture and apply these in a concrete situation is in part determined by their historical context, by the *Wirkungsgeschichte* of traditions within the group to which they belong, and by their own personality, their own possibilities for understanding, and their personal history, with psychological factors that may either foster or hinder a religious understanding.

In addition, the factor of subjectivity also influences our understanding. A text or social phenomenon always allows for more than one interpretation. Our own understanding must be tested intersubjectively by comparing it with the understanding of others, since some interpretations make more sense than others.

I also mention the factor of symbolical interaction that enters into religious communication. This refers to the mediation of a symbolic reality, aimed at spiritual experience and at providing meaning. Cognitive, as well as emotional and esthetic, dimensions of the person play a role in this respect. The Christian faith gives a deeper dimension to the social reality, as this is interpreted in terms of creation, redemption, and the eschatological perspective of the kingdom of God.

Finally, there is the ideological-critical factor. Or perhaps I should emphasize that the Christian faith, in particular, is susceptible to ideological influences and has often, consciously or subconsciously, been enlisted in the service of institutions that exert their power in society. The question of "cui bono" adds a critical moment of suspicion (Ricoeur) to our understanding, thus preempting "naive" interpretations.

This allows us to expand the hermeneutical circle, to which I briefly referred above, with a few additional elements. The following elements may be distinguished in the process of understanding: prejudgment — observation/experience — interpretation/discourse — discovering meaning — action.

We observe — whether we read a text or "read" a nontextual element from a cultural or social context — with a certain bias. This observation leads to a (religious) experience, which results in a particular interpretation of a small segment of reality. In our discourse with others, what we have internalized becomes part of a larger whole, and when that happens we find out whether it can withstand the test of intersubjective criticism. This learning experience brings meaning, and we integrate the experience in a symbolic reservoir of norms and values. This brings us full circle, and a new element has thus been added to our own (pre-) understanding.

F. de Lange suggests that the apostle Paul is a good example of how the so-called hermeneutical circle works: "After having been smitten by Christ (Damascus!), he is faced with the challenge of understanding what has happened to him. He has encountered something or someone who lays a claim on him and demands his abiding attention; the Christ-experience is more important than anything else. But the productive and creative work of Paul the theologian is needed in order to know what (or whom) he has experienced and what this experience means. The distance between our understanding and the original event of this Christ-encounter must be bridged by a process of interpretation. We must enter this circle of understanding, if we want to speak meaningfully about the religious claim this event lays upon us, and eventually to conjugate or inflect this in our own private grammar (the 'application'). . . . In Paul we also see how the interpretation of the Christ-event not only touches his ability to read and understand but also affects his total existence, and that the kerygma and our daily life help to explain each other and are inseparable from the unique state of being 'in Christ.' Theological hermeneutics is clearly not just a matter of exegesis, but also, at least, a matter of ethics" (1993, 43-44).

This identification of a number of distinct elements of the hermeneutical circle of understanding offers some rules for interpretation. It also provides the possibility to act in harmony with this in the theory-praxis relation. This may offer the basis for a more thorough and elaborate theory of the hermeneutical circle with regard to communicative action in proclamation, catechesis, and pastoral work. It also touches on the empirical perspective. This hermeneutical path that looks from within, which in itself already has an empirical character and allows for interpretive social scientific research, can be tested through inquiries that look from without.

10.5.4 Patterns of Interpretation

The considerable number of lines drawn in this chapter indicate that there can be no question of just one practical-theological interpretation of reality. Once again the search for truth leads to plurality. Several times I have referred to practical theologians who take one element of what I just surveyed. Reading prominent practical-theological books about, for instance, homiletics, catechesis, and poimenics, one discovers from whom a given author has borrowed certain concepts and what connections that author makes.

Here one may also distinguish between patterns of interpretation, which on the basis of the current situation serve as a meaning-dispensing framework and provide access to a praxis of faith and action. Modern practical theology offers many examples. They function within a specific model as a theological concept that can be dissected into various elements. That I must content myself with some examples points to the fragmentary character of these hermeneutical patterns of interpretation, which probably also should receive further serious study.

I mention, first, the theme of the kingdom of God, which has strongly emerged since the 1950s. This concept fits with the historical consciousness in the period of rebuilding after Word War II. Trusting God's future, it places considerable emphasis on human responsibility, often referred to by the term *stewardship*. The eschatological character of the kingdom encourages the anticipation of God's work in a praxis of hope and liberation (Moltmann).

One can argue that the theological concept of "the coming of the kingdom," as worked out in Herman Ridderbos's exegetical study (1950 [1962]), has during several decades, by way of an interpretive framework, put its stamp on Reformed preaching and served as a motivation for action. D. J. Louw (1984) develops a pastoral-theological concept based on the eschatological motif of victory. Van der Ven provides ethical content to the "*basileia* symbol" developed by biblical theology, with the help of the categories of Habermas (1990, 85ff. [1993, 69ff.]).

The covenant offers another concept that also suggests patterns of interpretation. It creates room for emancipation, human freedom, and responsibility. This emphasis on the covenant and relational thinking has an important place in more recent theology. Berkhof's (5.3.2) dogmatics offers a prime example. Following Berkhof, I chose the covenant as my key concept in the pastoral theology I proposed (1977). Ethical categories can also help us in our reflection on the covenant concept. It became a guiding principle in many discussions about sexual relationships (van Gennep 1972).

The discussion about *die Sache Jesu* (the Jesus-event) points the church to the salvific mystery of the death and resurrection of Jesus Christ. The memory motif of Metz (1977 [1980]) gives expression to the tension between remembering and expecting. This idea is used in particular by those who want to link the gospel with elements of the critical theory. The memory motif may also be connected with the heart of the Eucharist, as Lammens suggests in his study of the anamnesis as the "commemorative aspect" of the celebration of the Lord's Supper (1968).

When one refers to the church as the body of Christ, the emphasis is on the unity of the community and on the complementarity of the charismata. Or in an open community it may express more particularly a missionary concern, through the motif of "Christ existing as his church" (Bonhoeffer; see 5.2.3 above), in line with the ecclesiological model of "the church for others" (Schippers 1989, 13ff.).

The exodus model, which connects the notion of "God's people en route" (Vatican II) with a praxis of liberation, led H. Faber to a comparison of the "father's house model" and the "exodus model" in pastoral theology (1974, 64ff.). As an emancipatory motif, the exodus model significantly influenced the theology of the 1960s and 1970s, especially in connection with political and social themes. People are challenged to participate in the exodus, not to look back to the fleshpots of Egypt!

But since then the cultural climate has changed dramatically. The exodus leads to the desert. Inspired by the trends of the 1980s, characterized by a continuing secularization and a profound crisis of faith, Dingemans (1991, 92) suggests a new model: that of the exile. It is based on the reality of the exile, the hiddenness of God, and — like the exodus model — links the Christian faith with Israel.

J. Bodisco Massink, therapist and pastor, gives an example to illustrate how this manner of interpretation may play a role in his psychotherapeutic praxis: "Someone goes through a process of change and tells me about his difficulties. I can then have a moment of introspection and say: 'Yes, what does change in essence mean? What is the biblical model of a process of change?' That is the exodus story. What does the exodus story teach me? It takes effort to detach oneself from the bondage of one's situation and to leave the fleshpots. The process of detachment is risky. But then there is the joy that one is on the way to the promised land!

After three days, however, there is no more water and there is the cry, 'Moses, what do we do now?'" (Berger and Vossen 1993, 61).

A significant measure of theological creativity is apparent in the development of such patterns of interpretation. In a sense each pattern comprises a hermeneutical circle, in which the Christian tradition and the modern attitude toward life interact. This enables people to give meaning to their situation and to be inspired in their actions. Such patterns are indispensable if one is to interpret the current situation in the light of Scripture, and to bridge the gap between the text and the reader. This "action of understanding" (Ricoeur) is therefore essential for the mediation of the Christian faith in the praxis of society. All contextual factors, which have come to light through the hermeneutical circle, must be taken into account. Thus one finds an answer to the question "Who does what and why?"

A hermeneutical reading of more recent theology, as developed here in a tentative way — in agreement with what has been said in previous theological chapters (5 and 7) — appears to offer a perspective for a further hermeneutical development of practical theology.

10.6 Conclusion

This chapter has explained the foundation of a hermeneutical theory and has offered suggestions how a practical-theological theory might build on this foundation. It is important to realize what choices one makes and to justify these from the perspective of the various disciplines — theology, philosophy, and the social sciences. In any discussion of hermeneutics the language factor, as well as culture and history, requires considerable attention.

This completes our discussion of one of three circles that together determine the structure of practical theology. Although in my view of practical theology the hermeneutical theory occupies the most important place, the other two play a complementary role in a fully developed, integrative theology.

CHAPTER 11

The Strategic Perspective

The rise of the social sciences is closely related to the rapid changes in society. The practitioners of these sciences want first of all to understand and explain these changes. But they also discovered that they would be able not only to predict future developments but also to steer them, through management and planning. This led to the development of the strategic perspective in the action theories.

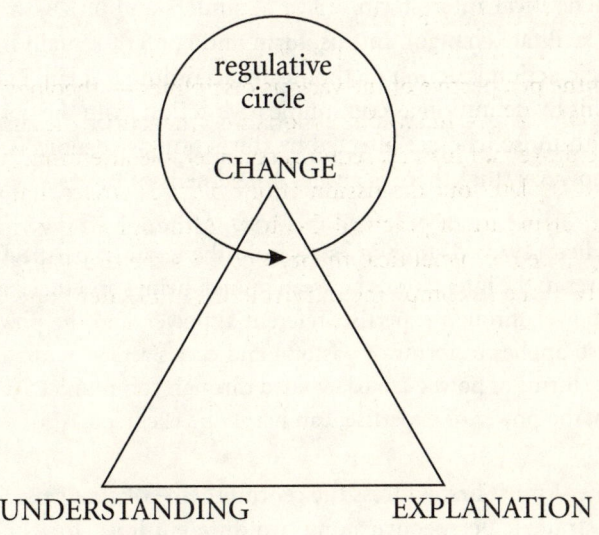

Figure 14: The strategic perspective

Practical theology as "the theory of the mediation of the Christian faith in the praxis of modern society" inevitably aims at change, through a process of management and steering. The strategic perspective links the "who does what" first of all with the "how" and the "for what purpose." This finds expression in one particular domain of life, the church, where people from their early years onward are guided and encouraged to assimilate the faith and make it the basis of life.

Calvin wrote in his *Institutes* (IV.1.4ff.) about God's work that "the church must be the mother for those who have God as their Father." The very term *mother* teaches that "there is no other way to enter into life unless this mother conceive us in her womb, give us birth, nourish us at her breast, and lastly, unless she keeps us under her care and guidance." For that reason "our weakness does not allow us to be dismissed from her school until we have been pupils all our lives. We see how God, who could in a moment perfect his own, nevertheless desires them to grow up into manhood solely under the education of the church." These are no longer our words and our metaphors, but they are a beautiful expression of what we mean when we refer to the church as a "learning community" (Schippers 1977).

The Christian faith works from the presupposition that people can indeed be changed and that our society can be renewed from the eschatological perspective of God's kingdom. Practical theology, which as a normative discipline regards this area of mediation and change as its object, combines in itself a hermeneutical interest (to arrive at understanding) with a strategic interest (to facilitate change). In this, form and content remain inseparable.

Strategic action is acting methodically according to plan. Practical theology sees this by definition as communicative action from the perspective of the actor with those who are affected by the action as cosubjects. One must recognize, however, that there is always an element of power.

A. van Servellen (1983) distinguishes — from the feminist perspective — four forms of power in the interactions between human beings and social groups: formal power, power through expertise, referential power, and the power of sanction. This also applies to forms of pastoral and ecclesiastical action. Even when three of these forms of power can be avoided through communicative action, the second form, the power of expertise, can hardly be excluded.

In this chapter I must first address the central theme of change (11.1). Then I explore the strategic perspective along two different lines, focusing on guidance and change of individuals (11.2) and on change with regard to social constructs and institutions (11.3). The regulative cycle functions as the foundational pattern of strategic action (11.4). Finally, I deal with the strategic perspective with a view to practical theology through two interconnected theories: the communication theory and the systems theory (11.5).

11.1 The Possibility and Desirability of Change

"Change" seems to be one of the secular doctrines of modern society. There are believers and unbelievers when it comes to change. Based on the historical-interpretive part (part I), one may distinguish between two currents of thought that are both rooted in the natural sciences: the first in physics, and the second in biology. The first compares society with a *mechanism,* and the second with an *organism.*

The mechanistic model views society as a conglomerate of autonomous individuals. Adam Smith (1723-1790), a famous economist, maintained that self-interest, which needs to be regulated by prudence and a sense of justice, is the main motivation (Manenschijn 1979, 235ff.). This model leads to individualism. The organic model, however, regards the whole as more than a sum of its parts. "This does not see the interconnectedness of the whole as problematic, as in the mechanistic model, but rather the autonomy of individuals" (Laeyendecker and van Stegeren 1978, 10). This model, which seeks to maintain or restore the organism, demands a certain degree of collective force to keep individuals on the desired track. But the two viewpoints may to some extent be combined, when the human being is regarded not solely as the creator but also as the product of social circumstances. The different positions lead to another view of humanity and the world. The one emphasizes the inevitable nature of things, while the other is more inclined toward intervention. The one opts for the education of the individual, while the other has a preference for various kinds of social work.

The individual line as well as the social line allows for a degree of belief in change. On the one hand psychoanalysis lays great stress on the idea that human conduct is largely predetermined. Change requires an intense process of raising the awareness of people so that they may detect and conquer the things that are part of human nature. This model is the product of the more pessimistic European culture. On the other hand humanistic psychology, with the motivational theory of Maslow as an example (1970), manifests a strong belief in a human's possibility for change and to work toward self-realization. This growth and development should in no way be obstructed. This fits with the cultural climate of the United States.

There are also differences from a social point of view. Some see the development of society as evolutionary, often in optimistic terms of progress. Others, depending on their position and political preference, have more of an eye for sudden revolutionary changes, which demand a management of change (the conservative option), or the fostering of revolutionary processes (the progressive option). A difference in vision thus leads to differences in opinion with regard to the action strategy that should be adopted. One thing, however, is clear: thinking about change can never be neutral, but always has a normative component. Once again one sees the links between practical theology and ethics (Browning 1991, 96ff.).

How does a theological theory of action deal with change? According to Berkhof (1973, 188ff. [1979, 178ff.]), theological anthropology calls attention on the one hand to self-realization and to "being there" for others in "love and freedom," but on the other hand to the oppressing reality of "guilt and fate." This view, which from the outset links one in a relational way with one's fellow humans, manifests neither the pessimism of determinism nor the optimism of self-realization. People can change, but only along the path of conversion. The idea of conversion may conjure up negative associations with revivals and preaching of hell and damnation. This is no doubt rooted in the thought that this involves nothing less than a "rebirth," as a gift of the Spirit. But it is more biblical to think, in the context of daily life, in terms of a daily conversion. "It cannot be for nothing that the *summons* to conversion is heard over and over in Scripture, that change is *commanded,* and that humans are *called* out of a state of sin and death into a new life" (Firet 1968, 259 [1986, 200]). According to Firet, conversion is a "fundamental change in the functioning of the mind" (1968, 261 [not in the Eng. trans.]). This demands an existential encounter with the Word, and points to the necessity of connecting strategic with hermeneutical insights in one's work with people.

One finds this same duality in the Bible with regard to change and renewal. This sinful world is burdened by the endless repetition of sin and the pervasiveness of evil, but the kingdom of God points to the final victory over all evil and to the ushering in of a kingdom of peace, characterized by righteousness. This kingdom is already present in this world through the reconciliation in Jesus Christ. It lives through the promise which is founded on the "Jesus is Victor" motif, says Karl Barth (IV/3.1, 188-89 [165-66]). Conversion, therefore, has political and social consequences. But Barth also warns against the sin of procrastination, which is somewhere between unwillingness and inability and is therefore difficult to combat. The manner in which the church acts in society demands normative reflection, even when this leads to polarization (e.g., in the sensitive case of the stationing of cruise missiles in the Netherlands in the

1980s) rather than to consensus and corporate action. This provides meaning and direction to "communicative action in the service of the gospel." Methods of exerting influence and strategies for change are not without values, but must be judged on the basis of what has been said above.

11.2 Agogic Thinking about Change

Agology is the discipline that deals with the professional management of intentional changes. It employs the social sciences but is anchored in philosophy. It is therefore a normative science. Its goal of assisting people reflects an anthropological perspective.

W. F. van Stegeren (1982) offers a detailed proposal of an emancipatory andragology in the context of the dilemma of "control and emancipation" (identified by van Nijk). She defines emancipation as follows: "Emancipation is a learning process with two aims: the *self-realization* of human beings and the *equality* of and between human beings and groups" (15). These aims are closely related. She distinguishes five aspects in this concept of emancipation: An individual aspect (becoming aware of one's own social position and relationships of dependencies), a group aspect (the emancipation of groups), and a political aspect (structures in society and policy making). In addition, the definition has an agogic aspect (the learning process) and an action aspect (focused on both goals). Referring to Habermas's interest in emancipation and his emphasis on dialogue (cf. 8.4.2 above), she arrives at the following definition: "Emancipatory andragology is a discipline that, in its theoretical reflection and research, deals with and supports the emancipation of individuals and groups" (19). This is based on a number of normative presuppositions that point to a concrete utopia. She gives content to this idea by enlisting the concept of a society with a threefold basis of justice, participation, and sustainability, as suggested by the World Council of Churches.

Van Stegeren builds on the work of A. J. Nijk, who at the end of the 1960s exchanged theology for a chair in agology, and who, until his premature death in 1982, put his stamp on the development of this discipline in the Netherlands.

In the course of time, Nijk opted for the critical theory. For there are action orientations that are false and must be unmasked. He referred to these as "myths," one of them being the myth of self-fulfillment: "This is the story of a small elite at the beginning of the nineteenth century and of a broader — but still relatively small — elite in the second part of the twentieth century" (1978, 201). He regarded philosophy as a means of producing and unveiling myths. This led him to human discourse as the basic form of andragogic action (1978, 353). Andragology, he maintained, is involved with action not directly but indirectly, through the story. This positions him in a critical-hermeneutical tradition with a pragmatic dimension. Action and narrative are the core concepts. This is A. J. Baart's analysis of the work of Nijk, with whom he shows much kinship, as is apparent from his dissertation about "stories." With "discourse as the workshop where actions are repaired" (Baart 1986, 24), Nijk placed less emphasis on education but more on helping: the therapeutic dialogue that he used "in the framework of meaning and action that characterizes the personal history of the client" (24). The important thing is that the client begins to tell her or his stories and can broaden her or his narrative repertoire. Once again the question of meaning is central in this critical-hermeneutical narrative andragology. Nijk referred in this connection to the spiritual concept of "personal piety."

It is clear that practical theology and agology are very close, and Firet's proposal to make discourse also the methodological basis for practical theology is hardly surprising (1987, 37). He thinks not of therapeutic sessions but of a "normal" conversation, referring to Berkhof, who qualifies revelation as an encounter event. Thus humans become enthralled in a process of encounter and understanding. After all, the Christian tradition is a narrative tradition! Action as conversation has an external and an internal structure (Ricoeur). Firet points to the following distinguishing factors: the situation, intersubjectivity, propositional content (it is about something), and the polarity of convention and spontaneity. The conventional element refers to a type of conversation, for example, a conversation between friends, a conversation aimed at instruction, a pastoral conversation, a discussion about work. Spontaneity has to do with the creative opportunity for emotions, sudden ideas, and so on. Once again I touch on the hermeneutical perspective described in the previous chapter.

The kinship with Nijk is also apparent in the manner in which Firet defined agogics as early as 1968: "Agogy is the act of functioning, with objective realism, in pure receptivity, discernment, and creativity, of one person in relation to another for whose humanization the agogue bears responsibility, *in order that* the other may learn to function humanly in a similar way" (295 [1986, 230]). It is fascinating to follow Firet as he further develops this definition. He sees interpersonal equality, even in pedagogic situations, as a condition for agogic action (203 [156]). Education can never be more than giving voice, with all modesty, to a process of personalization (222 [171]), even if this voice sometimes has its own peculiar sound or is at times antiphonal. Even when people receive help — in a relationship that is often characterized by an asymmetry of the parties — this incongruence should never be at the expense of the equality of the persons involved in that relationship (211 [162]). Firet assigns a central place to "the human being as spirit" (236 [182]), that is: "the whole human being" in his or her spiritual dimensions, the perspective of meaning and life orientation. The dynamic relationship of receptivity (empathy) and discretion (tolerance for the other) excludes pressure and coercion. Rümke's fundamental rule of "maximal empathy without loss of objectivity" will always apply (212 [163]). The core of the matter is that people will come to the point where they will "believe independently."

These are the basic principles for pastoral work, which give color to the various methods employed. Reciprocity is essential. The deeper structure of the relationship, whether disturbed or not, vis-à-vis the "Story of the Living One" (Schillebeeckx), can be heard in the human story. The pastoral exchange between brothers and sisters in the congregation differs from psychotherapy in its reciprocity. Being "accepted into the friendship of Jesus" characterizes mutual relationships, where friendship is not restricted to those one accepts as one's equals and to the boundaries of the private sphere (Moltmann 1975, 251-52 [1977, 224-25]). Forms of learning ignore the gaps between generations (Ploeger 1990, 589), when the young teach the old and vice versa. That church members experience themselves as subjects (Hendriks 1990, 49) is the basic presupposition for processes of change, which receive form and content in the context of the congregation. The proclamation of the Word can appeal to dependence only in relation to partnership. Agogic rules may thus be formulated that enable one to measure the critical-hermeneutical character of one's actions. Theological and agological concepts interact in the blending of hermeneutical and critical moments.

11.3 Strategies of Social Change

The other domain is that of social change. Once again we encounter normative questions regarding our view of society, the way in which we formulate the problems, goals, and positions when we choose to intervene. I follow in essence the pluralistic approach of Laeyendecker and van Stegeren (1978).

11.3.1 Social Problems

In dealing with social problems Laeyendecker and van Stegeren depart in the first instance from the pragmatic definition of Horton and Leslie: "A social problem consists of circumstances that affect a significant number of people in a way that is deemed undesirable, and about which something might be done through collective social action" (1978, 52). Practical theology also deals with social problems, either within the context of the church or through the involvement of the church with the needs and problems that occur in the various social settings of which one is part.

The definition refers to (a) objective circumstances, (b) which may be evaluated subjectively, and (c) which may be subsequently changed. That is a rather complex and vague situation. Something must be done on all three fronts. The circumstances demand elucidation. In addition, people must become aware of the undesirable character of the circumstances. In between is the phase of providing information. Values and norms come into play in the subjective evaluation. Through it all one hears the skeptical question whether the specific need is real or just imagined (59).

One's position in this depends, once again, on one's view of society as a whole. Is society understood from the viewpoint of the individual or vice versa? In other words: Does one operate on the basis of the autonomy of the individual, who can independently exert influence on the development of social frameworks? Or on the basis of a systems concept, in which the individual is embedded in a broader whole of which she or he is a mere component? Or, finally, on the basis of the predetermination of the individual's behavior through social circumstances according to a pattern of stimulus and response? The last view is represented in the behavioral sociology of George C. Homans (a psychologist in Boston and a colleague of B. F. Skinner). He believes that institutions change when it is found that they no longer function adequately (Laeyendecker and van Stegeren 1978, 38). There also are positions that combine different views, such as Marxism (4.2), which regards the human being as both the producer and the product of society. The Frankfurt School emphasizes more strongly the awakening of the consciousness of the subjects of history (43).

11.3.2 The Theory of Peter L. Berger

I believe it is important at this point to mention the dialectical views of Peter L. Berger, a sociologist of religion. In *The Sacred Canopy* he distinguishes three moments in the dialectical process: externalization, objectivation, and internalization. Externalization is anchored in the anthropological design of humankind. One becomes a human being through interaction. To be a human being implies "to bring to the outside, to externalize," a creative process.

The things that result from one's actions subsequently begin to lead an independent existence. A process of objectivation occurs and the objective reality then exerts a certain coercion. That objective reality in turn determines one's human consciousness through various processes of internalization. As a result one begins, at least to some extent, to identify oneself with that reality. This dialectic process must be seen in its close interaction. It is an ongoing process of socialization, in which humans change and constantly face new tasks in new situations.

Berger argues that social reality must be viewed as the ordering of experience. He gives due weight to communication and meaning. To provide meaning is a form of legitimizing. People legitimize their actions by appealing to tradition, science, or religion. Such legitimizations exert influence when they are generally recognized. They then create a credibility structure. Religion, as a philosophy of life and a worldview, provides the highest form of legitimization. Influencing the meaning systems thus constitutes an important factor for social change. A significant example of this was the struggle against apartheid in South Africa.

The question how religious traditions continue to provide meaning in modern society is of central importance. Berger sees three ways of providing meaning in a pluralistic situation; he refers to these with the words *deductive, reductive,* and *inductive* (1979, 60ff.). The deductive option stresses the authority of religious traditions in confrontation with modernity. The convictions are predetermined by traditions, to be transmitted from generation to generation. The reductive option reinterprets traditions in terms of modern secularism. It loses the perspective of transcendence, and the religious tradition is reduced to ethics. The inductive path follows one's own experiences as the ground for religious confirmation. The emphasis is on the question, Which experience in the context of the past is at the basis of a religious tradition? It then shifts to the experience of people today, in their present context. Subsequently, each is related to the other: criticism of the present situation on the basis of tradition is combined with a critical reflection of tradition on the basis of the present situation. This is the hermeneutical path, first tested by Schleiermacher (101), which in my opinion requires a bipolar approach of the theory-praxis relationship (9.1.2; 10.5.2).

Berger's approach is relevant when one attempts to answer how practical theology can contribute to the processes of social change. For, apart from the emphasis on relations of power and production, the perspective of meaning is essential. It is the theological point of contact with regard to processes of influencing and learning. This brings us back to the formulation of a hermeneutical theory, discussed in the previous chapter. Change in freedom always demands a change in mentality, referred to by Paul as "the renewal of our mind" (the spiritual direction), needed to ascertain the will of God (Rom. 12:2). This may become the focus of strategic action.

I prefer the inductive option. One should remember, however, that empirical studies among pastors and teachers indicate that pastors generally emphasize the deductive path, while teachers tend to follow the inductive strategy, often in combination with the reductive path (van der Ven 1993, 142-43 [1996, 158ff.]).

11.3.3 Choosing a Strategy

The choice of an appropriate strategy is of great importance. According to Laeyendecker and van Stegeren there are microstrategies, aimed at individuals, their behavior and attitude, with the expectation that these may lead to changes in society in general (1978, 78); and macrostrategies, aimed at changing the social system (91). Here the systems approach, which allows one to get an idea of the way in which the components are interrelated, is of significance. In this macroapproach norms and values also play a role, often formulated in general terms, such as justice, solidarity, equality, and democracy (92). Laeyendecker and van Stegeren rightly believe that micro- and macrostrategies should complement each other. Macrostrategies have to do with political measures and legislation. In countries with a separation between church and state, the influence of theology and religion in this area can only be indirect. Their influence is usually restricted to the domain of microstrategies. Laeyendecker and van Stegeren deal with these strategies in a systematic way. They distinguish between rational-empirical strategies, normative reeducational strategies, and power strategies (143).

The use of rational-empirical strategies presupposes that people are prepared to change their behavior when they perceive the desirability of such change (144). Humans as rational beings are the kind of persons the Enlightenment envisaged. This strategy aims to disseminate information, to provide knowledge, and to win others for particular ideas through an exchange of arguments. It communicates through the media, billboards, and television. Lectures with discussion periods, panels, and forums offer extra possibilities, in addition to information in printed form.

In the 1960s and 1970s we saw, also in the churches, an extensive culture of newsletters and newspapers, based on the optimistic expectation that people would be activated and would be motivated toward change if they were to receive adequate information about social problems. The contrary was, however, often the case. An example is the relation between the church and the peace movement (van Alphen et al. 1982). Research indicates that many who were challenged to support the peace movement felt under threat and pressure. The motivational theory of Maslow offers some insight in this respect. People find it difficult to change as long as some fundamental needs, such as the need for security, are not met.

This approach proved to be one-sided, and had to be complemented with normative-reeducational strategies. Humans are social beings, who share opinions with others, in part under the influence of the culture in which they live. Convictions grow through a process of socializing and internalizing. Freud pointed to the significance of unconscious factors. Change, therefore, must take place in a process that allows for the actor-perspective of all involved.

At this point one has several options. K. Lewin has summarized this process of change in the formula "unfreezing-moving-freezing." Learning through experience, pioneered by Paolo Freire (1970) in Brazil in an attempt to connect literacy with consciousness, has found followers elsewhere. E. Lange refers to this as a "language school for freedom" (1980). I must also mention the theme-centered interaction of Ruth Cohn (1983) and the context of group and training activities (Miles 1959).

Third, there are power strategies. The power structures are amply acknowledged in the analysis of problems. Marxists refer to a division between the oppressors and the oppressed. But social reality, in particular in a democratic state, is far more complex. Weber defined power as the ability to impose one's will on others, even when they refuse to cooperate. Laeyendecker and van Stegeren think in terms of "coercion — compliance — stabilization and/or reaction" (1978, 163). Power strategies imply pressure on the established order and on authorities who want to maintain the status quo.

Power strategies always require an evaluation of the damage to relationships in comparison to what is gained by the action. Seeking publicity almost always causes scandal. That is never pleasant, but the *skandalon* character of the gospel (1 Cor. 1:23) makes this often inevitable (Leudesdorff 1976, 185ff.).

Mohandas Gandhi opted for peaceful methods, whereas Che Guevara chose guerrilla warfare. Peaceful methods may consist of demonstrations, a refusal to cooperate, or actual interventions (Laeyendecker and van Stegeren 1978, 165). Demonstrations, such as those against nuclear weapons in the 1980s in the Netherlands, do have an impact on politics. The church can give further support through a "prophetic warning" to the government, for or against certain measures. Action groups, for instance, to protect the environment, give publicity to harmful developments and exert influence by doing so. The Green Peace organization is feared throughout the world. Amnesty International relentlessly pursues governments. The movement against apartheid has had a great impact on the events in South Africa. Consumer boycotts of certain products can have a significant effect on the producers. Blockades have proved their effectiveness. Civil disobedience is at times the method to follow. One example of this is churches providing asylum to protect refugees against deportation.

These three types of strategies complement each other and presuppose each other. A Christian view of society inspires Christians to participate in particular actions. The church can choose to be involved or to stay aloof.

11.4 Basic Pattern: The Regulative Cycle

The two previous sections bring us to the question of the method *(methodos)* of effectuating change. I respond to this question, in the context of the strategic perspective of a practical-theological theory of action, by turning to van Strien's regulative cycle, which clearly expresses the unique character of praxis-oriented thinking as the basis for strategic action (1986, 18ff.).

Van Strien mentions three characteristics of praxis-oriented thinking. (1) It is not generalizing but individualizing in nature and focuses on a specific situation. (2) It does not result in academic statements but rather in actions based on academic considerations. (3) Its interventions are guided by norms, since it wants to improve what is not good. He calls the resulting action cycle — as distinct from the empirical cycle — the regulative cycle (van Strien 1986, 19), with the following basic pattern: definition of the problem — diagnosis — plan — intervention — evaluation.

An example: A pastor-psychologist sees a couple who face serious difficulties in their marriage. He empathizes with their story (understanding) and helps them discover a particular communicative pattern that has led them in their relationship to react with mutual stereotypes — to a large extent dominated by fear and helplessness. His psychological expertise enables the counselor to suggest a diagnosis (explanation) and to develop a plan for action (change). He gives them a number of suggestions as to how they might relate to each other in a different way. These suggestions are based on a theory of learning he is acquainted with. In subsequent consultations he evaluates the experiences and adjusts the plan. The description of this case by the pastor-psychologist results, together with other case histories, in the formulation of a theory that undergirds the practice. Thus, following the regulative cycle will produce additional knowledge, which can be applied in other situations. This knowledge may then, with a view to generalization, be tested empirically.

The regulative cycle is not only hermeneutical in nature but also empirical, and must be critically approached, since normative moments play a role in each phase. Since mediative action holds a central place in practical theology, the link between hermeneutical and strategic action is essential: who does what, why, and how?

Based on this, practical thinking leads to forms of methodical and systematic action: starting from a particular situation, one will formulate a goal and determine the original situation, from which the process of change starts. In order to achieve this, one must give close attention to the sphere of experience of the individual or the individuals who are part of the process and who must always be viewed as the cosubjects. Any success of this enterprise depends to a high degree on their motivation and willingness to go through a process of change. Then one chooses a method to make sure that, starting from an analysis of the original situation, one will reach the goal that has been set. One develops strategies to organize the process of change that has been initiated, and one determines which contents will be dealt with in which phase of the process. An evaluation takes place upon completion.

This form of methodical action provides the basic pattern for discussions, working in groups, learning processes, and different kinds of adult education in a community, for instance, the church. One meets such action theories, in which one recognizes the pattern of the regulative circle, in the different domains of practical theology. It is necessary to provide feedback from the strategic to the hermeneutical and the empirical perspectives, as described in the practical-theological basic pattern (9.2.4). The hermeneutical perspective is apparent when the goal and the content are determined. Goal and content are based on the understanding of reality, from the perspective of God's dealings with the people. In determining the initial situation and the strategies, one can fall back on empirically acquired knowledge about the group one is addressing (for instance, young people in a certain age bracket) and on the results of comparable processes that have been researched. Thus one moves constantly within a triangle of change, understanding, and explanation (9.2.4).

11.5 Domains of Action in Practical Theology

One can distinguish several domains of action within practical theology. The action may be directed toward change in the relationship with the individual, the group (congregation), or the wider society. One can therefore speak of a differentiated practical theology. Appropriate strategies have been developed, on the micro-, meso-, and macrolevel, for each of these domains. Each domain demands its own strategic approach, for which various intervention techniques have been developed, such as a structured dialogue, theories of learning, working through rituals, theories of preaching, techniques for meetings, methods for church development, and organizational development. All these approaches require basic rules as formulated above. The actor-perspective must be central: approaching each person as a subject. Since mediative actions are the highest concern of any practical-theological theory of action, I describe each of these action domains in part III of this book.

In this section I need dwell on only two theories that reach further, since they cut as cross sections through the entire field of practical theology. They are therefore of great significance for an integral approach to the entire discipline. These are communication theory and systems theory. Because of the link between understanding and explanation, they complement each other and need each other in a practical-theological theory of action (9.2.4). Communication theory is built on the use of language (dialogue), while systems theory can be connected with the structural analysis of texts.

11.5.1 Communication Theory

Communication theory is of immense importance for any reflection on human action. It uses the insights of the discipline of linguistics, which are of importance for the development of a theory of action (8.5). The study of communication, however, shows that communication processes and communication systems are often very complex.

Cybernetics provides insight into this complexity. As a rule, organisms and organizations are in a homeostatic equilibrium. This means that adding more information usually causes a disturbance of that equilibrium. If one is to avoid protest, enough safety valves have to be provided before additional information can be allowed. Constant feedback ensures that the tension remains within acceptable limits (Riess 1973, 107ff.). Cybernetics is based on the presupposition that these processes can be controlled.

This "vital balance" in psychoanalytical sessions has become the object of inquiry through the work of Karl Menninger et al. (1963). The pragmatic approach in communication, to provide insight in interpersonal systems (spouses, groups), has been developed by P. Watzlawick et al. (1970). This brings us already into the sphere of systems theory, which I discuss in some detail in the next section.

Communication theory often starts with the classic formula of H. D. Lasswell: "*Who* says *what,* through which *medium,* to *whom,* with what *effect?*" (Riess 1973, 110). This is a variant of the general action model described above (9.2.3). This formula summarizes the action system. Four constitutive elements become apparent: the communicator (sender), the message, the channel (medium), and the recipient (receiver). This scheme applies foremost to situations of mass communication, which are characterized by "one-way traffic."

General accessibility is one of the key features of mass communication. That no one should be excluded as recipient is a major challenge for media productions, especially of religious programs.

Since the arrival of television, research has been done in this area also with regard to the possibilities of religious communication (e.g., Straver 1967; Hamelink et al. 1971; Jager 1971; Lammens 1974; van der Meiden 1980; Koole 1984; van der Goot 1989). From the perspective of the communicator, mass communication may be described as "making something public by means of symbols to achieve an intended effect" (van der Goot 1989, 39).

In many respects, however, interpersonal communication shows a totally different pattern. Here use of language as dialogue takes center stage. It is "two-way traffic" in a face-to-face situation. This form of communication may seem simpler, but it is extremely complex, as Riess (1973, 125) demonstrates in figure 15.

Riess's scheme may be clarified with the following example. When two people communicate, two different worlds meet. I think of a — not totally imaginary — situation of a Reformed pastor and a Muslim woman, here referred to as communicator (C) and recipient (R), respectively. They have been socialized in very different families, where the father and the mother (assuming that one is dealing with "complete" families) each puts his or her stamp on the development of the child (primary group). They have identified themselves with a group culture, with its specific norms and values (extended social system). Their communication is further colored by their social milieu. One party belongs to the established

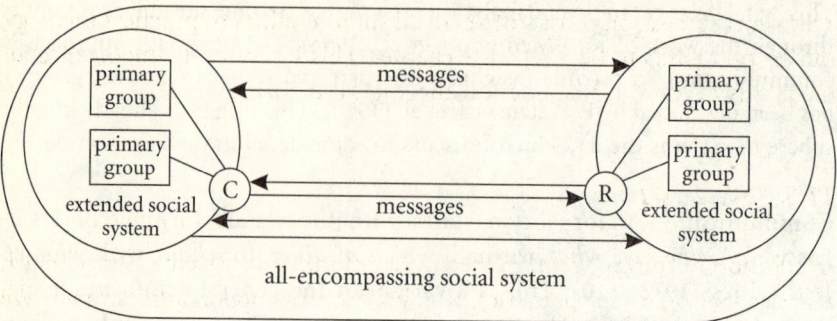

Figure 15: Interpersonal communication according to R. Riess

middle class, while the other is nearer to the bottom of society. In addition, both carry their own culture (dominant culture) or subculture (minority culture) with them. (This is all part of the "all-encompassing social system.") One has reason to wonder whether there can be any communication at all at a deep level under such circumstances. In this example the frames of reference are, indeed, totally different.

This conversation is primarily aimed at arriving at mutual understanding. One may refer to other forms of communication in the pastorate, catechesis, liturgy — of various situations of "communicative action in the service of the gospel." In all these situations one must take the factors of Riess's scheme into account. Berkhof calls dialogue or discussion a "means of grace" (1973, 376 [1979, 359]), which fits better in our cultural context than the sermon (Nicol 1990). A sermon is indeed a kind of monologue, but van der Laan (1989b, 154, seeking support from E. Lange) argues that even the sermon must, on a deeper level, be understood as dialogue. Group dialogue is often practiced in training situations (Lindijer and Lindijer-Banning 1977). Within the context of the church, and in particular in the pastorate, one finds pastoral counseling, the supportive dialogue with a therapeutic accent (Clinebell 1984).

The counseling session often follows the Rogerian tradition ("client-centered therapy") of empathy and congruence, based on the unconditional acceptance of the other (Rogers 1951). In the Netherlands this model was introduced by Faber and van der Schoot (1962 [1965]).

The model of learning through dialogue, often used in training situations, has a totally different scope (Dingemans 1986, 276ff.). Learning in the context of the Christian community, says Groome, requires dialogue (1980, 188).

This short discussion must suffice. In all subdisciplines of practical theology, this section tends to be a separate chapter. This indicates its importance for the praxis of the various practical-theological theories.

11.5.2 Systems Theory

In addition to communication theory I must mention systems theory, which also has its origin in cybernetics. It offers excellent opportunities to analyze different kinds of structures, to trace interconnections, and to adjust actions accordingly.

According to Keuning (1973, 46ff.), all system definitions have two things in common: an aspect of totality and an aspect of (inter-) relatedness. A system is defined as "an arrangement of components into a distinct, typical whole." Such a system does not really exist; it is a construct: something used to clarify a structure or process is regarded as a system (Firet 1987, 41).

At first sight, there appears to be a tension between a communicative approach from a hermeneutical perspective and the use of a systems theory, since the latter does not look at things from the inside, as one who participates in the communication, but from the outside. The difference is comparable to that between an interpretive and a structural analysis of "texts." But in this case also one should think in terms of complementarity. Systems theory complements communicative strategies and can be used to clarify certain situations and to bring the deeper structures of actions to the surface.

The concepts of system and systems theory are used in different ways in the literature. In this connection I ought to mention that an open-system theory as an explanatory model of communicative processes and organizational structures does not necessarily have to be linked to Habermas's distinction between system and lifeworld (8.4.2). The discussion between Habermas and, among others, Luhman about systems theory centers on the sociological theories that attempt to explain developments in society, in particular in the sectors of state and economy. A survey of this discussion is provided by Widdershoven (de Boer et al. 1988, 171ff.).

Systems theory is also applied as an instrument in practical theology (de Jongh van Arkel 1991). But I must add that practical theology is interested only in open systems, which maintain a relationship of reciprocity with their environment (Firet 1987, 41). This is particularly true for personality systems, social systems, and communication systems, such as a sermon or dialogue. In this connection Firet points out that an open-system design serves a communicative purpose.

Systems theory is applied in a number of areas. One example is in the work of the pastor. Trying to reconstruct a life story through an analysis of pastoral protocol (verbatim), by means of a structuralist reading, one might discover to what extent a personal history may be determined by the "system" of the family in which that person was raised. Family therapy is based on the presupposition that one should treat not just the individual but all members of the family, considering the manner in which distinctive "parts" (family members) of the "whole" interact in a stereotypical, and hence unfree, way (Richter 1970). As a result, the homeostatic equilibrium, which functions within the system, is disturbed, thus creating space for new relationships. Of course, the family system should not be detached from wider social contexts. Moreover, one must not forget that norms and values play a role in how family members interact (Ploeger 1989, 75).

The most important area of application is that of "church development." For instance, in his theory of a vital community Hendriks (1990, 101) uses the model of "parties within a system." Pasveer (1992) develops an open-system theory as a model for the development and nurture of a congregation. The congregation, as a web of relationships and as firmly attached to its environment, may be thought of as a system (57ff.). This enables one to analyze and diagnose its situation.

Like Hendriks, Pasveer also employs the "Systems Model" of the Center for Parish Development of P. M. Dietrich in Chicago (60ff.). He feels the model offers good prospects for diagnosis and feedback. He sees the danger, however, that the subject status of the congregation might be undervalued. In addition, the systems approach might reduce reality by making it manageable (221). He feels, nonetheless, that the systems approach is of great value in the area of church development.

11.6 Conclusion

The elaboration of the strategic perspective within a theory of action is of great importance for the development of practical theology. Strategic action must not be reduced to methodical action as the application domain of the various disciplines. If that happens, the hermeneutical perspective will be lost. Methods are never neutral but always imply a particular view of humanity and society. This demands fundamental-theoretical reflection on strategic action from a hermeneutical-critical perspective, in order truly to do justice to the people who experience the impact of the actions. The regulative cycle of praxis-oriented thinking holds a central place. Systems theory should never be detached from communication theory.

CHAPTER 12

The Empirical Perspective

Following the hermeneutical perspective and the strategic perspective, this chapter deals with the third — the empirical — perspective. This perspective has come more and more to the forefront since the empirical shift in practical theology in the 1960s.

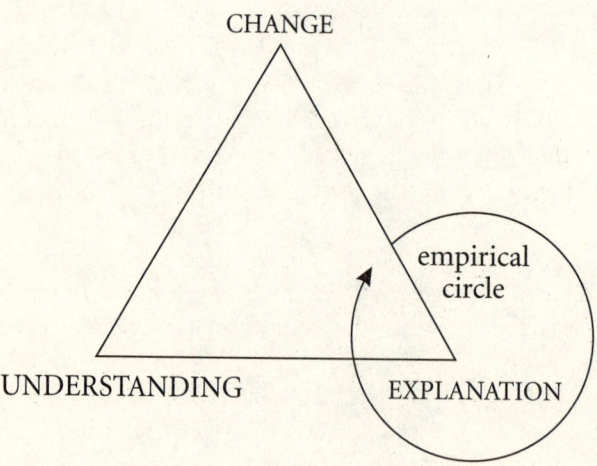

Figure 16: The empirical perspective

The empirical perspective connects the "who does what" primarily with the "where and when." Actions are always situational; they occur in time and space and have their unique context, determined by varying conditions and factors. Distanciation through empirical research clarifies this. If one takes the unity of understanding and explanation as a starting point, an empirical approach is not at odds with the hermeneutical and the strategic perspectives. For in the context of a theological theory of action, empirical testing has to do with the development of hermeneutical and strategic theories. This is apparent from the application of the empirical cycle in practical-theological research. Likewise, the hermeneutical perspective has strategic and empirical implications. With regard to the latter one might think of the *verstehende* (understanding) approach in the social sciences (10.3). The strategic perspective, in its turn, has hermeneutical and empirical implications, as is clear from the application of the regulative cycle (11.4).

The word *empiricism* derives from Greek *empeiria*, which means "experience." "Empiricism" is the term for an epistemological approach that attempts to show that all scientific knowledge is based on experience and can in all respects, through sense perceptions, be deduced from experience. This trend has been particularly popular in Anglo-Saxon philosophy, and it goes back as far as John Locke (1632-1704) and David Hume (1711-1776). Moreover, this type of thinking has a strong kinship with the natural sciences, while the principle of causality also plays an important role.

If practical theology really wants to be theology, it cannot be content with only an empirical approach, as is customary in religious studies. It must also deal with the normative claims embedded in the Christian faith tradition. But from the inception of practical theology it has been recognized that an empirical approach is of great importance for the practice of this discipline.

Through Schleiermacher (2.3), the key concept of experience acquires an important role in theology, and Nitzsch (3.4) was the first practical theologian to link this concept with the use of empirical methods. Here one can detect a relation with the anthropological shift within theology in general, which demands an increasing interrelatedness of revelation and experience. This line also leads me to choose an empirically oriented practical theology, which opts for a point of departure in the actual experiences of people and the situation of church and society, and is characterized by a theorizing approach that attempts to do full justice to empirical data (1.3).

I extend this line further in this chapter, choosing for limitation as well as concretization. The empirical perspective is of particular importance for research. I will show *in concreto* how practical theology can apply empirical methods. I will do this on the basis of a research proposal, a challenge every practical theologian has to face sooner or later. Here the empirical perspective provides the structure. One may, for instance, think of a proposal for a master's or doctoral thesis. This leads to questions of a theoretical nature, which I feel can best be addressed in this context.

I begin the discussion with a survey of various currents within empirical research (12.1). Next, I look at the preparations for a research project (12.2). Subsequently, I distinguish a number of different kinds of research (12.3), and I return to the links between the hermeneutical circle and the regulative and the empirical cycles (12.4). Finally, after having dealt with the aspect of problem definition (12.5), I discuss the further execution of a research project (12.6).

12.1 Currents within Empirical Research

Surveying the domain of empirical research, one must reckon with a considerable number of distinctions. The first has to do with the different research traditions. A tripartition is usually suggested: hermeneutical research, empirical-analytical research, and critical research. This division corresponds with the practical-theological currents of thought discussed in 9.4.2–9.4.4. In hermeneutical research one finds a strong preference for the *verstehende* (understanding) approach, which we studied in 10.3. Empirical-analytical research opts for the "hard" methodology of counting and measuring. The critical approach shows a preference for action-oriented research.

These three may be reduced to the general division into two categories in the social sciences: the choice in favor of the orientation of the human sciences, shared by the hermeneutical and the critical schools (10.3), or in favor of the orientation of the natural sciences.

I follow Swanborn (1987, 341) in his summary of the traditional differences between the two:

Natural sciences	Human sciences
quantitative	qualitative
positivistic	naturalistic
"from the outside in"	"from the inside out"
(spectator perspective)	(participant perspective)
objective	subjective
explanation	understanding
causal explanations	attribution of meaning

from facts and numbers	through those surveyed
structure-directed	process-directed
surveys and experiments	participatory observation, unstructured interviews, documents
variable language	common language
hard	soft

Those who are acquainted with research will appreciate that such a list of opposites represents intense discussions. For many would argue that both lists are based on premises in the philosophy of science that exclude each other. Others, however, tend to relativize the differences. This discussion is also carried over into practical theology; cf. Höfte (1990), van der Ven (1990 [1993]), Claessens and van Tillo (1990), Schippers et al. (1990). Four substantial studies in one single year! In previous chapters I dealt with this in a general way.

I believe that in practical-theological research these contrasts should not be made paramount. There are solid arguments to link the two traditions, as I earlier attempted to do on the basis of Ricoeur's theory of action (9.2). That is also what mostly happens in practice. For we are always faced with a theological content, which can be understood only hermeneutically, and we want to connect this with the praxis of faith and church, which can be accessed only empirically. The two traditions need each other and have their own requirements as they relate to each other. On the one hand, facts and figures may be accurate, but as abstractions of real life they may lead to a reduced rationality. This would suggest further qualitative research. On the other hand, interpretations are often extremely subjective and open to multiple explanations. Quantitative methods are therefore desirable as part of the research. Thus the differences are often merely gradations of emphasis.

Considering the kind of knowledge that is sought, one may differentiate among fundamental research, applied research, and technological development. This is simply a matter of classification: one category is not superior to the other. Fundamental research is aimed at increasing theoretical knowledge. Applied research, often in the form of research in connection with policies that are being pursued, is directed toward changing or improving a situation in the short term. Technological research focuses on the development of working models, for example, curricula for catechesis or models of church development. In the actual practice of practical-theological research one usually meets a combination of these. For research always aims to generate knowledge that will enable one to change the current situation into a more desirable situation, and this requires certain instruments.

12.2 Preparing a Research Project

In preparing a research project, one must always take into account the decisions to be made with regard to the topic to be studied, the unique character of practical-theological research, and the specific possibilities and limitations of the researcher.

12.2.1 Choosing a Topic

It is recommended to define, already early in the preparatory phase of the research, the preliminary topic that is to be studied in a scientific way. The first question is: What do I want to study? In asking this question, one should keep in mind that scientific research is foremost aimed at generating knowledge. Verschuren (1986, 19) reminds us that research first of all presupposes a *search*. Proposals for research projects are often introduced with the statement that one wants "to look at" or wants to "reflect in depth." That may be useful, but it is too meager for true research. The research proposal must answer questions regarding the why, what, where, and how.

Many choose topics with which they are already somewhat familiar. At times a graduate student or doctoral candidate is able to furnish a complete table of contents during the first meeting with her or his professor. This contains a systematic survey of what the person already knows. True research, however, aims at what one does *not* know but has aroused one's curiosity. This leads to the question how one can begin a search in a methodical manner, for example, through a study of the relevant literature or through a specific model of empirical research. It usually has to be a combination of both. Surveying the research that has already been done enables one to establish what is already known and what remains to be studied.

I am referring not just to research in general but to *scientific* research. That is, the question about what will be researched must be posed at a certain level of aggregation. This means that the problem must have enough coherence and must not suffer from internal contradictions. This will to a large extent determine the value of the study, which, taking certain additional conditions into account, should provide valid and reliable knowledge. It may be too much to ask for objective knowledge, but the study must at least result in intersubjective knowledge. This means that the statements about a certain aspect of reality made by researcher A can in principle be shared by researcher B or C (Swanborn 1987, 29).

Chance usually enters into the picture from the beginning if one takes a specific case as the starting point for research. This makes it difficult to arrive at valid conclusions. Yet such a description may result in added knowledge as it provides a profound insight in a given situation. But — just to give another example — describing how a course for catechesis is received and evaluated by a certain group is not automatically a piece of research. It may lead to a report that may help others to catch a new idea, but it does not result in valid knowledge. For the result might be quite different in another group led by another catechist. In such a situation one must work with a control group, and this leads to an approach not dissimilar to that of "quasi-experimental design" (van der Ven 1990, 147 [1993, 127-28]).

12.2.2 The Unique Character of Action Research

Another consideration is that practical-theological research is *action research*. Action is a very broad concept, as we saw in the differentiation between praxis 1 and praxis 2. Action research must at least have some relevance for mediative action. That may already be the case when the initial situation is studied. I will use a research topic as an example for the rest of this chapter.

One may, for example, decide to study the attitudes of the members of the Reformed Churches with regard to participating in the Communion service: frequency, manner of celebration, local variations, and so on. This information will be useful for further research that is more explicitly intended to establish whether — and under which conditions — participation in the Communion service can be improved.

Improvement of the situation toward the desired praxis is the underlying interest of practical-theological research. In this respect it differs from socioreligious research. The focus on mediative action must result in concrete suggestions for action.

Practical-theological research gives priority to practice-oriented research (van der Laan 1990, 271), the term used by Swanborn for this type of research. "In practice-oriented research a situation or process is studied that someone feels should be changed" (Swanborn 1987, 377). This does not coincide with the study of particular actions, where the researcher closely follows certain policy-induced interventions (385); in this instance "the field" is intimately involved with the study. Goals are often readjusted in the process. Due to the process-oriented character of the study, when improvements do occur it is often difficult to ascertain how these came about. It could be that they are the result not so much of the interventions but rather of the enthusiasm of the researcher and the increased engagement on the part of the persons who were studied.

For this reason, the results of this type of field research can usually not be generalized — a prerequisite for reliable knowledge. But also in practice-oriented research the action cannot be studied apart from the subject, whom one seeks to assist with a view to improving her or his action situation (van Tillo 1990, 34). Doing justice to the subject, who should not be reduced to a mere object of the study, together with the fact that one must deliver reliable research data, places high demands on the research procedures to be followed.

12.2.3 The Possibilities of the Researcher

In the preparatory phase consideration must be given to the reason for a particular study, and the likelihood that the researcher will be able to handle it successfully. Three questions must be posed: What can I handle? How do I limit the study? What are my own limitations?

What Can I Handle?

Why did I choose this topic? Can I handle it? These questions have a positive and a negative side. The first one is the easiest to answer. When one has met the problem a number of times in the books one has been reading or in actual practice, it would seem more probable that "there is something" that could be of interest for further study than would be the case if the topic was the result of sudden intuition.

At this point one should already think of the degree of difficulty the topic presents. If the topic leads to difficult exegetical questions, it would be unwise for someone who knows little of the original languages or exegesis to pursue it, unless one is willing to spend the time needed to remedy this deficiency in knowledge.

The subjective element is more difficult to judge, but it is no less important. What motivates me to select this research topic? Having too much of a personal involvement with the topic may be a hindrance once the study gets under way. That is a danger for those who research what they themselves experience as a problem, such as "religious doubt" or depression. But too great a distance from the topic may cause a gradual loss of motivation. Thus the question, Can I handle it? is realistic, for not being able to handle a topic means failure.

How Do I Limit It?

The question about one's own possibilities also involves establishing the limits of what one wants to study. Some research proposals would require the work of a lifetime, and others would take at least some years to complete. Both are unsuitable for a master's thesis.

Verschuren points in this connection to the bow-net principle: one opts for a particular limitation, and then makes a further selection among the various aspects. The rule is: "Choose a specific kind of topic, and then select some aspect of the attribute(s) of a specific element" (1986, 31). From the beginning it is important to go for something that is concrete and to establish clear parameters.

Someone who, for instance, wants to study the way in which church members experience their participation in the Communion service would do well to limit study to the experience of a specific group of people (e.g., of a certain age, belonging to a specific denomination) and to focus on one aspect of that experience, for example, that some people in Reformed circles tend to avoid the Communion service.

Where Lies My Competence?

Considering one's own possibilities, one should also consider in what areas one has reached a certain competence on the basis of earlier studies. This touches on where one situates the topic within practical theology and theology in general. How does the topic relate to this wider context? Does it relate primarily to the underlying theoretical framework, or rather to one or more of the subdisciplines?

The way in which the Communion service is "experienced" has dogmatic implications (the doctrine of the Lord's Supper, and, not to forget, the *ordo salutis*) and also church historical implications (Pietism) and touches on the subdisciplines of pastoral care (experience) and liturgy (celebration). Even in the preparatory phase, literature can be assembled from these various angles. A practical-theological topic also presents factors that need input from the social sciences:

the problem is found especially among a certain type of Christian in particular areas in the Netherlands (the "Bible belt"). Psychology of religion also comes into play: a particular type of spirituality, the experience of guilt, and the desire for a new birth and conversion. The choice of the research instruments raises the question which methods the researcher can competently handle.

This first inventory already indicates that even this narrowed-down topic has so many aspects that a more precise focus must be established.

12.3 Types of Research

In drawing up a research proposal, and in the course of research, the student has to face several methodological choices, which I will briefly discuss. In its simplest form a practical-theological study consists of the following elements: description, interpretation, explanation, and action. These elements call for each other in a reciprocal way and show the need to interrelate the hermeneutical, the strategic, and the empirical aspects. All phases of the study present aspects that touch on theology as well as on the social sciences. Thus it would be wise to opt, from the very beginning, for an interdisciplinary approach.

That a group of people experience the Communion service in this particular way (description) may be interpreted in such a manner, and may be explained after considering these various factors, which then leads to the following recommendations for pastoral action.

The formula is deceptively simple. One must remember, however, that the experience is due to a "prejudgment," in the sense of a prior conviction. Normative views play a role in the explanation, while the suggestions for action rest, at least in part, on a responsible interpretation of biblical-theological data. One must take into consideration normative elements in all phases of the study. One also faces some serious methodological questions. One may opt for a particular type of research: for the inductive or the deductive method, for qualitative or quantitative research, or for a combination of these. I must therefore briefly survey the various types of research: descriptive, explorative, and testing research.

A. D. de Groot (1961, 316) distinguishes five pure types: testing, instrumental-nomological research, descriptive research, explorative research, and interpretive-theoretical studies. The empirical research may then be reduced to three main types. One also may — and this is another important distinction — differentiate between descriptive and explorative research and studies that test specific hypotheses. One and the same study usually uses a combination: explorative-descriptive, explorative-explanatory, testing-descriptive, or testing-explanatory (van der Ven 1990, 146 [1993, 126]).

12.3.1 Descriptive Research

Descriptive research focuses on a systematic description of a topic on the basis of empirical data.

Studying the manner in which the Communion service is experienced, one soon discovers that this has to do with a certain aspect of a broader problem: differences in the way people experience their faith. Dutch Protestants may be categorized in different groups. Apart from those for whom outward experience is all-important, one finds orthodox, charismatic, evangelical, and liberal Christians. These groups are found in all major denominations. Descriptive research may attempt to chart these differences in the way in which faith is experienced, or on the basis of theological motifs or social characteristics. This knowledge will then help in extending this topic of the experience of the Communion service to a broader population.

Depending on the topic, descriptive research may also include the gathering of statistical data in order to describe a particular population. I also include under this heading those phenomenological studies that, through a method of *verstehen* (understanding), map out certain phenomena (de Groot 1961, 320). In many cases descriptive research characterizes the first phase, followed by either explorative or testing research. A prime example of this is the study of Firet and Hendriks (1986) about the "anonymous pastorate."

Good descriptive research is far from simple. When things tend to become somewhat cloudy, escape is often sought in enlisting the "explorative" concept. De Groot (323) speaks in this connection of a euphemism that conceals that it would have been better to organize the study along systematic objective-descriptive lines.

12.3.2 Explorative Research

Explorative research is a mixture between research that seeks to describe and that which seeks to test hypotheses, but it may have its own independent place when the researcher does not primarily want to explore the broader field or to register certain phenomena, but attempts to explain these, with a view to developing certain hypotheses on the basis of the findings. Likewise, case studies, like those on which Freud based the development of psychoanalysis and which continue to have great heuristic value (Stroeken 1985), belong to the explorative type (de Groot 1961, 322). Explorative research always aims at the formulation of a theory or of certain presuppositions, which might develop into hypotheses. This does not necessarily mean that these hypotheses can be tested. This is usually not the case for ideal-typical distinctions, unless they are such that they allow for empirical processing.

In contrast to descriptive research, explorative studies place the main accent on explanation and interpretation. Explorative research is especially useful when little is as yet known about a particular phenomenon, and no theory has yet been developed to explain it. Swanborn (1987, 155) refers in this connection to "milking the material" for whatever information it may contain. The first phases of this exploration are often more intuitive than methodical. The result is therefore limited to preliminary statements, models, or search strategies, for which one can adduce solid arguments. This is usually about as much as can be expected in a master's thesis.

De Groot (1961, 324) also regards factor analysis in empirical research as a typical explorative technique. This maps out the different variables and brings transparency to the reciprocal correlations.

For instance, it has been found that some key theological concepts play a role in the reflection on the way in which the Communion service is experienced, for example, guilt, reconciliation, conversion, community, obedience, judgment, eschatology, joy, new life, gratefulness. Not everybody uses the same terms. Some combinations are characteristic for certain types of people who attend the Communion service, and one of the hypotheses might be that, based on a number of factors that have been established, the decision not to participate in the Communion service is found predominantly among certain "theological types."

12.3.3 Testing Hypotheses

Characteristic for this type of research is "that a limited number (sometimes just one) of interrelated hypotheses, usually derived from a theory, are tested empirically" (de Groot 1961, 317). This is done mostly by surveying a representative sample, sometimes under experimental conditions.

The tests must give clarity whether certain relationships, which are thought to exist on theoretical grounds, can be detected in reality or in the human consciousness. Or they are used to prove the reality of a certain effect of specific actions on people. A sound academic suspicion ensures that this research seeks to falsify specific hypotheses. This is the only way to detect what can withstand criticism.

De Groot regards this type of testing as the real kind of empirical research, and uses this as the basis for his methodology. This research goes through the full empirical cycle of observation, induction, deduction, testing, and evaluation (de Groot 1961, 29ff.). "Observation" is the gathering and categorizing of empirical data, with a view to formulating hypotheses; "induction" has to do with the actual formulation of the hypotheses; "deduction" is the drawing of conclusions from these hypotheses, in the form of testable predictions; "testing" results in new empirical data, based on the outcome of the predictions; "evaluation" is the feedback to the theory, and also suggests issues for additional research.

Testing the hypotheses regarding the participants of the Communion service may show that the classification in different types finds little support in the actual practice of this service. The situation may be considerably more complex than anticipated, since most people in fact experience very little when they take part in the Communion service. This may raise the question to what extent a theological categorization is based on doctrinal prejudices, which receive unfortunate affirmation through pastoral action. This may then lead to suggestions for further research, as well as for a specific action.

12.3.4 Applications in Practical-Theological Research

Some questions arise when these various forms of empirical research are applied in practical-theological studies, in particular with respect to the link between a normative-hermeneutical approach, for which I earlier expressed my preference, and the various types of empirical research described above. The question seems justified whether the reality of faith and experience is accessible to this type of inquiry. Critics have wondered whether this would, in terms of Habermas (8.4.2), tend to lead toward a "constricted" rationality (Ploeger 1989; Höfte 1990; Claessens and van Tillo 1990). I will return to this important question, which I have already noted (8.4.3).

Van der Ven (1990 [1993]), whose views are close to those of de Groot and to whom such criticism has been addressed, bases his empirical research on a theological theory; he gives full attention to the hermeneutical and critical perspectives, and uses both quantitative and qualitative methods. This provides him with ample ammunition to defend himself against this criticism. On the other hand, it is undeniably true that some testing methods pay insufficient attention to the unique character of theological data.

I believe, however, that we must realize that, viewed from a theological perspective, empirical research through quantitative methods has its limitations. Researchers have to restrict themselves to data that are quantifiable and can be expressed in statistics. One may set out in percentages which groups share particular convictions, or which beliefs — which may be distinguished on the basis of theological theory — are held by certain groups of people. In this case one is dealing with cognitive things. One may even take one further step and categorize emotions and attitudes of people, and make them score on these aspects. But that seems to be the limit of quantitative research. The concepts and theories utilized in this type of research are not suitable if one wants to penetrate to deeper levels of consciousness. At this point assistance is needed from qualitative methods, employed from a hermeneutical angle (10.3). These may help to acquire a deeper insight in the unique character of a specific conviction.

Once again I refer to our example: the study of the reasons why people avoid the Communion service. In a certain phase of the research depth interviews will be needed to discover the essential nature of the particular kind of spirituality displayed by the people concerned, by listening to how they themselves experience this.

Another question arises: How can normative viewpoints receive enough attention in the context of empirical research? (a prerequisite for any normative-theological research). In a simple study consisting of three phases (description, explanation, action), this normativity may be expressed in the first phase in the process of developing a theological theory, in the second phase in designing the questionnaire and the interpretation of the data, and in the last phase in formulating the suggestions for action. In this connection I need to return just once more to the practical-theological structure of the three interrelated circles.

12.4 The Empirical Cycle in Its Relationship to the Regulative Cycle and the Hermeneutical Circle

De Groot states that the empirical cycle in fact rests on the experiential process that occurs in all people. Its first moment is observation. Something in the environment affects us, we sense something. This observation causes us to react to our environment. Several alternatives are available; we may react in various ways. These different ways of reacting may be tested to establish which alternative seems preferable. Life always retains something of a game of chess (the favorite game of de Groot). In this way we acquire experiential knowledge about the impact of a specific kind of reaction in a concrete situation. This leads to a preliminary "judgment," as a practical guideline for action. We now know the value of the various alternatives. Thus the path of "observation" — "experiencing" — "choosing" — "evaluating" (a variant of de Groot's categorization; 1961, 4) is completed. Having learned from experience we once again observe the surrounding reality, and the experiential cycle repeats itself. This touches every human being, for this is the way in which we "search" our life situation, whether or not we have any idea of "research."

The "use" of the empirical cycle in our daily experience can be with or without much reflection (de Groot 1961, 1ff.). As we follow our morning routine from getting up to having breakfast, not all of us will be aware of the role of the cycle of trial and error in our life. But those of us who during the rush hour try to go from the suburbs to the center of a city want to discover which route is the quickest at that particular time of the day. A comparison of such factors as distance, traveling time, pattern of traffic jams, and driving pleasure help us to consider the alternatives, from which we make a choice. This already points to some elements of research.

Empirical research is a conscious process of comparing and evaluating. We discover that certain distinctions are not necessarily opposed to each other. The basic pattern of the empirical cycle contains inductive as well as deductive moments, and the inductive and the deductive methods in research therefore never exclude each other but rather make room for each other. For this reason, this cycle is basic for all forms of research, whatever method one adopts, that of quantitative (de Groot) or qualitative (Wester 1987), of fundamental or praxis-oriented research.

Van Strien also states that de Groot's transitions between the "everyday cycle of trial and error" and the cycle of knowledge based on reflection are quite fluid. There are no clear demarcations between the thought processes and motifs in the various models of thinking and problem resolution. He sees the intervention on the basis of trial and error as a core moment in the regulative cycle (defining the problem — diagnosis — plan — intervention — evaluation), which he views as the basic cycle of all general learning and problem-solving behavior. In any case, the similarity is clear.

Swanborn rightly refuses to consider the regulative cycle of van Strien as an alternative for the empirical cycle (1987, 387). The regulative cycle does not primarily have to do with prediction and explanation but rather with propositions and change, and thus forms the methodological core of a strategic theory of action (11.4). But both cycles have a similar structure and complement each other in a practical-theological context.

One may now address the question how both cycles relate to the hermeneutical circle (10.5.3). In the hermeneutical circle action has a different connotation ("mental" action). It focuses on the interpretation of a meaning-providing tradition in relation to a *verstehende* (understanding) approach to reality. Here, once again, one faces the circle of trial and error. The path from understanding to explanation is that from guessing to testing. Whether an interpretation is valid depends in part on whether it holds up in a discourse where all arguments are considered, and whether it appears to be credible. The latter aspect becomes apparent in praxis.

The Christian faith has to do with orthodoxy in relationship to orthopraxis and orthognosis (Jonker 1983, 250ff.). This follows from the biblical statements that not only refer to "speaking" the truth, but also — in the Johannine writings — use such terms as "doing" the truth and "being" in the truth. Thus there is an intimate relationship between knowledge and action. Symbolic-interactionist research shows how a given context of awareness affects the interaction, as is clear from the study by Glaser and Strauss (10.3.1).

This again illustrates the link between the hermeneutical, the strategic, and the empirical perspectives. Motivational and content-related motifs, which occupy a prominent place in the strategic and empirical perspectives, derive from the hermeneutical perspective. Inversely, empirically acquired experience provides feedback for the hermeneutical perspective.

When one puts the three cycles side by side, some parallels become apparent from the structure of the circle of trial and error of mental processes (observing — suspecting — expecting — testing — evaluating; cf. de Groot 1961, 6):

hermeneutical circle	regulative circle	empirical circle
prejudgment	defining the problem	observation
observation/experience	diagnosis	induction/supposition
interpretation/discourse	plan	deduction/prediction
providing meaning	intervention	testing
action	evaluation	evaluation

The process in the first column serves first of all the kind of action that provides meaning, while that of the second serves systematic action, and that of the third testing action. Together they represent a conceptual triad: understanding — change — explanation.

In our daily practice of belief and action, we also face a circular process, with elements of all three. I would like to characterize this as: observation — experience — interpretation — providing meaning (faith) — choice — testing — evaluation. People observe something and this is registered as an experience, which they may interpret as a faith experience, and which may then lead to a choice that needs to be tested in actual life situations before it can be evaluated. As a well-founded expectation, a positive evaluation of this process will have an impact on other observations. Should the expectation be ill founded, one has lost an illusion but gained an experience.

In reflecting on this process of faith and action, with the intent of providing this with direction and guidance, one can recognize the figure of the circular process of the practical-theological methodology (9.2.4).

12.5 The Problem: Definition and Goal

After this short intermezzo we return to our journey along the various stages of the research project. We have now come to the point where the problem must be clearly defined. What questions do we want to see answered and what is the goal of the study? These aspects are at times defined in different ways. Defining the problem is here taken in a somewhat broad sense: it refers to a rather general description of the problem. On that basis, the goal of the study can be concretely formulated, followed by the question to which the study seeks an answer — preferably in a single sentence. Verschuren remarks that the term *problem* has two distinct meanings: "A *difficulty* with regard to a desirable situation in reality, and an *enigma* as a deficiency in our knowledge of that reality" (1986, 33). When we define the problem we use both meanings: the difficulty that needs to be addressed, which is then translated in the question regarding what knowledge is needed. The difficulty (the "why" of the study) finds further expression in the definition of the goal. Knowledge is needed to achieve that goal. The question of what is to be studied (the "what" of the study) is then further elaborated.

I apply this once again to the avoidance of the Communion service. In terms of praxis-oriented research, the problem may be stated as follows: How can attendance be improved in this situation where many avoid the Communion service?

This statement of the problem so far provides little direction. It seems to be a "do" question, something that is within the realm of things that could be done. I imagine that a pastor faced with such a situation, in her or his eyes an undesirable one, may well formulate the problem in this way. The question of *doing* must, however, be translated into one of *knowing*.

Therefore, the goal must be clearly stated: What do I want to achieve in this study? This question touches on the aspect of knowledge. I imagine that the question could now be answered in this way: I want to make recommendations, on the basis of practical-theological theories, with regard to pastoral action in situations where people avoid the Communion service.

Having answered "why," we can now formulate the "what": What is the question (possibly further divided into subquestions) that the researcher seeks to answer? This question may be formulated as follows: Which factors influence the phenomenon of avoidance of the Communion service? How are these to be evaluated? Under what conditions can one and should one exert influence on that practice?

One may, of course, pose the question in a different way. Formulated in this manner, the question is quite precise, but it remains rather open-ended. The situation must be analyzed. The aspect of evaluation has been included for two reasons. First, because normative theological factors play a role in this case; second, because the problem must be approached without bias. For it could be that what the church leaders refer to as an undesirable situation is in fact a matter of a deep conviction for the subjects concerned. Therefore the action perspective has also been formulated in an open manner, with the words "can one and should one." One should be concerned not only about effectiveness but also about legitimacy.

Having settled these matters, one can begin preparations for the actual research.

12.6 The Research

As the research project gets under way, the researcher must pay attention to the content of the study (the factors to examine), the execution of the research in a number of phases, and the choice of specific research methods.

12.6.1 The Content of the Study

A preliminary study usually precedes the formulation of the problem and of the goal. One has a general idea about the problem, through personal observation, conversations, and reading. Compiling a list of key words that might be of importance for the study is usually helpful for a library search, in order to discover what earlier research has taken place with regard to this specific problem and the specific target group. This produces a preliminary inventory of the literature on the topic, both in the area of theology and in that of the social sciences. This inventory leads to names of authors and institutions that may be able to provide further access to the topic or the target group. They can be contacted for additional information. This preliminary work leads to the conclusion that not enough is known about the problem and that further research is desirable. A more detailed survey of the literature enables the researcher to formulate the most important themes and aspects in the proposal.

In our example, this process will lead to the discovery that the problem of the avoidance of the Communion service is related to a specific population: the ultra-orthodox wing of the Reformed. For instance, one may concentrate the study on the orthodox modality in the Netherlands Reformed Church (Gereformeerde Bond) in a specific region (classis) where they are in the majority. It also has become clear that there is a theological aspect to consider: a specific way of dealing with Scripture, in particular with the words of Paul about being "unworthy" and "eating and drinking judgment on oneself" (1 Cor. 11:27-34) and the sanction for this in the final judgment. This text has had a unique *Wirkungsgeschichte* (history of effect) in the churches of the Reformation. One can detect this in several doctrinal teachings, in particular on such topics as predestination, providence, and the new birth. Historically, the topic brings one to the Pietistic movement and the experiential spirituality of these pietistic believers. Sociologists and psychologists of religion have made a considerable number of studies on this group of ultra-conservative Reformed Christians. All these data enable the researcher to formulate the theoretical framework for the study.

12.6.2 Execution of the Research in Phases

Having come to this point the researcher must plan the phases of the execution of the research. I would imagine that, in the case of a modest project such as a master's thesis, the researcher would use the inductive method, which is already to some extent reflected in the way the question of the "what" of the research has been defined: observation — description — analysis — reflection — suggestions for action. I refer to this as the hermeneutical path, which, however, demands a clear empirical elaboration.

The study may proceed as follows: After an introductory chapter with the definition of the problem, the statement of the goals, and the statement of the question to which an answer is sought, the first chapter will map out the theoretical framework of the study, in historical, sociological, and theological sections. The second chapter will deal with the empirical research, carried out on this basis, with a justification of the methodology, a description of what has been done, and a statement about the results. Keeping the theoretical framework in mind, the third chapter critically evaluates the results, with a view to pastoral action. A final chapter contains the conclusions of the study.

Another road is followed, after the first exploratory phase, if one opts for the empirical-analytic approach, as described in the context of empirical theology by van der Ven (1990 [1993]). If one conforms to the model of de Groot, the inductive phase is followed by the theological deduction: theological conceptualization, the theological-conceptual model, and theological operationalization. This leads to a questionnaire that is submitted to a representative sample of the group to be studied. The data are gathered for analysis, and the research is interpreted and evaluated.

A choice for field research requires that one move to the particular region, in order to share in the daily life of the people and to participate in their religious life. This has significant consequences for the organization in phases. One should note that such field research, if it is strictly scientific, may be well worth the effort but is also complex and time consuming (Schippers et al. 1990).

I have mentioned some theoretical possibilities. One must decide which method is most feasible, and justify that choice in the research proposal.

12.6.3 Research Methods

Finally, there is the matter of research methods. In our example one may opt for a quantitative study, a qualitative study, or both.

I refer to Swanborn (1987) for a survey of possible considerations. For a discussion of the quantitative method, see de Groot (1961) and van der Ven (1990 [1993]). For more information regarding the qualitative method, see van Strien (1986) and Wester (1987). Much of what I said earlier was based on their work.

I suppose that a broader study would lend itself more to the qualitative method. This involves the *verstehende* (understanding) approach, as discussed in 10.3. Participatory observation and depth interviews offer excellent possibilities. The interviews, developed on the basis of the theory, should be open, and should be structured only as far as the actual questions are concerned.

In our example, a limited, carefully selected number of individual believers will be interviewed, together with a few key leaders of the target group. Detailed preparations are essential, since the study deals with a relatively closed group, which is probably quite negatively disposed toward the study.

The relevant documents are analyzed by means of content analysis (Wester 1987, 91ff.), using current methods or a suitable computer program (e.g., Kwalitan). The study, which does not pretend to be representative, can be restricted to one specific location. As a result it may, for example, provide insight in the religious life of a usually quite homogeneous village community.

The results obtained do not automatically lead to suggestions for action. This requires reflection, based on available pastoral-psychological knowledge. It is also possible to involve a group of experts to determine what suggestions of action this material warrants. A discourse about the results strengthens the intersubjectivity of the study.

12.7 Conclusion

In this chapter I have, through an example, explained how an empirically oriented practical-theological study takes place, and have thereby contributed to the theory. Much of the research carried out by the Institute for Practical Theology at the Free University (Amsterdam) by and large follows this pattern. This shows that practical-theological research can be quite theological and empirical at the same time. Doing research is a difficult job. But as one works on a research project one may consult the vast amount of literature about each of the aspects discussed above.

This brings us to the end of part II of this book, which, I believe, has provided an adequate basis for the integrative approach to practical theology. The theory of action, developed in 9.2, is the core. This is rooted in the theological (chapter 7) and "action-theoretical" (chapter 8) character of practical theology, and finds further form in the hermeneutical (chapter 10), the strategic (chapter 11), and the empirical perspectives (chapter 12). These three perspectives need each other and complement each other; they are always present in practical-theological research.

We are now ready to proceed to the practice-theoretical part (III), which elaborates this theory in a differentiated way according to various action domains.

Domains of Action within Practical Theology

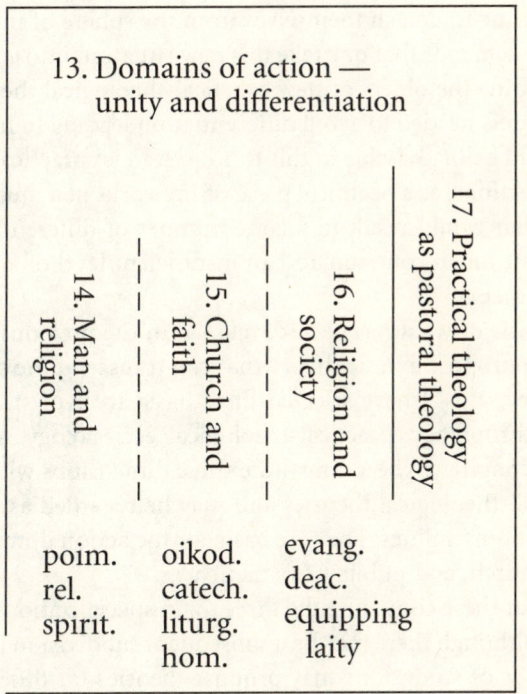

13. Domains of action —
   unity and differentiation

14. Man and religion

15. Church and faith

16. Religion and society

17. Practical theology as pastoral theology

poim.
rel.
spirit.

oikod.
catech.
liturg.
hom.

evang.
deac.
equipping
laity

Figure 17: Part III

Based on the two previous parts, this third part offers a further development with regard to the various action domains of practical theology. The approach is practical-constructive. This term is fitting with regard to making proposals for different disciplines. It refers to constructing, that is, designing and building. Models are developed on the drawing board, before they are tried out in actual practice, and tested by scientific methods. Such models are developed within the different practice theories, which focus on the actions of pastors and church officials, with a view to improving this mediative action.

The broad terrain of practical theology is here divided into three action domains: humanity and religion, church and faith, and religion and society. This division into three follows naturally from the differentiation principle that plays a fundamental role in the historical-interpretive part (part I). It has to do with the increased independence of the religious individual on the one hand, and of public religion on the other hand, vis-à-vis the church, which in the past, as the *corpus Christianum,* encompassed the entire sphere of church, state, and society. The secularization process has changed this situation dramatically. For one of the meanings of the concept of secularization is that new areas continue to detach themselves from the sphere of influence of the church. Reality demands that one take this new situation into account and allow it to determine the object of new practical-theological theories.

Integration is needed to avoid differentiation leading to fragmentation. I believe it would be inadvisable in this third part to let practical theology explode in all directions, as a beautiful piece of fireworks in a multicolored palette of light. That would result in a large number of different, insignificant theories, without much cohesion and an insufficient level of aggregation for proposing any theory.

On the basis of what has been developed in the previous parts, I must now attempt to propose a basic theory that can transcend the separate disciplines. To achieve this, I have selected three basic areas of study: practical-theological anthropology, practical-theological ecclesiology, and practical-theological diaconology. These constitute three dimensions within the entire field of practical-theological theories and may be regarded as cross sections of the various subdisciplines. They are basic for the action domains of the individual, the church, and public Christianity.

I think that these constitute the three main specializations within practical theology, although there may be a subsequent subdivision into a number of different fields of study. One may propose theories for different forms of pastoral and ecclesiastical action. They may be termed "practice theories" or "theories for practice" since they are linked — anthropologically, ecclesiologically, and diaconologically — at a higher theoretical level, and share in the development of fundamental practical-theological theory. Thus they play a distinct role in the work of practical theology.

In this third part I list ten different subdisciplines. Some I approach from an anthropological perspective, others from an ecclesiological or a diaconological point of view. The anthropological areas do, however, also share an ecclesiological and a diaconological aspect. Likewise, the ecclesiological specialties also have an anthropological and a diaconological aspect, while the diaconological specialties have an anthropological and an ecclesiological aspect. I deal briefly with each area. The most important theories for practice will be discussed at length in separate volumes in this series. Whether it is opportune to institutionalize all these specializations as distinct subdisciplines depends on a number of factors. The line followed in this book suggests as much integration as possible.

Finally, building on earlier chapters (6 and 9.4.5) I give attention to the development of a relevant pastoral theology. The work of the pastor is also experiencing a crisis in our time. Pastoral theology cannot solve this, but it can offer some clarifications for the reflection on the unique possibilities and limitations of the pastoral profession, and thus assist pastors in addressing questions of their identity and competence.

CHAPTER 13

Domains of Action:
Unity and Differentiation

In this chapter I move into the action domains of practical theology. The unity in theoretical proposals now undergoes a dispersion toward the various sectors and specialties. This does justice to the necessary differentiation in the discipline.

First, I pay attention to the differentiation principle, that, while recognizing the essential unity of the discipline, also allows for distinguishing different subdisciplines (13.1). Therefore, after evaluating other categorization principles, I opt for a moderate differentiation (13.2). In the elaboration of the principle I link the various perspectives that play a role in this book.

Once again I follow the division into three parts of the first part of this book. There I concluded that a differentiated practical theology must do justice to one's life as an individual, to life in social relationships, and to life in the broader context of society. These are three angles of approach to the praxis of modern society (praxis 2), which is the object of the mediation of the Christian faith (praxis 1). This determines the content of the next few chapters, which describe the action domains of "humanity and religion," "church and faith," and "religion and society." I then place this division against the background of developments within culture (13.3). The proposed differentiated practical theology relates to this in a critical way.

I realize that this link between the principles of integration and differentiation, for which this book has opted, raises tensions, not least for practical theologians themselves, who through teaching and research share in the further development of the discipline. They have to be not only specialists but to a large degree also generalists. That, finally, leads to the question of the competence of practical theology (13.4).

13.1 The Principle of Differentiation

As I enter on the description of the action domains, I move from the fundamental theory of practical theology to the developments of theories for the various specialties. As a result, the theoretical unity must give way to a degree of differentiation. It is important that in this section I extend the lines of the theory of action of part II. The various subdisciplines within practical theology can attain to academic status only if they can endure the test of a scientific theory of action. This makes it essential to avoid, in this final part, practical theology disintegrating into specialized theories, and to seek for a common theoretical denominator that transcends this thinking in purely practical terms.

In this book I have opted for an integrated way of "doing" practical theology. All who work within the discipline are, first, practical theologians and, second, specialists in a certain area. According to Firet (1980, 9), a chronic deficiency in our knowledge of the fundamental theories leads to an impoverishment of practical-theological activities and damage to the theological and academic character of the discipline. Each specialty tends to go its own way, focusing solely, with a view to daily practice, on a nontheological area. The pastoral theologian becomes a therapist, the catechist a specialist in didactics, the instructor of church development a social worker. They still meet in the corridors, but they no longer speak a common language. When the theories of the various specialties no longer have a firm footing in a foundational theory of action, says Firet (1980, 10), they deteriorate into "syncretistic banalities" (an expression from Foucault). Practical theology then becomes "praxeology," "a guideline for action" rather than a theory for action (Mette 1978, 321).

Firet believes (1980, 9) that practical theology has a threefold task in the theological department of the university: the development of a fundamental practical-theological theory, the development of various theories for practice, and providing training sessions. All three call for their own theories. I agree to a large extent with these assignments, but strongly emphasize the unity in the theoretical foundation.

The path I intend to follow is to a large extent determined by the academic task practical theology has to assume in our day and age. Comparing this book with a

"Grundriss der Praktische Theologie" in the German-speaking countries, the difference is immediately obvious. A. D. Müller (1950) devoted only 65 of his 375 pages to the *Grundlegung* (theoretical basis) of the discipline. The book then continues, after a discussion of the theology of the church offices, with a parallel treatment of the traditional subjects: liturgics, homiletics, catechesis, and poimenics. Rössler's *Grundriss* (1986) contains 300 more pages, manifests a new awareness of the issues it must address, offers a totally different organization of the various subjects, but also devotes only some 60 pages to the development of a fundamental theory. Likewise, the collected lecture notes of Schleiermacher (1850) offer 60 pages of introductory material. The subjects to be covered (mainly worship, sermon, and church order) are spread over two volumes.

The concept of "practice theory" usually presupposes a particular type of theory. Schippers agrees with ten Have: "A theory of practice states in a systematic way, and by means of a relevant set of concepts, what is needed for a satisfactory performance in a particular practice" (1990, 240). Others refer to "systematized knowledge gained from experience, together with a number of general rules for action" (ibid.). Schreurs (1990, 7) refers to an "attempt to formulate rationally defensible principles for a particular practice." These enable those who work in this practice to make decisions and justify their policies.

One finds such theories for practice also in the various subdisciplines of practical theology. They offer principles for action for liturgical, homiletic, catechetic, pastoral, and diaconal practice. Although I will not discuss these, I do want to emphasize that they are truly theological theories of action, which, in turn, contribute to the development of a fundamental theory, for instance in the areas of hermeneutics, communication, and empirical research. These subdisciplines are therefore part of science. The concept of a "practice theory" should not cause any misunderstanding on this point.

The next question is, How, within a basic theory, can one do justice to both the unity and the differentiation in practical theology? Over time a number of different suggestions have been made. I survey these briefly.

Firet (1968, 22 [1986, 12]) distinguishes initially between a "vertical" division of the different subjects and "horizontal" cross sections of the subdisciplines, in which he includes pastoral and church-related work. Later he questions even more strongly the classical categorization in subdisciplines. He begins to distinguish between a practical-theological communication theory and a practical-theological structural theory (1974, 10). In both cases he seeks to bring unity through the concept of action.

Others try to find the unity of practical theology in the concept of the church. O. Haendler speaks in his *Grundriss* (1957) along these lines of "practical theology as the structural theology of the present-day church." The manual of pastoral theology by F. X. Arnold et al. (1966ff.) is likewise built on the ecclesiological foundation of practical theology. A. D. Müller, referred to above, goes a step further and sees this unity in the realization of the kingdom of God in the church, and through the church in the world (1950, 13). P. Zulehner also opts in his book on pastoral theology for the "praxis of the church(es)" as the unifying principle (1989, 1:32). His prime concern, however, is with a situative, contextual theory of the "ecclesiogenesis," the birth of the church, which coincides with its praxis. He then distinguishes a "criteriology" (analysis of action goals), a "kairology" (analysis of the situation from a theological perspective), and a "praxeology," as the critical discussion of the concrete praxis.

Most American authors find the unifying factor in practical theology in the church and its "ministry" (Poling and Miller 1985; Mudge and Poling 1987). Don Browning's fundamental practical theology (7.5.2) goes much further. It comprises a descriptive, a historical, and a systematic theology leading to a strategic practical theology.

A modern variant of the principle of church structure is an approach that considers "church development" as a unifying, more or less overarching, theory of the various subdisciplines. For instance, van Kessel (1989, 12) refers to "church development as a general practical-theological basic theory." From the perspective of church development, with G. L. Goedhart (1984) one might divide the discipline by enlisting such verbs as "celebrating," "teaching," "serving," and "sharing."

The German literature also offers a more integrative approach. Bloth et al. (1981ff.) start from a matrix that allows for a horizontal and vertical positioning of the action goals (proclamation, catechesis, pastoral/diaconal care, leadership/organization) and the action domains (group, congregation, society). The activities may then be grouped in various cells. Otto's ideological point of departure prevents him from seeing the church as a unifying element. He works on the basis of "the complex relationship and the many-faceted manifestation of religion and church in society" (1986, 70). This results in an open system, in which "perspectives for reflection" (e.g., hermeneutics, didactics, ideological criticism, communication, symbolism) and "domains of action" (e.g., proclamation, worship, youth work, pastoral care) relate as "warp and woof" (see fig. 5 in chapter 7 above). Rössler (1986) works with a division into three: individual (religion, person, *diakonia,* pastoral activities) — church (church, offices, proclamation, worship) — society (institution, profession, catechism, congregations). In the background is the same differentiation principle, which I have also adopted in this book.

Thus there are more possibilities to show linkages than just through the traditional listing of subdisciplines. This book first pursues the unity of the theoretical framework as far as possible, in order to shift in this part to a moderate differentiation with regard to the action domains. This approach has similarities and dissimilarities with the authors mentioned in this section, as we will see below.

13.2 The Choice for a Moderate Differentiation

In this book I have chosen to link the differentiation principle and the integration principle. The differentiation principle follows from the differentiation process within praxis 2, the praxis of modern society (3.1.1). This principle is at the basis of the historical-interpretive approach in part I, which enables one to distinguish the spheres of the individual, the church, and society — viewed from the perspective of praxis 1, the mediation of the Christian faith — as three distinct action domains.

The integration principle is discussed in part II, which brought together the hermeneutical, strategic, and empirical perspectives in a practical-theological theory of action — theologically as well as methodologically (9.2). This theory is fundamental for the various forms of mediation of the Christian faith within the three distinct action domains. A link between the two principles results in a moderate differentiation in three steps.

The first step implies that one accept a relative distinction between the three domains of action, referred to as "humanity and religion," "church and faith," and "religion and society." These terms intend to describe the essence of the mediation of tradition and experience in various sectors of the society. In the context of the cultural development in Western Europe, which has been highly influenced by Christianity, one might speak of "individual Christianity," "institutional Christianity," and "public Christianity."

When we speak of the individual, we refer to *religion*, in this connection to be understood as religious experience, whether or not it is interpreted on the basis of the Christian tradition. When speaking of the church, we use the word *faith*, which presupposes a personal decision in favor of the Christian tradition. This receives form and content in the social environment of a group of believers. Speaking of society, we use "religion" in the sense of "religious behavior," as we refer to the ways in which people give public expression to their religion or faith, in worship services and through official position statements regarding moral or social issues. This parallels the three concepts of individual, institutional, and public Christianity. The term *individual Christianity* is based on the idea that in our society religious experience is often influenced by the Christian tradition, even though this does not always result in a personal conviction of faith. The term *public Christianity* points to the fact that many norms and values in society are rooted in a connection between Christianity and humanism. For the term *public religion,* see also 16.1.3.

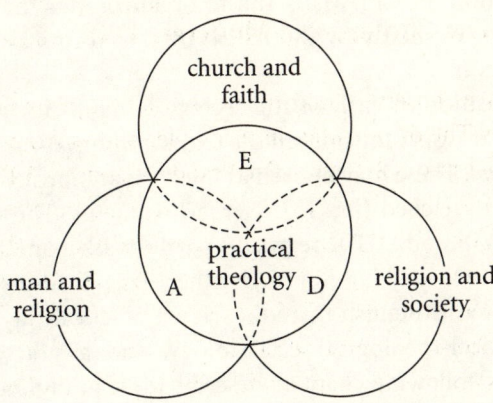

Figure 18: Differentiation with regard to action domains

The various sectors have been drawn as three partly overlapping circles. The fourth circle, in the middle, which covers segments of the other circles, comprises the praxis of practical theology (praxis 1). In all three sectors one confronts "communicative action in the service of the gospel" — the focus of the development of practical-theological theories.

The second step consists of the rather obvious presupposition that the mediation of tradition and experience in the sectors of the individual and of society — to the extent that this can be the case — to that of the church increasingly demands a specific practical-theological approach, separate from that of the church. In the sector of the church the mediation occurs in the sphere of faith, in the context of the Christian tradition, to which people in the church may be expected to relate. But the reach of church and faith is limited.

The story is often quite different when it concerns the individual. The forms of mediation have to be adapted to the private world of individuals who are looking for meaning in their lives. As a result of the secularization process, one finds that the identification with the Christian tradition is here much more vague. This is expressed through the more general label of "religion."

Other factors play a role in those forms of mediation that, on the basis of the Christian tradition, target processes of transformation in society. Here we refer to religion as "religious behavior." The influence of the church has also decreased in society in general. If there is any mediation, in the sense of exerting Christian influence, it is to a large extent due to the personal "radiation" of Christians and to organizations that let themselves be guided, either explicitly or implicitly, by the norms and values of the Christian tradition.

Communication in each of the sectors demands its own specific approach. For that reason, I introduced the terms *anthropological, ecclesiological,* and *diaconological.* These may be seen as the cross sections of practical theology. The figure I sketched (fig. 18) refers to segments. They were indicated with the letters A, E, and D. The segments partly overlap one another; this expresses the influence they have on each other. This distinction of three segments leads me to distinguish three theories: a practical-theological anthropology, a practical-theological ecclesiology, and a practical-theological diaconology. The following chapters describe these in outline.

The third step is to relate the various subdisciplines to this. I distinguish ten different areas. Some of these are established branches within practical theology, while some have usually not been recognized as separate subdisciplines. The latter aspect should not cause any objections. Rather, I would say the fewer subjects the better. In view of the desirable integration, it proves quite possible to combine different subdisciplines under the umbrella of practical theology.

I thus make a relative distinction between subjects and subdisciplines in practical theology. A subject has to do with a distinct area of knowledge. The subdisciplines result from the way in which theological education is organized. That many areas of theology have developed into separate subdisciplines has led to a significant fragmentation in contemporary theological studies. In part also as a result of the modular approach to education, students at times no longer see the forest for the trees. For this reason I am introducing this step-by-step approach in this section, which leads to a moderate differentiation.

Three of these subdisciplines are developed primarily from an anthropological perspective, four primarily from an ecclesiological perspective, and three primarily from a deaconological perspective. I most often use the terms that are commonly employed in the "encyclopedic" tradition, but will also coin some additional ones.

The primarily anthropological subjects are directed toward communicative action in relation to the individual. These include poimenics (pastoral theology and pastoral psychology), religious pedagogics, and spirituality. Poimenics gives a central place to theories concerning care for the individual; religious pedagogics concentrates its attention on religious education for young people, while the subject of spirituality deals specifically with the actual religious experience of people and how this can be influenced.

The primarily ecclesiological subjects are directed toward communicative action within, and on the basis of, the social structure of the Christian community. They are, in pairs: homiletics and liturgics, catechesis and church development. Celebration in the Christian community holds the central place in homiletics and liturgics. Catechetics, the transmission of the Christian tradition, and church development (oikodomics) focus on the nurture of the church to make it a living community concerned with the salvation of humanity and the world.

The primarily deaconological subjects are directed toward communicative action on the basis of the Christian tradition within various strata of society. The subjects are: deaconology, the theory of evangelism, and the equipping of the laity. Deaconology may be defined as the theory of the service to humankind and society through compassion and justice. The theory of evangelism refers to the theoretical basis for communicating the gospel through the church to its immediate environment, often largely consisting of people who have been alienated from the Christian tradition. The subject of equipping the laity intends to develop theories about the manner in which Christians may manifest Christian norms and values in everyday life.

This short description suffices for the moment. The following chapters offer a more detailed discussion. I must note the word *primarily* in the above definitions. With a view to the partial overlapping of the three segments, one subdivision is primarily anthropological, the other primarily ecclesiological, and the third primarily deaconological. But in each case the other perspectives also come into play. For instance, the perspectives of church and society cannot be missed in pastoral action, aimed at the individual; and church development, likewise, must take the needs of individual people into account and will also consider the development of the church as a service to society.

This approach also implies that, simultaneously, justice must be done to the perspective of individual autonomy, the perspective of the community, and the social perspective — and this always in a hermeneutical-critical sense.

This results in the following "map" for practical theology:

humanity and religion	church and faith	religion and society
practical-theological anthropology →		
	← practical-theological ecclesiology →	
		← practical-theological diaconology
• poimenics	• church development	• diaconics
• religious pedagogics	• catechetics	• theory of evangelism
• spirituality	• liturgics	• equipping the laity
	• homiletics	

My approach closely resembles that of Rössler in his works on modern Christianity ("Neuzeitliches Christentum," Rössler 1986, 78ff.; Nipkow, Rössler, and Schweitzer 1991, 48ff.): "We propose to make the principles from which the differentiated status of church praxis has been developed in modern times into the very principle of unity and organization of practical theology" (1991, 48). He uses "Neuzeitliches Christentum" (contemporary Christianity) as a descriptive concept. He distinguishes among "institutional Christianity," "public Christianity," and "individual Christianity." These three manifestations of contemporary Christianity have their own status but are also connected. "This threefold manifestation of contemporary Christianity has now given real shape and a specific meaning to the three major areas of concern for the church and for practical theology" (50).

13.3 The Impasse of Our Culture

The development outlined above is not without problems. I must therefore look in somewhat greater detail at the development in our culture, which to some extent lies at the root of this proposal for a tripartitioning. Already in part I (5.4), when I established my position, I referred to a degree of ambivalence. We may be modern people, but we often have a bad conscience. Here I recall some other considerations. Emancipation and individualizing may at times lead to individualism, but we cannot undo the Enlightenment. Even the Christian community is affected by rationalization and command-thinking, for the church is an organization like all others. Moreover, the church has been pushed back into the sphere of our private life and our free time, and it manifests a remarkable middle-class mentality. As a result there may be some tension between the church and the Christ-event ("die Sache Jesu"). Society has gained its independence from the church; the same is true for public Christianity, to the extent that it continues to exist in political and social organizations. They survive, in spite of secularization, but that in itself says little about their Christian content. In all three instances the ambivalence I noted in the relation of the Christian faith to society has to do with the tension between adaptation and resistance, between inculturation and cultural disobedience. Neither individuals nor the church can survive major cultural changes without some form of adaptation, but the credibility of the gospel poses its limits to this process of adaptation. The individual, as well as the church and Christianity, must go with the times, but they cannot totally disregard tradition. This tension-laden praxis becomes apparent when praxis 1 and praxis 2 are connected.

Scholars evaluate these developments differently, of course, and not all arrive at the same conclusions. The questions relating to this issue are extremely urgent, from a personal as well as from an ecclesiastical or political point of view. Two items from the newspaper that I read in the week when I was writing this chapter may serve as illustrations:

In his "Coornhert lecture" (for a society of "enlightened" law professionals), the Dutch politician H. van Mierlo (a Liberal Democrat) deals with the relationship between the citizen and the government (Trouw, Nov. 21, 1992). He argues that a radical change has occurred in our culture since the 1960s. This change comprises two major aspects: the de-ideologizing of politics and the individualization of the citizen. The great ideologies have collapsed. The ties between the individual sphere and the collective sphere have dissipated. This is true for the Dutch system of social organization on the basis of confessional orientations, as well as for the world of organizations and private initiatives. The church, which is part of this, has ceased to play its traditional role. The mediation between the individual and the collectivity no longer occurs through the traditional group. Van Mierlo feels that we must make a radical choice for the individual. This explains why feminism as an emancipation movement has been successful in our time. The emancipation process has a history of centuries, but it always attempted to work through groups. Van Mierlo believes that it would be incorrect to say that individualism fosters egoism and destroys solidarity. In this respect, he differs from his Christian Democratic colleagues Brinkman and Hirsch Ballin. The first regularly appeals to the "we" sentiment, while the latter calls for the restoration of public morality.

The second illustration is an interview in the Dutch Reformed weekly *Hervormd Nederland* (Nov. 21, 1992) in which Annelies van Heijst (a feminist theologian) speaks about her dissertation (1992). She chose "the loss of the self" as her theme, against the trends of feminism and its emphasis on self-realization and autonomy. She agrees with the book *De Wetten* (The laws) by Dutch novelist Connie Palmen, and sees "falling" as a positive disruption of the self. It represents the wish to be liberated from the burden of constantly having to realize oneself in a conscious and effective way. So much has gone wrong in our culture! She experiences a tension: "On the one hand, I want to work for a better world. I feel a kinship with the political left. On the other hand, I place great importance on what my mother called 'to be good for others.'" She views Auschwitz as the historical development of sovereign humanity. Autonomy is the result of a too grandiose view of humanity. She points to theories, such as that of Freud, that emphasize that humanity is not the master of its own home, and to philosophers, such as the Frenchman J. F. Lyotard, who claim that the end of "the grand narratives" has arrived. The ideologies are bankrupt.

While van Mierlo and van Heijst agree that "the grand narratives" of the ideologies no longer determine the thinking about society, they clearly differ in their evaluation of the individual. J. Peters, a sociologist of religion, comments on this discussion: "It is understandable that politicians and others would express their concern about this development. It is just a bit too easy to push this concern aside as 'moralizing'" (1993, 21). This concern also finds an echo in his definition of individualizing: "Individualizing means . . . that humans increasingly choose freedom, autonomy, and individual rights in all domains of life, and increasingly resist equality, leveling, and solidarity" (8). But, generally speaking, there has to be some degree of balance between freedom and equality.

These illustrations show a parallel with the cultural analysis of van Gennep (1989). He points to the gradual disappearance of ideologies, but also of the decline in the power of the church. But an ethical and political discussion must continue, if the utopia, the desire for justice, is to survive. "When we are no longer moved by a utopia, language will die and communication between humans will cease" (198). The church must unconditionally work to keep that discussion alive. This also applies to the representatives of the bankrupt ideologies. In this "ecumenism of enlightenment" — the term he uses for this discussion — much is at stake: freedom, justice, and equal rights. In this way he attempts to interest people in the public cause.

What can the church do in this respect? Van Gennep sees it as a major problem that the mediation between private life and public life has come to a standstill. He believes ideologies already came to their end around 1960 (1989, 224). In our postmodern time we must be content with "the small narratives" (Lyotard 1987, 220). Likewise, the church has retained little of its former power. Van Gennep pleads for a praxis "that succeeds in convincing the people that there is a form of authority that leaves humanity free" (1989, 242). God's power is totally different from human power. He quotes Bonhoeffer: "Only a suffering God is able to help" (367).

A side remark by way of clarification. I just used the term *postmodern*. In this book I do not differentiate between modern and postmodern. The difference is not necessarily one of contrast. Postmodern thinking, which is critical toward an optimistic Enlightenment thinking but nonetheless remains loyal to rationality, does not present a farewell from, but rather a radicalization of, modern thinking (cf. van Gennep 1989, 221). I use the general term *modernity*, and make a further distinction between the Enlightenment perspective and the critical perspective.

Contemporary society and the church, says van Gennep, are not prepared to engage in this discussion, because the intermediary structures have disappeared. Faced with the fact that everything in society tends to happen on a large scale, humans react by fleeing inward: individualism. For that reason the mesostructure is important. It serves as a buffer between state and society on the one hand, and individual and community on the other (247). It mediates between the collectivity and the individual and is important for the development of the personality, even though it can also become a breeding ground for prejudice. The social organization arranged according to the various confessions *(zuilen)* has often fulfilled that function, together with the church. Van Gennep searches for ways that will guarantee the survival of the humane tradition of Christianity and the Enlightenment. Following in the footsteps of Habermas, he thinks of "alternative institutions" that can offer resistance against the "colonizing" of the "lifeworlds" (263). Why could the churches not play this role? "Also in this respect we might expect more from a marginalized church than from a state church, a national church, or a church state" (264). Even though the church has lost much of its influence, there remains a desire for a mesostructural community (265), in particular where the subject status of humans is under heavy attack. "It is therefore of great importance that our society starts to rebuild its mesocultural order with regard to culture, economy, religion, and ideology" (268). The churches, but also the labor unions and the media, may play a role in this area.

This is an appealing plea. A choice for the division into three — of individual, church, and society — is not a matter of reticence but a solution that wants to relate positively to cultural developments, and wants to assign an important place to what happens in society in general, in particular to the church as a mesostructure.

The above is an attempt to give direction in the midst of understandable ambivalences. In this connection I am thinking of the arguments of van Gennep and of van Heijst. Attention for the individual should not be absorbed in an uncritical affirmation of autonomy. Humanity will have to find itself. I am thinking of H. Fortmann's description of mental health: "the ability (freedom!) to develop one's potential (e.g., in work) and to lose oneself" (1974, II, 361). This is a freedom in two directions: "self-realization and commitment." With respect to society, one indeed has to realize that the time of "the grand narratives" — of ideologies — is no more. But one should not lose the hope for a more peaceful and more just world. The utopia of the coming of God's kingdom should continue to be alive. That can also happen through "the small narratives" of movements, action groups, and church communities. As far as the church is concerned, it has the responsibility to search for a credible way of "being church," for new forms of Christian community, that call for a counterculture, against an extreme individualism and an anonymous bureaucratic collectivity. These are the main content lines I want to extend in the next few chapters.

13.4 Practical-Theological Competence

One other question demands attention in this chapter. I pleaded for a shift from the subdisciplines to a fundamental theory. This raises the question of (practical-) theological competence. Who is competent to act and judge?

At the Free University (Amsterdam) all graduate students in practical theology are required to take the same courses in practical theology, regardless of their specialization. All have to sit for two major exams, in theological theory and in methodology, before they begin to specialize in one or two subdisciplines. Both perspectives must feature in the thesis they write toward the end of their course work.

One would expect that as a result the student has acquired a practical-theological habitus and may be considered competent, even though her or his knowledge, insights, and experience are, of course, still limited. This distinction between competence in a narrow sense and in a broader sense (Neumann 1992, 352ff.), the tension between generalist and specialist, is manageable within certain parameters. The main aspect is "the basic qualification for theological and pastoral action" (355). This applies not only to graduate students in practical theology but to a large degree also for those who work on an academic level in this discipline.

A practical theologian is therefore both a generalist and a specialist. With the term *specialist* I want to underline that one can move within the practical-theological structure with its various circles (9.2.4) and that one has an elementary knowledge of the practical-theological theory. It is very difficult to master all the different fields. A specialization is needed not only in the area of practical theology but also with regard to such fields as dogmatics and ethics, (recent) church history, philosophy (of religion), psychology (of religion), sociology (of religion), (cultural) anthropology, agology, and empirical methodology. Such a list, which is far from complete, tends to give the students a feeling of just touching a few subjects in a superficial manner.

This is not only a problem for practical theologians but for theologians in general, who must always deal with a number of other disciplines besides their own. Here also I feel that anyone who considers her- or himself a theologian must first of all be a generalist, and only then a specialist, that is, an exegete, a systematic theologian, a church historian, or a practical theologian. Total withdrawal in a specialty is at the expense of the unity of theology and leads to a fragmentation of knowledge.

This also throws further light on the intradisciplinarity advocated by van der Ven (1985, 38). He believes that every theologian must be able to handle the theories, methods, and techniques of another discipline. This assignment should not be any reason for complaint, since it enriches the thinking of the scholar enormously. It becomes less threatening when the scholar shares this burden with fellow scholars. In taking this concept of intradisciplinarity on board, I am thinking primarily of group projects in which practical theologians can work closely together with social scientists, preferably even including in their midst someone with philosophical expertise.

All this has, of course, consequences for the way in which a team of scholars is constituted. It is impossible for one person to teach adequately in the entire field of practical theology. This may have been different within a deductive-theological concept, before the hermeneutical and empirical shift took place.

The future looks rather bleak. The decline in the number of students has led to a reduction in the teaching staff. As a result, only the complementary cooperation between institutions (cf. the report of the 1992 Commission on Theological Studies in the Netherlands) can assure competence in the various specialties.

An adequate theological department must, I believe, have at least five practical theologians. Two must deal specifically with the anthropological sector (a pastoral psychologist and a religious pedagogue), two with the ecclesiological sector (a church development expert and a specialist in liturgics and homiletics), and someone who primarily deals with the field of church and society (diaconology and evangelism). They must first of all be general practical theologians, while possessing expertise in one of the sectors mentioned.

13.5 Conclusion

In this chapter I sketched the outline for the third part of this book. The focus is on differentiation on the basis of a unity in theological theory. This differentiation is in three directions: individual, church, and society. It is supported by three theories from a fundamental theory: practical-theological anthropology, practical-theological ecclesiology, and practical-theological diaconology. One detects segments of circles that in part overlap each other, in which the various specialities may be positioned. Each of these has its own angle of approach, but they are linked through the three different perspectives. Contemporary culture forces one to place some clear emphases. I extend these lines in the next few chapters.

CHAPTER 14

Humanity and Religion

In this chapter I discuss the first of three distinct action domains of practical theology: the perspective of the individual in relation to the manner in which one gives meaning and significance to one's life by religious means. One is not alone in this world. For that reason the perspectives of church and society enter the picture. But the individual person should not be viewed from a purely ecclesiological frame of reference. This chapter does not address people as *church members* but as *people*. Practical theology here chooses its point of departure in the broad field of human religiosity.

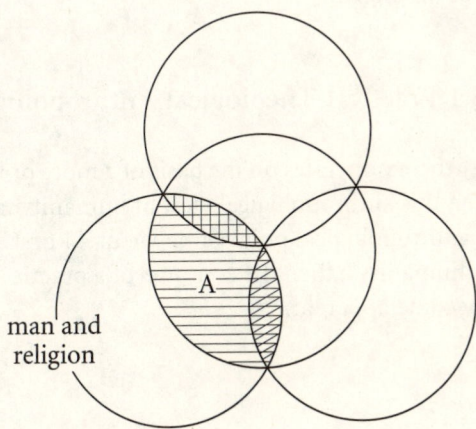

Figure 19: The anthropological segment

Focusing on people raises the matter of practical-theological anthropology as a bonding element for all specialties (14.1). The basic themes in this segment are subjectivity, meaning, religious development, and religious experience (14.2). From this perspective I then give attention to the subdisciplines of poimenics, religious pedagogy, and spirituality (14.3).

Since Schleiermacher, practical theology has been keenly interested in the experience of the individual. In our time we must recognize the relation with the process of individualization, which I have valued positively, in spite of ambivalent feelings (13.3). A recent study of young people, initiated by the Reformed Churches in the Netherlands and executed by the Institute of Practical Theology of the Free University in Amsterdam (Alma 1993), once again showed this necessity. Many young people see the faith their parents have transmitted to them as little more than an intellectual construct. Faith is an isolated area, associated with church and home, not with work, free time, school, and friends. The world in which young people live consists of a large number of subordinate worlds that are detached from one another. The differentiation in society leads to fragmentation of the world of experience. There will have to be space in the transmission of faith — which happens especially within the family — for "questioning and searching" rather than for "stating and knowing," and for the search for one's individual path. The church itself cannot contribute much in this process. But it will have to manifest itself as a recognizable community that leaves room for the unique experiences of individuals. The recommendations emphasize attempts to develop individual competencies within new social relationships (191). The individual competencies mentioned are a well-developed sense of self-worth, self-reflection, and flexibility. This line of thought corresponds with the differentiation principle of parts I and III of this book.

14.1 Practical-Theological Anthropology

Practical-theology theory operates on the basis of a more or less rational view of humanity. When this anthropological view of humanity takes center stage, one speaks of an anthropological point of departure. I first address this concept of "a view of humanity"; then the contours of a practical-theological anthropology will become apparent.

14.1.1 Views of Humanity

Practical-theological anthropology must recognize a number of quite divergent perspectives: of biology, philosophy, psychology, sociology, cultural anthropology, and systematic theology. It is difficult to combine all these approaches in one single theory. Moreover, systematizing may also occur at the expense of what has been called "an open view of humanity." On the basis of my orientation toward praxis, I will build on the concept of the "experienced" view of humanity.

What is a view of humanity? Kwant gives the following description: "I define a 'view of humanity' as a frame of reference at the disposal of people, allowing them to know how they must behave, what they must do and not do, and providing them with a norm by which to judge themselves and others" (1986, 10). Although in daily life this view of humanity that people supposedly have is rarely mentioned, it is clear that such a view functions in every society. It has most of all a social character. As people mature, they internalize the pattern of expectations of their environment. An image develops that tells one what one should be. Freud employs in this connection the rather striking term *Über-ich* (superego) (16).

Kwant distinguishes this view of humanity from the one that results from reflection and is expressed in language. This is the mythical view of humanity, the view of the popular story, religious tradition, or a particular theory. Thus, over time, Catholic, Calvinist, liberal, socialist, and humanistic views of humanity have arisen. These views have a historical character and are to a large extent determined by the culture in which they originated. They have a normative influence, often restricting the liberty of the people involved, since they submit them to the predominant thinking in a community. But people do not always experience it as such. Often they accept the demanding role pattern to which they submit as a voluntary choice or — in a positive sense — as a sacrifice.

The way in which such a view of humanity, which is the result of reflection, functions may be illustrated by referring to the many different contents that through the centuries have been given to the biblical notion of humanity as the image of God (Gen. 1:27ff.). The Catholic tradition teaches that the Fall hardly affected this image, while the Reformed tradition stresses how the image is all but lost as a result of the Fall, and the Jewish tradition focuses on concepts like choice and task. In the twentieth century, Jewish thinkers (5.2.5) like Buber (1958), Levinas (1969), and Heschel (Hartensveld 1988) give their own interpretations based on the world of their experience. Internalization of this religious heritage enables people to relate to life in various ways.

Philosophical anthropology places various accents, depending on whether personalism, existentialism, Marxism, or structuralism takes center stage (Bakker 1981). Berkhof concludes: "Through the centuries Christian anthropology has been a combination of biblical and contemporary thought patterns — in which, according to the designers, the first element was dominant, but as later generations saw it, the second" (1973, 189 [1979, 180]). This calls for prudence.

14.1.2 Choosing an Appropriate Combination

Practical-theological anthropology cannot offer much more than a combination of theological and social scientific insights that open a perspective for action. This perspective would suggest that one could also speak of andragogics.

The choices made in this book are always open for correction. Speaking theologically, with Berkhof (5.3.2; 11.1) I would like to emphasize that humans are "respondable," "made to" encounter God and respond to his love (1973, 191 [1979, 181-82]). Living in a relationship with God and fellow human beings endows one with a high degree of responsibility. The goodness of creation is not opposed to its preliminary and incomplete character, says Berkhof. Sin "is deeply rooted in the creaturely structure of the risky being called man" (198 [188]). "Love and freedom" have "guilt and fate" as their counterparts. Humanity also experiences the tension of goodness and preliminariness: "He cannot just be himself. He runs ahead of himself. One could also say that he 'is' precisely that which he is not (yet). His authentic existence lies above and ahead of him — as a promise or as a mirage? Faith says: as a promise; the creation is intended to be elevated and to become a world which is centered upon and which serves a radically new form of humanity, in conformity to the image of the glorified Christ" (179 [170]). In this line being human has everything to do with receiving and giving — in this order! — of *meaning*.

Kuitert refers in this connection to anthropological "floorboards" (1977, 74), in the sense of "primitive" faith, a basic trust. "Humans cannot help but have such a confidence-giving faith, as long as they are physically and mentally healthy" (83). Such "primitive" faith is in essence saving faith: faith that the human enterprise will end well (84).

From this perspective it is important for practical theology to offer a combination of viewpoints. I once called this a "basic anthropology" (1977, 82ff.). I used this term to refer to the entire person, the unity of body, soul, and spirit, of salvation and healing (Heitink and Veenhof 1990); being human as being "in relationship with," linked to the world around one; being human in its conscious and subconscious aspects; humans in their development, directed toward self-realization; humans with the convictions and values that drive them (1977, 108). To this I want to add the structuralist view of the de-subjectification under the influence of cultural and social factors.

I believe that the various points of view correct each other. Realizing, for instance, how unfree humans can react when under the influence of some subconscious factors enables one to relativize "the myth of self-realization" (Nijk 1978). Knowing about the cultural imprisonment of the subject ensures that one does not overestimate the aspect of autonomy. In addition, practical-theological discourse puts these viewpoints in a theologically critical perspective. In this the concept of "freedom" plays an important role, as is apparent from the fact that ever since Augustine and Pelagius, through Luther and Erasmus, the theme of the "freedom of the will" has dominated the anthropological discussion up till the current debate about autonomy and heteronomy.

One must always keep in mind that the view people have of themselves in their mutual communication must always have priority over interpretations of the view of humanity. This demands from field-workers a maximum of receptivity. They must not prematurely interrupt people's stories with theoretical constructs. This is the only way to do justice to the subject status of the other. The reflection on the view of humanity, in this context the view of humanity of practical-theological anthropology, functions as the frame of reference and does not come to the forefront until the moment when it becomes desirable to clarify the experiences through shared interpretation.

14.2 The Anthropological Segment

Having chosen this combination of viewpoints, I must now fill out the details of the anthropological segment of practical theology. First, I must take a critical look at the central place allotted to the individualized subject. Then I can further discuss the aspects of meaning, religious development, and religious experience. These three in combination constitute the core of practical-theological anthropology.

14.2.1 Toward a Critical Subjectivity

To counter the dominance of the ecclesiological paradigm, Henning Luther (1992) recently made his own contribution to the anthropological shift in practical theology in his proposal for "a practical theology of the subject," which has remained in fragmentary form because of his early death. He criticized the kind of practical theology that makes the church the prime subject (Nitzsch), as this presents one with "a subject without subjects," while it should always focus on people (9).

Against a central place for the pastor as the subject, he emphasized the lay perspective (15). He was interested in how concrete individuals deal with religion and faith in their own private world and personal history, and how religion can contribute to the process in which the individual becomes a subject.

The term *subject* is, however, charged with a suspicion of individualism. He therefore took a critical stance toward an aggressive and egoistic interpretation of subjectivity (62). He also distanced himself from identity concepts that emphasize the identification with oneself (155). The question of the self thus demands a critical-emancipatory content. Subjectivity is in essence directed toward a relationship with others. In this context he referred to Habermas and Levinas, who define the subject not in terms of a monologue but in terms of relationships. Luther paid ample attention to the study of (auto-) biography. In recent years one often detects this interesting theme in practical theology. One has the best chance of truly understanding a person, also as a believer, from her or his biography, that is, from the way in which a person sees her- or himself.

One encounters a further radicalization of the subject in the work of B. Höfte. He points out that the critical dialogue with modern humanity occurs initially through categories borrowed from existentialism and personalism (1990, 59). Within a context dominated by the middle-class subject, he stresses the contribution that can be made toward making the poor into subjects (131). This emphasis on solidarity is needed in order to counter an "antisocial individualism" (H. Luther).

Solidarity is, however, a word to be used with caution. My experience indicates that practical theology here meets its boundary. For many years I have tried, through research and internships for students, to look at society "through the eyes of the underprivileged." This has indeed been a learning experience, but it has been only partly successful. One remains an outsider, unless one is prepared to live among the poor and to share fully in their lives. Yet there are other ways to bridge some of the gap between the middle-class subject and the poor as subject. Even a practical theology that realizes its own limitations can contribute in this area (Schippers et al. 1990). This results in a critical subjectivity that enables one, from a privileged position, to engage in the needs of society.

14.2.2 The Meaning of Life

The core question practical-theological anthropology must address is that of the meaning of life. This question has acquired an extreme urgency in modern times. It is not a question born of luxury, but one rooted in anxiety and despair. Haarsma points out that this question arises in a culture where people lack nothing as far as material things are concerned, and is asked by people who seem to be in perfect health. But this does not mean that each individual must answer this question separately, nor that this is only a subjective problem (Haarsma 1991, 35). The quest for meaning has to do with the deep alienation people experience in our culture. Durkheim's term for the internal disarray of society, anomy, which leads many to despair and at times to suicide, shows that this rosy picture concerns only the external aspects of society.

Haarsma also refers to the "gratuitous" character of meaning, or in other words: the Christian faith is not just about "giving" meaning but also about "receiving" meaning. He pleads for a further elaboration of a theology of grace in that direction, and for the restoration of the esthetic categories in the doctrine of grace, categories that refer to the "enjoyment" of faith, so that people can be truly happy with their faith. The quest for meaning is related to the quest for God and demands a further definition of content on the basis of the Christian faith. The quest also refers to the other. Being together with brothers and sisters makes people realize: I need you. Haarsma concludes: "It is in this respect that the church can offer people meaning, and I think it is this type of meaning they enjoy" (1991, 53).

Here one detects the critical perspective of the quest for meaning. It is apparently not a matter of coincidence that there are more psychological needs in society than ever before, and that even social workers and therapists begin to realize that more than mere psychological help is required (Kuilman and Uleyn 1986). Questions like "Why do I live?" and "What will give me hope?" transcend psychological reality. These questions refer to "the human being as spirit" (Firet 1968, 236 [1986, 182]), and to what Fortmann calls "degrees of depth in the concept of mental health" (1974, 2:351). The quest for meaning is rooted in one's view of life and springs from that dimension which Tillich describes as "ultimate concern" (1968, 1:14).

When discussing a practical-theological theory of action, it is important to understand through what psychological process people find meaning. Research shows that "significant others" play a major role in this respect (Alma 1993, 44). Interaction with others provides sources of meaning in one's life that help one to respond to existential questions. Which sources of meaning are enlisted depends on one's personal life history (biography) and on the specific situation a person finds oneself in. This requires attention in pastoral action for the unique life story of the other, in a common search for the person's sources. The narrative tradition in pastoral theology and pastoral psychology (Andriessen and Heitink 1985; Gerkin 1986), which establishes along hermeneutical lines a link with the story of Scripture (humanity as a "living human document"), uses this approach.

14.2.3 Religious Development

When people succeed in giving religious meaning and significance to their lives, they do this on the basis of a religious development that has taken place in their lives. One of the tasks of a basic anthropological theory is to understand this process of religious development as a prerequisite to developing instruments for assisting young and old people in this aspect of their lives.

In recent years several theories about this have been developed, the one by James W. Fowler (1981) being the best known. Fowler has reported on his research about the "stages of faith." "Faith" is here defined as "finding meaning" or "life orientation," whether religious or secular. Fowler searches for points of agreement with others and combines in his model cognitive development theories (Piaget, Kohlberg) with the identity theory of Erikson. He distinguishes six stages in faith development: the stage of intuitive-projective faith (age 4-7), the mythical-literal faith (age 7-11), the synthetic-conventional faith (age 11-17), the individuative-reflective faith (age 17 and older), the conjunctive faith, and finally the universal faith. Each phase builds on the previous one.

This faith development has several crucial moments. Those who do not succeed in moving from phase 2 to phase 3, from a mythical to a conventional faith, soon turn away altogether. The transfer from phase 3 to phase 4 is even more important. There it becomes apparent whether someone grows from a conventional faith to a personal conviction of faith.

Should one at this point make any further distinction between boys and girls? The experts do not agree. Carol Gilligan (1982) argues that research has shown that boys and girls show different patterns of socialization and identify with father or mother each in their own way. R. Bons-Storm (1986, 350) agrees. "Men experience their selves and the world around them on the basis of *separation* and the need for autonomy within a certain hierarchy." The situation is different for girls. "Girls grow up with the basic values of *bonding,* warmth, psychosomatic wholeness." Bons-Storm believes that this also results in a different experience of the relationship with God. Therefore, the unique experiences of women must receive special pastoral attention from the specific perspective of "women's ways of knowing" (Belenky et al. 1986). Though recognizing the value of Gilligan's research, the feminist theologian C. J. M. Halkes (1984, 114ff.) places other accents. She refuses to turn the gender difference into an anthropological point of departure. She feels that the words *male* and *female* must be accompanied by a thousand quotation marks, as they are the results of thousands of years of socialization and internalization. In a period of emancipation a strong accent on the uniqueness of each gender is defensible (116); but, looking toward the future, she prefers a transformative model, in which female values gradually develop into human attitudes that transform the "linear" male models of thinking.

14.2.4 Religious Experience

Finally, I must discuss the psychology of religious experience. In recent decades religious-psychological research has provided more insight in this area. Based on studies by Adorno and by himself, J. Weima points to the difference between extrinsic and intrinsic religiosity (1981, 45ff.). Extrinsic religiosity is accompanied by prejudices. These disappear when religion is internalized into a personal conviction. In the first instance, one often sees merely an objective, doctrinal, at times authoritarian, faith. In the second instance, the person matures and acquires a living faith. This, in a way, parallels the shift from Fowler's third phase to his fourth phase.

It is important for a foundational theory to recognize the conditions under which religious experience originates. The factor of interpretation here plays a major role. In experience — since Schleiermacher a central topic in any discussion about the subject — a cognitive moment is connected with an affective moment (Firet 1975, 213). Together they constitute an experiential process. Religious experience always presupposes a religious frame of reference, says Weima, who in this connection refers to theories of attribution (1981, 81ff.). There are subjective experiences and cognitive factors, the latter determining the meaning one gives to the former. This is referred to as "attribution of meaning." Hjalmar Sundén (1966), a Swedish psychologist of religion, distinguishes in his role theory between role assumption *(Rollen-übernahme)* and role absorption *(Rollenaufnahme)*. For instance, a man who takes the Bible as his frame of reference may identify with Abraham (a radical break with one's past) and in so doing will experience, at some point in his life, a religiously experienced choice. This is the assumption of a role. But, at the same time, he takes the role of God, that is, he anticipates the biblical promise that God will bless him on this path and will make him a blessing. One and the same reality is experienced in different ways. Sundén refers to this with the expression "exchange of phases."

Weima argues that subconscious factors also come into play. He refers to the archetypes of C. G. Jung, which mark the path of human individuation and lead toward the archetype of the "Self." Indeed, Jung here recognizes the presence of "immanent transcendence" (Weima 1981, 267). A psychologist can go no further. Whether this results in an experience of the divine depends, theologically speaking, on whether the work of the Spirit, as the gift of God, is involved in this process.

Weima further distinguishes between autocentric and allocentric observation (1981, 211). The concern is here with a cultural perspective. On the one hand, the first form has to do with the "object of use" perspective. This is a form of control that is part and parcel of a capitalistic society. On the other hand, allocentric observation refers to a way of observing that allows for being subjected to outside influence. This demands a receptive attitude, an exercise in openness, impressionability, and wonder. Fortmann refers in this connection to a "second primitiveness," a receptivity that has passed through reflection (1974, 344). For a critical discussion, see O. Jager (1987, 161), who prefers to speak of a "second house of bondage" experience: "Having experienced liberation we are once again united with those who are still in bondage." This is a critical moment in speaking of religious experience.

Finally, the theme of religious experience must be related to that of mental health (Fortmann 1974, vol. 3b). There is healthy as well as unhealthy faith, and it belongs to the task of practical-theological anthropology to provide insight in this matter, so that people may learn to distinguish between the two. Based on many years of supervising experience, W. Zijlstra (1989) is able to offer a number of effective models. He follows the polar approach of F. Riemann (1975), who distinguishes four basic forms of anxiety, which he subsequently links with the personality that is too dependent in contrast to that which is too independent, and with the type that is too free in contrast to the type that is too predetermined. This provides insight in the "credit" and "debit" side of various ways in which people experience their faith, as encountered in the pastoral practice.

14.3 Subdisciplines

From the perspective of the subject one can distinguish three subdisciplines: poimenics (or pastoral theology and pastoral psychology), religious pedagogics, and spirituality. The model of the circles (13.2) presupposes that the church and social factors also play a role. But in this section I emphasize the subject sphere.

14.3.1 Poimenics

Poimenics encompasses the theory about the pastorate for individuals or groups. In my proposal for a pastoral theology (Heitink 1977), I left the traditional ecclesiological framework and chose my point of departure in anthropology: the pastorate as encounter, as an incarnational experience. This occurs against the horizon of society and in community with the Christian congregation. It does justice to the two other perspectives: the diaconological and the ecclesiological.

Pastoral action in and from the Christian community occurs at three levels: for fellow members, as church development, and as assistance. These three aspects complement each other. The pastorate as assistance is defined as "the helping relationship between the pastor and people, with a view to finding a way — in the light of the gospel and in community with the church of Christ — with regard to the questions of faith and life" (75). This professional pastorate makes extensive demands regarding the subject-subject relationship. It comprises both the pastorate in the congregation and the intramural spiritual care in such institutions as hospitals and prisons.

The pluralizing process in theology has led to a plural pastoral-theological practice. Eight different streams may be distinguished: a kerygmatic stream (pastorate as proclamation, Thurneysen), the Calvinist stream (visitation and discipline), the sacramental stream (auricular confession), the hermeneutical stream (the encounter perspective), the pastoral-counseling movement (clinical pastoral training), charismatic pastoral care (ministry of healing, inner healing, K. J. Kraan 1983ff.), evangelical pastoral care (in which the fundamentalist orientation of J. E. Adams 1970 plays a major role), and the political pastorate (attention to political and social factors). For these streams, see Heitink 1992, 541-42.

In the literature one finds that, on the basis of historical studies, four functions of the pastorate are distinguished (Clebsch and Jaekle 1964). The healing function links the pastorate with various forms of psychotherapy. Here the Rogerian approach to pastoral counseling finds wide application. The second function, sustaining, refers primarily to forms of dealing with crisis and loss. In this context, the model of thinking in phases of coping with loss, based on studies by Elizabeth Kübler-Ross (1969), is well known. The third function, guiding, seeks to help people in making responsible decisions and choices on the basis of their inner convictions. Here the processes of awareness raising and learning play a major role; they point to the emancipatory character of pastoral action. The fourth function, reconciling, ties in with the alienation between human beings and between humanity and God, with broken or problematic relationships, and with conflicts that hamper normal interaction. Reconciliation is not always the result of striving for harmony; in many cases it does not occur without conflict.

Since the 1960s the theory of the pastorate has seen a rapid development, mainly due to the influence of clinical pastoral training. Pastoral training is provided at different levels, for pastors, theology students, and volunteers in pastoral work. Empirical research into the effects of various forms of pastoral action has only just begun.

14.3.2 Religious Pedagogics

The subdiscipline of religious pedagogics presents a number of developments, both within and outside practical theology. The literal meaning of the term *religious pedagogics* is "the theory of guiding the child with regard to his service to God" (Ploeger 1993). The subdiscipline can be developed by pedagogues who are interested in learning about religion. This is the situation at some universities, but in most cases the topic is taught by theologians and experts in religious studies. In the latter case, the approach is not from the perspective of the Christian faith, but from a broader perspective of a religious attitude, or from a pluralistic perspective, where Christianity is seen as just one of the world religions.

At the Dutch universities not run directly by the state, the subdiscipline has acquired its own place, separate from catechetics, which is more directly linked to the church. But it has remained in the domain of practical theology. Here the domain of action is not restricted to religious education in the schools, but attention is also paid to religious education at home. It also branches out into Christian youth work.

Two factors have contributed significantly to a rapid development of the subject in recent decades. The first is the problematic situation of the transmission of faith in a secular society. Parents are looking for assistance with regard to the question how they can give their children a religious or Christian education in this time, when even their own ties with the church have become looser. Studies about youth acquire their own place, since young people build their own private world at an early age and develop ties outside the family with their peer groups. Alma's study (1993) about faith in the world of young people provides valuable insights. It also shows that studies about youth have received considerable attention from religious psychologists.

The second factor is the position of religious education as a separate subject in the school curriculum, and the need to train specialist teachers for this subject. This training must be of high quality in view of the difficulties that the subject faces in the present cultural environment. Many young people are not very motivated for this part of their studies, and since it is not part of the final exams they hardly take it seriously. In such a situation good teachers are a necessity. With a view to the situation in the schools, religious pedagogues give ample space to religious didactics, aimed at various educational methods in different types of schools and at young people of different age groups.

The subdiscipline may be developed along several lines. Ploeger (1993) refers to a humane-spiritual pedagogics, taking its point of departure in the subject. The emancipation of the "burgher" having been completed, this approach focuses on "the poor" and "the rich" in their pedagogic relationships to each other. Van der Ven wrote a "critical introduction to religious didactics" (1982). In the United States Groome (1980) bases his approach on the life story of young people, while Schipani (1988) establishes a link with liberation theology. K. E. Nipkow (1975-82) is the most prominent religious pedagogue in Germany. He is professor of pedagogics and religious pedagogics and has his roots in the school of Klafki, who connects an orientation toward the human sciences *(Bildung)* with a critical theory.

14.3.3 Spirituality

In most recent times the subject of spirituality also seems to have developed into a separate subdiscipline. Here the cultural situation again plays an important role. The revival of spirituality points to "fundamental deficiencies" in contemporary culture, as is apparent from such central themes as "wholeness, integration, meaning-providing frameworks, community, and personal identity" (Laeyendecker 1990, 21). Religious experience evaporates and the often-used expression "eclipse of the divine" points to the oppressing reality of God's absence. Maintaining and recovering personal faith thus becomes a separate domain for attention and action.

The term *spirituality* has a French background. It was initially used only in Catholic circles. But since the publication of C. Aalders's book on spirituality (1969), the word has become more and more acceptable in the world of Dutch Protestantism.

Firet refers to spirituality as "the structural principle of church and theology." He gives this definition: "Spirituality is a personal and/or corporate, fundamental, more or less continuous life orientation of a religious nature" (1987, 172). This leads to a second element. A fundamental life orientation cannot survive without "actions directed at increasing awareness, clarification, and strengthening that orientation, by giving form to a way of life based on that orientation." He mentions in this connection prayer, meditation, and participation in celebration. These give tangible expression to an action domain for theory and research, with a view to spiritual guidance.

Steggink and Waaijman (1985) propose a working hypothesis that offers a clear conceptualization. This working hypothesis of spirituality in dialogue links theological and nontheological disciplines. The authors conceive of spirituality as a combination of factors that do not derive from each other (79). These factors are: spirit of the times, that is, that each culture breathes its unique atmosphere and has its own basic mood or sense of life; basic inspiration as the foundational stimulus that motivates people; the self, the unique personality and one's identity and life story; internalization, a process that allows people truly to own an experience; myth, as the source of spirituality, the secret of being bonded in the work of the Spirit (80ff.).

In our time one must give attention to differences in spirituality and a plurality of ways of experiencing faith, in particular among Protestants. Within the church as well as in movements outside the church one can detect not only a mystical or experiential spirituality, but also, among others, conservative, charismatic, evangelical, and sacramental spiritualities, as well as a spirituality that is critical of social structures. One must also pay attention to the channels of the mediation of spirituality, such as, in particular, language and story, as well as symbol and ritual. With respect to the story, one finds that "bibliodrama" (Andriessen and Derksen 1985) and working with "life images" (Zuidgeest 1986) have acquired their definite place. Since the introduction of rituals in psychotherapy (van der Hart 1978), in situations of transition and consolidation working with rituals has also found a place in pastoral work (Lukken 1986). Finally, I want to mention the interest in pilgrimages, retreats, faith workshops (Schreurs 1990), and prayer workshops, particularly in Catholic circles.

This development allows one to speak of a separate action domain and, in principle, of a distinct subdiscipline. These considerations would seem to justify the teaching of spirituality as a separate course in the theological curriculum. But one could also argue that it should find a place within such subdisciplines as pastoral psychology, religious pedagogics, liturgics, and church development.

14.4 Conclusion

A practical-theological anthropology is part of the central theory of practical theology. The domain of humanity and religion has become differentiated vis-à-vis the church, partly as a result of the individual's quest for independence. The process of subjectivizing, which can be viewed from different perspectives, has rendered the faith situation in modern society rather problematic, but has also created new possibilities. As a result of the ongoing secularization, religious development and experience have become important themes. We must ensure that the ties with the work of the church remain, and these developments have to be critically evaluated from the perspective of society.

CHAPTER 15

Church and Faith

In this chapter I deal with the second action domain that can be distinguished within practical theology: the domain of the church as the community of believers. One of the problems in ecclesiology is the tension between doctrinal and empirical statements about the church. This tension-laden relation constitutes the starting point for practical-theological ecclesiology, which begins its work by looking at the church "from the bottom up."

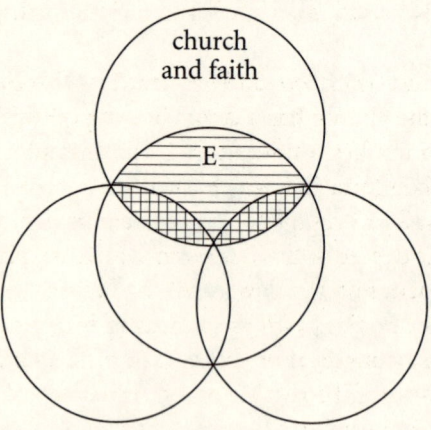

Figure 20: The ecclesiological segment

I already referred to this approach to the church when I discussed in previous chapters such topics as the disappearance of the mesostructures, the deterioration of the plausibility structure, and the move of the church to the private world. This is empirical language, which is also heard in statistics of people who leave the church, and of worship attendance and participation in catechesis.

This language is in a dialectical tension with the biblical-theological statements about the church. Such statements are based on the reality of the Spirit and employ terms that, considering the present situation, seem to reflect the ideal rather than reality. In this chapter I do not attempt to remove that tension, but rather want to make it fruitful with a view to ecclesiastical action. This is possible in a practical-theological ecclesiology (15.1) by critically relating the insights of theology and the social sciences as converging options. Referring to the church as *koinonia* indicates the direction.

Along this line, the ecclesiological segment (15.2) is fleshed out in further detail with themes about the developments in the church within our culture. This has an impact on the discussion of the subdisciplines that are relevant for this domain (15.3): church development, catechetics, liturgics, and homiletics. These are primarily ecclesiological subjects. They deal with church attendance, the teaching that takes places, and the development of the church. Since the church is of and for people and fully shares in the developments in society, one can also view these subjects from an anthropological and a diaconological perspective.

15.1 Practical-Theological Ecclesiology

I first define what must be understood by "practical-theological ecclesiology" and which view of the church has a direct bearing on this subject.

This approach implies a limitation. I concentrate on how the church functions in a local congregation, which usually is part of a national denomination. In what follows I presuppose a considerable degree of autonomy of the local church. The degree of this autonomy varies within different denominations, since it depends on the power that is reserved, within a church's organization, for higher bodies (such as councils of bishops or synods). Therefore the situation in a congregationalist system of church governance differs from a presbyterian-synodal structure or a hierarchical structure. I am therefore guilty of a certain oversimplification that does not do full justice to the reality in every situation.

Of course, one might follow another road. In this regard the structural-functionalist model that van der Ven (1993 [1996]) applies to the church might be helpful. This model is based on four core functions of the church: identity, integration, policy making, and management. "Identity has to do with the convictions, vision, and mission of the church. Integration points to cohesiveness, uniformity, and pluriformity in the church. Policy making refers to the development of programs and projects. Management, lastly, is concerned with personnel, finances, and other resources of the church" (1993, 79 [1996, 78]).

Van der Ven maintains that the church has relations with all four dimensions of society: cultural life, social life, political life, and economic life. He positions the church within the cultural dimension.

I have also distinguished these four dimensions in part I of this book. But, taking my starting point in the differentiation with respect to individual, church, and society, I decided on another route. This led to seeing the church in its social functioning, from the perspective of praxis 1, primarily as a social-cultural institution. This results in a slimmed-down ecclesiology, befitting the modest place of the church in today's world. In fact, referring to the church as a social entity is in itself a form of modernity, as we saw earlier (3.4). Ecclesiology is a nineteenth-century phenomenon. In earlier types of society it was unusual to picture the church as a social institution (Kaufmann 1989, 14).

15.1.1 Ecclesiastics

A practical-theological ecclesiology should pay systematic attention to the way in which the church functions. Firet introduces in this connection the term *ecclesiastics*, a term already used by Muurling (1860, II, 505) to refer to the discipline that deals with the organization, the governance, and the daily life of the church, in relation to its essence and destiny. Firet describes ecclesiastics as:

- the theological theory of the social manifestation of the Christian faith,
- the actualization of a possibility inherent in the promise,
- and the fulfillment of a commission that has been received
- in a particular social and cultural situation (1986, 589).

The theological core, "the possibility inherent in the promise" and "the commission that has been received," points to the work of the Spirit. For that reason, Firet feels it is justified to speak of an "applied" pneumatology.

One must be able to link this ecclesiastic discipline to systematic-theological ecclesiology. As the definition indicates, its unique character lies in the tension-laden relation with empirical reality. For instance, when one speaks of the attributes of the church — the *notae ecclesiae* — unity, catholicity, holiness, and apostolicity, one may well ask to what empirical reality these terms refer, and how this reality might better conform to the gifts that are enshrined in these *notae*. It might be possible that a new situation could lead to a new understanding of these *notae* (Henau 1989).

This tension is most palpable in the well-known "is" statements, in the statements of faith about the church. For example, what does the word *is* mean when it is said that "the church *is* a missionary movement," or "the church *is* the body of Christ"? It may easily assume the meaning of an imperative: "is" stands for "should be." This tends toward legalism. This "is" functions differently when one sees it as referring to a possibility that has been entrusted, to be realized in actual practice ("a commission that has been received").

If one wants to give full attention in ecclesiastics to the way in which the church functions, one would be advised to think in terms of problem definition, diagnosis, and goal. For example, in attempting a definition of the problem, this tension between "ideal and reality" may receive concrete expression in one particular theme. One may, for instance, think of a complaint of some church members, verbalized in a letter to the church board, that "the church lacks a sense of community." These church members are apparently thinking of some norm of how such a community should be, and have concluded that the situation does not comply with the norm. The problem is further analyzed in the diagnosis: What exactly is the problem? Once again the viewpoints of theology and of the social sciences must be brought together. To return to our example: What exactly does one mean by "the lack of a sense of community"? What does "community" mean theologically? Does this refer only to the social function of the church? Does the church still have a social role? Are there tangible factors that make it more difficult for this church, with its particular composition and accommodation, to be "a community" than for other churches? Do the people even want to belong to such a community? What are the obstacles? In this way, analysis can bring clarification. In formulating a goal one addresses how this church can develop a plan to better answer to its real purpose.

15.1.2 *Concept of the Church:* Koinonia

Understanding the church as "the social manifestation of the Christian faith" leads one to a central concept in a biblical-theological ecclesiology: the idea of *koinonia*. What was said regarding one's view of humanity also applies, mutatis mutandis, for one's view of the church. It serves (in a variant of Kwant's definition) as a frame of reference for the congregation for its actions and as a criterion for self-assessment.

With reference to Avery Dulles (1974), Weverbergh (1992, 135ff.) lists the following views of the church: the church as a salvific institution, the church as community, the church as sacrament, the church as witness, the church as servant. He traces the ecclesiological attributes, the functional and empirical characteristics, and those that are related to the theory of action that belong to each of these views. Here one recognizes the trinity of the hermeneutical, the empirical, and the strategic. This, indeed, gives the way in which the church functions its central place.

In this section I follow the hypothesis of U. Kuhnke (1992): When one focuses on how the church functions, one needs only one concept: that of the congregation as *koinonia*. He believes that practical theology needs an option that can lead to a critical reconstruction of the identity of the congregation, and that the *koinonia* option can serve that purpose (16). The credibility of the Christian faith depends on whether Christians succeed in developing a kind of life in which the weaknesses of the modern lifestyle are diagnosed and overcome (21).

With Bäumler (1984) — and with credit to Habermas (8.4) — Kuhnke positions the local church where the social systems and the daily experience of its church members intersect. Problems in daily life offer points of contact for a communicative praxis in the church. Thus the church may manifest itself as "a community of people who have been liberated" (E. Lange 1980). Conformity to the structures of society ("resembling the world," as people would have said in the past) implies the danger that the church might lose its unique vision on reality (43). A Christian church is born where Christians engage in the discourse of identity (97). *Koinonia* contributes to the genesis of a communicative identity (100).

The *koinonia* concept, which may be understood in a normative sense, is not identical with the other basic functions of the church: *martyria, diakonia,* and *leitourgia. Koinonia* transcends, permeates, and connects these three, as Kuhnke (106) shows in his discussion with Zerfass (Bäumler and Mette 1987, 363). The *koinonia* concept comprises, as it were, the basic functions of *martyria, diakonia,* and *leitourgia.* This is characteristic for a community that exhibits solidarity while celebrating the remembrance and being engaged in the needs of the world.

This may be further clarified by referring to some New Testament data. The earliest Christian churches were house churches, as is apparent from the epistles (1 Cor. 16:19; Rom. 16:3ff.; Phlm. 2) and from the book of Acts (10:1-11, 18; 16:15, 32-34). This is also supported by the Synoptic tradition (Luke 10:5-6; Matt. 10:12-13). These assemblies were rooted in the traditional Jewish celebrations of, for instance, the Sabbath or the Passover feast. In addition to the house churches, the people met in the synagogue, the place for study.

A house church consisted of a relatively small group, with a "lot of interaction, personal contacts, affective relationships, common goals and norms, differentiated role patterns, and solidarity over and against the environment" (Kuhnke 1992, 113). Within the social community reigned the proclamation of Christian freedom that is given in baptism: "There is neither Jew nor Greek, slave nor free, male nor female, for you are all one in Christ Jesus" (Gal. 3:28).

Acts 2:42 presents the paradigm of such a community: "They devoted themselves to the apostles' teaching and to the *koinonia*, to the breaking of the bread, and to prayer." This was accompanied by a sharing of earthly goods in solidarity, for "they had everything in *koina*" (v. 44). This renders *koinonia* into a critical concept. In celebrating the meal, the community with the Lord and with one another is realized, with a view to a praxis of discipleship.

With these and other data Kuhnke undergirds his hypothesis of *koinonia* as the preferred option to reconstruct the identity of the Christian church in a critical sense (100). This, he believes, offers a converging option, which relates Christian views and those of the social sciences to each other along dialectical lines.

15.1.3 An Integrative Concept

Kuhnke's suggestion not only leads to a simplification of the ecclesiological discussion, but also offers possibilities for a much-desired integration. *Koinonia* as a core concept in a practical-theological ecclesiology connects anthropological and diaconological aspects. It presents an answer to the subject-less subject. Church members are participants (van Nijen 1983) and are taken seriously as subjects. One is here dealing with a concept of critical participation that, from the sphere of private life, stimulates a countermovement against a purely functional or even elitist view of society, which is always ready to trap people in our day and age. Besides the anthropological, there is also the diaconological aspect. This community wants to exhibit solidarity; it wants to pay attention to "the poor" (the marginalized groups) and understands that a different way of dividing resources is needed if one wants to have a more just society. It is open toward critical groups and women's movements that have turned their back on the traditional church.

Moreover, several functions of the congregation are united in this single concept. Acts 2 shows the unity of teaching, celebrating, and serving. The subdisciplines I have distinguished — church development, catechetics, liturgics, and homiletics — find an integrative motif. In developing a congregation one would hope that the element of learning would play a significant role (Schippers 1977), while its heart would beat in the liturgy. Understanding the church as *koinonia* implies a critical attitude toward a functional isolation and bureaucratization of the church as organization.

Finally, the *koinonia* concept offers an integrative view with respect to such false contrasts as confession against apostolate, the people of God against the body of Christ, the church looking inward against the church looking outward, and pastoral action against mission-inspired action. For that reason this concept can provide direction when one tries to respond to questions that arise within the ecclesiological segment.

Extensive practical-theological research (Hendriks et al. 1987) has shown how small groups are of great value in church development. Viewed from the perspective of *koinonia* this is important to note. But the same research also indicates that many small groups suffer from "institutional vagueness," which greatly reduces their influence in the church as a whole (85). Their potential for church development far exceeds the use that the church makes of such groups.

15.2 The Ecclesiological Segment

If one takes the *koinonia* concept as the directive when looking in more detail at the ecclesiological segment, a number of dilemmas the churches face become apparent. Here one discovers the tension between biblical-theological statements about the church and the actual situation. But these dilemmas also help one to see how the present state of the church, after the collapse of the *corpus Christianum,* offers possibilities to realize new forms of "being church" on a smaller scale that are closer to the *koinonia* concept.

The choice one makes at this point leads to the following questions: Should one, in the present situation, opt for an established church or a minority church? Should one emphasize plurality or unity? Should one continue to focus on the parish structure or on other forms of presence of the church? Does one think of a church "from the top down" or "from the bottom up"? Further discussion will show that these questions are interrelated and must be understood against the background of developments in society (3.1) and of the process of secularization that so heavily affects the churches (3.3.3).

15.2.1 Established Church or Minority Church?

The aporetic situation of church and theology in our time would suggest that "the church as a cognitive minority" (P. L. Berger 1967) may be called a "generative" theme (Heitink 1988, 28ff.). There is a link with Bonhoeffer's letters from prison (5.2.3), which recognize the emancipation of humanity and stress the need for a nonreligious interpretation of the gospel, and therefore demand a renewed attention for the *disciplina arcani*. In that way he gives content to a "church for others."

It may surprise the reader that, having defined the broad anthropological approach in the previous chapter, I opt in my ecclesiology for a seemingly narrower concept. Yet one does not exclude the other. One can have an open eye for the broad spectrum of religious experience and simultaneously opt for a church with clear boundaries, which requires commitment. This gives expression to the conviction that, in spite of the disappearance of the mesostructures, there will continue to be a group of people who are prepared to give form to a critical counterculture on the basis of a Christian inspiration of faith.

As the church relinquishes its old pretenses and accepts its de facto minority position in society, it can learn to see with new eyes, with those of other minorities around it. That could lead to a reinforcement of the *koinonia* character of the church.

A survey of practical-theological literature shows that the idea of a minority church does not find much support in German literature. It is too much associated with the idea of an "elitist cell" or an "in-group" (Drehsen 1988, 310). For a careful defense of the idea of an established church, see Daiber (1977, 220ff.). Some American authors plead for a restoration of the "public church" in their country, where the situation is quite different from that in Europe. In the Dutch context, K. A. Schippers views the minority position as a combination of a sense of reality and modesty (1989, 190ff.), but he also poses some critical questions. He fails to see how this model can be realized without succumbing to the danger "that this minority position becomes an alibi, with the result that the deepest intention of the church — a church for others — is turned around and the church becomes a church for itself, and to the danger that it loses its mission" (192). He adds to this idea of "a minority church for others": "in the realism of the Spirit." We already learned (13.3) that van Gennep expects more from a marginalized church than from a state church or an established church.

This theme will not disappear from the ecclesiological discussion at any time in the foreseeable future. The unique tradition of each denomination also plays a role. For instance, the Netherlands Reformed Church has a tradition of a confessing *national* church, while the Reformed Churches in the Netherlands have in the past opted for a confessing church — what in fact was a church with a *confession,* a difference that seems to have been obliterated by historical developments. Would it be possible to link the two traditions in such a way that preference for a confessing church would not be at the expense of the ideal of serving a whole nation?

15.2.2 Plurality and Unity

The pluralism in society (3.1.2) also has its impact on the church. In his manual Rahner already indicates that "a considerable pluralism is arising, that can no longer be institutionalized and regulated by church leaders" (Arnold, Schuster, and Rahner 1968, 3:232). Not all people are aware of the cultural situation. Van Kessel (1982, 75) notes that few people in the working class have any idea of critical theology, but that some "young (semi-) intellectuals, who, having shared in the blessing of the bourgeois welfare state, feel almost suffocated; they have come to a critical awareness and are no longer at peace with, in particular, the structural violence in our society." In view of developmental theories, for instance, those of Kohlberg (Ploeger 1989, 54ff.), this does not sound unreasonable. As a result, one may find in all religious communities traditional but also modern and critical believers, each with his or her own worldview and ideas about God, humanity, and church. This leads to a permanent discussion about the nature of truth (Heitink 1984). I refer to this as pluralism.

The concept of pluralism marks a new phase in the way the church deals with differences of opinion. It can no longer operate on the basis of discipline and excommunication, resulting in schisms. Pluralism requires a new attempt to do justice to the relation between truth and unity, in part based in the conviction that many theological issues are rooted in nontheological factors. The debate in the churches about nuclear weapons was an example of how much pain and struggle the acceptance of this situation may cost. "A pluralistic situation in a group of people that wants to be a recognizable community will, by definition, be a situation of conflict" (Firet 1977, 95).

This makes plurality a practical-theological theme par excellence. Ernst Lange (7.5.1), who has given in-depth study to this kind of conflict, searches for a possibility to organize conflicts in such a way that polarization can be avoided: consensus through conciliarity (1980, 164). This refers to a democratic model (the council model) for a discussion between equal subjects, based on the shared hope — in the awareness of the presence of the Spirit — that this will help in the search for truth. It requires a willingness to learn together and from each other in a congregation that is open to new discoveries. Likewise, in a practical-theological study about conflict management, Hendriks and Stoppels (1986) point to the value of the learning model.

15.2.3 Parish and Presence

The next dilemma raises the question whether there is room for other forms of "being church" in addition to the tradition of territorial division (parishes or local churches). In this context many today refer to "the presence of the church" (Schippers et al. 1990). I choose those words because they represent more than a principle of division. They also represent a spiritual attitude or mentality.

Ernst Lange, to whom I just referred, is critical in this sense toward the parish concept. For many centuries the church has presented itself through the parish church. It consists of a symbiosis between the Christian congregation and the civil community, in the context of the closed microsociety of a village or a small town (1981, 66ff.). The church is in the very center of life. In this setting the conscience of the people is shaped. The authority system of society is internalized. People know what they are and are not allowed to do; they know their boundaries. Lange therefore speaks of a "parochial conscience." This conscience proves to be extremely limited when it comes to the acceptance of new experiences. It offers little room for learning and change. Together with the indestructible basic pastoral model (6.2) it continues, at least to a certain extent, to determine the often rather conservative character of the traditional congregation.

Most congregations that have been able to go through a process of renewal are, also in our situation, categorical communities, base communities, or mentality communities, which attract people from a wider region. H. Luther saw the city as the "theater of everyday life" (1992, 211). One finds new forms of Christian community and presence in particular in cities. These communities are often liturgical breeding grounds, where new types of celebration and a treasure of new hymns are born. People come from afar to participate. But in most denominations they can hold membership only in the local congregation that covers the geographical area where they live, and the church has made only a hesitant beginning with what has been called "the perforation of parish boundaries."

These remarks may lead to the question whether it would not be wise to be more flexible with regard to territorial boundaries. Dingemans (1987, 29) points out, however, that this is a matter of principle for the Reformed Church in the Netherlands: "We do not choose a church, but we are chosen by the Lord through the church that is present where we happen to be." But this principle can no longer do justice to the growing plurality. The development of new forms of "being church" is therefore an important theme in practical-theological ecclesiology. Once again the *koinonia* concept can provide direction.

15.2.4 Church from the Top Down or from the Bottom Up?

The last dilemma is that of the church "from the top down" or "from the bottom up." In the Catholic Church, hierarchy and doctrinal authority are still powerful controlling mechanisms. The movements for renewal in the 1960s in Dutch Catholicism could be reversed by the pope through episcopal appointments. Their criticism of the church left many church members with only a partial identification (Haarsma 1991, 157ff.).

In his ecclesiological proposal Dingemans emphasizes strongly the autonomy of the local congregation. He does opt for the territorial principle, but on the strict condition that there must be room for more than one form of worship. Differentiation is possible if several local congregations do things together or cooperate on a regional level (1987, 81). The term *local* must therefore not be interpreted too narrowly.

Dingemans wants to stress that over and against control from the top down, "the local congregation *is the church in the fullest sense*" (81). The "local" congregation is a conciliar entity, where no one rules over the other. The democratic "council" of all members has a central place (83). He thus chooses a structure that is based on the local church. A wide variety of congregations is the result. The unity and catholicity of the church are assured at the level of the classis (a regional body). The synod is not a meeting of ministers and elders but of local churches. But others reject this approach, which offers significant possibilities for church development, as sheer independentism.

The report of the Reformed Churches in the Netherlands entitled *Kerk in perspectief* (Church in perspective; 1969) refers to the congregation as "the bearer of all intentions of the church." The church is a charismatic community and the *ekklēsia* is the subject of the ministries. This offers a church structure that does away with a clergy-oriented church and strengthens the *koinonia* character of the congregation.

It is clear that thinking from the top down or from the bottom up largely determines the structure of a church community. It is therefore an essential theme for practical-theological ecclesiology.

15.3 Subdisciplines

Celebration and learning belong to the core functions of the congregation as *koinonia;* the congregation must be open to what happens in the surrounding world. Its development and structure must be directed toward this end. I distinguish four subdisciplines within the domain of church and faith: church development (oikodomics), catechetics, liturgics, and homiletics.

15.3.1 Church Development (Oikodomics)

Church development is a relatively new subject within practical theology. Its genesis is related to the ecclesiological shift in practical theology I referred to earlier, from the clergy to the congregation. The study of this area is presently at times referred to by the Greek term *oikodomics,* the building of a house, based on the biblical image of the church as a "spiritual house" with the church members as "living stones" (1 Pet. 2:5).

Firet defines oikodomics (in the broader context of ecclesiastics) as:

- "the theological theory of the initiation and guidance of processes directed toward the functioning of the congregation
- in a particular situation,
- in accordance with its possibilities
- and its calling,
- and of processes aimed at the creation of adequate structures for this functioning" (1986, 590).

This subdiscipline borders on that of canon law, which in Germany is sometimes incorporated in practical theology under the name "cybernetics" (A. D. Müller 1950, 67). Speaking about the church as a missionary-diaconological community suggests a relation in content with such subdisciplines as diaconology and evangelism theory. The question is then how the church can be developed in such a way that it can fulfill its goal.

Hendriks (1990, 26) feels that this subdiscipline is still in its infancy, as is apparent from the fact that all kinds of aspects and viewpoints are still being considered without a clear systematic approach. This is partly the result of the limited degree of integration between a normative and an empirical approach, and of the fact that most authors try to deal not with the congregation as a whole but usually with only one or just a few aspects. Long-term integration of viewpoints and action domains into one theory certainly seems possible. Hendriks mentions as the most important aspects: goal, identity, and essence on the one hand, structure and process on the other hand.

As far as content is concerned, this subdiscipline initially needs to be guided by a view of the church that has been developed within ecclesiastics. One such model might be that of the "church for others" (Schippers 1989, 13ff.). But other factors also come into play. One usually discovers five elements in any theory of church development, says Weverbergh (1992, 73): views of God, views of humanity and society, church models, leadership models, and models of methodical action. At the core is a process of transformation, as is apparent in the description given by van Hooijdonk: "Church development assists the local community of Christian believers, as a matter of their own responsibility, to live toward a new faith community that is in closer harmony with the discipleship of Christ, and is open to the questions of modern people" (1985, 16).

The development of models for the revitalization of the congregation is part of the process of formulating a relevant theory. Hendriks (1990) has developed a model that shows how five factors together promote this new vitality: a positive climate, stimulating leadership, an adequate structure (relationships between individuals and between groups), inspiring goals and attractive tasks, and a stimulating conception of identity.

"Congregational studies" have a high profile in the United States. In this context several types of congregations may be distinguished (Wheeler 1990, 67ff.). The "survey-guided development" has a prominent place in church development (Dietterich 1987; Dudley 1991). At the same time a number of studies, from different perspectives, appear in German. Schneider (1982) finds his basis in the basic anthropological needs, while Bäumler (1984) has a communicative point of view; Möller (1987-90) writes from a historical and systematic perspective, and Schwarz Sr. and Jr. (1987) from a charismatic angle. All these studies fail to give due emphasis to empirical aspects.

15.3.2 Catechetics

Learning is an essential experience for the congregation, as it is for any individual or community — comparable to eating and drinking. It is impossible not to learn (Dingemans 1986, 64). It is therefore hardly surprising that the theme of "the congregation as a learning community" or, better still, as "a community of learners" has acquired a central place in catechetical theories. Schippers (1977, 22) provides the following definition: "A congregation as a learning community is a congregation that views its situation as one of continuous learning; such a congregation will therefore establish an intentional and systematic learning process, in which the church members recognize themselves through the combination of faith and experience on the one hand, and of themes and relationships on the other hand, and will integrate the results of this learning process in its policies."

An important point in this definition is that this learning is not limited to catechesis for young people, but is viewed as a core function of the entire congregation. Recent forms of home catechesis where young and old learn from each other and teach each other provide a good example. Faith learning is intergenerational (Ploeger 1993). The relational aspect and the experiential aspect are also important. A "learning community" aims at a long-term process for all concerned, with social interaction and experiential knowledge as important facets.

Several versions of this model are in use (Ploeger 1993, 6ff.). Some emphasize "congregational pedagogics" (Foitzik 1992), while others stress "adult education," based on methods utilized in social work, and others again prefer to approach the learning process as an emancipatory process inspired by liberation theology (Freire 1970); finally, some opt for the Jewish study model.

Dingemans (1986) makes an important distinction between mathetics as "learning how to believe" and catechetics, defined as "the professional didactics of organizing learning processes around faith." Catechetics differs from religious pedagogics in its focus on learning in the context of the congregation. The catechesis for the youth has a central place in this, as Schippers indicates: "Catechesis is a fundamental task of the congregation and must therefore be supported by the congregation. As part of a complete youth-pastoral approach, and in combination with other educational and instructional activities, the catechesis will create situations for teaching and learning that will encourage the younger members and others to understand themselves before God and to grow into mature Christians and active church members" (1982, 41). This demands a catechetical work plan.

In the past in Protestant churches this learning culminated in a public confession of faith, when the child had reached "the age of discernment." In Calvin's time this was around age ten. In subsequent centuries the confession of faith (confirmation) gradually shifted to around or even above the age of twenty. This shift was caused by two factors: the emphasis on the inner experience of faith (Pietism), and later the discovery by developmental psychologists (e.g., Erik Erikson) of the "moratorium" in the phase of adolescence. Today the number of young people who have been "confirmed" has strongly declined and the institution itself has come under discussion. This is partly the result of the growing tendency to admit very young children to the Communion table. These developments urgently require clear catechetical strategies.

The Netherlands Reformed Church and the Reformed Churches in the Netherlands have launched a significant initiative: a three-year course for the laity in a large number of cities, usually taught by pastors.

The Roman Catholic Church in the Netherlands has a different catechetical tradition. The children are prepared for their First Communion at the elementary school. This instruction used to be given by clergy, but is nowadays the responsibility of the teacher. A distinction is sometimes made between "experiential catechesis," "liberation catechesis," and "Bible catechesis" (Dingemans 1986, 193-94).

Catechetics as an academic subject covers mainly reflection on goals, motivation, course contents, work forms, learning processes, and curriculum. In recent years, the changes in church and culture have also heavily affected the character and content of this subdiscipline.

15.3.3 Liturgics

Following some others, Lammens (1968, 22) makes a certain distinction between liturgical studies and liturgics. Liturgical studies focus on a study of the literature and the history of the liturgy. In the Catholic tradition liturgical studies are considered to be part of either the historical or the systematic subjects. The historical study by Wegman (1991) may serve as an introduction. Liturgics connects with the contemporary situation and prepares the building blocks for the theory of the content and shape of the church's liturgy. It is therefore a practical-theological subdiscipline. Golterman (1951) has given a succinct definition: "Liturgics is the theory of liturgy." Vrijlandt (1987) offers a (Protestant) introduction on the subject. It should be noted in passing that this is an area where the Protestant and the Catholic traditions differ more than anywhere else.

The research domain, the celebration of the liturgy, is described by van der Laan (in a reader used at the Theological University in Kampen) in practical-theological parlance as a collective term for "all those ritual and devotional forms and actions that assist us in communicating with divine reality." He defines the character of this area of study in these words: "It derives its unique character from the communicative event between God and humans, in so far as this takes place in ritual and devotional acts."

An important focus is the ritual of Sunday worship and the several constitutive elements of the service. The Catholic Church has always used a liturgical year and reading rosters, but the Protestant churches have only in more recent times shown a renewed interest in these (Lammens 1970). The Dutch Council of Churches now provides an ecumenical order for the entire year that gives attention to the Jewish roots of the liturgy embedded in the worship of the synagogue (Boon 1970).

The distinct liturgical traditions — the Roman Catholic, Eastern Orthodox, Lutheran, Calvinist, and Anglican — also receive due attention. In the Protestant tradition the ministry of the Word develops along a separate track, detached from the celebration of the Eucharist. In addition to the ministry of the Word, the celebration of the sacraments, in particular baptism and Communion, have become more prominent. It signals substantial ecumenical progress that the Reformed and the Catholic traditions are beginning to close the gap at this point. Apart from the Sunday worship services, one now sees also other services, such as "teaching" services and services "of hours" (vespers in particular). Other themes include prayer and hymnology. Finally, the special services, for weddings and funerals, must be mentioned. Here liturgics and poimenics meet. If liturgics is approached from an anthropological perspective, it also overlaps with the area of spirituality.

Liturgics thus covers a broad field of inquiry. For the moment the emphasis is mainly on historical research. This fits with an approach to liturgy that prefers to seek inspiration in the ancient Christian traditions. Whether these are suitable for modern people is a question that is not sufficiently raised. More research must be done into the experiences of people who participate in these celebrations. Do they really participate? What appeals to them? What causes resistance? Practical-theological research has shown that many church members do not experience the worship service as meaningful (Hendriks and Rijken-Hoevens 1976). One must also realize that a major percentage of the population has become alienated from the Christian tradition. This also calls for an anthropological shift. The phenomenological study of M. Josuttis (1991) may point in the right direction. He describes church worship from the perspective of the participant, through such acts as going, sitting, seeing, singing, hearing, eating. When the liturgy is approached in this way, as a "form of actual life," feelings of alienation are more easily recognized.

15.3.4 Homiletics

The sermon has a place of its own in the liturgy. The recent developments in the domain of homiletics must be seen against the backdrop of the anthropological shift in theology as a whole. Proclamation held center stage in dialectic theology (5.2.1). Barth's dictum: "Good dogmatics, good theology, good sermons" was broadly respected. The sovereignty of the Word and the belief that humans cannot freely dispose of that Word constituted a theological premise with little room for a practical-theological approach to homiletics. The *Predigtlehre* (sermon theory) of R. Bohren (1971) comes closest to that tradition. But Bouwer (1992) shows in his hermeneutical-homiletical study of the theology of H. Ott, Barth's successor in Basel, that something new can spring forth from the Barthian tradition when it is combined with existential interpretation.

The homiletical theory current in his time explains the reaction of Bastian (1968), who wants to free the sermon from its dogmatic claim by focusing on the sermon as a communicative event. This allows for an important place in homiletical theory for the situation of the listeners. This line is extended with regard to the theory of preaching by E. Lange (1968). He emphasizes that in the tension between tradition and modern situation — of *Verheissung* (promise) and *Anfechtung* (temptation), as he defines this tension theologically — the sermon must be viewed as *neues Wort* (a new word) (van der Laan 1989b). If the struggle of sermon preparation does not make it possible to say something new, it is better to say nothing at all. Lange has elaborated his theory in a series of "sermon studies." His central thesis is that the exegesis of the homiletical situation and the exegesis of the text stand in a tension-laden relation to each other.

The Dutch homiletics of Dingemans (1991) is likewise constructed from the point of view of the listener. He gives ample attention to the hermeneutical aspects, as well as to the communicative situation and the process of sermon preparation. Among the different types of sermons *(kerygma, didachē, martyrion, homilia)*, he prefers the ancient form of the homily, which demands interaction. He also provides a typology of the audience. He agrees to a large extent with van der Laan (1989a) in his discussion of the sermon-preparation process. The best way of taking the audience seriously is to involve them from the very beginning in discussions or even in the preparation of the sermon itself. Thomas (1978) has developed a model for this.

Looking at the current situation in homiletics, also from an international perspective, one can see similar accents in Germany in the work of Dannowski (1985) and Zerfass (1987), in South Africa in the work of Pieterse (1991), and in the United States in the pragmatic homiletics of Buttrick (1987). Other American studies from the viewpoint of the listener include Craddock (1971) and Long (1989). Van der Geest (1978) offers a different perspective. He explores the experiences of the listeners by enlisting the method of sermon analysis that has been developed by the representatives of the school of Clinical Pastoral Training. Daiber (1991) has done empirical research on sermons. Content analysis also offers excellent possibilities for research, as is apparent in R. Bos's (1992) study about possibilities for identification in sermons based on Old Testament texts.

15.4 Conclusion

A practical-theological ecclesiology is a basic element of pastoral theology. Its development, in relation to and as counterpart of the ecclesiology of systematic theology, is still in its infancy. It is clear that one can refer to the congregation as the subject only if one has actual subjects in mind. Otherwise one falls into a new kind of docetism (Thielicke 1965, 67). The core themes of ecclesiastics have to do with the actual functioning of the church in the context of modern culture. The most important question might well be how the church may give voice to a counterculture.

CHAPTER 16

Religion and Society

The third action domain to be distinguished within practical theology is that of the Christian presence in society. This is sometimes referred to as a form of "public Christianity," which is still visible in society in spite of the modernizing process. This is the least developed of the three action domains. Practical theology has in the past always been firmly inward-looking, in spite of what the "grand narratives" might suggest.

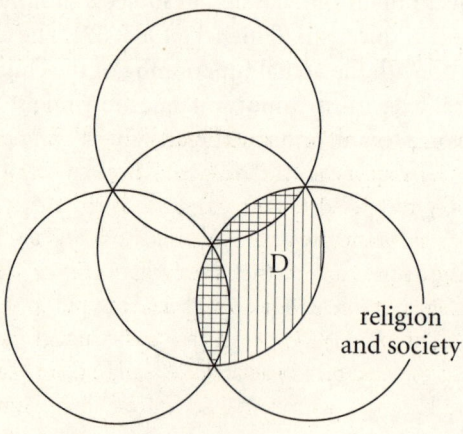

Figure 21: The diaconological segment

Those who are in search of a practical-theological diaconology (16.1) will have to content themselves with fragments. We are nowhere near a systematic treatment of this third domain. This chapter traces some outlines that may help in the development of a vision regarding this public domain, which must be regarded as a specific field of action. As a result of differentiation and secularization, the reduced sphere of influence of church and religion has been accompanied by forms of Christian presence that are detached from the church.

This forms the basis on which the diaconological segment is developed. The focus is on some core themes (16.2) that have an impact on the three subdisciplines that may be distinguished: the theory of evangelism, diaconate, and the equipping of the laity (16.3).

16.1 Practical-Theological Diaconology

For this field I have coined the expression *practical-theological diaconology*, which calls for some justification (16.1.1). Next I distinguish between different models (16.1.2) and survey the public domain (16.1.3).

16.1.1 The Concept of Diaconology

The term *diaconology*, coined as a parallel for anthropology and ecclesiology, is somewhat a term of convenience. It is open to misunderstandings and fails to do justice to all intentions that play a role in public Christianity.

Kuyper employs the expression "diaconological subject" for practical theology as a whole. The object of inquiry is "the *diakonia*," the service of the church. With Kuyper this is mostly restricted to the activities of the clergy, even though the concept of ministry is broadened to the priesthood of all believers. Roscam Abbing describes the entire task of the church as *diakonia* (1950). For him the term *diaconology* refers not to the work of the deacons but to that of the ordained minister (1980, 38). Philippi (1975) detects the basic rule of the kingdom of God in Jesus' challenge to the disciples to act as *diakonoi* (e.g., in Matt. 20:26). The essence is "serving" in humility, as opposed to "ruling," based on the new order in which "the last" become "the first." This applies not only to the disciples but to the whole church. *Diaconology*, derived from the verb *diakonein*, therefore seems a defensible term. It refers to the humble work of serving at table (e.g., John 12:2), but also, in a broader sense, to the service to fellow humans (Luke 22:26-27), with the use of all the charismata, for the well-being of all (1 Cor. 12:5-7).

Philippi therefore rightly speaks of "a fundamental principle" that determines the "order and structure of the new church" (1975, 100). This is true for the basic attitude of the corporate church ("church for others"), as well as for that of the individual believer. He agrees with Berkhof (1973, 429 [1979, 410]), who sees the focus on the world as the third aspect of "being church." The church mediates Christ to the world. This is its missionary-diaconal presentation. Berkhof calls this a "bridge-event" (430 [411]). He refers in this connection to the missionary theology of H. Kraemer, A. A. van Ruler, and also J. C. Hoekendijk (1964), who calls the church "the function of the apostolate." This theological approach is closely tied to that of the World Council of Churches, as Margull (1959) shows in his survey.

In our day and age we must conclude that many of the bridges between church and society have been blown up, and that almost all now depends on the "personal commitment" of individual Christians and their service in organizations and movements. We continue to sense resistance against forms of ecclesiastical Christianity that seem to be characterized by imperialistic rule rather than by altruistic service. For that reason we should emphasize that this service will only be modest. It would therefore be better to refer to it with the term *presence*. People may expect of a follower of Christ that "he or she is there in Christ's name, that is, with attention for people, caring for them, and looking after their well-being" (Pop 1967, 109). In many cases there is no longer a direct tie to the church or an explicitly Christian label for these forms of presence. The Christian character rather plays an implicit role as the motivation of the participants.

In the sections below I survey several existing models of understanding the relationship between church and society, the remains of public Christianity, and the renewed attention for the theme of public morality.

16.1.2 Models

The oldest model is that of the theocracy, "a type of societal life whose ethical, juridical, and cultic dimensions were governed by what God had in mind for his people" (Berkhof 1973, 523 [1979, 502]).

Israel provides the biblical example. Theocracy received a new chance when the church became the state church. The Roman Catholic Church tried to achieve its theocratic ideals through the controversy between church and state. Calvin also wanted a theocracy. One finds an echo of this in article 36 of the Dutch Confession of Faith. This article appeals to the government to maintain law and order, to defend the true religion, and to care for the social aspects of life. Ph. J. Hoedemaker developed a new form of theocracy. His vision of "the entire church and the entire nation" was the opposite of what A. Kuyper wanted. In Hoedemaker's theocratic ideal, the church proclaims the Word for the benefit of the whole people, and the state is willing to submit to this Word. Van Ruler thinks about the relationship between church and state along similar lines: "It is impossible to define a simple division of terrain and labor between the two" (1945, 368).

Kuyper (4.3; 5.1.3) left no doubt about his opinion: "The state church is something of the past" (Langman 1950, 111). The re-Christianization of the people would have to be achieved by other ways. He opted for a more limited, confessional church, because of the secularization of the state and the deplorable situation in the church. This resulted in his strategy of antithesis, which would lead in the Reformed world to an "ideological automatism" (Berkhof 1961, 118). His differentiation between the church as *an institution* and as *an organism* opened the way for the establishment of Christian organizations (van der Werf 1960), in the domains of church, state, and society. As time went by, the Catholic Church, with its traditional preference for theocracy, made a similar choice: for the model of Catholic organizations, on the basis of the principle of subsidiarity as expressed in the *Quadragesimo anno* (1931).

The model of the two kingdoms is linked to the Lutheran tradition. God exercises his lordship in this world in two ways: "conserving as the sustaining Lord, and salvific as the redeeming Lord" (Jentsch 1965, 261). In the kingdom to the right Christ reigns by his Holy Spirit through Word and sacrament. In the kingdom to the left ordinances are in force (marriage, occupations, government) to maintain a barrier against sin. This distinction coincides partly with that between gospel and law. The Christian has a different role in each of these kingdoms: the Christian is "a person who belongs to Christ" or "a person who belongs to the world." Forgetting that the two kingdoms belong to the one Lord may easily lead to the danger that the public will live "according to its own laws."

This model has found a modern proponent in H. M. Kuitert (5.3.1). Against the zeal of political theologians, he maintains that classical theology has never been willing to put the Sermon on the Mount in a political context (1985, 141 [1986, 112]). He does not attempt to make the context ("black-white/freedom-oppression/man-woman and similar social and political questions") part of a theory of preaching "the Christian message of salvation" (142 [113]). Christians are involved with this in other ways as they experience God, who as the Creator sustains his world. The church deals with eternal bliss, but society presents many other kinds of bliss, that is, aspects of well-being. "The one kingdom is not the other" (147 [117-18]). The principles that must govern political and social actions cannot be read from the Gospels; they emerge from creation. "One does not have to be a Christian to know what good action is" (149 [120]).

Yet another model, that of the church for the world, is rooted in Barth's doctrine (5.2.1) of the atonement and in his ecclesiological proposal of "calling, sending, commissioning, and serving" (Barth 1932ff., IV/3.2:553ff. [1936ff., IV/3.2:481ff.]). This concept of service in no way contributes to a greater role for the church or for Christianity in society; the same is true for the somewhat similar model of the church for others, as suggested by Bonhoeffer (15.2.1) and E. Lange (1981) and discussed earlier. In this case the principle of solidarity plays the primary role.

Barth's thinking has also exerted a major influence in the Netherlands. From the perspective of hope, Barth regarded humans as *christianus designatus,* that is, *christianus in spe.* Even *extra muros ecclesiae* one finds "true words" as "parables" of God's kingdom. In its service to the world, the church must not be patronizing: "Patronage means the human exercise of power by men against other men as though they were objects. It means the treating of others, however benevolently, as so much material for one's own abilities" (IV/3.2:950 [829]). True humanity becomes visible in the relationship of Christians with others, who do not yet know the secret, in that "we find a simple solidarity" for the others, and "unreservedly take up their case" (140 [125]). A critical theory can hardly be more critical than this theology! In the Netherlands this led to a "breakthrough" in the Christian organizations. Antithesis and confessional categorization make room for solidarity in cooperative ventures with people with different worldviews in "a meaningful complementarity."

Thinking in terms of complementarity may lead one to the model of Christianity outside the church (Rendtorff 1969). Rendtorff argues that this distinction between public and private Christianity occurs first in the Enlightenment (13). Public Christianity is rooted in the free choice of the private citizens. This leads to a distanced relationship to the church through a nondoctrinal Christianity of free individuals. The Enlightenment positively contributed to the broadening of the horizon and giving people more room to move (53).

Theologians have reacted to this in various ways. Over and against the "no salvation outside the church," one might suggest that "the world is not so bad after all"

(Kuitert 1964, 55). Dorothee Sölle has given wings to this idea of "the church outside the church" (76). Karl Rahner has made some influential suggestions from a Catholic perspective. He speaks of humanness as "anonymous Christianity" (69). Outside the church one encounters people who are en route to salvation, who should be recognized as "anonymous Christians." Thus our shared humanity becomes a basis of hope for collaboration.

The model of political theology offers a proposal for an "ethic of the revolution" (ter Schegget 1972). This has consequences for the church. Ter Schegget refers to the church as the "partisan of the poor": "The Christian community does not get involved in party politics, but it does take a political stand, in favor of the poor, the oppressed, the discarded. The church supports the poor, is a friend of the proletariat, and stands with those who are have been left to themselves. The deaconological work of the church cannot remain politically neutral" (1971, 29). This model receives its inspiration both from dialectic theology and from liberation theology. Van Hoogstraten (1986) offers a version of this latter variant for the "free West."

These models show how one can describe the relation between Christianity and society by the use of various "theological views of society." These are closely related to "views of the church." A further debate might clarify the available options. In this book I come closest to the model of "the church for others," but in so doing I want to do justice to anthropological motifs on the one hand (assigning meaning, religious experience), and a critical orientation on the other hand. In the new situation the connecting lines between religion and society do not usually run via the church as an institution, but via the input of individual Christians.

16.1.3 The Public Domain

The choice one makes has consequences for one's position as a Christian in the public domain and for whether one wants to plead for a public morality. American publications, in particular, focus on themes like "public philosophy" and the "public church." "Public" refers to the forum or arena where matters of common interest are decided. "Public" has a wider connotation than "political." Those who plead for the public cause have in common that they demand a restoration of public life, against the tendency toward individualism and privatization. They look for commonalities within the plurality of the many diverse life orientations. This may be done by clearly separating what unites people in some vague commonality from what divides them as controversial. The latter aspects are then banished to the private sector. Another, less restrictive, possibility is that of a public discourse where arguments on all sides can be heard. Both approaches are found among the supporters of a "public philosophy."

According to S. Griffioen in his analysis of this development (1990, 183), "public" has two meanings. The first meaning is that of becoming public, in the sense of becoming generally known. But since the Enlightenment a second meaning has gained much importance. It is the rendering of Latin *publicus,* referring to what is part of the *res publica,* the common interest. The Christian faith has a pretension in both directions. It wants to bring things out into the open that are good for all people. In the Netherlands the Christian religion has received official recognition through Christian education, Christian democracy, and Christian social thought (Woldring and Kuiper 1980; Kouwenhoven 1989). The supporters of these organizations that care for these interests feel that their organizations should be the first to play a leading role in this respect. Griffioen believes that privatization is an irreversible process, and the Christian Democratic politician L. C. Brinkman reminds us that "we ought to let the 'we' sentiment of the 1990s conquer the 'I' sentiment of the 1980s" (speech published in Trouw, Nov. 27, 1992, as a reaction to the individualism of van Mierlo; cf. 13.3).

In the United States, this "public philosophy" is promoted in Catholic circles by C. Murray (Griffioen 1990, 189-90), while Martin Marty pleads for a "public church." The covenant theology of Althusius, a Dutch Calvinist, provided Marty with the inspiration for a "public covenant." Such a covenant must express the collective responsibility for the public domain. In particular, Robert Bellah has studied the side effects of individualism and appeals to all to accept responsibility for the public domain (Bellah et al. 1985, 297-307). He refers to the American situation, where civil religion is accorded an important place. In this thinking, religion, as a mixture of Christianity and Republicanism, binds the nation together. In Western Europe public religion has lost much of its influence. Even more than before it is the personal presence, as a form of public Christianity, that counts.

The problems in modern society have become such that it must be one of the first tasks of a practical-theological diaconology, together with ethics, to contribute to the public cause. Christians may not abandon the public domain to others. They should be just as much concerned about common interests and public morality.

This perspective may well lead to a reevaluation of the special pastoral care in hospitals and other institutions, in psychiatry and forms of mental health care in the community, in penitentiaries, in the military, and in commercial enterprises. Many pastors feel very lonely in their work. Ecclesiastical thinking tends to undervalue these activities in the margin of the church. But if one thinks from the perspective of society, one must conclude that these pastoral workers occupy important outposts and beachheads, where the church puts out its feelers to a world it cares about for Christ's sake.

16.2 The Diaconological Segment

I select four areas in the diaconological segment of practical theology that demand attention. These represent matters of extreme urgency in the social, political, and economic sectors of society. In the economic sector the labor question is the most important problem. A significant social theme in our society is that of equal treatment for groups in minority positions. A number of illustrations will further clarify the theme of the relationship between church and politics. Finally, I touch on the question of how one can give substance to one's moral responsibility for society.

16.2.1 The Labor Question

The first theme is that of labor. One sees in our society a growing divide between those who have work and those who do not have work. This has to do with unemployment, the aging of the population, and the increasing number of those who live on some social benefit payment. Paid work has become more scarce, partly due to automation, and should be split more equitably between men and women. Women have a much shorter history on the labor market and, as a rule, find themselves in a more vulnerable position.

But even unpaid work must be distributed more equitably. The sector of volunteer work has grown enormously in recent years. This is often heavy work that carries major responsibilities. Examples are: working in a community center, serving as a hostess in the polyclinic of the hospital, as the "buddy" of a patient with AIDS, or as a companion for someone who wants to die at home. The church is a wholesale provider of volunteers not just for its own work, which usually remains unpaid, but also for refugee work, third-world shops, Amnesty International, and other groups and organizations with goals that deserve the church's sympathy.

A lot of volunteer work is a heavy burden particularly on the shoulders of women, who by choosing to care for their family have left the labor market and are subsequently unable to return to paid work. If regular employment and volunteer work were distributed more fairly, there would be hope that both would be considered as "normal" forms of labor.

In Heerlen a research project that has already resulted in some important studies indicates that work constitutes an important theme for practical theology. The church has withdrawn into the private world where the people live, and as a result it is no longer involved with a central part of life: the work of the people. It must therefore make an intentional effort to develop the theme of labor in church development activities and catechesis for adults. Labor is clearly an important aspect of personal identity, but identity must be accompanied by solidarity (Schrojenstein Lantman 1990, 197-98). It is important for the church to meet with organizations in society if it wants to know what problems people face who, for instance, can no longer work because of illness or disability (Verbraak 1990). These groups of disadvantaged people must be able to count on the solidarity of others.

Unfortunately, the number of chaplains in commercial enterprises — who truly represent the church in the world of labor — had to be reduced for financial reasons.

A remarkable initiative is that of theologians and their families who opt for manual labor and a modest income, and move to a working-class neighborhood. They help in building a new kind of community, with values other than competition and rationality (van der Kolm 1991). The training these theologians provide in this environment for theology students and pastors is of great importance for those who want to learn to see society from the bottom up.

16.2.2 Equal Treatment

Article One of the Dutch Constitution, carved in marble in a low bench in front of the new Parliament building in The Hague, underlines the right of protection for all, irrespective of race, religion, gender, or sexual inclination. This fundamental right must be translated into equal treatment for all, especially for minorities in our society. The term *minority* should not be taken in its numerical sense, but rather as the opposite of the concept of dominance. Hendriks (1981, 50ff.) defines a minority as a subgroup that — regardless of its size — has little power and is subject to prejudice. The counterpart of a minority is the "dominant" group whose social identity accords with what society regards as the ideal.

This theme first of all impacts on the equal treatment of men and women. Women not only find themselves in a disadvantaged position, but also face the challenge of having to cope with a sexist climate that is rather unfriendly toward women. These situations call for a special ministry for women. In this context forms of sexual violence come to light that are often religiously legitimized (Imbens and Jonker 1985).

Equal treatment also involves the position of homosexuals and lesbians in society. They continue to be discriminated against because of their sexual inclination. A report of the Dutch Council of Churches states that emancipation would make them assertive. Unfortunately, the climate for them in the church is worse than that in society as a whole. Gay and lesbian theologians still find it difficult to find employment in the ministry.

Equal treatment also has an impact on people of other races (i.e., non-Caucasian) or religions (i.e., non-Christian) who are part of our increasingly multicultural society. In this day and age we confront images of skinheads and arson in homes for asylum seekers. The stranger can no longer feel secure in our midst. Illegal immigrants are particularly vulnerable. The inner cities often become centers of racism. It is in the public interest to bring these developments to a halt by our collective efforts.

Finally, one sees discrimination based on age. Many of the elderly in our society experience this when they have to leave the labor process prematurely. Many also find that increasingly stricter age limits are applied to social functions.

Thus equal treatment is in many ways a hot item. It offers many opportunities for the church and for individual Christians to get involved for the public cause.

16.2.3 Church and Politics

Article 5 of the draft Constitution for the proposed United Protestant Church of the Netherlands says: "The church confesses each time anew, in its celebrations, words, and actions, Jesus Christ as Lord of the world, and thus calls for a renewal of life in culture, state, and society. Together with other churches it testifies for people and authorities of God's promises and commandments." Here the political responsibility of the church finds clear expression. The further elaboration will to a large extent depend on the model (16.1.2) that gives concrete shape to this responsibility. The following two examples may serve as illustrations.

The first example is that of nuclear arms. The Synod of the Reformed Churches in the Netherlands went on record on March 7, 1984, as follows: "All confidence in and threats with nuclear weapons, which would cause massive destruction among the population, is at odds with a life of discipleship in Christ, who did not destroy until the end, but loved until the end." It decides "to charge the moderamen [the day-to-day leadership of the church] to admonish the government and Parliament . . . to refrain from any further step in the nuclear arms race (such as the installation of cruise missiles) and to give great urgency to the political process aimed at the disappearance of nuclear weapons systems." Other churches have issued similar statements. When such pronouncements are made, the tensions between church and authorities run high — finding expression, in particular, in mass demonstrations — while polarization in the churches also increases. No one could in those days foresee that today's world would be quite different! A careful analysis (Hendriks and Stoppels 1986) gives one reason to doubt, however, that this was a propitious conflict, seen from a practical-theological perspective.

Another example reflects a greater actuality. In many countries the matter of church asylum for refugees is being discussed. The "Sanctuary Movement" in the United States offers the primary example. From time to time congregations — even some that belong to relatively conservative denominations — permit refugees to seek safety in their church buildings (Browning 1991, 23ff.). This has also happened a number of times in the Netherlands, thus providing the discussion about the establishment of places of "sanctuary," and about acts of civil disobedience, with some test cases (Mattijsen 1987). Even though there is no official right of asylum, until now the Dutch authorities have not tried to arrest refugees, who had no further legal recourse and had found refuge in church buildings.

These examples show how this area of tension between church and politics provides an important field of inquiry for practical theology.

16.2.4 Moral Responsibility

Finally, I must mention personal moral responsibility as a contribution to public morality. This touches on the way society is organized and the area of legislation. Here one is directly involved with norms and values, and has the possibility to translate one's inner convictions into concrete influence. In the areas discussed above — labor, equal treatment, politics — we also encountered moral questions. But these were predominantly in the area of social ethics. In this section we must confront some questions that are more in the realm of personal ethics (Rothuizen 1973, 26).

The medical ethics problems immediately spring to our attention. As a result of the progress of medical science, the gray areas between life and death have been considerably widened, and human responsibility now has to deal with some new moral issues. The problem may be summarized as follows: "We live longer and die longer" (Zulehner 1990, 3:30). This is borne out by the fact that, on the average, people live longer than in the past, and the lives of elderly or sick people can be considerably prolonged through medical interventions. But this brings us to the question: Is everything that is possible also allowable? (Kuitert 1989a).

The question whether a prolongation of life is always desirable is at the core of the debate about euthanasia. Other related topics are: the choice for abortion if a child is expected to be handicapped, or ending the life of patients in a coma or of a newborn that has little chance of survival, as well as the demand for assisted suicide, in particular of psychiatric patients. Many are wrestling with these questions and find themselves in serious moral dilemmas.

Christianity is heavily involved in these discussions for several reasons: first, because of the realization that each human being is a unique creature of God, whose life deserves to be protected; second, because of the conviction that through God's grace even death can be overcome; finally, because of our faith that God does not want people to suffer (Schillebeeckx 1977, 656ff. [1980, 715ff.]). This demands a praxis of resistance against suffering, as well as a willingness to help people in — and, in extreme cases, from — their suffering when this proves to be unbearable. For instance, AIDS patients would find their ordeal less formidable if they knew that, should this situation arise, their doctor would not fail them at the decisive moment.

In cooperation with medical ethics, pastoral theology can make a major contribution with regard to pastoral care, but also assist medical doctors and nurses and others who are faced with immense responsibilities. The hospital chaplain is usually a member of the medical-ethics committee of the institution in which she or he serves.

Besides the area of medical ethics I must also mention that of sexual morals. The changes in sexual morals have had major consequences for the social fabric of our society. The last few decades have seen nothing less than a sexual revolution. Sexuality, marriage, and reproduction have been detached from one another as a result of new means of contraception. The percentage of divorces has dramatically increased. In contrast to the past, the modern family is now a small unit, an island in society. Other ties of blood relationship also have become much looser. Other forms of cohabitation have made their appearance: homosexual relationships, LAT (living alone together) relationships, single-parent families. Under the influence of feminism the traditional role patterns in the family have also drastically changed.

16.3 Subdisciplines

One may point to three subdisciplines in the domain where Christianity and society meet: theories for evangelism, diaconology, and the equipping of the laity.

16.3.1 The Theory of Evangelism

The theory of evangelism is usually regarded as part not of practical theology but of missiology. This categorization is undesirable, however, if this subdiscipline is supposed to formulate theories for missionary practice. For classifying this under missiology would give practical theology an excuse to limit itself to internal church matters. As a result, evangelism would have to forfeit the support of empirical practical-theological theory and the power this would be able to provide. This subdiscipline languishes rather often, since evangelism in the form of open-air meetings, distribution of tracts, revival campaigns, and so on is almost a thing of the past.

I therefore agree totally with Verkuyl (1978, 53) that evangelism belongs "without any doubt" to practical theology. He provides the topic with the following working formula: "The theory of evangelism is the academic support for the communication of the gospel of the kingdom of God, from the basis of the entire church congregation, in its own environment through the proclamation of the gospel, through fellowship, through *diakonia*, and through participation in the struggle for justice. In addition, it provides critical reflection on old and new methods and techniques, on new experiments, and on organizational forms, church structures, relationship and lifestyle patterns, which assist or should assist in this task" (50-51). With regard to the last statement, van der Meiden remarks: "Evangelism without a practical communication theory is like a ship in dry dock" (1973, 110).

F. de Lange, who teaches this subject in Kampen, sketches its development within the Reformed tradition as a movement from technique to hermeneutics. In this he follows the interpretation theory of Ricoeur, which also occupies a central place in part II above. He describes evangelism as "a hermeneutic of the gospel, in its discourse with modern Western culture" (1993, 40), in search for places where God can be spoken of in a liberating way.

In our time I see three specific areas for which theories for practical intervention may be developed. The first area is the communication by a local church (or, in an ecumenical setting, by the local churches) in *their direct environment.*

Hardly any work has been done on a theory how a more public Christianity might be developed. It would be worth the effort to survey possibilities for encounter in a systematic way. The church may want to send a message of welcome to all who move to a city or village, with information about what the church(es) and Christianity have to offer. It may engage in publicity in free advertising papers, mentioning key addresses where people can get help in various circumstances. It may organize public meetings about topics of general interest. The church may also decide to produce religious programs for the local radio or TV station. It can also contribute to cultural life by making the church building available for concerts or exhibitions.

Second, I would like to point to the mass media — to a study of matters that relate to press, radio, and TV. Jager (1978, 135) poses three preliminary questions: Are radio and TV suitable for evangelism? If so, is the gospel suitable for this new form of publicity? If so, are the churches adequately equipped to use these new forms of evangelism? These are critical questions that give some indication of the type of study that might be needed in this area. More research would be desirable (van der Goot 1989).

Third, I want to mention the area of urban missions. This is a new specialty that has mainly developed in an ecumenical context. It seeks to experiment with new forms of Christian mission in modern society (Schippers et al. 1990, 217). In the Netherlands this approach has been translated into some missionary projects in old inner-city areas, where problems like poverty, unemployment, discrimination against minorities, and racism are more predominant than elsewhere. Claerbaut (1983) explains what happens in the American situation. Among other things, he shows how the church is caught in a "middle-class" mentality, which carries the acute danger of "victim blaming" (174).

Surveying these three areas, I can only conclude that evangelism still has an important role to play, even in a secularized society.

16.3.2 Diaconics

Diaconics — as distinct from diaconology — may be defined as the study of the activities of the church's diaconate. Until quite recently, these activities were mostly concentrated on the problem of poverty. The work of the diaconate simply consisted of care for the poor.

In the early Christian church the diaconate was intimately connected with the liturgy, as is apparent in the *agapē* celebrations (1 Cor. 11:20ff.). In the Middle Ages the *caritas* (as was by then the common name) became more independent. The emphasis shifted to the virtuous character of good deeds. Calvin restored the social diaconate, on the basis of Acts 6:1-7. Only the Calvinist tradition has seen a clear institutionalization of the diaconate. In view of the lack of scriptural support for this, Berkhof calls it a "blessing in disguise" (1973, 390 [1979, 372]).

We saw (4.3) how as a result of the social question the church is no longer able to cope with the poverty in society, and how care for the poor acquires a rather conservative character (Heitink 1982). After World War II the church lost its task of caring for the poor at home, as social legislation was introduced, and thus was able to direct its attention toward global poverty. Modern studies tend to emphasize that the diaconate needs to focus on the combination of compassion and justice. In our time one distinguishes three specific domains for work: the diaconate in the local congregations, in the society in which one lives, and for the world.

The rise of the diaconate for the local congregation is related to the ecclesiological shift: from the ordained ministry to the laity. The members are the subject of the service the church offers (Hendriks 1973). It is the task of the deacons to equip the church members for service. But the diaconate in the local church seems to acquire an increasingly internal function, as the church members are more and more regarded as the object rather than as the subject of the diaconate. The attention goes primarily to the sick and the elderly in the church, while the diaconate should in fact primarily embody the care of the church for those within its reach in the society that surrounds it.

For that reason, more recently a distinction is often made between the diaconate of the local congregation and that for society at large. When the church draws a social map of its surroundings, it will get a picture of the needs in its immediate environment. Those in a city differ from those in rural areas. But everywhere, wherever people live, health care, social services, welfare work, and psychiatric help begin to show deficiencies as a result of spending cuts. At the same time, a division is making itself felt between, as it is euphemistically called, the active and nonactive. In reality, there are less-privileged groups everywhere who are feeling the cold, as the social "cover" (Hattinga Verschure 1977) is gradually withdrawn. Society becomes less user-friendly. This is an area where the church, together with others, must consider what it can do.

Finally, the diaconate has a global dimension, in relation to mission and development work. That world is primarily the third world, but it includes the fourth world in Europe and the second world of the former Eastern-bloc countries. In the Communist era many churches in the West were paired with churches in the East. The "world diaconate" can find expression in concrete projects that emphasize "sharing on a global scale." The youth may also be actively involved in such projects.

One sees a revival of the study of this field in a number of new manuals that have appeared in the last decades: in the United States by Barnett (1979), in Germany by Turre (1991) and Schibilsky (1991), in the Netherlands by Tieman and Zunneberg (1990) and Noordegraaf (1991), and in Catholic circles by H. Spee (1992).

16.3.3 Equipping the Laity

It is with a certain degree of reluctance that, in this last section, I call attention to courses for the equipping of the laity. This is not an established sub-discipline. It does, however, concern a neglected area that may well gain in importance, considering the differentiation that has occurred in our society. Kuyper had a prophetic vision when he included "instruction for the laity" in his "encyclopedia." More than fifty years later Kraemer wrote his book about "the forgotten office in the church" (1960). He wrote about the place and the calling of the laity, that is, of the "ordinary" church member.

This philosophy is based on the biblical thought of the "priesthood of all believers" (1 Pet. 2:9) — a better term than the neo-Calvinist "office of the believer," which suffers from a strong intrachurch connotation. The concept of "laity" is tainted by the contrast of clergy versus laity, which regards a nonordained status as a deficiency. In popular usage the word often has a negative undertone. The "layperson" is the nonexpert, the one without specific training. But the Greek word *laikos* refers to membership of the people *(laos)*, in biblical terms of the "people of God." As such, it is a title of honor.

I would gladly exchange the expression "equipping of the laity" for something better, but the matter itself is of practical-theological relevance. It has to do with those activities that equip Christians to perform their task in society.

In this context, one may first of all think of the situation in which people live: the family, the circle of friends, the living conditions. Next, one may think of the work sphere. The church may initiate discussions with certain groups of professionals about values and norms that are relevant for their line of work, and about the ways in which they, in their situation, can give form and content to their Christianity. As examples I mention such professional groups as teachers, medical doctors and other medical personnel, military personnel, business people, and scientists. The church often has only a limited idea of the challenges people in such professions face, and these professionals often feel that their faith has but little relevance for their daily work.

I am also thinking of the equipping of church members for administrative functions in the various organizations in society that attempt to give form and content to social life in certain sectors of society. Here one may think of labor unions, school boards, youth organizations, women's organizations, sports clubs, and political parties. It is important for the church as well as for the individuals involved that one give more thought to how one may make a Christian contribution in these areas.

Finally, I want to mention other movements of more recent origin in which many church members serve as volunteers. Examples include the peace movement, the ecological movement, refugee work, and Amnesty International. To these one could add volunteer work in crisis centers, homes for addicts, shelters for abused women, and so on. This work requires a strong motivation, as well as a lot of stamina to bear the many frustrations. Can the Christian faith serve as a source of inspiration, and can practical theology contribute in keeping the vision of the wholeness and integrity of humanity and creation alive?

In all these instances one is faced with two-way traffic, with a movement of mutual equipping. The church needs the experiences of all these people in its task of reflecting on the words of the gospel on the basis of the concreteness of daily life. The workers in turn benefit from a church that empathizes, supports, and assists in reflecting on the questions raised in the context of their work, on the basis of the values and norms of the gospel. All this may result in conciliary experiments that offer perspectives for the future.

Working along these lines, one will clarify how much expertise the church possesses in its members. The oft-repeated complaint that the church has no expertise in the areas of politics, economics, or social action is silenced the very moment the church allows its members, who are experts in their own fields, to speak.

It would, of course, be possible to include the area of the equipping of the laity in other subdisciplines that cover the teaching role of the church, or with pastoral care, the diaconate, or church development. But experience has taught that equipping for a task in society is not maximized if it is not treated as something in its own right. The Evangelical Academies in Germany provide a good example of how this may be done (Wolfaardt 1971). One may also point to the Multidisciplinair Centrum voor Kerk en Samenleving (MCKS, Multidisciplinary center for church and society) in Driebergen, the Netherlands.

16.4 Conclusion

The domain of religion and society is the most neglected area in practical theology. Yet a practical-theological diaconology offers many suggestions for responses to the questions that must be addressed. The Christian faith has much to say about the way in which society is organized and functions. The subdisciplines of evangelism and diaconics need further strengthening. It merits consideration to assign a separate place to the field of equipping the laity.

CHAPTER 17

Practical Theology as Pastoral Theology

One other professional domain within practical theology demands attention: pastoral theology. Chapter 6 dealt with the history of pastoral theology, often regarded as the precursor of practical theology. In chapter 9 we encountered the pastoral-theological current as one of the five streams in practical theology (9.4.5). This chapter offers a more systematic treatment of the content of present-day pastoral theology as an important branch of practical theology. From its inception, pastoral theology has focused on the role of the various offices in the life of the church. Since I have discussed the role of the congregation in the previous chapter in some detail, I now deal in particular with the role of the pastor. Here I use the term *pastor* as a collective epithet for all ministers, priests, and pastoral workers who work in the church, with the church as their base. Although not all churches have introduced the ordination of women, I include both male and female pastors.

From the outset I stress that this chapter does not signal a return to a traditional "pastoral theology." But I regard pastoral theology as an important part of practical theology, since this branch is to a large degree responsible for the professional training of pastors. Considering the high demands of the pastoral profession, special attention on pastors and their work is necessary. But attention on the pastor should not occur in isolation. I see the ministry as one of the charismata in a "charismatic" church. All work in the church is not identical, but it is of equal value. Giving special thought to the role of the ministry should, in my view, not lead to a view of the church in which the ministry dominates. In order to avoid misunderstandings, I must first underline this fundamental principle. The role of the pastor deserves further discussion, with the preunderstanding that she or he functions within a community, in reciprocity with all who contribute to the development of the church.

I first point to the unique character of the pastoral profession (17.1) and on that basis distinguish among the ecclesiastical character (17.2), the professional character (17.3), and the personal character (17.4) of the pastoral profession.

17.1 The Uniqueness of the Pastoral Profession

In this section I discuss the pastoral profession by looking at the concepts of identity (17.1.1) and competence (17.1.2). The first element applies mostly to the person, and the second to the profession of that person. But the two concepts complement each other.

17.1.1 The Identity of the Pastor

The term *identity* refers to a sense of personal wholeness. The question arises: Can a person have a sense of fulfillment in this profession? When speaking of the identity of the pastor, I am asking whether a woman or a man, as a human being, and as a believer and a theologian, can thrive in her or his role as a pastor. One may make a certain distinction among personal identity, pastoral identity, and theological identity. Two questions are paramount in this connection: Who am I? What am I supposed to do? (Riess 1973, 78).

With regard to this personal identity, I can build on the views of Erik H. Erikson (1968, 91ff.). There is continuity in the different phases of human life. Erikson speaks of the "epigenetic principle." Humans grow and develop on the basis of a "ground plan." One phase presupposes the other and builds on it. Each phase brings new challenges. If one cannot cope with these challenges, a crisis results. Viewed from the perspective of human development, a crisis can be understood as "a backlog of homework" or as "unfinished business" (Andriessen 1974, 155ff.). Some things may have been insufficiently integrated and cause a tension between, for example, the person and the ministerial role, or theology and faith. This tension may create confusion.

Kruijne (1977, 249) has compared the personal history of pastors with Erikson's theories and has concluded that internal psychological factors dominate when a pastor faces an identity crisis. The reason is that the pastor has not achieved an adult sense of maturity. Of course, one must realize that the three states of existence — of being simultaneously a pastor, a believer, and a human being — constantly interact, as stimuli and obstructions, while external factors of a social or theological nature may add to the crisis.

Female pastors face another problem. Identity is usually acquired through a process of identification and experiment (de Wit and van der Veer 1979, 161). The first aspect demands a model of a pastor with whom one can identify. The latter aspect demands sufficient room for the person to have enough experiences to allow for a personal interpretation of the pastoral role. Research among female pastors has repeatedly indicated that this model may not have been available to them (Heitink 1985). Women cannot rely on a long tradition of role models. This is a disadvantage as there is little to learn from predecessors, but it may also prove to be an advantage, as one can largely shape one's own role. Patterns of expectation may, however, often be such that little room for experimentation is left, since male pastors constitute the models on the basis of which female pastors are judged. As a result, in many denominations female pastors feel tolerated rather than accepted. An additional aspect in the Catholic Church is that female (and male!) pastoral workers have fewer rights than their ordained colleagues.

Apart from developmental and sociopsychological factors, other elements also come into play. Pastors have to give a theological account of their work if they are to integrate theology and science in their work. They also have to establish a fruitful relationship with the institutional church: critically and in solidarity. They have to learn how choices of faith and psychological factors in their personal life interact, to enable them to be more open for others. They have to solve any tensions that may exist between their church role and their personal expertise. They must be able to represent the church in a more and more secularized society, with all the difficulties this entails.

All these factors combined determine the identity of the pastor. It becomes increasingly difficult to shape such a personal identity, as church and faith are less and less self-evident in our society, and the old, traditional landmarks of clergy, tradition, role, and behavior are no longer self-evident. Supervision and monitoring are now absolutely vital. On this point this chapter offers little more than some cognitive clarification. But even that is important.

17.1.2 The Competence of the Pastor

The second aspect that determines the unique character of the pastoral profession is that of competence. To establish some clarity, I follow van der

Spijker (1984, 18ff.) in differentiating between two meanings of the term *competence:* being authorized and having certain skill. Pastoral competence thus consists of "being authorized to" and "being knowledgeable about." The competencies of authority include legal, traditional, and archetypical competence. The pastoral profession demands authorization from the institutional church, identification with the tradition, and acquisition of the spirituality that goes with this symbolic function. "This authority gives the pastor the right and the permission to be what he or she must become: a pastor." In addition, one may distinguish three kinds of competencies with relation to ability: pastoral-theological skills, communicative skills, and personal skills. A combination of these three is necessary if one is to mediate the knowledge of God's encounter with human beings to others. It is the combination of wisdom and knowledge, in community with others, and in loyalty to oneself (1984, 21). The pastor acquires these skills in interaction with the entire congregation.

I believe these distinctions are helpful, since they show the connection between authorization (clergy) and competence, focused on the integration of calling and profession, person and church office, knowledge and skill. On this basis in pastoral theology one may distinguish three approaches to the pastoral profession: that of the ecclesiastical character (17.2), of the professional character (17.3), and of the personal character (17.4).

17.2 The Ecclesiastical Character

Holding a church office is an important factor for the pastoral identity. I highlight the significance of holding a church office, the value presently attached to such an office, and the authority the church invests in the pastoral profession.

17.2.1 The Significance of Holding a Church Office

As spiritual gifts, church offices are rooted in a charismatic community (6.1). The Bible does not refer to the word *office,* with its clerical associations, but prefers the word *diakonia* (service). But the New Testament also — in the Pastoral Letters — points to another aspect, as holding an office "in Christ's name."

Schillebeeckx (1979, 68) emphasizes the remarkable fact that in the New Testament these church offices did not develop in the context of the Eucharist or the liturgy (in its more limited sense), but emerged in the context of apostolicity. They are rooted in the need for proclamation, and for people who can lead and build the church: "A sacralistic-mystical foundation for the priesthood (the church office) in the liturgy cannot be defended on Biblical grounds" (69). This would not change until the eleventh and twelfth century, when leading the "corpus Christi verum" (the true body of Christ) acquires another meaning. Until then the body of Christ was understood as the body of believers. From the Middle Ages onward, however, the body was defined as "the eucharistic body of Christ." This led to a mystical sacralization of the priesthood.

The Reformation returned the office in the church to normal, human proportions. In the Calvinist tradition church members may receive the office of elder or deacon. Together with the minister(s), they form the "church council," in which they are a solid majority. This enables them to put their stamp on church policy. The administering of the sacraments, however, remains the prerogative of the minister.

Berkhof sees the essence of the office as representation. Representing Christ (1973, 400 [1979, 382]), those who hold a church office are called constantly to remind the church of its special purpose. Berkhof distinguishes three theological approaches to the offices in the church: the Catholic or high-church type, characterized by the ordination that sets the person apart from and above the congregation; the classical Reformed type, which positions the office as separate from the church but also in the midst of the church, with its authority limited by the priesthood of all believers; and the free church or low-church type, which regards holding a church office as not essentially different from the office of all believers (398 [380]). In the Netherlands the second, Calvinist, type predominates. Ridderbos summarizes this in the following words: "The office . . . is from Christ and through the church" (1966, 534 [1975, 478]). From the 1960s onward the major Protestant churches have opened the offices for women, even though the local congregation may decide whether they want a woman as their minister.

17.2.2 The Current Esteem for the Church Office

In our time the esteem for church office fluctuates like the value of the dollar: up and down. For a while it may rise in the appreciation of the people, but shortly afterward its stock may fall sharply. The "rate" of the office is apparently susceptible to cultural influences. In the 1960s democratization went wild and the prestige of traditional authorities was under stress.

Holding office in the church was seen as a full-time expression of the priesthood of all believers. But lately society is back to dotting the *i*'s and crossing the *t*'s, recognizing that it cannot exist without rules and regulations. A brochure of the Dutch Protestant churches that are preparing for a merger states that the church office is more than a special form of the "general" role of the Christian: "The church offices must be accepted as a special gift of Christ to his people, as a special instrument to offer a unique experience of his presence." This seems close to the shift to which Schillebeeckx pointed.

The Lima Report (or BEM Report: Baptism, Eucharist and Ministry) appeared in 1982 as a document of the World Council of Churches, in cooperation with the Roman Catholic Church. Care was taken to position the office in the midst of the community of believers. Those who hold a church office are referred to as representatives of Christ who proclaim his message of atonement to the community. The report distinguished three different types of officers: bishops, presbyters, and deacons. The emphasis was on the office as separate from the community of believers.

Most Protestants consider this report as rather "high church." But the interesting thing is that, like Calvin, the BEM Report underlined a threefold pattern. It goes back to the second and third centuries, when "a threefold pattern of bishop, presbyter, and deacon became established as a pattern of ordained ministry throughout the church" (III, §19). Of those three the bishop holds the highest rank. The Protestant minister more resembles the presbyter, with some priestly traits. The deacon has the lowest position. But this hierarchical vista leaves no room for the elder — "the pawn that once checkmated the pope" (O. Noordmans).

The report offers a reasonable compromise of the various traditions, but one may wonder whether this is the way forward. Would it not be better to choose a pluralistic approach and respect the views on church governance of other churches and to allow different systems to coexist?

Holding a church office is a somewhat controversial aspect of the pastor's identity. Governing bodies decide whether someone will be invited to a church office and what conditions apply. The Catholic Church refuses to ordain women and married men. This limits the possibilities of identification for young people, and as a result fewer feel a call to the ministry. Protestant theologians have to face evaluation committees or must sign confessional statements that they often support only partly. Holding church office may thus easily evoke feelings of selectivity or pressure that are difficult to reconcile with the original character of a charisma. Reflection on the image of the church office is much needed.

17.2.3 The Authorization from the Church

The pastoral profession has always been linked with authorization by the church. Those who do this work do so in the context of the Christian community, which stimulates, legitimizes, and criticizes. This provides some balance for the concept of being called. Having a calling is not just a personal sense of feeling called but also implies a recognition of that call by the church. This recognition ensures that the church is not left at the mercy of the subjectivity of the one who claims to be their pastor. This is the reason why, even in New Testament times, the people have been warned against unauthorized itinerant preachers. Even in the case of the prophetic gift, a process of intersubjective testing is needed (1 Cor. 14:29).

The churches of the Reformation added a further restriction. Recognition by the church is possible only when the person has received a theological education at a university or other similar institution for higher learning. This has to do, in particular, with the requirement that the pastor should possess adequate knowledge of Hebrew, Greek, and Latin, to be able to read the Scriptures and the church fathers in their original languages. A church that gives the highest emphasis to proclamation must have the guarantee that its servants have access to the sources. One might raise the question whether this has encouraged the intellectualization of the Christian faith.

The Catholic Church largely follows the same route. In the 1960s the Dutch Catholic Church transferred the seminary education to the universities, even though the dioceses have maintained a parallel system.

In recent decades this policy has been eroded by the differentiation of church and society. This is especially true for specialized ministries. Pastors in hospitals, institutions, or prisons have a dual identity to some extent. They derive their mission from the church, while their professionalism is determined by their employing institution. Differentiation has driven a wedge between the two. The bodies that provide the funding make their own decisions, also when hiring pastors. This stands to reason, as neither these institutions nor their leaders are tied to the church, and the salaries are often paid from public funds. Financial or other reasons at times lead to the employment of pastors without the academic training normally required by the churches. As a result these pastors are not recognized by the church and are not allowed to lead in official celebrations. But it is usually difficult to avoid this in their line of duty.

It should be possible to employ persons without a university education in various pastoral functions. I believe that the church should not have any valid objections. But this requires an agreement between the churches and, for instance, the government ministries that supervise the institutions concerned, with regard to minimum requirements for pastoral functions and the ecclesiastical status of those pastoral workers. This is needed to protect the pastoral profession with its complicated entanglement of competencies with regard to authorization and skills.

17.3 The Professional Character

A second aspect I distinguished was professional character. To be a pastor means having a profession that in our time needs constant professionalization. This raises questions with regard to the skills that are essential and the need for further education and in-service training.

17.3.1 Professionalization

The very word *professionalization* evokes such strong associations with the process of rationalization that one can easily miss the ecclesiastical root of the word: the profession (promise, vow) at the time of one's entry into the priesthood. Admittedly, in the past some professional codes were in operation, for example, the requirement of confidentiality in the context of the sacrament of auricular confession, regulated by Lateran IV (1215) (Lebacqz 1985, 16). In that sense, even in the past there were professional elements in the ministry, in particular in the Roman Catholic Church, which regulated the administering of the sacraments in every detail. The churches of the Reformation were somewhat uneasy about the relationship between regulations and God's sovereign acts through Word and Spirit. Righteousness by faith brought all human action into question. Moreover, the development of a professional group of "clergy" was at odds with the emphasis on the priesthood of *all* believers.

From the 1960s onward one sees an ever enlarging "market for well-being and happiness" (Achterhuis 1980), cared for by new professionals: agogic specialists, psychologists, therapists, and social workers. Siegers and Haan (1983, 46) define professionalization as the process whereby certain activities (which are important for society) are compressed into societal functions. This implies a new demarcation of their task, the development of specific knowledge and skills, and the formulation of educational requirements. They list these four characteristics of professionalization: specialization, expertise, power, and institutionalized social assistance.

In the 1960s this tendency toward professionalization was initially welcome in church circles. With the decline in prestige of the traditional ministry, this expertise-based authority was seen as a possible response to the crisis situation. This was particularly the case in the Catholic Church. In his inaugural lecture Schreuder (1964) pleaded for professionalization and referred to a "professional underdevelopment" of the pastoral profession. This, he believed, had made the priesthood unattractive for intellectuals and the new middle class. Nowadays it is important what one can do and how one performs, rather than what one is. "Our society regards someone who holds a higher profession, without being a true professional, as an outlaw" (1964, 11). In particular in the area of more specialized pastoral care, where pastors have to compete with other professionals, the cry for professionalization became louder. Professionalization occupied an important place in the new pastoral-theological curriculum at the University of Nijmegen (1964). Here no isolated professionalization was sought, but one that was "embedded in the spirituality of the pastor," says Haarsma (van der Ven, ed., 1985, 15ff.). Likewise, in Protestant theological education internships, supervision, and mentoring acquire a place, though with some theological reservations (Heitink 1977, 367ff.).

Critics look at professionalization differently. Assistance creates needs and makes people dependent, says Achterhuis. Illich, an ex-priest, is happy to use the comparison between clergy and profession: "He sees professionals as a new kind of clergy, who first tell people about their needs, then inform them about what their salvation requires, and finally deliver the required product themselves" (Achterhuis 1980, 123).

In the United States, but also among some in the Netherlands, there is less worry about the side effects of this new product. But Alastair V. Campbell also points to the danger of the "professional captivity of pastoral care" (1985, 43). He believes that the church cannot operate without professionals, but it must know what it does, otherwise it moves beyond "a calculated risk." He mentions a few of those risks. Professionalism has an impact on the nature of the pastoral relationship. A counseling situation does not provide for real reciprocity. He refers to a discussion between Rogers and Buber about the "I and Thou." Such a pastoral relationship is a matter of roles, of the one who gives and the one who receives assistance. It is functional, but one might raise the question whether a friendship relationship does not more accord with the way people in the church are supposed to relate to each other.

Campbell also points to the imbalance of influence and power in such a relationship. If things are done right, the counseling situation offers the client protection without making him or her emotionally dependent. But expertise always implies power of one over another. Campbell also mentions the danger of intellectualism. The pastorate should be rooted in the giving and receiving of love, while professionalism tends to develop relational expertise through the use of psychological knowledge, which by its use of language alone (the agogical and therapeutic jargon) already creates distance. It also easily results in a gap between professionals and volunteers.

Thus, as Campbell remarks, the phenomenon of professionalization gives rise to some ambivalence. If pastoral work is done in a serious manner, it cannot refuse to become "professional," but that does not remove the tension between this development and the unique identity of the Christian community. With this ambivalence in mind I speak about the challenges and limits of professionalization.

17.3.2 Pastoral Skills

Speaking about pastoral skill, I am thinking first of all of the "average" pastor who has had a theological education. This expresses itself in the context of her or his professional activities in hermeneutical expertise. The pastor attempts to understand the reality of humanity and the world in the light of Scripture and tradition (7.4; 10.5). With Firet I may speak of the hermeneutical moment in the pastoral work, according to the "modes of kerygma, didache, and paraklesis" (1968, 54ff. [1986, 39ff.]). The fundamental context is that of the congregation. Schippers (1989, 114) confirms this: "The pastor is the hermeneut."

This finds primary expression in proclamation and celebration. From the perspective of the church, the core of the pastor's function is embedded in one's hermeneutical-liturgical competence. But, as we saw, this cannot be detached from an agogical-communicative competence. By this I mean one's ability to provide leadership to the church through various forms of communicative action, such as celebrations, meetings, working in groups, and personal discussions. Firet (1968, 131ff. [1986, 99ff.]) refers to the "agogic moment in the work of the pastor," and Schippers (1982, 107) states: "The minister is an agogue."

On the basis of further differentiation I see room for three variants within the pastoral profession, in which pastors can acquire a certain level of professionalism. These three specializations are built on pastoral, educational, and organizational competence, respectively. For those who work in a team in regular pastoral work, such a professional differentiation offers many advantages. It allows for the work in the congregation to be cared for along three lines of expertise. A division of work along geographical lines is complemented by assigning tasks on the basis of specialization. The crucial element is to equip the church itself for what it is supposed to be: a missionary community that continues to learn and is ready to serve. Some speak in this connection of the "agogizing of the pastoral profession" (Scholten 1982, 59), that is: "the equipping of others for tasks in the church becomes one of the core functions of the pastor in his congregation or parish." The church becomes the subject, and the pastor moves "in the second line," as the one who gives support in the background rather than being in the forefront.

Three aspects of "being church" are at issue in this threefold specialization. This differentiation largely parallels the threefold division of the domains of action developed in the previous chapter, around the individual, the group, and society.

Pastoral competence demands specialization in the area of the pastorate. Continuing education through postacademic training and supervision is essential. In this connection one should think not only of pastors who serve congregations but also of those who want to improve their skills in the pastorate in hospitals and other institutions. For the latter category a course in clinical pastoral training is usually a prerequisite.

Educational competence demands specialization in the area of religious instruction to young people and adults, in the church and outside the church. Apart from catechesis and adult education in the church and the development of the church as a place of learning, one may think of religion teachers, social-cultural workers, and similar professions. Another area of professional activity is the broad domain of theological education at different levels. A background in religious pedagogics, didactics, and agogics is a prerequisite.

Organizational competence focuses on the analysis of structures and processes in society, taking account of the aspects of power, injustice, and poverty — in particular in that segment of society called church. An expert in this field may lead in developing the church into a community in which people can reach their full potential. I intentionally refer to the link between the development of the church and the development of society. The two aspects must interact in a critical way. Pastors with this specialization can find their field of labor in the local church but also as chaplains in commercial organizations, in activities related to neighborhood development, and so on. A training in the dynamics of urban and industrial society is here of major importance.

17.3.3 Education and In-Service Training

I already alluded to some educational and training requirements in the previous section. Further comments may be helpful. Entrance to the pastoral profession is subject to a completed academic education, preferably at the university level. Within this education a fair degree of specialization may be offered toward pastoral, educational, or organizational work.

A major part of the training needed for the pastoral profession has to be acquired through postacademic courses and in-service training. Each of the various denominations has its own rules and programs. A mentoring system during the first years in the pastorate and supervision for specific projects are also useful. It would be good if all pastors, whether working in the congregation or in a specialized area, were to receive, after a few years of experience, some training in clinical pastoral formation.

17.4 The Personal Character

I now turn to the demands the pastoral profession makes on the person of the pastor (17.4.1), and, in close connection with this, on the spirituality of the pastor (17.4.2).

17.4.1 The Person of the Pastor

The matter of suitability for the pastoral profession is a separate question that demands attention. It has often been pointed out that many psychologically troubled persons seem to be attracted to the ministry. W. J. Berger (1968, 135ff.) writes on the basis of the research that he has done that church authorities must be very clear in their statements about the requirements for the ministry. This study concludes, however, that the problem of neurotic instability is not worse than among other comparable groups.

Protestant churches quite often face the problem that ministers resign after a few years. This says something about the exacting nature of this profession, but also about the spiritual health of some of the individuals concerned. That is why some churches insist that the suitability of candidates for this work should already be evaluated during their schooling. This presents problems because adolescents tend to experience significant development during their years of study. So far the Protestant churches have not required a psychological test before appointing a pastor, even though this is a widely accepted process in the case of other comparable professions. I believe that the pastoral profession is made too special by rejecting such a test.

In his two-volume pastoral theology Josuttis (1982, 1988) pays ample attention to the requirements with regard to the person of the pastor. Most of these have already been mentioned in the previous sections. But I should add two aspects. First, there is the aspect of sexuality and relationships.

The Roman Catholic Church requires celibacy from its priests. Hoenkamp-Bisschops (1991, 105) concludes that celibacy does not do damage to a person's psychological health, if three conditions are met: freedom of choice, a normal affective development, and a positive motivation for this way of life. In our culture this last aspect is often missing. She describes three different ways of handling the requirement of celibacy. Some opt for an intimate sexual relationship without actually living with a partner. Others stick to their vow of celibacy without too much difficulty. Another group never makes a clear choice and tries — with varying degrees of success — to obey this rule as best as they can. Five practical theologians in Germany have recently pointed to the crisis situation in the pastoral situation, at least in part due to the continued insistence of the church on celibacy (Mette 1992). The situation in the Netherlands is quite similar.

Intimacy and sexuality are important themes for all pastors. Many ministers seem to be married to their congregations, at the expense of the relationship with their partner. Many marriages of pastors therefore end in divorce. In addition, more recently one hears warnings about the danger of "sexualizing" pastoral relationships. A pastoral relationship may lead to a considerable degree of intimacy. In a time when the distance between the pastor and her or his members has decreased, sexual contacts may more easily occur. The symbolic function of the pastoral office and the fact that the pastor has easy access to the homes of church members may play a role in this respect. It would be good if there were a professional code, as is the case for other "helping" professions, to counter the danger of sexual abuse in pastoral relationships. In recent times complaints about the misuse of such relationships are on the increase. In some cases hot lines have been set up where victims can receive help.

Finally, I must mention the impact of the pastoral profession on the family life of the pastor. Living in a parsonage often means "living in a glass house" (Riess 1992). There are constant visitors. Incoming telephone calls make the family members aware of the repeated emotional appeals to which the pastor is subjected. In many cases the spouse of the pastor is also expected to play a role in the life of the congregation. Children are branded as "pastor's kids" and are supposed to behave accordingly. Thus life in the parsonage has its own tensions that are often hardly noticed by the environment.

17.4.2 The Spirituality of the Pastor

As a final point I need to discuss the spirituality of the pastor as a "professional believer," who, just like others, experiences periods of darkness of the soul. The constant appeal, week after week, on the personal faith of the pastor — just think, for instance, of the many prayers the pastor has to offer — may turn a joyful occupation into a heavy burden.

The practical theologian E. Lange wrote a moving chapter about "faith and temptation in the daily life of a church pastor" (1976). This touches on a classic theme in the theology of the Reformation: the God who remains silent and hides himself. Of course, this may affect not only pastors but all believers. This crisis is the core of temptation, but also a source of faith. Here Luther discovered the heart of the gospel: the justification of the godless. For centuries this temptation has been repressed by assuming that faith is automatic. Lange believes that an innovative approach to the pastoral profession, through professionalization, must be accompanied by a spiritual approach. Many pastors become frustrated by the fact that they must do so many things for which they possess no skills. Lange refers to this as "malaise" rather than "temptation." But in our day and age feelings of inefficiency and incompetence often go together with the sense that God is no longer there. Lange calls this the "Sisyphus feeling." He quotes a complaint of a priest in one of Graham Greene's novels: "I have never been able to really help anyone." Some survive this feeling by consciously establishing some distance, while others escape in a culture of meetings. But this temptation cannot simply be overcome by action. Or, to put it in Reformation words: No one is justified by works.

Lange pictures the local congregation as a "corporate victim of our time." The typical congregation has no "backbone" or "advance party." Many are unfree and long for liberation. Lange refers to this, in line with "the culture of silence" (P. Freire), as the "inability to speak." "They have plenty of words. But these words leave certain things unsaid. One can talk about technical progress and visit a supermarket together. But these words do not speak of suffering and joy, loneliness and passion, hope and anxiety. One cannot really communicate with them" (Lange 1976, 191). For that reason the spiritual dimension demands attention "in, with, and under" (a sacramental formula!) the innovative aspect. Only in solidarity with those who suffer is a path opened up to face temptation. I believe this points to the need of integrating professionalism and spirituality.

In addition, I want to mention the concept of "mystagogic" pastoral care, which has been developed in Catholic circles (Knobloch and Haslinger 1991). Significantly, the concept of "mystagogics" (introduction into mysteries), which long led a marginal existence, has become extremely popular since the 1980s. The concept arises from the *disciplina arcani* of the early church, a term we encountered earlier with Bonhoeffer (5.2.3). In his *Handboek* (Manual) Rahner already pleads for a new form of mystagogics (Arnold, Schuster, and Rahner 1966ff.). For him this is a matter of a basic attitude. Leading people to faith requires a real encounter with believers. Mystagogics stands for leading people to the mystery of the merciful self-revelation of God. A human being that transcends him- or herself may hope to reach that point.

For Protestant theologians, in particular, it has been quite a discovery to find that there are spiritual exercises like steps on a mystical path. These exercises of prayer and forms of meditation lead to a deeper experience of personal faith, which is indispensable in the pastoral profession.

17.5 Conclusion

One meets the uniqueness of the pastoral profession in the tension of identity and competence. Pastoral competence is practical-theological competence (13.4) that focuses on the practice of the congregation. Along these lines of ministry, profession, and person, the contours of a pastoral theology emerge. Pastoral theology must be seen as a distinct subdiscipline within practical theology.

This brings us to the end of part III, in which I have opted for a moderate differentiation of action domains within practical theology. Our society presents us with three partly overlapping domains of action: "humanity and religion," "church and faith," "religion and society." In the context of the fundamental theory of practical theology I have worked this out in three directions: practical-theological anthropology, practical-theological ecclesiology, and practical-theological diaconology. On this basis one may distinguish a number of fields or "theories for practice," which separate volumes in this series dedicated to practical theology will examine.

Bibliography

Aalders, C. *Spiritualiteit: Geestelijk leven vroeger en nu*. The Hague, 1969.

Aalders, M. J. *Ethisch tussen 1870 en 1920*. Kampen, 1990.

Achelis, Chr. *Lehrbuch der praktischen Theologie*. 2 vols. Freiburg, 1880.

Achterhuis, H. *De markt van welzijn en geluk*. Baarn, 1980.

Adams, J. E. *Competent to Counsel*. Philadelphia, 1970.

Adorno, T. W., E. Frenkel-Brunswik, D. J. Levinson, and R. N. Sanford. *The Authoritarian Personality*. New York, 1950.

Adriaanse, H. J., H. A. Krop, and L. Leertouwer. *Het verschijnsel theologie: Over de wetenschappelijke status van de theologie*. Meppel, 1987.

Alma, H. *Geloven in de leefwereld van jongeren*. Kampen, 1993.

Alphen, M. van, et al., eds. *Kerk en vredesbeweging*. Kampen, 1982.

Andriessen, H. C. I. *Groei en grens in de volwassenheid*. 2d ed. Nijmegen, 1974.

Andriessen, H. C. I. *Leren aan ervaring en supervisie*. Nijmegen, 1975.

Andriessen, H., and G. Heitink. *Het wordt kil in de kerk: Pastoraal-theologische en pastoraal-psychologische overwegingen*. The Hague, 1985.

Andriessen, H., and N. Derksen. *Bibliodrama en pastoraat*. The Hague, 1985.

Arnold, F. X., H. Schuster, and K. Rahner. *Handboek van de pastoraaltheologie: Praktische theologie over de kerk in haar huidige situatie*. Hilversum, 1966ff.

Augustine. *Belijdenissen*. Trans. G. Wijdeveld. Baarn and Amsterdam, 1985. [*Confessions*. Trans. H. Chadwick. Oxford, 1991.]

Austin, J. L. *How to Do Things with Words*. Cambridge, Mass., 1962.

Baart, A. J. *Verhalen: De dialoog als grondmodel van het maatschappelijk activeringswerk*. Hilversum, 1986.

Bakker, J. T. "Sleutelwoorden uit Berkhofs geloofsleer," *Gereformeerd theologisch Tijdschrift* 76 (1976) 141-61.

Bakker, J. T. "Om de Naam/Om het leven: K. H. Miskotte," *Gereformeerd theologisch Tijdschrift* 84 (1984) 198-218.

Bakker, R. *Wijsgerige antropologie van de twintigste eeuw.* Assen, 1981.

Banning, W. "Lijnen van ontwikkeling tot 1940," in T. T. ten Have, ed., *Vorming, handboek voor sociaal-cultureel vormingswerk met volwassenen.* Groningen, 1966.

Baptism, Eucharist and Ministry. Geneva, 1982.

Barnett, J. M. *The Diaconate: A Full and Equal Order.* 1979. New York, 1981.

Barth, K. *Die Kirchliche Dogmatik.* 4 vols. Zurich, 1932ff. [*Church Dogmatics.* Trans. G. W. Bromiley et al. Edinburgh, 1936ff.]

Bastian, H. D. "Vom Wort zu den Wörtern," *Evangelische Theologie* 28 (1968) 25ff.

Bastian, H. D. *Theologie der Frage: Ideen zur Grundlegung einer theologischen Didaktik und zur Kommunikation der Kirche in der Gegenwart.* Munich, 1969.

Bäumler, C. *Kommunikative Gemeindepraxis: Eine Untersuchung ihrer Bedingungen und Möglichkeiten.* Munich, 1984.

Bäumler, C., and N. Mette. *Gemeindepraxis in Grundbegriffen: Ökumenische Orientierungen und Perspektiven.* Munich and Düsseldorf, 1987.

Bavinck, H. *Gereformeerde dogmatiek.* 4 vols. 1895ff. 4th ed. Kampen, 1928-30.

Bayreuther, E. *Geschichte der Diakonie und Innere Mission der Neuzeit.* Berlin, 1962.

Beerling, R. F., S. L. Kwee, J. J. A. Mooij, and C. A. van Peursen, *Inleiding tot de wetenschapsleer.* 6th ed. Utrecht, 1980.

Beld, A. van der. *Filosofie van het menselijk handelen.* Assen, 1982.

Belenky, M. F., et al. *Women's Ways of Knowing: The Development of Self, Voice, and Mind.* New York, 1986.

Bellah, R. N., R. Madson, W. M. Sullivan, A. Swidler, and S. M. Tipton. *Habits of the Heart: Individualism and Commitment in American Life.* Berkeley, 1985.

Belzen, J. A. van. *Rümke, religie en godsdienstpsychologie.* Kampen, 1991.

Berg, J. H. van den. *Psychologie van het ziekbed.* 1952. 12th ed. Nijkerk, 1967.

Berg, J. H. van den. *Kroniek der psychologie.* Nijkerk, 1973.

Berg, J. H. van den. *Dieptepsychologie.* 5th ed. Nijkerk, 1975.

Berger P. L. *The Sacred Canopy.* Garden City, N.Y., 1967.

Berger, P. L. *A Rumor of Angels.* Garden City, N.Y., 1969.

Berger, P. L. *The Heretical Imperative: Contemporary Possibilities of Religious Affirmation.* Garden City, N.Y., 1979.

Berger, W. J. *Beoordeling van geschiktheid voor het priesterambt.* Nijmegen and Utrecht, 1968.

Berger, W. J., and J. J. M. Vossen. "Pastor aan en RIAGG," *Praktische Theologie* 20 (1993) 57-74.

Bergh, W. van den, H. Hoekstra, and N. A. de Gaay Fortman. *Olie en wijn in de wonden: Beschouwingen over het diakonaat.* Harderwijk, 1888.

Berkhof, H. "Antithese en solidariteit" (1956), in J. M. van Veen, ed,. *Naar de wereld van morgen.* Vol. 2. Amsterdam, 1961.

Berkhof, H. *Christelijk geloof: Een inleiding tot de geloofsleer.* Nijkerk, 1973. [*Christian Belief.* Trans. S. Woudstra. Grand Rapids, 1979.]

Berkhof, H. *Bruggen en bruggehoofden.* Nijkerk, 1981.

Berkhof, H. *200 Jahre Theologie: Ein Reisebericht.* Neukirchen, 1985. [*Two Hundred Years of Theology: Report of a Personal Journey.* Trans. J. Vriend. Grand Rapids, 1989.]

Bethge, E. *Dietrich Bonhoeffer: Theoloog — christen — tijdgenoot.* Baarn, 1968. [*Dietrich Bonhoeffer: Man of Vision, Man of Courage.* Trans. E. Mosbacher et al. Ed. E. Robertson. New York, 1970.]

Biemer, G., and J. Siller. *Grundfragen der Praktischen Theologie.* Mainz, 1971.

Biesterveld, P. *Het hooge belang der ambtelijke vakken.* Kampen, 1894.

Biesterveld, P. *Het object der ambtelijke vakken.* Wageningen, 1902.

Birnbaum, W. *Theologische Wandlungen von Schleiermacher bis Karl Barth: Eine enzyklopädische Studie zur praktischen Theologie.* Tübingen, 1963.

Bloth, P. C., et al. *Handbuch der Praktischen Theologie.* Gütersloh, 1981ff.

Bloth, P. C. "Praktische Theologie," in G. Strecker, ed., *Theologie im 20. Jahrhundert.* Tübingen, 1983, 389-493.

Boer, Th. de. *Grondslagen van een kritische psychologie.* Baarn, 1980. [*Foundations of a Critical Psychology.* Trans. T. Plantinga. Pittsburgh, 1983.]

Boer, Th. de. *De God van de filosofen en de God van Pascal: Op het grensgebied van filosofie en theologie.* The Hague, 1989.

Boer, Th. de, et al. *Hermeneutiek: Filosofische grondslagen van mens- en cultuurwetenschappen.* Meppel and Amsterdam, 1988.

Bohren, R. "Praktische Theologie," in Bohren, ed., *Einführung in das Studium der evangelischen Theologie.* Munich, 1964, 9-32.

Bohren, R. *Predigtlehre.* Munich, 1971.

Bohren, R. *Dass Gott schön werde: Praktische Theologie als theologische Ästhetik.* Munich, 1975.

Bohren, R. *Prophetie und Seelsorge: Eduard Thurneysen.* Neukirchen, 1982.

Boisen, A. T. *Out of the Depths: An Autobiographical Study of Mental Disorder and Religious Experience.* New York, 1960.

Bolkestein, M. H. *Zielszorg in het Nieuwe Testament.* The Hague, 1964.

Bonhoeffer, D. *Sanctorum Communio: Eine dogmatische Untersuchung zur Soziologie der Kirche.* Munich, 1986. [*The Communion of Saints: A Dogmatic Inquiry into the Sociology of the Church.* New York, 1963.]

Bonhoeffer, D. *Gemeinsames Leben.* 1939. 11th ed. Munich, 1964. [*Life Together.* Trans. J. W. Doberstein. London, 1954.]

Bonhoeffer, D. *Verzet en overgave.* Rev. ed. Baarn, 1972. [*Letters and Papers from Prison.* Ed. E. Bethge. Rev. ed. New York, 1972.]

Bons-Storm, R. *Kritisch bezig zijn met pastoraat: Een verkenning van de interdisciplinaire implicaties van de practische theologie.* The Hague, 1984.

Bons-Storm, R. "De rib, de appel en de pastor," *Praktische Theologie* 13 (1986) 346-56.

Bons-Storm, R. *Hoe gaat het met jou? Pastoraat als komen tot verstaan.* Kampen, 1989.

Boon, R. *De joodse wortels van de christelijke eredienst.* Amsterdam, 1970.

Borg, M. ter. *Een uitgewaaierde eeuwigheid: Het menselijk tekort in de moderne cultuur.* Baarn, 1991.

Bos, R. *Identificatie-mogelijkheden in preken uit het Oude Testament.* Kampen, 1992.

Bouwer, J. *Hermeneutics and Homiletics: The Relationship between Proclamation and Existence in the Theology of Heinrich Ott and the Implications Thereof to Homiletics.* Amsterdam, 1992.

Brand, A. "Weber, Max," in *Sociologische Encyclopedie.* Utrecht, 1978, 805-14.

Bremmer, R. H. *Herman Bavinck als dogmaticus.* Kampen, 1961.

Bremmer, R. H. *Herman Bavinck en zijn tijdgenoten.* Kampen, 1966.

Browning, D. S. *A Fundamental Practical Theology: Descriptive and Strategic Proposals.* Minneapolis, 1991.

Browning, D. S., ed. *Practical Theology.* San Francisco, 1983.

Bruin, J. *Kerkvernieuwing: Een praktisch-ecclesiologisch onderzoek naar de betekenis van "Gemeenteopbouw" voor de Nederlandse Hervormde Kerk.* Zoetermeer, 1992.

Buber, M. *Ich und Du.* Leipzig, 1923. [*I and Thou.* Trans. R. G. Smith. 2d ed. New York, 1958.]

Bucer, M. *Over de ware zielzorg.* 1538. Trans. H. J. Selderhuis. Kampen, 1991.

Burger, C. *Praktiese teologie in Suid-Afrika.* Pretoria, 1991.

Busch Keiser, I. *Het protestantsch leeraarambt in deszelfs ganschen omvang: een handboek der praktische godgeleerdheid.* Groningen, 1833.

Buttrick, D. *Homiletic: Moves and Structures.* Philadelphia, 1987.

Buytendijk, F. J. J. *De vrouw: Haar natuur, verschijning en bestaan. Een existentieel-psychologische studie.* Utrecht, 1958.

Caldwell, C. F. *Pastoral Theological Hermeneutics: A Quest for a Method.* Notre Dame, Ind., 1978.

Calvin, J. *Institutie of onderwijzing in den Christelijken godsdienst.* 3 vols. Ed. A. Sizoo. 3d ed. Delft, 1956. [*Institutes of the Christian Religion.* Trans. F. L. Battles. 2 vols. Philadelphia, 1960.]

Campbell, A. V. *Professionalism and Pastoral Care.* Philadelphia, 1985.

Chopp, R. S. *The Praxis of Suffering: An Interpretation of Liberation and Political Theologies.* New York, 1986.

Chopp, R. S. "Practical Theology and Liberation," in L. S. Mudge and J. N. Poling, eds., *Formation and Reflection: The Promise of Practical Theology*. Philadelphia, 1987.

Claerbaut, D. *Urban Ministry*. Grand Rapids, 1983.

Claessens, P. W. M. *Het omgekeerde leren: Van vraag naar antwoord*. Kampen, 1988.

Claessens, W. F., and G. van Tillo, eds. *Van beneden naar boven: Een nieuwe richting in de praktische theologie*. Kampen, 1990.

Clebsch, W., and C. R. Jaekle. *Pastoral Care in Historical Perspective*. Englewood Cliffs, N.J., 1964.

Clinebell, H. *Basic Types of Pastoral Care and Counseling*. Nashville, 1984.

Cohn, R. C. *Van psychoanalyse naar temagecentreerde interactie: Bouwstenen voor een pedagogisch systeem voor onderwijs, vorming en hulpverlening*. 2d ed. Baarn, 1983.

Craddock, F. *As One Without Authority*. Nashville, 1971.

Dahm, K.-W. *Beruf Pfarrer: Empirische Aspekte zur Funktion von Kirche und Religion in unserer Gesellschaft*. Munich, 1971.

Daiber, K.-F. *Grundriss der Praktischen Theologie als Handlungswissenschaft*. Munich, 1977.

Daiber, K.-F. *Predigt als religiose Rede: Homiletische Ueberlegungen im Anschluss an eine empirische Untersuchung*. Predigen und Hören 3. Munich, 1991.

Dannowski, H. W. *Kompendium der Predigtlehre*. Gütersloh, 1985.

Dekker, G. *Godsdienst en samenleving: Inleiding tot de studie van de godsdienstsociologie*. Kampen, 1987.

Dekker, G. *De stille revolutie: De ontwikkeling van de Gereformeerde Kerken in Nederland tussen 1950 en 1990*. Kampen, 1992.

Dieterich, P. M. *Survey-Guided Development for Church Vitalization*. Chicago, 1987.

Dingemans, G. D. J. *In de leerschool van het geloof: Mathetiek en vakdidaktiek voor catechese en kerkelijk vormingswerk*. Kampen, 1986.

Dingemans, G. D. J. *Een huis om in te wonen: Schetsen en bouwstenen voor een Kerk en een Kerkorde van de toekomst*. The Hague, 1987.

Dingemans, G. D. J. "Praktische theologie als een academische discipline," *Nederlands theologisch tijdschrift* 43, no. 3 (1989) 192-212.

Dingemans, G. D. J. *De tijd van de verborgen God*. The Hague, 1990.

Dingemans, G. D. J. *Als hoorder onder de hoorders . . . . : Een hermeneutische homiletiek*. Kampen, 1991.

Dongen, J. C. van. *Vervreemding en dienst: Verkenning van een Diaconia Alienatorum*. The Hague, 1964.

Douwes, P. A. C. *Armenkerk: De Hervormde diaconie te Rotterdam in de negentiende eeuw*. Schiedam, 1977.

Drehsen, V. *Neuzeitliche Konstitutionsbedingungen der Praktischen Theologie:*

Aspekte der theologischen Wende zur sozialkulturellen Lebenswelt christlicher Religion. Gütersloh, 1988.

Drehsen, V. "Praktische Theologie als Kunstlehre im Zeitalter burgerlicher Kultur," in K. E. Nipkow et al., eds., *Praktische Theologie und Kultur der Gegenwart.* Gütersloh, 1991.

Drews, P. *Das Problem der Praktischen Theologie: Zugleich ein Beitrag zur Reform des theologischen Studiums.* Tübingen, 1910 (partly included in Krause 1972).

Dudley, C. S. *Basic Steps toward Community Ministry.* New York, 1991.

Duijker, H. C. J., and A. C. Dudink, *Leerboek der psychologie.* 2d ed. Groningen, 1970.

Dulk, M. den. *De geboorte van de praktische theologie.* Leiden, 1992.

Dulles, A. *Models of the Church.* 1974. Expanded ed. New York, 1987.

Erikson, E. H. *Identity: Youth and Crisis.* New York, 1968.

Es, J. J. van. *Spreken over God: letterlijk of figuurlijk.* Amsterdam, 1979.

Faber, H. "Een nieuw theologisch model," in H. H. Berger et al., eds., *Tussentijds.* Tilburg, 1974, 61-74.

Faber, H. *Profiel van een bedelaar: Pastor zijn in een veranderende samenleving.* Meppel, 1975.

Faber, H., ed. *Pastoraat — balans en perspectief.* 2 vols. Kampen, 1983-84.

Faber, H., and E. van der Schoot. *Het pastorale gesprek.* Utrecht, 1962. [*The Art of Pastoral Conversation.* New York, 1965.]

Farley, E. *Theologia: The Fragmentation and Unity of Theological Education.* Philadelphia, 1983.

Farley, E. *The Fragility of Knowledge: Theological Education in the Church and the University.* Philadelphia, 1988.

Firet, J. *Het agogisch moment in het pastoral optreden.* Kampen, 1968. [*Dynamics in Pastoring.* Trans. J. Vriend. Grand Rapids, 1986.]

Firet, J. *Praktische theologie als theologische futurologie.* Kampen, 1968.

Firet, J. "De plaats van de praktische theologie in de nieuwe strukturen van de theologische wetenschap," *Rondom het Woord* 12 (1970) 325-43.

Firet, J. "De situatie van de praktische theologie," *Praktische Theologie* 1 (1974) 4-10.

Firet, J. "Godservaring in het Interim," in *Ad Interim, opstellen voor R. Schippers.* Kampen, 1975.

Firet, J. "De plaats van de praktische theologie binnen de theologische faculteit," in C. P. van Andel et al., eds., *Praktische theologie.* The Hague, 1980.

Firet, J. "Kroniek van de praktische theologie," *Praktische Theologie* 13 (1986) 579-94.

Firet, J. *Spreken als een leerling: Praktisch-theologische opstellen.* Kampen, 1987.

Firet, J., and J. Hendriks. *Ik heb geen mens: De anonieme pastorale relatie.* The Hague, 1986.

Firet, J., and H. J. M. Vossen. *Klinische Pastorale Vorming: Balans and perspectief.* (*Praktische Theologie* 18 [1991] 137-270.)

Firet, J., et al. *Pluraliteit in de kerk.* Kampen, 1977.

Foitzik, K. *Gemeindepädagogik: Problemgeschichte eines umstrittenen Begriffs.* Münster, 1992.

Fortmann, H. *Wat is er met de mens gebeurd? Over de taak van een vergelijkende cultuurpsychologie.* Bilthoven, 1971.

Fortmann, H. M. M. *Als ziende de Onzienlijke: Een cultuurpsychologische studie over de religieuze waarneming en de zogenaamde religieuze projectie.* 2 vols. (1, 2, 3a, and 3b). 1964-68. 2d ed. Hilversum, 1974.

Fowler, J. W. *Stages of Faith: The Psychology of Human Development and the Quest for Meaning.* San Francisco, 1981.

Fowler, J. W. "Practical Theology and the Shaping of Christian Lives," in Browning 1983, 148-67.

Frankl, V. E. *Der Mensch vor der Frage nach dem Sinn: Eine Auswahl aus dem Gesamtwerk.* Munich and Zurich, 1979.

Freire, P. *Pedagogy of the Oppressed.* Trans. M. B. Ramos. New York, 1970.

Friedman, E. H. *Generation to Generation: Family Process in Church and Synagogue.* New York and London, 1985.

Gadamer, H.-G. *Wahrheit und Methode: Grundzügen einer philosophischen Hermeneutik.* 1960. 2d ed. Tübingen, 1975. [*Truth and Method.* 1975. 2d ed. Trans. J. Weisenheimer and D. G. Marshall. New York, 1989.]

Geertz, C. *The Interpretation of Cultures.* New York, 1973.

Geest, H. van der. *Du hast mich angesprochen: Die Wirkung von Gottesdienst und Predigt.* Zurich, 1978.

Genderen, J. van, et al., eds. *Ten dienste van het Woord: Opstellen aangeboden aan W. H. Velema.* Kampen, 1991.

Gennep, F. O. van. *Mensen hebben mensen nodig: Een studie over sexualiteit en nieuwe moraal.* Baarn, 1972.

Gennep, F. O. van. *De terugkeer van de verloren Vader.* Baarn, 1989.

Gerkin, C. V. *Widening the Horizons: Pastoral Responses to a Fragmented Society.* Philadelphia, 1986.

Geukema, R., M. Sikkel, and H. Zijlstra. *De akseptatie voorbij: Een nieuwe visie op de voortgaande bezinning over kerk and homosexualiteit.* Voorburg, 1989.

Geulen, D., ed. *Perspektivenübernahme und sociales Handeln: Texte zur social kognitiven Entwicklung.* Frankfurt, 1982.

Gilligan, C. *In a Different Voice: Psychological Theory and Women's Development.* Cambridge, Mass., 1982.

Girard, R. *The Scapegoat.* Trans. Y. Freccero. Baltimore, 1986.

Goddijn, W. *De beheerste kerk: Uitgestelde revolutie in R. K. Nederland.* Amsterdam, 1973.

Goedhart, G. L. *Gemeenteopbouw: Om dienende, vierende, lerende and delende gemeente te worden.* Kampen, 1984.

Golterman, W. F. *Liturgiek.* Haarlem, 1951.

Goot, Y. van der. *Publiek en persoonlijk: Aspecten van de pastorale verantwoordeliikheid van de omroep.* Kampen, 1989.

Gräb, W. "Godwin Lämmermann, Praktische theologie als kritische oder empirisch-kritische Handlungstheorie?" *Themen der Praktischen Theologie* 19 (1984) 55ff.

Greimacher, N. "Das Theorie-Praxis-Problem in der Praktischen Theologie," in Klostermann and Zerfass 1974, 103-19.

Greive, W. *Praxis und Theologie.* Munich, 1975.

Griffioen, S. "'Public Philosophy' en religieus pluralisme," in *Cultuur als partner van de theologie: Opstellen voor G. E. Meuleman.* Kampen, 1990.

Groome, T. H. *Christian Religious Education: Sharing Our Story and Vision.* San Francisco, 1980.

Groot, A. D. de. *Methodologie: Grondslagen van onderzoek en denken in de gedragswetenschappen.* 1961. 8th ed. The Hague, 1975.

Grözinger, A. "Offenbarung und Praxis: Zum schwierigen praktisch-theologischen Erbe der Dialektischen Theologie," *Theologie und Kirche* 6. Tübingen, 1986.

Grözinger, A. *Praktische Theologie und Aesthetik.* Munich, 1987.

Grözinger, A. *Die Sprache des Menschen: Ein Handbuch Grundwissen fur Theologinnen und Theologen.* Munich, 1991.

Haarsma, F. *Geest en kerk.* Utrecht, 1967.

Haarsma, F. *De leer van de kerk and het geloof van haar leden.* Utrecht, 1968.

Haarsma, F. "Supervision: ein Modell von Reflexion kirchlicher Praxis," in Klostermann and Zerfass 1974, 609-24.

Haarsma, F. *Morren tegen Mozes.* Kampen, 1981.

Haarsma, F. *Kandelaar en korenmaat: Pastoraaltheologische studies over kerk and pastoraat.* Kampen, 1991.

Habermas, J. *Erkenntnis und Interesse.* 1968. 5th ed. Frankfurt, 1979. [*Knowledge and Human Interests.* Trans. J. S. Shapiro. Boston, 1971.]

Habermas, J. *Theorie des kommunikativen Handelns.* 2 vols. 1981. Repr. Frankfurt a/M., 1988. [*The Theory of Communicative Action.* 2 vols. Trans. T. McCarthy. Boston, 1984-87.]

Habermas, J. *De nieuwe onoverzichtelijkheid en andere opstellen.* Meppel and Amsterdam, 1989.

Haendler, O. *Grundriss der Praktischen Theologie.* Berlin, 1957.

Halkes, C. J. M. *Zoekend naar wat verloren ging: Enkele aanzetten voor een feministische theologie.* Baarn, 1984.

Hamelink, C. J., et al. *Kerk en massamedia.* Baarn, 1971.

Häring, H. "De laatste zekerheid van een verlichte theologie," *Gereformeerd theologisch Tijdschrift* 92 (1992) 93-106.

Hart, O. van der. *Overgang en bestendiging: Over het ontwerpen and voorschrijven van rituelen in psychotherapie.* Deventer, 1978.

Hartensveld, F. *Het concept mens in het denken van Abraham Joshua Heschel and de betekenis daarvan voor onderwijs and opleiding.* Amsterdam, 1988.

Hartvelt, G. P. *Omgaan met het verleden: Tussen ja-zeggers en nee-zeggers.* Kampen, 1981.

Hattinga Verschure, J. C. M. *Het verschijnsel zorg: Een schets van het verschijnsel zorg.* Lochem, 1977.

Heitink, G. *Pastoraat als hulpverlening: Inleiding in de pastorale theologie en psychologie.* Kampen, 1977.

Heitink, G. "De armen hebt gij altijd bij u: Een hoofdstuk uit de geschiedenis van het gereformeerde diakonaat," in *Bewerken and bewaren, studies voor K. Runia.* Kampen, 1982.

Heitink, G. "Pastoraat en veranderend geloven," in J. Boendermaker et al., eds., *Doen wat er te doen staat: Denken over pastoraat.* The Hague, 1984, 55-65.

Heitink, G. "De vrouwelijke pastor in het pastoraat," *Praktische Theologie* 12 (1985) 399-415.

Heitink, G. "Secularisatie en het individuele geloofsleven," in G. Dekker and K. U. Gabler, eds., *Secularisatie in theologisch perspectief.* Kampen, 1988a.

Heitink, G. *Om raad verlegen, doch niet radeloos . . . : Ervaringen van aporie bij de beoefening der praktische theologie.* Kampen, 1988b.

Heitink, G. "Ontwerp van een empirische theologie: Naar aanleiding van: J. A. van der Ven, *Entwurf einer empirischen Theologie,*" *Praktische Theologie* 18 (1991) 525-38.

Heitink, G. "Pastorale zorg," in Schaeffer 1992.

Heitink, G., and J. Veenhof, eds. *Heil, heling, gezondheid.* The Hague, 1990.

Henau, E. *De kerk: Instrument en teken van heil.* Leuven and Amersfoort, 1989.

Hendriks, J. *De emancipatie van de gereformeerden.* Alphen aan den Rijn, 1971.

Hendriks, J. *Overal waar mensen zijn: Een diakonale gemeente.* Kampen, 1973.

Hendriks, J. *Emancipatie: Relaties tussen minoriteit en dominant.* Alphen aan den Rijn, 1981.

Hendriks, J. et al., *De kleine groep en de opbouw van de gemeente.* Kampen, 1987.

Hendriks, J. *Een vitale en aantrekkelijke gemeente: Model en methode van gemeenteopbouw.* Kampen, 1990.

Hendriks, J., and A. L. Rijken-Hoevens. *De kerkdienst: Sociologisch onderzoek naar opvatting en oordeel over de kerkdienst.* Amsterdam, 1976.

Hendriks, J., and S. Stoppels. *Uitspraak tegenspraak samenspraak: Het profetisch spreken van de kerk als pastoraal handelen.* Kampen, 1986.

Heyer, C. J. den. *Exegetische methoden in discussie.* Kampen, 1978.

Heyer, C. J. den. "Struktuur-analyse," *Gereformeerd theologisch Tijdschrift* 79 (1979) 86-110.

Hiltner, S. *Preface to Pastoral Theology.* New York, 1958.

Hiltner, S. *Theological Dynamics.* New York, 1972.

Hoekendijk, J. C. *De kerk binnenste buiten: Keuze uit zijn werk.* Amsterdam, 1964.

Hoenkamp-Bisschops, A. *Celibaat: varianten van beleving. Een verkennend onderzoek rond ambtscelibaat en geestelijke gezondheid.* Baarn, 1991.

Höfte, B. *Bekering en bevrijding: De betekenis van de Latijns-amerikaanse theologie van de bevrijding voor een praktisch-theologische basistheorie.* Hilversum, 1990.

Hollweg, A. *Theologie und Empirie: Ein Beitrag zum Gespräch zwischen Theologie und Sozialwissenschaften in Deutschland.* 2d ed. Stuttgart, 1971.

Hoof, J. J. van. "Symbolisch interactionisme," in *Sociologische encyclopedie.* Utrecht, 1978, 3:710-15.

Hoof, P. van. *Intermezzo: Kontinuïteit and diskontinuïteit in de theologie van A. A. van Ruler.* Amsterdam, 1974.

Hoogstraten, H-D. van. *Het gevangen denken: bevrijdingstheologie voor het "vrije Westen."* Kampen, 1986.

Hooijdonk, P. van. *Inleiding in het kerkelijk opbouwwerk.* Baarn, 1985.

Imbens, A., and I. Jonker. *Godsdienst en incest.* Amersfoort, 1985.

Jager, O. *Verkondiging en massamedia.* Kampen, 1971.

Jager, O. *Schrale troost in magere jaren: Theologische kritiek in maatschappelijke krises.* Baarn, 1976.

Jager, O. "De omroepmedia," in J. Verkuyl, ed., *Inleiding in de evangelistiek.* Kampen, 1978, 135-46.

Jager, O. *Geloven wordt onwennig: Naar een tweede primitiviteit.* Baarn, 1987.

James, W. *The Varieties of Religious Experience.* Repr. London, 1974.

Jelsma, A. J. *Tussen heilige and helleveeg: De vrouw in het christendom.* The Hague, 1975.

Jentsch, W. *Handbuch der Jugendseelsorge.* Vol. 2: *Theologie.* Gütersloh, 1965.

Jong, O. J. de. "Vier eeuwen domineeswerk," in *Over de predikant.* Utrecht, 1969.

Jong, O. J. de. *Nederlandse kerkgeschiedenis.* 2d ed. Nijkerk, 1978.

Jongh, J. T. van Arkel de. "Ekosisteemdenke as meta-teorie in die praktiese teologie," *Praktiese theologie in Suid-Afrika* 6, no. 1 (1991) 61-75.

Jongkind, B. L. *De heiliging van Gods Naam: Verzet and overgave in het lijden van het joodse yolk.* Kampen, 1991.

Jonker, H. *Theologische praxis, problemen, peilingen en perspektieven bij kenterend getij.* Nijkerk, 1983.

Jonker, W. J. *Als een riet in de wind . . . : Gedachten naar aanleiding van de huidige discussie rondom het ambt.* Kampen, 1970.

Josuttis, M. "Die Bedeutung der Kirchensoziologie fur die Praktische Theologie," *Verkündigung und Forschung* 12 (1967) 159.

Josuttis, M. *Praxis des Evangeliums zwischen Politik und Religion: Grundprobleme der Praktischen Theologie.* Munich, 1974.

Josuttis, M. *Aspekte einer zeitgenössischen Pastoraltheologie.* Vol. 1: *Der Pfarrer ist anders.* Munich, 1982.

Josuttis, M. *Aspekte einer zeitgenössischen Pastoraltheologie.* Vol. 2: *Der Traum des Theologen.* Munich, 1988.

Josuttis, M. *Der Weg in das Leben: Eine Einführung in den Gottesdienst auf verhaltenswissenschaftlicher Grundlage.* Munich, 1991.

Jüngel, E., Karl Rahner, and Manfred Seitz. *Die Praktische Theologie zwischen Wissenschaft und Praxis.* Munich, 1968.

Kaptein, R., and P. Tijmes. *De ander als model en obstakel: Een inleiding in het werk van René Girard.* Kampen, 1986.

Katz, R. L. *Pastoral Care and the Jewish Tradition: Emphatic Process and Religious Counseling.* Philadelphia, 1985.

Kaufmann, F. X. *Religion und Modernität.* Tübingen, 1989.

Kerk in perspectief: Rapport van de commissie gemeentestructuur van de Gereformeerde Kerken. Leusden, 1969.

Kessel, R. van. "Arbeid en pastoraat: Een meditatieve analyse," *Praktische Theologie* 9 (1982) 67-79.

Kessel, R. van. *Zes kruiken water: Enkele theologische bijdragen voor kerkopbouw.* Hilversum, 1989.

Keulartz, J. *De verkeerde wereld van Jürgen Habermas.* Amsterdam, 1992.

Keuning, D. *Algemene systeemtheorie, systeembenadering en organisatietheorie.* Leiden, 1973.

Kierkegaard, S. *Schotschriften tegen gevestigde kerkelijkheid.* Ed. W. R. Scholtens. Baarn, 1980. [*Attack upon "Christendom."* Trans. W. Lowrie. Repr. Princeton, 1968.]

Kierkegaard, S. *Jezus als dwarsligger: Dagboeknotities.* Ed. W. R. Scholtens. Baarn, 1981.

Klapwijk, J. "Abraham Kuyper over wetenschap en universiteit," in C. Augustijn et al., eds., *Abraham Kuyper: Zijn volksdeel, zijn invloed.* Delft, 1987, 61-94.

Klostermann, F., and R. Zerfass, eds. *Praktische Theologie heute.* Munich and Mainz, 1974.

Knippenberg, M. van. *Dood en religie: Een studie naar communicatief zelfonderzoek in het pastoraat.* Kampen, 1987.

Knippenberg, M. van. *Grenzen: Werkplaats voor pastoraaltheologen.* Kampen, 1989.

Knobloch, S., and H. Haslinger. *Mystagogische Seelsorge.* Mainz, 1991.

Kolm, G. J. van der. *"Eigenlijk geloof ik niets": Theologie in de praktijk van fabriek en volkswijk.* Kampen, 1991.

Koole, W. J. *Kan televisie troosten? Levenshulp als pastorale omroepbijdrage.* Hilversum, 1984.

Korthals, M., ed. *Wetenschapsleer: Filosofisch en maatschappelijk perspectief op de natuur- and sociaal-culturele wetenschappen.* Meppel and Amsterdam, 1989.

Kouwenhoven, A. *De dynamiek van christelijk sociaal denken.* Nijkerk, 1989.

Kraan, K. J. *Genezing en bevrijding.* 3 vols. Kampen, 1983ff.

Kraemer, H. *Het vergeten ambt in de kerk: Plaats en roeping van het gewone gemeentelid.* The Hague, 1960.

Krause, G., ed. *Praktische Theologie: Texte zum Werden und Selbstverständnis der praktischen Disziplin der evangelischen Theologie.* Darmstadt, 1972.

Kruijne, T. *De pastor en zijn identiteit in het geding.* Groningen, 1977.

Kübler-Ross, E. *On Death and Dying.* New York, 1969.

Kuhn, T. S. *The Essential Tension.* Chicago, 1977.

Kuhnke, U. *Koinonia: Zur theologischen Rekonstruktion der Identität christlicher Gemeinde.* Düsseldorf, 1992.

Kuilman, M., and A. Uleyn. *Hulpverlener en zingevingsvragen.* Baarn, 1986.

Kuiper, F. H. *Op zoek naar beter bijbels onderwijs.* Amsterdam, 1977.

Kuitert, H. M. *De spelers en het spel.* Amsterdam, 1964. [Eng. trans. *Signals from the Bible,* 1972.]

Kuitert, H. M. *Wat heet geloven? Structuur and herkomst van de christelijke geloofsuitspraken.* Baarn, 1977.

Kuitert, H. M. *Alles is politiek maar politiek is niet alles.* Een theologisch perspectief op geloof and politiek. Baarn, 1985.

Kuitert, H. M. *Filosofie van de theologie.* Leiden, 1988.

Kuitert, H. M. *Mag alles wat kan? Ethiek en medisch handelen.* Baarn, 1989a.

Kuitert, H. M. *Autonomie: een lastige laatkomer in de ethiek.* Amsterdam, 1989b.

Kuitert, H. M. *Het algemeen betwijfeld christelijk geloof: Een herziening.* Baarn, 1992.

Kunneman, H. *Habermas' theorie van het communicatieve handelen: Een samenvatting.* Amsterdam, 1983.

Kunneman, H. *De waarheidstrechter: Een communicatietheoretisch perspectief op wetenschap and samenleving.* Meppel, 1986.

Kuyper, A. *Encyclopedie der Heilige Godgeleerdheid.* Kampen, 1894.

Kuyper, A. *Het sociale vraagstuk en de christelijke religie.* Amsterdam, 1891.

Kwant, R. C. *Mensbeeld als referentiekader.* Amersfoort, 1986.

Laan, J. H. van der. "De praxis van de praktische theologie," in G. Heitink et al., eds., *Voortgang.* Kampen, 1979.

Laan, J. H. van der. "Hoe maak ik een preek?" *Postille* 41 (1989a) 7-18.

Laan, J. H. van der. *Ernst Lange en de prediking.* Kampen, 1989b.

Laan, J. H. van der. "Evaluatie met het oog op praktisch-theologische theorievorming," in K. A. Schippers et al., *Kerkelijke presentie in een oude stadswijk.* Kampen, 1990.

Laarhoven, J. van. *De kerk van 1770-1970.* Nijmegen, 1974.

Laeyendecker, L. "Spiritualiteit en moderne cultuur," in J. Beumer, ed., *Als de hemel de aarde raakt: Spiritualiteit and mystiek.* Kampen, 1990.

Laeyendecker, L. "Godsdienst: een nadere omschrijving," in Schaeffer 1992.

Laeyendecker, L., and W. F. van Stegeren. *Strategieën van sociale verandering.* Meppel, 1978.

Lammens, G. N. *Tot zijn gedachtenis: Het commemoratieve aspect van de avondmaalsviering.* Kampen, 1968.

Lammens, G. N. *Liturgische jaarorde en kerkelijke kalender.* Kampen, 1970.

Lammens, G. N. *Liturgie and massamedia.* Kampen, 1974.

Lämmermann, G. *Praktische Theologie als kritische oder als empirisch-funktionale Handlungstheorie?* Munich, 1981.

Lange, E. "Glaube und Anfechtung im Alltag eines Gemeindepfarrers," in E. Lange, *Predigen als Beruf.* Stuttgart, 1976.

Lange, E. *Sprachschule fur die Freiheit: Bildung als Problem und Funktion der Kirche.* Munich, 1980.

Lange, E. *Kirche für die Welt: Aufsätze zur Theorie kirchlichen Handelns.* Munich, 1981.

Lange, E., ed. *Zur Theorie und Praxis der Predigtarbeit.* Stuttgart and Berlin, 1968.

Lange, A. de. *J. H. Gunning Jr., Brochures en brieven uit zijn Leidse tijd (1889-1899).* Kampen, 1984.

Lange, A. de. *De verhouding tussen dogmatiek en godsdienstwetenschap binnen de theologie. Een onderzoek naar de ontwikkeling van het theologiebegrip van J. H. Gunning Jr. (1829-1905).* Kampen, 1987.

Lange, F. de. *Grond onder de voeten: Burgerlijkheid bij Dietrich Bonhoeffer.* Kampen, 1985.

Lange, F. de. *Een burger op z'n best: Dietrich Bonhoeffer.* Baarn, 1986.

Lange, F. de. *Individualisme: Een partijdig onderzoek naar een omstreden denkwijze.* Kampen, 1989.

Lange, F. de. *Onszelf als een ander: Evangelistiek van techniek naar hermeneutiek.* Kampen, 1993.

Langman, H. J. *Kuyper en de volkskerk.* Kampen, 1950.

Lascaris, A. *Uitzicht voor een oude wereld: West-Europa op een keerpunt.* Kampen, 1987.

Lasch, C. *The Culture of Narcissism: American Life in an Age of Diminishing Expectations.* New York, 1979.

Lebacqz, K. *Professional Ethics: Power and Paradox.* Nashville, 1985.

Lehmann, K. "Das Theorie-Praxis-Problem und die Begründung der Praktischen Theologie," in Klostermann and Zerfass 1974, 81-103.

Leudesdorff, R. "Der christliche Skandal," in Zerfass and Greinacher 1976, 185-90.

Levinas, E. *Totality and Infinity: An Essay on Exteriority.* Trans. A. Lingis. Pittsburgh, 1969.

Lewin, K. *Grundzüge der topologischen Psychologie*. Stuttgart, 1968.

Lindijer, C. H., and J. Lindijer-Banning. *Groepsgewijs: Een boek over groepen in de kerk*. The Hague, 1977.

Lindijer, C. H. *Pastor and therapeut: Wat kan pastoraat leren van psychotherapie?* The Hague, 1984.

Long, T. *The Witness of Preaching*. Louisville, 1989.

Loo, L. F. van. *"Den arme gegeven . . ." Een beschrijving van armoede, armenzorg en sociale zekerheid in Nederland, 1784-1965*. Amsterdam, 1981.

Louw, D. J. *Pastoraat in eskatologische perspectief*. Kaapstad, 1984.

Lukken, G. *Geen leven zonder rituelen: Antropologische beschouwingen met het oog op de christelijke liturgie*. Hilversum, 1986.

Luther, H. *Religion und Alltag: Bausteine zu einer Praktischen Theologie des Subjekts*. Stuttgart, 1992.

Lyotard, J.-F. *Het postmoderne weten*. Kampen, 1987.

Manenschijn, G. *Moraal en eigenbelang bij Thomas Hobbes and Adam Smith*. Amsterdam, 1979.

Marcuse, H. *One Dimensional Man: Studies in the Ideology of Advanced Industrial Society*. Boston, 1964.

Margull, H. J. *Theologie der missionarischen Verkündigung: Evangelisation als oekumenisches Problem*. Stuttgart, 1959.

Marheineke, Ph. *Entwurf der praktischen Theologie*. Berlin, 1837.

Marheineke, Ph. "Uebersichtliche Einleitung in die Praktische Theologie," *Zeitschrift für spekulatieve Theologie* 2 (1837) 162-82. (Repr. in Krause 1972, 39-47.)

Marquardt, F. W. *Tambach nu: De christen in de maatschappij, Karl Barth*. Zeist, 1978.

Marty, M. E. *The Public Church: Mainline — Evangelical — Catholic*. New York, 1981.

Marx, K., and F. Engels. *On Religion*. New York, 1964.

Maslow, A. H. *Motivation and Personality*. 2d ed. New York, 1970.

Mattijsen, D., ed. *De kerk als vrijplaats wereldwijd*. Delft, 1987.

McCann, D. P., and C. R. Strain. *Polity and Praxis*. New York, 1985.

McNeill, J. T. *A History of the Cure of Souls*. New York, 1965.

Meer, F. van der. *Augustinus de zielzorger: Een studie over de praktijk van een kerkvader*. 3d ed. 2 vols. Utrecht, 1957.

Meeuws, H. "Wat bezielt de praktisch-theoloog?" in H. H. Berger et al., eds., *Tussentijds*. Tilburg, 1975, 294-316.

Meiden, A. van der. *Mensen winnen: De overdracht van de boodschap*. Baarn, 1973.

Meiden, A. van der. *Alleen van horen zeggen . . . : Bouwstenen voor een communicatieve theologie*. Baarn, 1980.

Menninger, K., M. Mayman, and P. Pruyser. *The Vital Balance: The Life Process in Mental Health and Illness*. New York, 1963.

Mette, N. *Theorie der Praxis: Wissenschaftsgeschichtliche und methodologische Untersuchungen zur Theorie-Praxis-Problematik innerhalb der praktischen Theologie.* Düsseldorf, 1978.

Mette, N. *Der pastorale Notstand: Notwendige Reformen für eine zu kunftsfähige Kirche.* Düsseldorf, 1992.

Mette, N., and H. Steinkamp. *Sozialwissenschaften und Praktische Theologie.* Düsseldorf, 1983.

Metz, J. B. *Glaube in Geschichte und Gesellschaft.* Mainz, 1977. [*Faith in History and Society: Toward a Practical Fundamental Theology.* Trans. D. Smith. New York, 1980.]

Meuleman, G. E. *De Godgeleerdheid volgens de Wet op het Hoger Onderwijs van 1876.* Amsterdam, 1982.

Meuleman, G. E. *Theologie aan de universiteit.* Kampen, 1991.

Michielse, H. C. M. *De burger als andragoog: Een geschiedenis van 125 jaar welzijnswerk.* 2d ed. Meppel, 1978.

Miles, M. B. *Learning to Work in Groups: A Program Guide for Educational Leaders.* New York, 1959.

Miskotte, K. H. *Als de goden zwijgen: Over de zin van het Oude Testament.* 1956. 2d ed. Haarlem, 1966. [*When the Gods Are Silent.* Trans. J. W. Doberstein. New York, 1967.]

Mitscherlich, A. *Auf dem Weg zur vaterlosen Gesellschaft.* Munich, 1963.

Möller, Chr. *Lehre vom Gemeindeaufbau,* 1/2. Göttingen, 1987-90.

Moltmann, J. *Theologie der Hoffnung.* Munich, 1964. [*A Theology of Hope.* Trans. J. W. Leitch. New York, 1967.]

Moltmann, J. *The Church in the Power of the Spirit: A Contribution to Messianic Ecclesiology.* Trans. M. Kohl. New York, 1977.

Mudge, L. S., and J. N. Poling, eds. *Formation and Reflection: The Promise of Practical Theology.* Philadelphia, 1987.

Müller, A. "Praktische Theologie zwischen Kirche und Gesellschaft," in Klostermann and Zerfass 1974.

Müller, A. D. *Grundriss der praktischen Theologie.* Gütersloh, 1950.

Müller, J. "Die Pastoraltheologie innerhalb des theologischen Gesamtkonzepts von Stephan Rautenstrauch (1774)," in Klostermann and Zerfass 1974.

Muurling, W. *Practische godgeleerdheid.* 1851ff. Groningen, 1860.

Neidhart, W. *Psychologie des Religionsunterrichts.* 2d ed. Zurich, 1967.

Neumann, K. "Theologische Kompetenz als Ausbildungsziel?" *Der evangelische Erzieher* 44 (1992) 352ff.

Neven, G. W. *Tijdgenoot en getuige: Opstellen over de theologie van dr. O. Noordmans.* Kampen, 1980.

Neven, G. W. "Schleiermachers erste Auflage von *Der Christliche Glaube,*" *Berliner theologische Zeitschrift* 10 (1993).

Neven, G. W. *Oepke Noordmans, voorloper van een theologie van onze tijd.* Driebergen, n.d.

Nicol, M. *Gespräch als Seelsorge: Theologische Fragmente zu einer Kultur des Gesprächs.* Göttingen, 1990.

Niebergall, F. *Praktische Theologie: Lehre von der kirchlichen Gemeindeerziehung auf wissenschaftlicher Grundlage.* 2 vols. Tübingen, 1918/1919.

Nijen, J. J. van. "Gemeenteleden als deelgenoten," in J. M. Vlijm, ed., *Buitensporig geloven.* Kampen, 1983.

Nijk, A. J. *Secularisatie Over het gebruik van een woord.* Rotterdam, 1968.

Nijk, A. J. *Beheersing en emancipatie.* Alphen aan den Rijn, 1972.

Nijk, A. J. *De mythe van de zelfontplooiing and andere wijsgerig-andragologische opstellen.* Amsterdam and Meppel, 1979.

Nipkow, K. E. *Grundfragen der Religionspädagogik.* 3 vols. Gütersloh, 1975-82.

Nipkow, K. E., D. Rössler, and F. Schweitzer. *Praktische Theologie und Kultur der Gegenwart: Ein internationaler Dialog.* Gütersloh, 1991.

Nitzsch, C. I. *Praktische Theologie.* 3 vols. Bonn, 1847-57.

Nitzsch, C. I. "Universalgeschichtlicher Ansatz, Methode und Einteilung der praktischen Theologie" (1847), repr. in Krause 1972, 71-81.

Noordegraaf, A. *Oriëntatie in het diakonaat.* Zoetermeer, 1991.

Noordegraaf, H., and H. Tieleman. "Kerken, economie en het sociale vraagstuk," in Schaeffer 1992, 313-39.

Noordmans, O. *Zondaar en bedelaar.* Amsterdam, 1946.

Noordmans, O. *Verzamelde werken.* Kampen, 1978ff.

Ontginningswerk, bijdragen voor dr. Wybe Zijlstra. Kampen, 1985

Oosterzee, J. J. van. *Praktische theologie.* Utrecht, 1877/78.

Otto, G. *Praktisch-theologisches Handbuch.* Hamburg, 1970.

Otto, G. "Praktische Theologie als Kritische Theorie religiös vermittelter Praxis — Thesen züm Verständnis einer Formel," in Klostermann and Zerfass 1974.

Otto, G. "Godwin Lämmermann, Praktische Theologie als kritische oder als empirisch-funktionale Handlungstheorie?" *Themen der Praktischen Theologie* 17 (1982) 148ff.

Otto, G. *Grundlegung der Praktischen Theologie.* Munich, 1986.

Otto, G. *Handlungsfelder der Praktischen Theologie.* Munich, 1988.

Palmer, Chr. von. "Pastoraltheologie" (1859), repr. in Krause 1972, 81-99.

Palmer, P. J. *The Company of Strangers: Christians and the Renewal of America's Public Life.* New York, 1981.

Palmer, R. E. *Hermeneutics: Interpretation Theory in Schleiermacher, Dilthey, Heidegger, and Gadamer.* Evanston, 1969.

Pannenberg, W. *Wissenschaftstheorie und Theologie.* Frankfurt a. M., 1973. [*Theology and the Philosophy of Science.* Trans. F. McDonagh. Philadelphia, 1976.]

Päschke, B. "Praktische Theologie als kritische Handlungswissenschaft," *Theologia practica* 6 (1971) 1-13.

Pasveer, J. *De gemeente tussen openheid en identiteit: Een open-systeemtheorie als model voor de gemeente ten dienste van haar opbouw.* Gorinchem, 1992.

Peters, J. *Individualisering and secularisering in Nederland in de jaren tachtig: Sociologie als contemporaine geschiedsbeschrijving.* Nijmegen, 1993.

Peukert, H. *Wissenschaftstheorie — Handlungstheorie — Fundamentale Theologie: Analysen zu Ansatz und Status theologischer Theoriebildung.* Düsseldorf, 1976.

Peursen, C. A. van. *Cultuur in stroomversnelling. Strategie van de cultuur.* Amsterdam, 1976.

Philippi, P. *Christozentrische Diakonie.* 1963. 2d ed. Stuttgart, 1975.

Pieterse, H. J. C. *Gemeente en prediking.* Kaapstad, 1991.

Piper, H. C. *Gesprächsanalysen.* Göttingen, 1973.

Ploeger, A. K. *Diskurs: De plaats van geloofservaringen binnen de rationele handelingstheorie van Jürgen Habermas.* The Hague, 1989.

Ploeger, A. K. "Voorbij tolerantie en emancipatie: Het intergeneratief leer- and leefproces in de kerk," *Praktische Theologie* 17 (1990) 576-97.

Ploeger, A. K. *Inleiding in de godsdienstpedagogiek.* Kampen, 1993.

Plomp, J. *De kerkelijke tucht bij Calvijn.* Kampen, 1969.

Poeisz, J. J. *Traditie en vernieuwing in caritatieve organisaties.* Meppel, 1968.

Poling, J. N., and D. E. Miller. *Foundations for a Practical Theology of Ministry.* Nashville, 1985.

Pop, F. J. *Zo is God bij de mensen.* The Hague, 1967.

Ramsey, I. T. *Religious Language: An Empirical Placing of Theological Phrases.* London, 1957.

Rau, G. *Pastoraltheologie.* Munich, 1970.

Rebel, J. J. *Pastoraat in pneumatologisch perspectief: Een theologische verantwoording vanuit het denken van A. A. van Ruler.* Kampen, 1981.

Reenders, H. *Alternatieve zending: Ottho Gerhard Heldring en de verbreiding van het christendom in Nederlands-Indië.* Kampen, 1991.

Rendtorff, T. *Christendom buiten de kerk.* 1969. Repr. Baarn, 1973.

Richter, H.-E. *Patient Familie.* Reinbek, 1970.

Ricoeur, P. *Interpretation Theory: Discourse and the Surplus of Meaning.* Fort Worth, 1976.

Ricoeur, P. *Hermeneutics and the Human Sciences.* New York, 1981.

Ricoeur, P. *Oneself as Another.* Trans. K. Blamey. Chicago, 1992.

Ricoeur, P. *From Text to Action.* Evanston, 1991.

Ricoeur, P. *Tekst en betekenis: Opstellen over de interpretatie van literatuur.* Trans. M. van Buuren. Baarn, 1991.

Ridderbos, H. *De komst van het koninkrijk: Jezus' prediking volgens de synoptische evangeliën.* Kampen, 1950. [*The Coming of the Kingdom.* Trans. H. de Jongste. Ed. R. Zorn. Philadelphia, 1962.]

Ridderbos, H. *Paulus: Ontwerp van zijn theologie.* Kampen, 1966. [*Paul: An Outline of His Theology.* Trans. J. R. de Witt. Grand Rapids, 1975.]

Riedel, M. *Verstehen oder erklären? Zur Theorie und Geschichte der hermeneutischen Wissenschaften.* Stuttgart, 1978.

Riemann, F. *Grundformen der Angst: Eine tiefenpsychologische Studie.* 10th ed. Munich, 1975.

Riesman, D., N. Glazer, R. Denney, *The Lonely Crowd: A Study of the Changing American Character.* New York, 1950.

Riess, R. *Seelsorge: Orientierung, Analysen, Alternativen.* Göttingen, 1973.

Riess, R. *Haus in der Zeit: Das evangelische Pfarrhaus heute.* Munich, 1992.

Rogers, C. *Client-Centered Therapy: Its Current Practice, Implications, and Theory.* Boston, 1951.

Roscam Abbing, P. J. *Diakonia: Een studie over het begrip dienst in dogmatiek and practische theologie.* The Hague, 1950.

Roscam Abbing, P. J. *Predikantswerk in verband met communicatie- en leertheorie.* The Hague, 1980.

Rössler, D. "Praktische Theologie," in Wintzer 1982.

Rössler, D. *Grundriss der Praktischen Theologie.* Berlin, 1986.

Rothuizen. G. Th. *Wat is ethiek?* Kampen, 1973.

Rothuizen, G. Th. *Een bezige bij of de gereformeerde zede bestaat niet meer.* Kampen, 1980.

Rozendal, R., ed. *Wie ben ik dat ik dit niet doen mag?* Kampen, 1987.

Ruler, A. A. van. *Kuypers idee ener christelijke cultuur.* Nijkerk, 1940.

Ruler, A. A. van. *Religie en politiek.* Nijkerk, 1945.

Ruler, A. A. van. *Reformatorische opmerkingen in de ontmoeting met Rome.* Hilversum, 1965.

Ruler, A. A. van. "De bevinding, proeve van een theologische benadering," in *Verzameld werk.* Nijkerk, 1971, 3:43ff.

Runia, K. *In het krachtenveld van de Geest.* Kampen, 1992.

Sauter, G. *Theologie als Wissenschaft.* Munich, 1971.

Sauter, G. "Der Praxisbezug aller theologischen Disziplinen," in Klostermann and Zerfass 1974.

Schaeffer, H., ed. *Handboek godsdienst in Nederland.* Amersfoort, 1992.

Schegget, G. H. ter. *Partijgangers der armen: Avantgarde van Gods revolutie.* Baarn, 1971.

Schegget, G. H. ter. *Het beroep op de stad der toekomst: Ethiek van de revolutie.* Haarlem, 1972.

Schegget, G. H. ter. "Kornelis Heiko Miskotte ter nagedachtenis," *Voorlopig* 10 (1976) 304-5.

Schegget, G. H. ter. *Kernwoorden bij Marx.* Baarn, 1977.

Schelsky, H. "Ist die Dauerreflexion institutionalisierbar? Zum Thema einer modernen Religionssoziologie," *Zeitschrift für Evangelische Ethik* 1 (1957) 153-74.

Schelsky, H. *Einsamkeit und Freiheit.* 1963. Repr. Düsseldorf, 1971.

Schian, M. *Grundriss der Praktischen Theologie.* Giessen, 1922.

Schibilsky, M. *Kursbuch Diakonie.* Neukirchen, 1991.

Schillebeeckx, E. *Jezus: het verhaal van een levende.* Bloemendaal, 1975. [*Jesus: An Experiment in Christology.* Trans. H. Hoskins. New York, 1979.]

Schillebeeckx, E. *Gerechtigheid en liefde: genade en bevrijding.* Bloemendaal, 1977. [*Christ: The Experience of Jesus as Lord.* Trans. J. Bowden. New York, 1980.]

Schillebeeckx, E. *Tussentijds verhaal over twee Jezus boeken.* Bloemendaal, 1978. [*Interim Report on the Books Jesus and Christ.* Trans. J. Bowden. New York,1981.]

Schillebeeckx, E. "Basis en ambt: Ambt in dienst van nieuwe gemeentevorming," in *Basis en Ambt.* Bloemendaal, 1979, 43-90.

Schillebeeckx, E. *Mensen als verhaal van God.* Baarn, 1989. [*Church: The Human Story of God.* Trans. J. Bowden. New York, 1990.]

Schipani, D. S. *Religious Education Encounters Liberation Theology.* Birmingham, Ala., 1988.

Schippers, K. A. *De gemeente als leergemeenschap.* Kampen, 1977.

Schippers, K. A. *Werkplaats catechese: Doelbepaling en organisatie jongeren-catechese.* Kampen, 1982.

Schippers, K. A. *Er zijn voor anderen.* Kampen, 1989.

Schippers, K. A., et al. *Kerkelijke presentie in een oude stadswijk.* Kampen, 1990.

Schleiermacher, F. *Over de religie: Redevoeringen tot de ontwikkelden onder haar verachters.* Ed. A. A. Willems. The Hague, 1990. [*On Religion: Speeches to Its Cultured Despisers.* Trans. R. Crouter. New York, 1988.]

Schleiermacher, F. "Ueber die Einrichtung der theologischen Fakultät" (1810), repr. in Krause 1972.

Schleiermacher, F. *Kurze Darstellung des theologischen Studiums zum Behuf einleitender Vorlesungen.* 1811. Darmstadt, 1973. [*Brief Outline on the Study of Theology.* Trans. T. N. Tice. Richmond: Knox, 1966.]

Schleiermacher, F. D. *Die praktische Theologie nach den Grundsätzen der evangelischen Kirche im Zusammenhang dargestellt.* Ed. J. Frerichs. Berlin, 1850. [Partial translation: *Christian Caring: Selections from Practical Theology.* Trans. J. G. Duke. Ed. D. H. Stone. Philadelphia, 1988.]

Schneider, G. *Grundbedürfnisse und Gemeindebildung.* Munich and Mainz, 1982.

Scholten, R. G. "Het pastorale beroep," in G. Dekker et al., *Kerk, godsdienst en samenleving.* Assen, 1982.

Scholtens, W. R. *Alle gekheid op een stokje: Kierkegaard als psycholoog.* Baarn, 1979.

Schoof, T. M. *Aggiornamento: De doorbraak van een nieuwe katholieke theologie.* Baarn, 1968.

Schoonenberg, P. "Charismata: talenten waar de Geest mee speelt," in van der Ven, ed., 1985.

Schreiter, R. J. *Constructing Local Theologies.* New York, 1985.

Schreuder, O. *Het professioneel karakter van het geestelijk ambt.* Nijmegen and Utrecht, 1964.

Schreurs, A. *Spirituele begeleiding van groepen: Bijdrage tot een praktijktheorie voor geloofspractica.* Kampen, 1990.

Schröer, H. "Inventur der Praktischen Theologie" (1969), repr. in Krause 1972, 445-59.

Schrojenstein Lantman, R. J. M. *Arbeid ter sprake: Een pastoraaltheologische verkenning ten dienste van gemeenteopbouw en volwassenencatechese.* Hilversum, 1990.

Schulz, W. "Aufgaben der Didaktik," in D. C. Kochan, ed., *Allgemeine Didaktik, Fachdidaktik, Fachwissenschaft.* Darmstadt, 1970.

Schwarz, F., and Chr. A. Schwarz. *Theologie des Gemeindeaufbaus: Ein Versuch.* Neukirchen, 1987.

Searle, J. R. *Speech Acts: An Essay in the Philosophy of Language.* Cambridge, 1969.

Servellen, A. van. *Macht van de onmacht: Hoe vrouwen met macht omgaan.* Amersfoort, 1983.

Siegers, F., and D. Haan. *Handboek supervisie.* Alphen aan den Rijn, 1983.

Siemerink, J. A. M. *Het gebed in de religieuze vorming.* Kampen, 1987.

Sölle, D. *Choosing Life.* Trans. M. Kohl. Philadelphia, 1981.

Spee, H. *Diaconie. Een hartszaak.* Op zoek naar profielverdieping voor diaconaat aan de basis van de geloofsgemeenschap. Kampen, 1992.

Spiegel, Y. "Praktische Theologie als empirische Theologie," in Klostermann and Zerfass 1974, 178-95.

Spijker, A. M. J. M. H. van der. *Pastorale competentie: Mogelijkheden and moeilijkheden van het pastor zijn.* Heerlen, 1984.

Steck, W. "Friedrich Schleiermacher und Anton Graf — eine ökumenische Konstellation Praktischer Theologie?" in Klostermann and Zerfass 1974, 27-42.

Stegeren, W. F. van. *Welzijn en emancipatie: Ontwerp van een emancipatorische andragologie.* Meppel, 1982.

Steggink, O., and K. Waaijman. *Spiritualiteit en mystiek.* Nijmegen, 1985.

Steinkamp, H. *Sozialpastoral.* Freiburg im Breisgau, 1991.

Stevense, H. *Sociaal-kultureel werk: Een verkenning naar de teorie and de metoden.* Bloemendaal, 1979.

Stollberg, D. *Therapeutische Seelsorge.* Munich, 1969.

Störig, H. J. *Geschiedenis van de filosofie.* 2 vols. 1959. 18th ed. Utrecht, 1985.

Straver, C. J. *Massacommunicatie en godsdienstige beïnvloeding.* Hilversum, 1967.

Strien, P. J. van. *Praktijk als wetenschap: Methodologie van het sociaal-wetenschappelijk handelen.* Assen, 1986.

Strijd, K. "Pastoraat — in dienst waarvan?" in M. B. Blom et al., eds., *Gestalten van pastoraat*. Amsterdam, 1978.

Stroeken, H. *Freud en zijn patiënten*. Nijmegen, 1985.

Sundén, H. *Die Religion und die Rollen*. Berlin, 1966.

Swanborn, P. G. *Methoden van sociaal-wetenschappelijk onderzoek*. New edition. Meppel, 1987.

Tawney, R. H. *Religion and the Rise of Capitalism*. 1926. Repr. Harmondsworth, 1937.

Tennekes, J. *Symbolen en hun boodschap*. Assen, 1982.

Thielicke, H. *Lijden aan de kerk: Een persoonlijk woord*. Wageningen, 1965.

Thomas, J. *Het luistert nauw: Het gesprek over de preek tussen gemeente en predikant*. Kampen, 1978.

Thomassen, J. *Heilswirksamkeit der Verkündigung: Kritik und Neubegründung*. Düsseldorf, 1986.

Thurneysen, E. "Rechtfertigung und Seelsorge," *Zwischen den Zeiten* 6 (1928) 197-218.

Thurneysen, E. *Die Lehre von der Seelsorge*. 2d ed. Zurich, 1957. [*A Theology of Pastoral Care*. Trans. J. A. Worthington et al. Richmond, 1962.]

Tieman, W. A. Z., and H. Zunneberg. *Bevrijd tot verbondenheid: Actueel diakonaat*. The Hague, 1990.

Tillich, P. *Systematic Theology*. 3 vols. London, 1968.

Tillo, G. van. "Over de plaats van kwalitatieve analyse in het praktisch-theologisch onderzoek," in Claessens and van Tillo 1990.

Tracy, D. "The Foundations of Practical Theology," in Browning 1983, 61-83.

Trimp, C. *Communicatie en ambtelijke dienst*. Groningen, 1976.

Turre, R. *Diakonik: Grundlegung und Gestaltung der Diakonie*. Neukirchen, 1991.

Uchelen, N. A. van. "Bijbeluitleg volgens de 'Amsterdamse school,'" *Gereformeerd theologisch Tijdschrift* 79 (1979) 201ff.

Ultee, W., W. Arts, and H. Flap. *Sociologie: Vragen, uitspraken, bevindingen*. Groningen, 1992.

Veenhof, J. "De pastor als medewerker van God: Zelfstandigheid in pneumatologisch perspectief," in F. H. Kuiper et al., eds., *Zelfstandig geloven: Studies voor Jaap Firet*. Kampen, 1987.

Veltkamp, H. J. *Pastoraat als gelijkenis*. Kampen, 1988.

Ven, J. A. van der. *Kritische godsdienstdidaktiek*. Kampen, 1982.

Ven, J. A. van der. *Pastoraal tussen ideaal en werkelijkheid*. Kampen, 1985.

Ven, J. A. van der. "Practical Theology: From Applied to Empirical Theology," *Journal of Empirical Theology* 1 (1988) 7-27.

Ven, J. A. van der. *Entwurf einer empirischen Theologie*. Kampen, 1990. [*Practical Theology: An Empirical Approach*. Trans. B. Schultz. Kampen, 1993.]

Ven, J. A. van der. *Ecclesiologie in context*. Kampen, 1993. [*Ecclesiology in Context*. Grand Rapids, 1996.]

Ven, J. A. van der, ed. *Toekomst voor de kerk? Studies voor Frans Haarsma.* Kampen, 1985.

Ven, J. A. van der, and W. Rooijakkers, "Vernieuwing in de klinische pastorale vorming," *Praktische Theologie* 16 (1989) 329-50.

Verbraak, E. *Arbeidsongeschikten in beweging: Een toetssteen voor de theologie van de arbeid van M.-D. Chenu en de nieuwe politieke theologie van J. B. Metz.* Hilversum, 1990.

Verkuyl, J., ed. *Inleiding in de evangelistiek.* Kampen, 1978.

Verschuren, P. J. M. *De probleemstelling van een onderzoek: Handleiding voor het maken van de probleemstelling voor een onderzoek, scriptie, nota of artikel.* Utrecht and Antwerpen, 1986.

Vossen, H. J. M. *Vrijwilligerseducatie en pastoraat aan rouwenden.* Kampen, 1985.

Vossen, H. J. M. "De ontwikkeling van een empirisch-theologisch statuut in de praktische theologie," in W. Logister et al., *Twintig jaar ontwikkelingen in de theologie, tendensen en perspectieven.* Kampen, 1987.

Vossen, H. J. M. "Onderzoek naar schoolcatechese en kommunikatie," *Praktische Theologie* 15 (1988) 94-109.

Vossen, H. J. M. "Klinische Pastorale Vorming als religieus-communicatief leerproces," *Praktische Theologie* 18 (1991) 176-97.

Vree, J. *De Groninger godgeleerden: De oorsprongen en de eerste periode van hun optreden (1820-1843).* Kampen, 1984.

Vrijlandt, M. A. *Liturgiek.* Delft, 1987.

Watzlawick, P., J. H. Beavin, and D. D. Jackson. *De pragmatische aspecten van de menselijke communicatie.* Deventer, 1970.

Weber, M. *Gesammelte Aufsätze zur Religionssoziologie.* Vol. 1. 1920. Repr. Tübingen, 1978. [*The Protestant Ethic and the Spirit of Capitalism.* Trans. T. Parsons. New York, 1930.]

Wegman, H. A. J. *Riten en mythen: Liturgie in de geschiedenis van het christendom.* Kampen, 1991.

Weima, J. *Reiken naar oneindigheid: Inleiding tot de psychologie van de religieuze ervaring.* Baarn, 1981.

Werf, J. van der. *Kerk en christelijke vereniging.* Amsterdam, 1960.

Wester, F. *Strategieën voor kwalitatief onderzoek.* Muiderberg, 1987.

Weverbergh, R. *Bouwen met beelden: Onderzoek naar theorie en praktijk van kerkopbouw.* Baarn, 1992.

Wheeler, B. G. "Uncharted Territory: Congregational Identity and Mainline Protestantism," in M. J. Coalter et al., eds., *The Presbyterian Predicament.* Westminster, 1990.

Wijngaarden, H. R. *Hoofdproblemen der volwassenheid: De psychische ontwikkeling tussen twintig en veertig jaar.* 1950. 5th ed. Utrecht, 1969.

Willms, B. *Revolution und Protest, oder Glanz und Elend des bürgerlichen Subjekts.* Stuttgart, 1969.

Wintzer, F., ed. *Praktische Theologie*. Neukirchen, 1982.

Wit, J. H. de. *Leerlingen van de armen*. Amsterdam, 1991.

Wit, J. de, and G. van der Veer. *Psychologie van de adolescentie*. 1977. 4th ed. Nijkerk, 1979.

Woldring, H. E. S., and D. Th. Kuiper. *Reformatorische maatschappijkritiek*. Kampen, 1980.

Wolfaardt, J. A. *Kerklike konfrontasie-oorde: 'n deskriptiewe, analitiese studie met die evangeliese akademies as model*. Groningen, 1971.

Zahrnt, H. *Wachtend op God: De Duitse protestantse theologie in de twintigste eeuw*. Utrecht, 1967. [*The Question of God: Protestant Theology in the Twentieth Century*. Trans. R. A. Wilson. New York, 1969.]

Zerfass, R. "Praktische Theologie als Handlungswissenschaft," in Klostermann and Zerfass 1974, 164-78.

Zerfass, R. *Grundkurs Predigt*. Düsseldorf, 1987.

Zerfass, R., and N. Greinacher, eds. *Einführung in die Praktische Theologie*. Munich and Mainz, 1976.

Zezschwitz, G. von, *System der praktischen Theologie: Paragraphen für academische Vorlesungen*. Leipzig, 1876.

Zijderveld, A. C. *De theorie van het symbolisch interactionisme*. 1973. 2d ed. Meppel, 1975.

Zijlstra, W. *Klinisch pastorale vorming, een voorlopige analyse van het leer- and groepsproces van zeven cursussen*. 1969. 2d ed. Assen, 1973.

Zijlstra, W. *Op zoek naar een nieuwe horizon: Handboek voor Klinische Pastorale Vorming*. Nijkerk, 1989.

Zuidgeest, P. *Levensbeelden: Markante metaforen in het levensverhaal, aanknopingspunten voor pastorale begeleiding en hulpverlening*. Kampen, 1986.

Zulehner, P. *Pastoraltheologie*. 4 vols. Düsseldorf, 1989-90.

Index